WORLD 2.0

WORLD 2.0
A HISTORY

From Enlightenment to Terrorism and Beyond

JELLE PETERS

Odyssea Publishing

Cover image document: The United States Declaration of Independence. First published July 1776.

Cover image map: Map of Turky [sic], Arabia and Persia. Created by Guillaume de L'Isle, 1721. First published in *A New General Atlas*, John Senex, London: D. Browne, 1721. Library of Congress Geography and Map Division Washington, D.C.

Published by Odyssea Publishing.
Layout and index by Merijn de Haen
Book design by Derek Bishop
Maps by Michael Athanson

ISBN: 978 90 810821 8 1

If you have a question about the book, want to read more from the author, or stay informed about upcoming books by the author, go to jellepeters.com. The site also features a challenging history quiz, for those who dare.

For my parents

ACKNOWLEDGMENTS

I would like to thank Gert van Essen, who was kind enough to read the first version and provide valuable insights, my mother, for her meticulous reading and equally valuable points, my wife Maaike, for all her helpful suggestions after first having to listen to me reading the entire book to her and subsequently reading a revised version herself—not to mention having to listen to countless tales of a work in progress—Merijn de Haen, for his corrections and excellent layout, Derek Bishop, for creating an amazing cover, Michael Athanson, for doing a fantastic job on the maps, the great people of cafe Le Bouquet d'Alésia, in the 14th arrondissement of Paris, where I spent many hours writing, researching and editing while consuming hundreds of espressos, the equally wonderful staff of the French Roast cafe on Broadway, for offering a little piece of Paris in New York City's Upper West Side, and last but certainly not least all the friends who had to sit through yet another enthusiastic anecdote about the intricacies of this or that tiny footnote. You are all the best.

TABLE OF CONTENTS

TABLE OF MAPS

"ALL RIGHT THEN," SAID THE SAVAGE DEFIANTLY,
"I'M CLAIMING THE RIGHT TO BE UNHAPPY."

Aldous Huxley, *Brave New World*, 1931

Prologue

LOOKING AT OUR HISTORY, WE ARE EASILY tempted into disparaging our forefathers for their mistakes and mis-guidedness. In readily condemning slavery, warmongering, genocide, fascism, racism, sexism, and all those other 'isms', we celebrate our own enlightened world, our shining city upon a hill.

But when our descendants will one day look back on us—as they inevitably will—they will likely see our time as part of a larger movement, one that gained traction in late 18th century North America, later spread to Europe, South America, Africa and Asia and was still ongoing in the 21st century. A paradigm-shifting revolution, originally ignited by a radical idea that shattered ancient beliefs and founda-tions, one of the core concepts of the Age of Enlightenment:

All men are created equal.

A statement that has proven to be a veritable Pandora's box for reactionary forces the world over, and which in many ways is as radical today as when it was cemented in the Declaration of Independence of the United States, in 1776.

Considering the times of the Enlightenment philosophers who first formulated this radical departure from the age-old belief that all men are *not* created equal, one wonders whether they really foresaw—let alone accepted—the far-reaching implications that were 'baked in the cake', so to speak. For the same basic argument that makes the nobleman equal to the peasant—their both being human—is just as potent an argu-ment against any other form of discrimination, be it based on race, religion, gender, or sexual preference, to name a few.

We can hardly blame them if they failed in this respect though, not least since every generation since has struggled with the social implications of that seemingly simple and innocuous statement, including our own. Think only about the long fight to end slavery in the 19th century, the women's rights movements of the 19th and 20th century, the Civil Rights Movement of the 1950s and 60s and the dogged prevalence of discrimination based on gender, race and sexual preference at the beginning of the 21st century.

Similarly, we continue to struggle with its political implications, like the disturbing fact that, given the right to choose their government, the people do not always opt for benevolent democracies, but also regularly back violent, oppressive, even genocidal dictatorships.

In replacing authoritarianism with individualism as the foundation of society, in giving everyone a voice and more equal access to knowledge and the available resources, the idea of human equality has thus emerged as the most disruptive force in the history of mankind, producing a cascade of political, social and technological revolutions that would likely never have occurred tapping only the potential of the few.

Consequently, at the beginning of the 21st century the individual has become more independent, more powerful, more promising and more dangerous than ever before.

PART I
REVOLUTION!

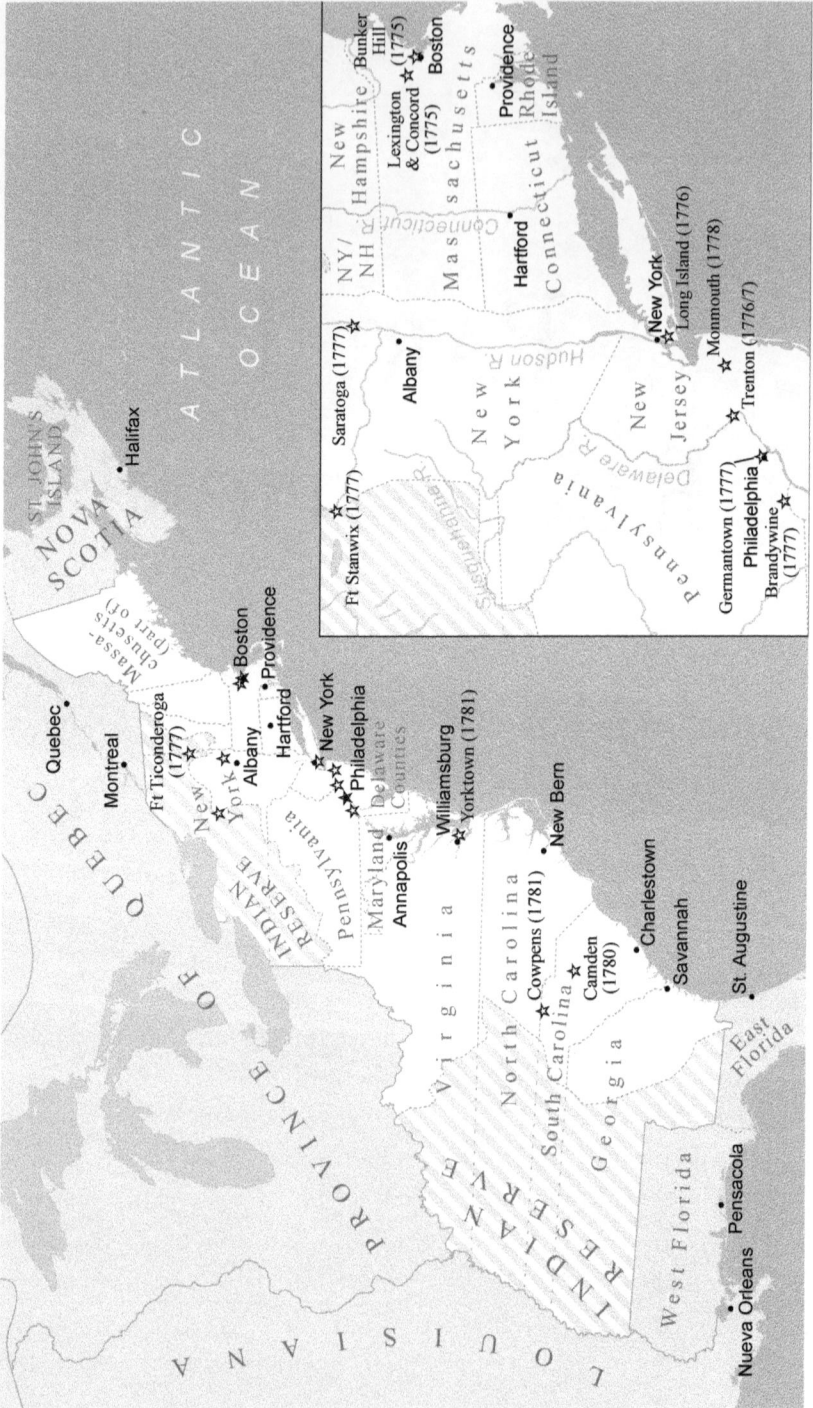

Map 1: Britain's Thirteen Colonies, c. 1775

1

WE THE PEOPLE

"Yesterday the greatest question was decided which ever was debated in America; and a greater perhaps never was, nor will be, decided among men. A resolution was passed without one dissenting colony, that these United Colonies are, and of right ought to be, free and independent States..."

John Adams, July 3, 1776, letter to Abigail Adams

ON NOVEMBER 9, 2012, AN ONLINE PETITION was created on the 'We the People' section of the White House website, asking to grant Texas the right to secede from the Union and form its own, independent nation.[1] In a short time, more than 125,000 people signed the petition, well above the bar of 25,000 the White House had set for a petition to qualify for an official response.

That response was a 522 words long, polite, eloquent but nevertheless resounding 'no'. Apart from the inescapable reflection on the (supposed) will of the founding fathers, the response also harked back to the Civil War of 1861–65, in which more than 600,000 Americans had died and which, according to the response, *"vindicated the principle that the Constitution establishes a permanent union between the States"* (Carson, "Our States").[2]

There is no doubt Texas could survive on its own—as a country it would have the 12th largest economy in the

---

1   The petition was titled *"Peacefully grant the State of Texas to withdraw from the United States of America and create its own NEW government."*

2   Of course, invariably, vindication is the privilege of the victorious.

world—nor would it be the first time for the Lone Star State to be called a country, since it had also been a nation in its own right after winning its independence from Mexico in the Texan Revolution of 1835–36.[3] But back then, the freshly minted Republic of Texas soon asked to be annexed by the United States and in 1845 was admitted as the 28th State, formally relinquishing its sovereignty on February 19, 1846, just shy of ten years after having been founded (Stephens, 108). A short fifteen years later, in a remarkable twist, Texas decided its future lay outside the Union after all and seceded, only to be forced to rejoin after losing the Civil War.

In 1868, the U.S. Supreme Court ruled that individual states did not have a right to secede.[4] No doubt King George III of England (1738–1820) would have agreed, though he would have probably preferred to avoid the word 'states' when talking about his colonies on the Atlantic coast of North America, a.k.a. the Thirteen Colonies.

Not only was secession of the 'Colonies and Plantations in North America' wholly unthinkable to King George III, it almost seemed he felt personally wronged by those *"dangerous and ill designing men"* in open rebellion, when he stated in the Proclamation of Rebellion, issued on August 23, 1775, that they were *"forgetting the allegiance which they owe to the power that has protected and supported them"* (qtd. in MacDonald, 189–90).

The proclamation came after numerous petitions from the colonists asking King George III to intervene in Parliament on their behalf, as they felt wronged by several laws they had

---

3   According to the U.S. Bureau of Economic Analysis, the Gross state product of Texas was $1.532 trillion in 2013, which would make it the world's 12th economy, ranking just below Canada (BEA, "Texas"; IMF, "Report").

4   In Texas v. White - 74 U.S. 700 (1868), Chief Justice Salmon P. Chase wrote that *"The Constitution, in all its provisions, looks to an indestructible Union composed of indestructible States"* (725).

had no part in drafting but that were nevertheless relentlessly enforced by the king's ministers. As late as July 1775, the Continental Congress had sent a petition to the king, humbly beseeching *"your majesty, that your royal authority and influence may be graciously interposed to procure us relief from our afflicting fears and jealousies, occasioned by the system before mentioned* [i.e., the king's ministers]" (qtd. in Morse, 187).

In the same petition, the colonists also sought to assure the king that they remained *"Attached to your majesty's person, family, and government with all devotion that principle and affection can inspire, connected with Great Britain by the strongest ties that can unite societies, and deploring every event that tends in any degree to weaken them, we solemnly assure your majesty, that we not only most ardently desire the former harmony between her and these colonies may be restored, but that a concord may be established between them upon so firm a basis as to perpetuate its blessings (..)"* (qtd. in Morse, 186) .

King George III never formally received the petition, but his Proclamation of Rebellion, issued shortly after the colonial representatives had delivered their petition in person to Lord Dartmouth, Secretary of State for the Colonies, could be considered as a reply of sorts (Brown, 31–32).[5]

The seeds of conflict had been sown long before though, nurtured by a fundamental difference of interest between the colonies and the mother country. The latter thought it should first and foremost benefit from the colonies, not be burdened by it. In other words, the colonies should turn a profit, plain and simple. Otherwise, why would a country go

---

5   The position of the British might have further hardened in the weeks that followed by the publication of an intercepted letter from John Adams to James Warren, written on July 24, 1775—i.e., a few weeks *after* the Olive Branch Petition had been sent to England—and published in *Lloyd's Evening Post* and *British Chronicle*, 18-20 September (Taylor, 89–93). In the letter Adams advocated that the colonists should first prepare for war and independence and only then negotiate for peace and reconciliation, thus clearly contradicting the conciliatory tone of the official public statements of the Continental Congress (Brown, 29–30; Taylor, 89–93).

through all the trouble of settling a colony in the first place? For the colonists, meanwhile, that which at first had perhaps been nothing more than a place to make a living, a refuge from religious persecution, a second chance, had over time become their home.

Friction between England and its American colonies went back to the 17th century, when British mercantilist policies forbade all trade outside the empire, blocking the American colonists from trading with Dutch, French and Spanish merchants.[6]

From 1651, the British government enacted a series of laws known as the Navigation Acts, designed to protect English merchants against foreign rivals, especially the Dutch, who, after the conclusion of their Eighty Years' War with Spain in 1648 were quickly becoming the world's dominant trading nation. The 80 laws that were imposed on American colonial trade between 1650–1750 required an ever growing number of goods to be shipped by English and American ships, via English ports (Nester, 76). Mercantilism protected English merchants and enriched the state, but it hampered economic growth in the colonies and forced high-priced, inferior products on the colonists.

An example was the Molasses Act of 1733, which imposed a high tax on molasses imports from non-British colonies, to protect the sugar trade from the British West Indies against competition with sugar from the French West indies. The policy threatened to destroy New England rum production—the region's largest and most prosperous industry—but the Crown was more concerned about the French West Indies growing at the expense of the British West Indies than it was about the livelihood of the American colonists.

---

6   The Crown's first mercantilist act for the colonies goes back as far as 1621, when it ordered Virginia to export its tobacco only to English ports (Nester, 76).

The only way the New England colonists could save their businesses was by resorting to smuggling molasses, which they did in great numbers. For a while the English government tried to enforce the act, without much success (Miller, "Origins", 99). The failure of the Molasses Act was an early sign that the American colonies were not going to accept any and all new taxes without putting up a fight.

Things heated up after the end of the Seven Years' War, in 1763.[7] Fought between several European powers in Europe, North America, South America and India, its result was a complex reshuffling of colonial possessions, most notably in North America, where New France was divided between Great Britain and Spain. All French lands east of the Mississippi River—including Canada, Acadia and part of Louisiana—went to Great Britain, while the larger part of Louisiana went to Spain.[8]

Though the war had gone well for Great Britain, it had also been pretty much bankrupted by it. To pay for the war and the continued presence of British troops in North America after its conclusion, several new taxes were imposed on the colonies, which in turn invoked growing irritation among the colonists.

There was the Sugar Act of 1764, reintroducing a tax on the import of non-British molasses. The Currency Act, also of 1764, prohibiting the colonies from issuing paper money as legal tender for public or private debts, thus protecting British merchants from being paid in colonial currency but also creating a money shortage throughout the colonies, hampering economic growth (Allen, 98). The Quartering Act of 1765, ordering local governments of American colonies to

---

7   The North American part of the Seven Years' War is known as the French and Indian War.

8   Spain returned Louisiana to France in 1800, but three years later Napoleon sold the territory to the United States (known in the U.S. as the Louisiana Purchase), thus permanently ending French colonial rule on the North American mainland.

provide accommodations for British soldiers, together with *"fire, candles, vinegar, and salt, bedding, utensils for dressing their victuals, and small beer or cyder, not exceeding five pints, or half a pint of rum mixed with a quart of water, to each man, without paying any thing for the same (…)"*.[9] And of course the Stamp Act of 1765, requiring that printed materials such as legal documents, newspapers and magazines were produced on special paper from London that carried an embossed revenue stamp.

The Stamp Act particularly infuriated the colonists, because it was a tax based entirely on activities within the colonies, a so-called 'internal tax', as opposed to an 'external tax', which was more trade related, such as tariffs.[10]

The Act led to violent street protests in several colonies. In Massachusetts, the house of Lieutenant Governor Thomas Hutchinson was vandalized by an angry mob. In Rhode Island, the houses of stamp distributors suffered a similar fate and in New York posters were put up warning people not to distribute or use stamped paper if they valued their house, person and possessions. Many colonists also took to systematically boycotting British goods out of anger over the new taxes (Northrup, 53).

In October 1765, nine of the thirteen colonies sent representatives to New York City to participate in the Stamp Act Congress. It was the first time elected representatives from several colonies came together to discuss a joint reaction to the British Parliament. The resulting Resolutions of the Stamp Act Congress (a.k.a the Declaration of Rights and Grievances) asserted that there should be no taxation

---

9   Quartering Act of 1765. Art. VI, VII.

10   The relevance of any distinction between 'internal' and 'external' tax was debated both in England and in the colonies. The English doubted American opposition to the Stamp Act was really based on it being an 'internal' tax, but by using this as a chief argument—as Benjamin Franklin did, among others— repeal of the act was perhaps made more palpable for Parliament (Morgan, 283–87).

without representation, and that since the colonies were not represented in Parliament, Parliament did not have the right to tax the colonists, only the colonial assemblies had that right.[11]

It was the same fundamental question that had plagued England a century earlier: who has the right to tax the people? Back then, the dispute had been between the king, who claimed absolute rule based on the divine right of kings, and Parliament, which claimed that only the representatives of the people could pass new taxes. It had led to civil war, chaos, revolution, the beheading of one king and the ousting of another, before Parliament had finally been victorious in the Glorious Revolution of 1688.

Of course this time around, in dealing with the grievances of the colonists, Parliament was on the other side of the argument. Enlightenment called for government with consent of the governed, for democracy and the rule of law, principles Parliament had based its own resistance on during the civil wars and the Glorious Revolution but which now served as legal foundation for the American colonists and *their* resistance.

The colonists argued that since they were not represented in Parliament, they should not be affected by its laws, least of all be taxed by it. That would be a breach of their rights as Englishmen.[12] Parliament, on the other hand, held that the colonists were 'virtually represented', because members of Parliament had the right to speak for all British subjects, not just for those districts that had elected them. (Of course in

---

11   Resolutions of the Stamp Act Congress, articles 3,4,5. October 19, 1765 (MacDonald, 136–39).

12   Resolution two of the Resolutions of the Stamp Act Congress emphasized the colonials' rights as Englishmen by stating that "*his majesty's liege subjects in these colonies, are entitled to all the inherent rights and liberties of his natural born subjects, within the kingdom of Great-Britain*" (qtd. in MacDonald, 137).

reality this virtual representation existed in name only, since politicians rarely cater to those who cannot vote for them).

Because the colonists had no representation in Parliament, they had zero control over new legislation and felt wholly at the mercy of this small group of people more than 3,000 miles away. Samuel Adams (1722–1803), a politician in colonial Massachusetts and one of the leaders of the early revolutionary movement, perhaps best formulated that fundamental fear of the colonists with regards to British tax policy in the Americas in a statement drafted in May 1764, writing: "*For if our Trade may be taxed why not our Lands? Why not the Produce of our Lands and every thing we possess or make use of? This we apprehend annihilates our Charter Right to govern and tax ourselves – It strikes our British Privileges, which as we have never forfeited them, we hold in common with our Fellow Subjects who are Natives of Britain: If Taxes are laid upon us in any shape without our having a legal Representation where they are laid, are we not reduced from the Character of free Subjects to the miserable State of tributary Slaves.*" (qtd. in Cushing, 5).[13]

Both the Sugar Act and the Stamp Act were repealed in 1766—mostly because boycotts were hurting British trade—but at the same time Parliament explicitly asserted its right to tax the colonies by passing the Declaratory Act (on the same day it repealed the Stamp Act), which stated that Parliament "*had, hath, and of right ought to have, full power and authority to make laws and statutes of sufficient force and validity to bind the colonies and people of America, subjects of Great Britain, in all cases whatsoever.*" (qtd. in MacDonald, 140).

At this point, the colonists were still not seeking independence from Great Britain, merely a greater freedom to govern

---

13   Part of a set of written instructions for the Representatives of the Massachusetts House, following the Boston Town Meeting in May 1764. The complete text can be found in: *The Writings of Samuel Adams*, IV Volumes, 1:1–7, edited by Harry A Cushing.

themselves. Of course the more freedom a colonial people are allowed in governing themselves the less colonial they become, begging the question whether the colonists would have been satisfied even if Parliament had granted them the right to tax themselves. Then again, perhaps the colonists were still a bit like teenagers during those 1760s and early 1770s, longing to be free of their parents but not quite ready yet to move out of the house.

So far, both sides were unhappy with the other but neither one was willing to bring it to the next level. The colonists grumbled and sent petitions, while Parliament repealed some of its most provocative laws but at the same time reaffirmed its right to legislate and tax the colonies.

Then, in 1767, Parliament passed the Townshend Acts—named after Charles Townshend, the chancellor of the exchequer—a series of laws that, among other things, slapped tariffs on a number of goods imported by the colonies, such as paper, paint, lead, glass and tea, all items the colonists were only allowed to buy from Great Britain (MacDonald, 144).[14] Needless to say the Townshend Acts became very unpopular among the colonists.

In Boston, Massachusetts, British troops had to be stationed to protect the officials charged with enforcing the hated laws.[15] The presence of British soldiers only increased the tensions in Boston though and on March 5, 1770, things got badly out of hand when an angry mob threatened a group

---

14   The idea behind the Revenue Act of June 29, 1767 (7 Geo. III c. 46) was that the Crown still needed to replenish its coffers from the expensive Seven Years' War and that the repeal of the Stamp Act and the reduction of the land tax simply required another source of revenue. Townshend thought that by framing the Revenue Act as an external tax the colonies would not object to it, but this proved to be a fallacy, since the tax was still imposed on the colonists without consulting them (MacDonald, 143).

15   Two regiments, elements of a third and accompanying artillery arrived on October 1, 1768. Two more regiments began arriving in November. Samuel Adams later said that the arrival of these troops had convinced him that America must become independent (Alexander, 65).

of nine soldiers, some of whom lost their nerve at one point and fired into the crowd without orders. Three people were killed instantly, eight others were wounded, two of whom later died of their wounds. Following an official inquiry, the soldiers were tried in a court of law.[16] Six of them were acquitted, two were convicted of manslaughter but received only a branding on their thumb after John Adams success-fully invoked an exception enabling leniency (Allison, 50).[17] Captain Thomas Preston was tried separately and acquitted, because the jury did not believe he had ordered his troops to fire (Allison, 39–40).

The Boston Massacre brought the civil unrest to a new level and the subsequent occupation of the city by British troops convinced some early revolutionaries that full independence was now the only solution. Memory of the massacre was kept alive by annual commemorations and fiery pamphlets, thus preparing the ground for more incidents, such as the attack on the British customs schooner HMS Gaspée, two years later.

The HMS Gaspée was attacked, looted and set ablaze in June 1772 after it had run aground in Warwick, Rhode Island.[18] It was not the first time a British customs vessel had been attacked by the colonials, but it was the first time the Crown decided to try the raiders for high treason (Bartlett, 51–52).[19] Ultimately no one was tried though, because the

---

16   The soldiers were defended by John Adams, who would later become one of the Founding Fathers of the United States and its second president. Adams was a lawyer by trade.

17   The exception, *benefit of clergy*, went back to medieval times. The brand-ing of the thumb was to ensure a convict would only invoke the exception once (Allison, 50).

18   For a detailed description of the event by eyewitness Aaron Briggs, see: *A History of the Destruction of His Britannic Majesty's Schooner Gaspee in Narragansett Bay, on the 10th June, 1772* (Bartlett, 84–87).

19   Source contains a portion of a letter from Secretary of State for the Colonies Lord Dartmouth to the Governor of Rhode Island, Joseph Wanton, informing the latter of the intent of the Crown to consider the act as *"high*

Royal Commission of Inquiry could not obtain sufficient evidence against any individual colonist.

A year later, a group of angry Bostonians boarded three ships full of taxed tea from Britain and dumped the entire cargo of tea in the Boston Harbor.[20] Known as the Boston Tea Party (December 16, 1773) it in turn elicited a harsh response from Parliament in the form of the Coercive Acts— a.k.a the Intolerable Acts—meant to punish Massachusetts and especially Boston for its resistance. The Acts severely restricted Massachusetts' self-governing rights, closed Boston Harbor until Britain had been compensated for all the tea the Bostonians had dumped in the harbor, ordered British soldiers to be tried in Britain instead of the colonies and allowed governors to house British soldiers in the homes of citizens without their consent.[21]

The colonies responded by forming the First Continental Congress, meeting in Carpenters' Hall in Philadelphia between September 5-October 26, 1774. Twelve of the thirteen colonies (Georgia being the exception) sent a total of 56 members from their colonial legislatures. On October 14, the members adopted a Declaration of Rights and Grievances, outlining their grievances and their objections against the Coercive Acts and their intent to enter into a *"Non-Importation, Non-Consumption, and Non-Exportation Agreement or Association"* (i.e., a boycott), until their grievances were addressed and resolved ("Journals of the Continental Congress", 19–22). The Congress also agreed to prepare a *"loyal address to his majesty"*, and to meet again

---

treason, viz.: levying war against he King." (qtd. in Bartlett, 51).

20   In several other colonies, protesters had succeeded in forcing the tea consignees to resign and return the tea ships to England, their cargo still on board, but in Boston, Thomas Hutchinson—Governor of the Province of Massachusetts Bay and a staunch Loyalist—had refused to let the tea ships return to England with their cargo.

21   The Coercive Acts were four separate punitive measures, the Boston Port Act, the Massachusetts Government Act, the Administration of Justice Act and the Quartering Act (MacDonald, 150–62).

the following year if the grievances had not been attended to ("Journals of the Continental Congress", 22).

When the Second Continental Congress indeed convened in Philadelphia the following year, on May 10, 1775, the American Revolutionary War had already begun. Three weeks earlier, on April 19, British Army regulars seeking to capture and destroy the militia's military supplies, had clashed with the Massachusetts militia at Lexington and Concord.[22] The first shots were fired at North Bridge, close to the town of Concord, an event the poet Ralph Waldo Emerson later epitomized as "the *shot heard 'round the world*".[23] The result of the battles was a surprising colonial victory.

But even though the war was already underway, the outcome of the Second Continental Congress was not a done deal. In fact, several members still wanted to try and come to reconciliation with the Crown. So, on July 8, 1775, the Olive Branch Petition was sent to the king, in a final attempt to mend the already severely broken fence.

But King George III's 'answer' in the form of the Proclamation of Rebellion made it clear to all that there was no more turning back, and in the months that followed Congress slowly but surely moved toward the only logical outcome in the face of a war that was already being waged.[24]

---

22   The militia had been warned of the approaching British by Bostonian silversmith Paul Revere. The Battles of Lexington and Concord were fought in Middlesex County, Province of Massachusetts Bay, not far from Boston.

23   As the first verse of Emerson's "Concord Hymn" goes: *By the rude bridge that arched the flood | Their flag to April's breeze unfurled | Here once the embattled farmers stood | And fired the shot heard round the world.* The phrase would later also be used for the assassination of Austrian Archduke Franz Ferdinand by Serbian nationalist Gavrilo Princip, in Sarajevo, June 1914, which ignited World War I.

24   That King George III had already decided not to try to resolve things with the colonists through negotiation, becomes clear from his correspondence with British Prime Minister Lord North. In September 1774—while the First Continental Congress was in session—he wrote that " *the die is now cast, the colonies must either submit or triumph*" (qtd. in Black, 215). And two months later, in another letter to North: "*The New England governments are in a state*

On July 2, 1776, the Second Continental Congress finally approved a resolution of independence and on the 4th of July it adopted the Declaration of Independence.[25]

But although the Thirteen Colonies now officially considered themselves a new nation, independence would not be given, it had to be won.

The early stage of the war did not go very well for the Americans. The invasion of the province of Quebec for instance, which had begun in August 1775 with the dual aim of preventing the British to invade from the North and convincing the French-speaking Canadians to join the revolution, ended in disaster. And while the Continentals did succeed in chasing the British from Boston in March 1776, the opposite happened a few months later in New York, when the Continental Army under General George Washington was badly defeated at the Battle of Long Island, on August 27, less than two months after the United States had officially declared its independence.[26]

After the battle, Washington managed to retreat from Brooklyn Heights to Manhattan, but another two lost battles later—at White Plains and Fort Washington—he decided to withdraw from New York altogether. The Continentals were subsequently chased across New Jersey by General Lord Cornwallis until they crossed the Delaware river and retreated into Pennsylvania, in December 1776 (Stedman, 223).[27]

Following the American retreat the British retired for the winter, but in a surprise move Washington then crossed the

---

of rebellion....blows must decide whether they are to be subject to this country or independent." (qtd. in Black, 215).

25   The original document is actually titled *The unanimous Declaration of the thirteen united States of America*. The term 'Declaration of Independence' is not mentioned in the text.

26   Washington's army suffered 1,000 casualties during the battle, while another 1,000 were captured.

27   Charles Stedman served under Generals Sir William Howe and Marquis Charles Cornwallis during the American Revolutionary war.

Delaware again, in the night of December 25th, and defeated the British-hired Hessian forces at Trenton, New Jersey. A few days later Washington crossed the river a third time, this time defeating British reinforcements under Cornwallis. The victories gave the colonials a much needed morale boost.

The real turning point of the war came in the fall of 1777, when General John Burgoyne's invasion army was decisively defeated at Saratoga, New York, by the Continental Army under General Gates, resulting in the surrender of some 6,000 men, the capture of 73 guns and thousands of muskets, as well as powder and cannon balls (Luzader, 339–40).[28] The victory convinced the French to actively join the war, after they had already supported the revolutionaries with loans, donations, technical assistance, gunpowder and ammunition (Luzader, x-xi). The Spanish and the Dutch later also joined as active contributors to the American war effort, further hampering the British (Luzader, x-xi).

More than anything else, the British strategy depended on the might of its navy and colonial support from the loyalists. The latter factor ultimately proved to be small and ineffective though, while British naval power was eventually checked by the French at the Battle of the Chesapeake (a.k.a. Battle of the Capes, September 5, 1781), a decisive French victory of great strategic value, as it prevented both reinforcement and evacuation of General Cornwallis' army in Yorktown, Virginia, where it was besieged by a joined American and French Army.

Two weeks before the Battle of the Chesapeake, General Washington and Comte de Rochambeau, the commander of the French Army, had marched from Newport, Rhode Island. Washington had gone to great lengths to make the British believe the American-French army was headed for

---

28   General Burgoyne's army had also suffered about 1,000 casualties in the two battles of Saratoga.

British occupied New York City—including fictitious correspondence and summoning provisions, boats etc., for a drive against New York—but the real goal was Yorktown (Greene, 18).

On September 14, 1781, Washington arrived in Williamsburg, about fifteen miles from Yorktown. Somewhat later additional troops arrived and on September 28 Washington had Yorktown surrounded with a force of 18,000 men, made up of French and American regulars plus militia (Greene, 79).[29] Cornwallis and his 9,000 strong army were trapped (Greene, 79, 33).[30]

With the British cornered, the Americans and French started bringing their artillery in position, further weakening British morale with the promise of a forthcoming brutal bombardment, which on October 9 indeed began (Washington himself fired the first cannon). After a few days of relentless shelling, the British organized a desperate, if valiant, attack on the allied cannons, but after spiking six of them they were pushed back to Yorktown.

On October 17, Lord Cornwallis resigned in the hopelessness of his situation and asked for terms. Two days later the British officially surrendered, though Cornwallis himself was not present at the ceremony of surrender, delegating the duty of surrendering his sword to Brigadier General Charles

---

29   According to Greene, the nominal strength of the French Army was 8,600, that of the Continental Army 8,280 and that of the militia 5,535 (Greene, 77–79). But he also estimates that some 1,500 Continentals and 600 French regulars *were absent due to sickness or other reasons at any given time*, and that the effective strength of the militia was not more than 3,500, which is how he arrives at an estimated 18,000 strong American-French army (Greene, 77–79).

30   Greene states that mid-September 1781 the nominal strength of Cornwallis' army was 9,700—including 840 seamen who were part of the British ships anchored at Yorktown—but in the months leading up to the siege, Cornwallis himself reported that the effective strength fluctuated between 5,000–5,500, though this excluded the 840 seaman and the Hessian mercenaries (Greene, 33).

O'Hara (Lengel, 343). Apart from its strategic importance and the surrender of 8,000 British soldiers, the victory at Yorktown also came with considerable spoils, including 244 pieces of artillery, a number of transport ships, almost 3,000 muskets, 80,000 musket cartridges and an abundance of food supplies (Lengel, 308–09).

The Battle of Yorktown was the last major engagement of the American Revolutionary War, though several smaller battles would follow. Four months after Yorktown, on February 27, 1782, the British House of Commons voted to end the war in America. Negotiations began soon after and a preliminary Treaty of Paris was signed that same year, on November 30.[31]

The United States of America had secured its independence as a new nation, but exactly what kind of nation it would be remained a struggle for decades. Initially, the idea was for the United States to be a confederation of sovereign states. Consequently, its first constitution, the Articles of Confederation of 1777 (adopted March 1, 1781) gave almost no power to the federal government, except where foreign policy and defense were concerned. The Articles did not even call the United States a nation, speaking instead of a *"firm league of friendship"* ("Articles", art. III).

Recognizing the dangers of an overly weak central government, nationalists such as Alexander Hamilton, James Madison and John Jay pushed for more power at the federal level. The result was the U.S. Constitution of 1789, with the first ten amendments (a.k.a the Bill of Rights) attached to it, to assuage fears for an overbearing federal government. But the friction between those favoring states' rights and those advocating a strong federal government remained.

And so, within a century after the adoption of the Declaration of Independence, Americans from the states of Virginia, North Carolina, South Carolina, Arkansas,

---

31   The formal Treaty of Paris was signed on September 3, 1783, and ratified by both sides early 1784.

Tennessee, Missouri, Kentucky, Mississippi, Florida, Alabama, Georgia, Louisiana and Texas would fight for their independence once again. Only this time they lost, thus vindicating the principle *"that the Constitution establishes a permanent union between the States"*.

2

FROM A FIRM LEAGUE OF FRIENDSHIP TO A MORE PERFECT UNION

"Let Americans disdain to be the instruments of European greatness! Let the thirteen States, bound together in a strict and indissoluble Union, concur in erecting one great American system, superior to the control of all transatlantic force or influence, and able to dictate the terms of the connection between the old and the new world!"

Alexander Hamilton, The Federalist Papers,
No.11, November 24, 1787

IN APRIL 2010, THE FATE OF EUROZONE member state Greece hangs in the balance. Its sovereign debt rating has just been slashed to junk bond status, following the admission by the Greek government that Greece's financial situation is much worse than previously reported. After performing its own analysis, Eurostat, the European Union's statistical bureau, finds that the Greek budget deficit is not five but a staggering fifteen percent, while the Greek national debt is also revised upward, from 113 to 130 percent.

The junk bond status sends the already high interest rate on Greek government bonds into the stratosphere, effectively shutting Greece out of the bond markets. No longer able to issue new government bonds, the country is in danger of default. Desperate for a lifeline and out of options, Greece turns to Brussels and asks for a loan.

The other Eurozone countries are not too keen to help profligate Greece. Fiscally conservative countries like Germany, the Netherlands, Austria and Finland are especially loath to help a country that over-borrowed and overspent for years while they themselves took pains to run a fiscally responsible budget.

Time is quickly running out though, because in the weeks that follow, the Greek crisis threatens to spread to other financially vulnerable Eurozone countries, like Portugal, Ireland, possibly even Spain and Italy—the latter two the world's 12th and 8th largest economy, respectively.[1] And with many financial institutions so heavily invested in European government bonds, another systemic crisis—like the one that occurred after the collapse of Lehman Brothers in September 2008—suddenly seems perilously close.

On May 2, 2010, Germany is the last country to cave and agree to a €110 billion bailout package for debt-stricken Greece, albeit under strict conditions. Greece has to implement tough austerity measures, privatize €50 billion worth of government assets and implement a host of (long overdue) structural economic reforms. The Greeks grumble, protest, strike and sigh, but it is clear they have no choice. They simply cannot afford sovereignty anymore.

In the late 18th century, several American states faced the same problem. The American Revolutionary War—though won—had left the U.S. federal government with a debt of $39 million and the individual states with a total debt of $21 million, an enormous amount of money for the time (Dewey, 56). Some states, like Virginia, had relatively small debts, but others owed a boatload and were nowhere near repayment. Massachusetts and South Carolina, for instance, each had debts of over $4 million (Miller, "Alexander Hamilton", 242).

Massachusetts was particularly mired in economic problems. Part of its economy was agriculture-based, while the area around Massachusetts Bay was merchant-based. After

---

1   In 2010, according to IMF data.

the war had ended, European traders began to demand payment in hard currency from Massachusetts merchants, who in turn started to demand payment in hard currency from their local customers, many of them farmers (Szatmary, 19–20). As there was a shortage of such currency, many farmers and small businesses simply could no longer buy anything.

In a country just refreshed by revolution the first task of any new government is to prevent another. The risk is very real, because in the immediate aftermath of a rebellion the state is still weak. There could be a counter-revolution—perhaps supported by a neighboring state ceasing upon the opportunity to increase its influence—or a new rebellion, fueled by even more radical revolutionaries or disgruntled veteran revolutionaries.

The latter is what happened in Massachusetts in August 1786, when a violent uprising broke out as a result of the ongoing economic depression of Massachusetts and the harsh fiscal policies of a state government desperately trying to pay off its huge debt (Richards, 87–88).[2] In the months that followed, Shays' rebellion—named after one of the rebel leaders, Revolutionary War veteran Daniel Shays—threatened to topple the Massachusetts government, greatly alarming the governments and legislatures of the other states as well.[3]

---

2   In *Shay's Rebellion: The American Revolution's Final Battle*, Leonard Richards writes that the taxes levied by the in 1785 elected Governor James Bowdoin "*were now much more oppressive - indeed, many times more oppressive - than those that had been levied by the British on the eve of the American Revolution*." (88).

3   The rebellion was largely put down in February 1787, with very few casualties on either side. Most of the rebels were pardoned. Two rebel leaders were hanged, but Daniel Shays himself was pardoned. Though Shays' rebellion convinced many prominent revolutionaries that a stronger central government was needed, Thomas Jefferson, apparently undisturbed by the rebellion, wrote in a letter to a friend on September 13, 1787: "*We have had 13 states independent 11 years. There has been one rebellion. That comes to one rebellion in a century and a half for each state. What country before ever existed a century and*

In September of that same summer of 1786, delegates of five of the thirteen states met in Annapolis, Maryland, to discuss how to improve the constitution of the United States, the Articles of Confederation.[4] At the Convention, Alexander Hamilton, representative from New York and a long-time proponent of a much stronger federal government, drafted a resolution proposing the individual states appoint Commissioners "*to meet at Philadelphia on the second Monday in May next, to take into consideration the situation of the United States, to devise such further provisions as shall appear to them necessary to render the constitution of the Federal Government adequate to the exigencies of the Union*", in other words to work out the deficiencies of the Articles of Confederation ("Proceedings of Commissioners", Sept. 14). The resolution was passed unanimously by the 12 attending delegates.

To be sure, the Articles of Confederation had been created only ten years earlier, between June and early July 1776, during the same weeks the Declaration of Independence had been drafted.[5] The war had already begun and the last thing most members of Congress wanted was to exchange a strong, tyrannical government on the other side of the Atlantic for a strong, tyrannical government on *this* side of the Atlantic. The Articles of Confederation therefore focused on

---

a half without a rebellion?" (qtd. in Ford, 362). Jefferson goes on to argue that a rebellion warns rulers "*that their people preserve the spirit of resistance*" and that "*The tree of liberty must be refreshed from time to time with the blood of patriots and tyrants. It is it's natural manure*" (qtd. in Ford, 362).

4   Though known as the Annapolis Convention, the meeting was formally titled 'Meeting of Commissioners to Remedy Defects of the Federal Government'.

5   The June-July 1776 version of the Articles of Confederation was the first draft.The final draft was prepared in the summer of 1777 and sent to the individual states for ratification by the Second Continental Congress in November 1777. The Articles were ratified five years later, on February 2, 1781 (ceremonial ratification on March 1, 1781).

individual states' rights and limiting the powers of the federal government.

The states wanted to work together where they felt they had to, such as in defending their borders, establishing and maintaining diplomatic relations, negotiating commercial agreements with foreign powers and deciding disputes between states, but retain sovereignty in everything else.

Strictly speaking, the United States of America was not even a country according to the Articles of Confederation. It was a confederacy, meant to provide a *"firm league of friendship"* between individual states.[6] In dividing power and responsibilities between the federal government and the individual states, the Articles left no doubt about who was to have the upper hand. Article II of the Articles stipulated that *"each state retains its sovereignty, freedom, and independence, and every power, jurisdiction, and right, which is not by this Confederation expressly delegated to the United States, in Congress assembled."*

Under the Articles, the United States did not have a president, king, emperor or any other head of state, no executive agencies, no judiciary and no tax base. The federal government could not even collect customs duties after a bill to this effect was vetoed by Rhode Island in 1782 (Risjord, 198). Vetoes like this effectively crippled the Congress of the Confederation, because most of the legislation it proposed needed unanimous approval from all thirteen states.

Since Congress was not able to collect taxes, it could only *request* money from the states, not demand it. But the states were much more concerned with paying down their own

---

6   Article III of The Articles of Confederation and Perpetual Union: *"The said States hereby severally enter into a firm league of friendship with each other, for their common defense, the security of their liberties, and their mutual and general welfare, binding themselves to assist each other, against all force offered to, or attacks made upon them, or any of them, on account of religion, sovereignty, trade, or any other pretense whatever."*

debts and rarely paid up.[7] Congress did have the right to print money, but because it lacked ways to raise actual revenue, these 'Continental Dollars' quickly depreciated in value. As early as 1779, General Washington lamented in a letter to the President of Congress that "*A wagon-load of money will scarcely purchase a wagon-load of provisions*" (letter qtd. in Sparks, 227–29). No wonder the phrase 'not worth a continental' made its way into everyday vocabulary as denoting something utterly worthless.

Though the Confederation Congress was charged with declaring war and maintaining the peace—one of its few powers—it had no money to maintain an army. After the war had ended the Continental Army was largely disbanded, and from June 1784 only 80 enlisted men and a few officers remained (Waddell, 23). Additionally, Congress called on the states to provide 700 soldiers from their respective militias for one year service on the frontier (Bennett, 3). The weakness of the post-war Continental Army caused the British to linger longer in the frontier forts than the Treaty of Paris allowed for.[8]

Complaints about the ineffectiveness of the federal government had been growing since the early 1780s, as had momentum to amend the Articles of Confederation to strengthen the federal government and curb the power of the individual states. Support for a stronger federal government was voiced by the so-called federalists, with Alexander Hamilton, James Madison, John Jay, George Washington, John Adams and Benjamin Franklin among them.[9]

---

7   In fact, the main reason Rhode Island vetoed the impost amendment that would have given Congress the power to collect customs duties, was that its *own* tax system subsisted mainly on impost duties on imported goods, part of which it used to pay off its debts (Risjord, 198).

8   Apart from the inability and/or unwillingness of raising a proper national army, the individual states also showed a lack of coordination in foreign policy, making it impossible to retaliate effectively against British mercantilist policies.

9   Hamilton, Madison and Jay were also the authors of a series of articles

FROM A FIRM LEAGUE OF FRIENDSHIP TO A MORE PERFECT UNION — 43

The federalists contended that Congress should decide by majority instead of unanimity and have the right to tax, that the federal government should have an executive branch, led by a chief executive, and that there should be a federal bank, which would assume the national debt, including the debt incurred by the individual states during the Revolutionary War.[10]

Anti-Federalists, like Samuel Adams, the revolutionary from Boston, Patrick Henry, the Virginian who had led opposition against the Stamp Act of 1765 and is still famous for the phrase *"Give me Liberty, or give me Death"*, and James Monroe, also from Virginia and later the fifth President of the United States, were dead set against a strong central government. They feared the 'chief executive' would evolve into a king of sorts and that states' and citizens' rights would be increasingly trampled by an overbearing, omnipotent federal government.

But although strong opposition to the federalist viewpoint remained, a Constitutional Convention nevertheless convened in Philadelphia on the 'second Monday in May',

---

called 'The Federalist' (1787–88), later known as The Federalist Papers, which promoted the ratification of the (new) U.S. Constitution. Though the effect of The Federalist Papers on the ratification debates in the individual states—particularly in the state of New York, where the articles were initially published—is hard to discern, its impact on the U.S. judicial system has been notable, with 291 quoted mentions in the Supreme Court by the year 2000 (Chernow, 260). The political influence of the three authors is also hard to overestimate. Hamilton went on to become the first U.S. Secretary of the Treasury, Madison the fourth President of the United States and Jay the first Chief Justice of the United States.

10   After Alexander Hamilton became the first Secretary of the Treasury on September 11, 1789, he proposed that the federal government assume all state debts incurred during the Revolutionary War. Apart from giving the federal government more power, this would also increase the creditworthiness of the United States and free the individual states of a burden some were unable to shake off. States that had already paid most of their debts, most notably Virginia, objected, but a complex compromise ensured the narrow passage of Hamilton's plan on July 26, 1790. Part of that compromise was Hamilton's support for moving the national capital to the banks of the Potomac River, the border between Virginia and Maryland (Miller, "Alexander Hamilton", 250–51).

1787, as had been agreed to at the Annapolis Convention the previous year.[11]

A majority of the delegates agreed that the current state of affairs demanded fundamental changes. Providing a fearsome real-life example of what could happen if the states kept insisting on going at it alone, the events of Shays' rebellion—though largely suppressed by the time the Constitutional Convention began—must have surely contributed to this feeling.

George Washington for instance, reacting to Shays' Rebellion in a letter to Henry Lee on October 31, 1786, wrote: "*You talk, my good Sir, of employing influence to appease the present tumults in Massachusetts. I know not where that influence is to be found; and if attainable, that it would be a proper remedy for the disorders. Influence is no Government. Let us have one by which our lives, liberties and properties will be secured; or let us know the worst at once.*" (letter qtd. in Fitzpatrick, 33–35).[12]

Though the task of the Constitutional Convention had originally been to "*render the constitution of the Federal Government adequate to the exigencies of the Union*", the final version of the document the delegates of the Constitutional Convention agreed to on September 17, 1787 was not an improvement of the existing constitution but an entirely new constitution.[13]

Moreover, rather than following the procedure for constitutional revision as laid out in the Articles of Confederation—requiring all thirteen states for ratification—the new

---

11   Very few delegates actually made it on time though and it took until May 25 before a full quorum of seven states was reached.

12   Henry "Light-Horse Harry" Lee had served as a cavalry officer in the Continental Army during the American Revolution. He was also the father of Robert E. Lee, the later general and commander of the Army of Northern Virginia during the American Civil War.

13   Quote is from the Annapolis Convention Resolution, September 14, 1786 ("Proceedings of Commissioners").

constitution stated in article VII that *"The Ratification of the Convention of nine States, shall be sufficient for the Establishment of this Constitution between the States so ratifying the Same."* ("Constitution").

Strictly speaking, the Constitutional Convention was of course out of order bypassing the ratification procedure of the Articles of Confederation like this, but what choice did it have?[14] No amendment to strengthen the federal government had ever been agreed to by all thirteen states, and here an entirely new constitution was proposed whose chief aim it was to increase the power of the federal government at the cost of states' rights. It would have had no chance of passing unanimously, even though most Americans recognized the need for change.

Defending the Convention's choice to supersede the Articles' strictures, James Madison, one of the principal Framers of the new constitution, argued in The Federalist No. 40 *"that in all great changes of established governments, forms ought to give way to substance; that a rigid adherence in such cases to the former, would render nominal and nugatory the transcendent and precious right of the people to "abolish or alter their governments as to them shall seem most likely to effect their safety and happiness"".*[15]

To legitimize the proposed ratification process, the Framers asked the Confederation Congress in a separate resolution to forward the proposed constitution to the state legislatures and that the state legislatures in turn call special elections for their ratifying conventions. This way, the decision of

---

14   Article XIII of the Articles of the Confederation stated that *"the Articles of this Confederation shall be inviolably observed by every State, and the Union shall be perpetual; nor shall any alteration at any time hereafter be made in any of them; unless such alteration be agreed to in a Congress of the United States, and be afterwards confirmed by the legislatures of every State."*

15   *The Federalist No. 40. On the Powers of the Convention to Form a Mixed Government Examined and Sustained.* James Madison. New York Packet. January 18, 1788. The quote Madison uses is from the Declaration of Independence.

ratification would lie with the people rather than with the state legislatures, contrary to the ratification procedure that had been followed with the Articles of Confederation. It was an important distinction, because, as Madison had explained at the Convention: *"the difference between a system founded on the Legislatures only, and one founded on the people, [is] the true difference between a league or treaty, and a Constitution."* (qtd. in Elliot, 398).[16]

Congress debated whether or not it should simply forward the constitution to the states without commenting on it, or instead debate it clause by clause and perhaps send a plan of its own to the states as well, alongside the constitution as proposed by the Convention (Maier, 53–59). But in the end Congress unanimously decided to grant the request of the Convention and forward the document unamended and un-commented to the individual states.

In the months that followed, the pros and cons of the new constitution were debated in public meetings, newspaper articles and pamphlets, with anti-federalists arguing that the document was illegal—on account of its supersedence of the ratification rules of the Articles of Confederation—and lacked guarantees of citizens' rights, while the federalists contended that the failure to adopt the constitution would surely lead to (more) anarchy and rebellion.[17]

But the anti-federalists were at a definite disadvantage, having to defend something that clearly was not working according to the vast majority of the people. Perhaps most people therefore ultimately decided in favor of the new con-stitution on the same grounds as Benjamin Franklin, who, at the end of the Convention, had said: *"There are several parts of this Constitution which I do not at present approve, but I am*

---

16   Debates in the Federal Convention, Monday July 23, 1787.

17   Though the Federalists were against a Bill of Rights, arguing that the inclusion of specific citizens' rights was unnecessary since the constitution did not ask the people to give up any rights, they nevertheless agreed to include a Bill of Rights as soon as the constitution was ratified.

not sure I shall never approve them."(…) "Thus I consent, Sir, to this Constitution because I expect no better, and because I am not sure, that it is not the best. The opinions I have had of its errors, I sacrifice to the public good." (qtd. in Elliot, 617–18).[18]

Ten months later, the first nine states had approved the Constitution, after which the key states of Virginia and New York both narrowly voted in favor of the Constitution as numbers ten and eleven. North Carolina ratified the Constitution in November 1789, after a Bill of Rights had been proposed in Congress. Finally, Rhode Island, the last holdout, having already rejected the Constitution, called a convention in 1790 and ratified it on May 29 of that same year by the narrowest of margins, 34 against 32.

But although the federalists had won the battle for the founding principles of the 'more perfect union' with the adoption of the Constitution, they had not won the war. Over the next two centuries, the federalists and anti-federalists would continue to come into conflict over states' rights vs. supremacy of the federal government, most notably and devastatingly during the American Civil War of 1861–65.[19]

The question whether to be a less influential part of something larger or a more independent part of something

---

18   Debates in the Federal Convention, Tuesday September 17, 1787.

19   Another example is the resistance of several southern states to racial integration in schools during the 1950s and 60s, even after the Supreme Court in 1954 ruled in favor of such integration in Brown v. Board of Education. More recently, conservative groups have mounted resistance against the Affordable Care Act of 2010 (a.k.a. 'Obamacare'), calling the comprehensive healthcare reform legislation unconstitutional on several points, most notably its requirements that states participate in the expansion of Medicaid or risk losing Medicaid funding and that citizens secure medical insurance or face a penalty (the so-called individual mandate), which conservatives argued exceeded Congress's taxing power. In its 2012 ruling in *National Federation of Independent Business v. Sebelius*, the Supreme Court upheld the constitutionality of most of the ACA's provisions, including the individual mandate, but did strike down the provision that forced states to participate in the expansion of Medicaid.

smaller has continued to play a significant role throughout the existence of the United States—indeed from its earliest beginnings. To many Americans it may have seemed (seem) as though they were (are) drawn into that 'something larger' against their will. Having to join the 'more perfect union' following the Constitutional Convention of 1787, being forced to rejoin that union after the Civil War and being sucked into two—largely European—wars in 1917 and 1941.

The world of today—and the outcome of both World Wars—would have likely looked very different though, had a Confederate United States retained its Articles of Confederation.

Over the last few decades, the same question has also become increasingly important in the European Union, where individual states continue to jealously guard their sovereignty, even though most of them realize further integration is a necessity if the bloc is to remain a serious global player in an ever more globalized world.

Think historians will one day write about how the problems of debt-laden Eurozone member states like Greece, Portugal and Ireland contributed to a Constitutional Convention in Brussels that led to the United States of Europe?

Neither did most Americans in the 1780s.

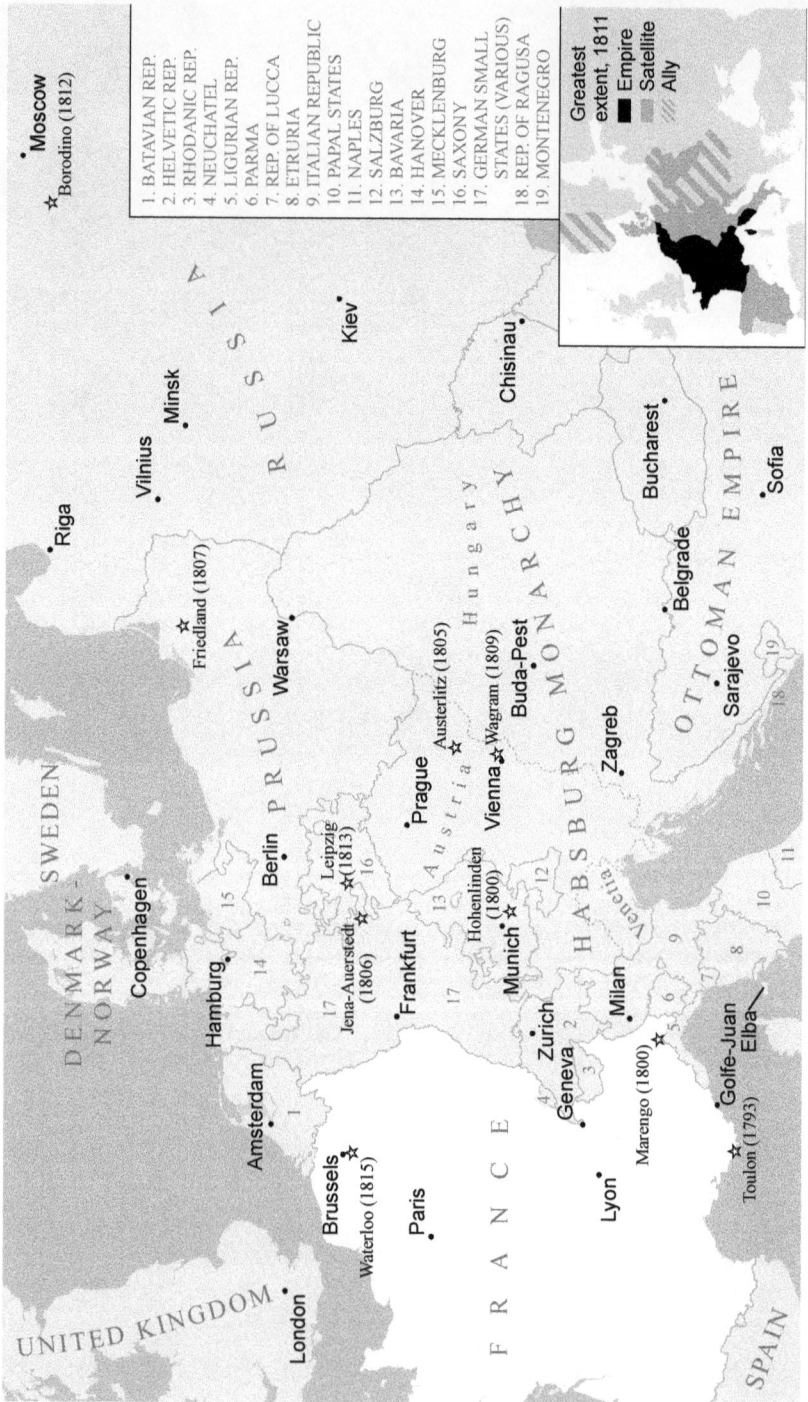

Map 2: The French Empire in Europe, c. 1803

Key:
1. BATAVIAN REP.
2. HELVETIC REP.
3. RHODANIC REP.
4. NEUCHATEL
5. LIGURIAN REP.
6. PARMA
7. REP. OF LUCCA
8. ETRURIA
9. ITALIAN REPUBLIC
10. PAPAL STATES
11. NAPLES
12. SALZBURG
13. BAVARIA
14. HANOVER
15. MECKLENBURG
16. SAXONY
17. GERMAN SMALL STATES (VARIOUS)
18. REP. OF RAGUSA
19. MONTENEGRO

Greatest extent, 1811
- Empire
- Satellite
- Ally

3

THE LITTLE CORPORAL

"Henceforth, until the enemies have been driven from the territory of the Republic, the French people are in permanent requisition for army service. The young men shall go to battle; the married men shall forge arms and transport provisions; the women shall make tents and clothes, and shall serve in the hospitals; the children shall turn old linen into lint; the old men shall repair to the public places, to stimulate the courage of the warriors and preach the unity of the Republic and hatred of kings."[1]

Convention Nationale, August 23, 1793

WHAT DO THE BATTLE OF TRAFALGAR, A burning Moscow and the islands of Elba and Saint Helena have in common? They would all feature in a new theme park dubbed Napoleonland (Schofield, "Napoleon"). Plans for the park include reenactments of the taking of the Bastille—the event that ignited the French Revolution and would later enable Napoleon to shine—the naval Battle of Trafalgar and the crossing of the Berezina River during Napoleon's disastrous retreat from Russia, complete with frozen corpses of soldiers and horses lying on the side of the road, or so is the plan (Schofield, "Napoleon"). Other ideas for attractions in the park are computerized exhibits of Napoleon's many achievements, high-tech simulations of his most important battles and reconstructions of sites that played an important

---

1   Translated from French and quoted in Stewart, *A Documentary Survey of the French Revolution* (473).

part in Napoleon's life, such as the Pyramids and the Gates of Moscow (Schofield, "Napoleon").

The plan is to build Napoleonland at the site of the Battle of Montereau, 55 miles southeast of Paris, where the French Emperor achieved one of his last victories. Initiator Yves Jego, deputy mayor of Montereau: *"Napoleon is the best-known French figure in the world. He's someone who in 15 years changed the history of the world. In two centuries, 80,000 books have been written about him. Yet we don't have a dedicated museum to him in France."* (qtd. in Chrisafis, "Vive la révolution").

That is because the French are rather ambivalent towards Napoleon, and not entirely without reason. On the one hand, the fiery Corsican brought France stability after it had been ravished by the Reign of Terror following the French Revolution.[2] He also enacted many reforms that solidified the ideas of Enlightenment that had been at the heart of the revolution, such as opening education to everyone, creating a code of clear and accessible laws that made everyone equal under the law, institutionalizing religious freedom, establishing the French central bank, reforming the bureaucratic system and ending feudalism.

But, on the other hand, an estimated 1,000,000 Frenchmen lost their lives in the Napoleonic Wars, through battle, disease and the Russian winter (Bodart, 131–33). Napoleon also reinstated slavery in France's overseas colonies and opined that women should simply marry and have children, nothing

---

2   In *The Incidence of Terror during the French Revolution: a statistical interpretation*, Donald Greer writes there were 16,594 official death sentences carried out during the Reign of Terror, between September 1793 and July 1794, but that the total death toll would likely rise to 35,000–40,000 if those who died in prison or were summarily executed are included (Greer, 37–38). Greer put the total number of political prisoners during the Reign of Terror at perhaps 500,000 (Greer, 29). Given the conditions in French prisons at the time, his total number of deaths from imprisonment and execution without trial seems on the conservative side. For a discussion of death toll estimates in different French regions, see Greer 25–37.

else.[3] And although most French people did not have much of a problem with slavery or sexism 200 years ago, they do now. And of course in the end Napoleon also lost, making the British Empire—France's perennial foe—the undisputed dominant world power of the nineteenth century, a period known as the Pax Britannica.

Still, to put all the French casualties of the Napoleonic Wars on Bonaparte's tab would be all too easy, as they were in many ways a continuation of the French Revolutionary Wars, instigated against the newborn French Republic by several European monarchs who feared French revolutionary ideas could become a threat to their own power base.

Things had started heating up in August 1791, when Holy Roman Emperor Leopold II and Frederick William II of Prussia—having followed the developments in France with a wary eye and spurred on by the French émigrés who had packed their bags in time—called upon all European nations to unite against the French Republic and restore Louis XVI fully to the throne.[4-5]

The French Republican government took the joint declaration as an imminent declaration of war—not altogether far-fetched, though in reality it was not—and decided to act first. On April 20, 1792, France declared war on Austria, which had just entered into a formal alliance with Prussia two months earlier. When the French further aggravated the situation by executing Louis XVI, on January 21, 1793—his wife Marie

---

3   The Law of 20 May 1802 revoked an earlier law that had abolished slavery in all French colonies.

4   The so-called Declaration of Pillnitz, named after Pillnitz Castle, where Frederick William II and Leopold II issued their united call to arms.

5   In the period following the storming of the Bastille on July 14, 1789, Louis XVI had already been largely stripped of his powers, remaining king in name only. He subsequently sealed his fate with a botched escape attempt to Austria—his wife Marie-Antoinette's home country—in June 1791. Louis XVI was officially deposed on September 21, 1792, but by then he had already been arrested and sent to the Temple, a medieval fortress in Paris.

Antoinette would follow him a few months later, on October 16—Portugal, Spain, Great Britain, several Italian city states and the Dutch Republic joined the Holy Roman Empire and Prussia in their coalition against the French Republic. France was surrounded on all sides, or, to be more precise, the French Revolution was.

Desperate to survive, the French revolutionary government came up with the idea of total war, which, at the time, was at least as revolutionary in warfare as the idea of democracy was in (French) politics. Later conceptualized by military strategist Von Clausewitz and German World War I general Erich Ludendorff, it meant the conscription of the entire population and all its available resources to achieve victory.[6] In order to mobilize as many soldiers as possible, France introduced the so-called *levée en masse* (general conscription), the first modern nation state to do so. When Napoleon came to power a few years later, he simply inherited this greatly expanded army.

Due to France's massive efforts, it was victorious in the Revolutionary Wars fought between 1792–1802 and was even able to expand its territory. By then, Napoleon had already proven himself to be an exceptionally brilliant military commander and seized power as First Consul in a classic *coup d'etat,* in 1799. But when the wars started, he had just been a captain in the French revolutionary army.

Being from minor nobility—his father had been the Corsican Representative at the court of Louis XVI—Napoleon had been given a few chances early in life not open to everyone in the *Ancien Régime,* such as attending the elite *École Militaire* in Paris. But in the years after the revolution young Napoleon advanced himself through talent, ambition and

---

6   *Vom Kriege* (On War), Carl von Clausewitz, 1832. *Der Totale Krieg* (The Total War), Erich Friedrich Wilhelm Ludendorff, 1935.

hard work and would in that respect epitomize the love child of Enlightenment and Revolution.[7]

The first time history took note of his military talent was in 1793, during the siege of Toulon, an important naval port city in southern France that had revolted against the Republican government and had turned itself over to the British. Napoleon had just been promoted artillery commander of the besieging republican forces there, thanks to some connections.[8] After evaluating the situation, he conceived a plan to capture a hill from where the British ships in the harbor could be bombarded by his artillery, which would force the British to leave (Englund, 63–64). Napoleon's plan was executed and indeed led to the capture of the city. As a reward, the 24 year old artillery commander was promoted to the rank of Brigadier General and put in charge of the artillery of France's Army of Italy (McLynn, 76–77).

Two years later, in October 1795, royalists rose in rebellion against the National Convention to protest the new Constitution.[9] Paul Barras, general of the Army of the Interior and future member of the *Directoire,* appointed Napoleon to command the ad hoc defense forces at the Tuileries Palace—where the Convention was seated—based on the young general's achievement at Toulon.[10] True to his field of expertise, Napoleon used artillery against the royalist

---

7   Napoleon graduated from the *École Militaire* in 1785, after one year instead of the customary two. Just turned sixteen, he was one of the youngest officers in France and the only Corsican lieutenant of artillery (Englund, 23).

8   One key connection was fellow Corsican Antoine Saliceti, representative at the National Convention and former Corsican proconsul. Saliceti also introduced Napoleon to Augustin Robespierre, brother of Maximilien Robespierre, the leader of the Jacobin faction, which controlled the Republican government during the Reign of Terror of 1793–94 (Englund, 63, 67).

9   The rebellion is known as *13 Vendémiaire*, named after the first month in the French Republican calendar. The date corresponds with October 5, 1795 in the Gregorian calendar.

10   The *Directoire* would be the French government from November 1795 until November 1799.

rebels in the streets of Paris, killing 1400 of them. Rebellion over (McLynn, 94–96).[11]

A grateful *Directoire* rewarded Napoleon with the command of the Army of Italy. Wasting no time, Bonaparte invaded Italy in 1796, decisively defeated the Austrian forces there and subsequently invaded Austria itself, forcing the Austrians to sue for peace. The resulting Treaty of Leoben gave France control of most of Northern Italy and the Austrian Netherlands (present-day Belgium).

In August 1797, Napoleon proposed a military expedition to the Levant to conquer Egypt, arguing this would enable the Republic to better protect its trade interests in the Indies, while simultaneously frustrating the British ones.[12]

The expedition started auspiciously enough, with Napoleon and his army disembarking in Alexandria, Egypt, on July 1, 1798, and quickly taking the city. But on the march for Cairo his army was met by a large force of Mamluks, the military caste that ruled Egypt semi-autonomously (Egypt was officially a province of the Ottoman Empire at the time).

Because the Mamluk cavalry greatly outnumbered the French cavalry, the French could do little more than maintain a strict defensive position. To that effect, Napoleon devised a defensive tactic whereby his soldiers would form large hollow squares, with cavalry and supplies in the center and artillery at the corners (Herold, 98). At the Battle of Shubra Khit, and a few days later at the Battle of the Pyramids, the Mamluks tried to penetrate the French defenses with large-scale cavalry charges, but were repelled each time, suffering massive

---

11   The Scottish historian Thomas Carlyle would later say that Napoleon had quelled the rebellion with a *"whiff of grapeshot"* (Carlyle, 892). The phrase is sometimes (incorrectly) attributed to Napoleon himself.

12   The idea was to send an army from the Egyptian city of Suez to link up with the forces of Tipu Sultan, the ruler of Mysore, a kingdom in southern India (Roberts, "Long Duel", 18–19). As Napoleon had noted a decade earlier: *"Through Egypt we shall invade India, we shall reestablish the old route through Suez, and cause the route by the Cape of Good Hope to be abandoned."* (qtd. in Roberts, "Long Duel", 18–19).

casualties in the process. At the Battle of the Pyramids alone, the Mamluks suffered 10,000 dead, against only twenty-nine Frenchmen (McLynn, 178–79).

Napoleon achieved several other decisive victories in both Egypt and Syria, but an outbreak of the bubonic plague severely reduced his army. Worse, or at least equally bad, was the defeat of the French fleet by the British Royal Navy at the Battle of the Nile (August 1–3, 1798), cutting off resupplies and the way home—or at least for the troops it did, not for Napoleon himself.

With a now weakened army preventing him to achieve further greatness in Egypt and alarmed by rising political instability at home, Napoleon decided to return home, even though he had not received orders to do so. Leaving command of the Oriental army in the hands of general Kléber, Napoleon departed from Cairo on August 22, 1799, on the French frigate Muiron.[13]

That same year, on November 9, Bonaparte led a *coup d'etat* overthrowing the *Directoire* and securing his own election as First Consul (i.e., dictator), thus becoming the most powerful man in France just before the turn of the century.

Soon after becoming First Consul, Napoleon defeated the Austrians in the Battle of Marengo (June 14, 1800), in northwestern Italy, leading the Habsburg Empire to quit Italy altogether.[14] The victory also strengthened Napoleon's political

---

13   Though the French occupied Egypt for only three years, it would have a considerable impact on the country. Apart from his soldiers, Napoleon had also brought a small army of scientists with him—mathematicians, historians, archeologists, naturalists, chemists—who not only learned a lot about Egypt's rich history but also infused the Middle Eastern region with knowledge from the modern world.

14   Around 1800, the Habsburg Empire was a composite monarchy, made up of several countries and provinces located mostly in Central and Eastern Europe, ruled by the same monarch, the Holy Roman Emperor, from the House of Habsburg. The Habsburg Empire would be replaced by the Austrian Empire in 1806, in the aftermath of the disastrous defeat at the Battle of Austerlitz (1805), after which Napoleon reorganized most of the Habsburg Empire's

position at home. A few months later, General Moreau (a rival of Napoleon who would later be exiled) won the Battle of Hohenlinden, another decisive French victory over the Austrians, and Bavarians, which effectively ended the War of the Second Coalition.

On March 27, 1802, the British signed a peace treaty with the French as well, though it was destined to be short-lived, even if the parties to the Treaty of Amiens faithfully promised to "*carefully avoid every thing which might herafter affect the union happily re-established*", as article one stated (qtd. in "Official papers", 56). Signed by Napoleon's older brother Joseph Bonaparte and Lord Cornwallis—the same who had surrendered to the American and French forces at Yorktown in 1781—it would last only a year and was to be the only peace time between England and France in the period 1793–1815.

During that period, a grand total of seven coalitions would march against revolutionary France and Napoleon. At first mainly to restore the French monarchy, later to stop Napoleon from taking over Europe. The British were the main driver behind these coalitions, which is hardly surprising considering the two countries' long history of animosity and rivalry, going back centuries, all the way to the Hundred Years' War of 1337–1453, perhaps even to Norman nobleman William the Conquerer's conquest of England in 1066. Though Britain maintained a relatively small army during the Napoleonic Wars, it ruled the waves with its formidable Royal Navy and also heavily subsidized other coalition powers who fielded armies against "Boney", as the English liked to call Napoleon (Hall, 22, 113).[15]

Of the seven wars the various coalitions fought against France, the first five ended with a French victory. The wars

---

German possessions into the Confederation of the Rhine, a collection of French client states.

15   One of the coalition powers that received millions of pounds in British subsidies was Russia, which, between 1812–15 was paid a grand total of more than £6.8 million (Hartley, 77).

of the first two coalitions had started before Napoleon had seized power, but he was still largely responsible for ending them favorably for France.

The War of the Third Coalition was kicked off with Britain declaring war on France, in May 1803 (thus 'un-establishing' the happy union again). During the next two years the British heavily lobbied several other European countries to join them, which—helped along by various French political blunders and provocative actions—Sweden, Russia and Austria finally did mid-1805.[16]

It would be a short war though, because at the Battle of Austerlitz (December 2, 1805), Napoleon, who had crowned himself Emperor of the French exactly one year earlier, defeated a numerical superior Russo-Austrian army in such a total way that it ended the Third Coalition right then and there.

The battle was a tactical masterpiece, in which Napoleon deliberately weakened his right flank to entice the allied forces to attack it, while holding his main force out of sight. When the allies took the bait, Napoleon's main force recaptured strategic higher ground on the right flank and from there attacked the allied center, now weakened from its attack on the French flank. After breaking the allied center, Napoleon's forces encircled it from the rear and mopped it up (Fremont-Barnes, 19). Russian and Austrian casualties numbered around 27,000, of which 15,000 dead, out of a combined army of 73,000, while the French had close to 9,000

---

16   One such blunder was the execution of Louis Antoine de Bourbon, Duke of Enghien, on March 21, 1804, after he had been falsely implemented in a royalist conspiracy. Being a member of the House of Bourbon and a royalist who had fought against the French Republic, Napoleon considered the Duke a potential danger to the stability of his government (Burke, 158–61). The young Duke's death shocked the European aristocracy. Sweden cut off diplomatic relations with France after the incident. Another provocative move by Napoleon was letting himself be crowned king of Italy in May 1805, which ticked off the Austrians, who considered Northern Italy within their traditional sphere of influence.

casualties, including 1,300 dead, out of an army of 67,000 (Chandler, 432).

The Fourth Coalition was decisively defeated through victories at the Battles of Jena (1806) and Friedland (1807), the Fifth Coalition ended with the Austrian defeat at the Battle of Wagram (1809).

Napoleon was master of Europe, occupying and/or controlling Spain, the Dutch Republic, Italy, a slew of German kingdoms, duchies, principalities and towns, Denmark, Austria, Switzerland, and a large part of present-day Poland. The wars that the European powers had brought to the French Republic to restore the monarchy had thus turned around and bit them in their *derrières,* so to speak. The general conscription that revolutionary France had introduced to survive the first two coalitions against it, had grown into an army of over 2,500,000 men and given a highly intelligent, ambitious, energetic, charismatic military commander the chance to rise to the occasion and do what he did best: wage war.

Napoleon's military genius lay not so much in revolutionizing warfare but in its innovation, notably through improved tactical organization, flexibility and mobility. One such innovation was grouping divisions into multiple smaller army corps, comprised of infantry, artillery and cavalry, capable of functioning as miniature armies and operating independently. The movements of these different army corps could be highly deceptive to the enemy, while their logistical burden was obviously lighter than that of a bigger army. As a rule, Napoleon dispersed his corps while on the march, so that they could help each other when an advantageous position to give battle emerged.

In Napoleon's own words: "*Here is the principle of war - a corps of 25,000–30,000 men can be left on its own. Well handled, it can fight or alternatively avoid action, and maneuver according to circumstances without any harm coming to it, because an opponent cannot force it to accept an engagement but if it chooses to do so it can fight alone for a long time."* (qtd. in Chandler, 154).

In addition to his aptitude for (military) innovation and command, Napoleon was also highly energetic—habitually working eighteen to twenty hours a day—and gifted with a photographic memory. One anecdote goes that while on campaign in 1805, one of his subordinates could not locate his unit. While his aides were searching through maps and papers, the emperor effortlessly cited the unit's current location to the officer, as well as where it would be for the next three nights, what its strength was and what the embarrassed officer's military record was. And this out of an army of 200,000 men, with all the units on the move (Dean, "Napoleon").

But there were also mistakes. Like the Peninsular War (1807–14), in which Napoleon fought the Spanish, Portuguese and British for control of the Iberian Peninsula. It evolved into a costly guerrilla war, draining French resources while achieving little. As Napoleon would later lament in his memoirs: *"All the circumstances of my disasters are connected with that fatal knot: it destroyed my moral power in Europe, rendered my embarrassments more complicated, and opened a school for the English soldiers. It was I who trained the English army in the Peninsula."* (qtd. in Las Cases, 135).[17]

And then there was the disastrous invasion of Russia in 1812, aimed at forcing that vast country to the East to commit to the Continental System, a large-scale embargo against Great Britain.

As Napoleon's *Grande Armée* advanced through Western Russia in the summer of 1812, the Russians deployed a combination of Fabian and scorched earth strategy, continuously retreating while simultaneously burning, dispersing and

---

17   *"Spanish ulcer"* was another, not so flattering moniker Napoleon used for the Peninsular War (Rose, 173).

destroying all the resources, luring the French further and further into the Russian Empire.[18]

On September 7, 1812, the Russians finally engaged the French, at the Battle of Borodino. Though Napoleon won the battle, he did not succeed in destroying the Russian army—a failure that may have lost him the war. Losses were heavy on both sides, but of course unlike the Russians, the French could not replenish their forces.

A week later Napoleon entered an empty Moscow. Its citizens had evacuated, food stores had been destroyed or plundered. To make matters worse, the governor of the city had left behind a police detachment whom he had charged with burning the city to the ground, as the French learned after catching a Russian police officer (Caulaincourt, 121). [19]

A month later, with no victory in sight and worried about the political stability at home, Napoleon began his retreat through the winter wonder landscape of a hostile Russia. But what began as the disappointing retreat of an undefeated army quickly morphed into a death march, claiming hundreds of thousands of lives through hunger, disease, drowning (while crossing the Berezina river), incessant attacks on the rearguard and of course the cold. Eventually, only 112,000 returned to France at the end of 1812, out of the 680,00 strong army (including 68,000 non-combatants) that had begun the Russian campaign.[20]

---

18   The Fabian strategy is named after Roman dictator Fabius Maximus, who, against Hannibal Barca and his Carthaginian army, which invaded the Italian peninsula in 218 BCE, deployed a strategy of avoiding large, pitched battles while constantly harassing the enemy through small skirmishes.

19   Armand de Gaulaincourt was a general in Napoleon's army who accompanied him on his Russian campaign as Officer of Horse, meaning he was in charge of the horses of Napoleon and his guard. Gaulaincourt was still working on his memoirs when he died. The work was lost but eventually rediscovered after World War I and published for the first time in 1935.

20   Of the 612,000 combatants, 100,000 were killed in battle, 200,000 died of hunger, exhaustion, cold, or disease, 100,000 were captured, 50,000 ended up in hospitals and another 50,000 deserted. Of the 68,000 non-combatants, about

With the French army now severely weakened and Napoleon's reputation of invincibility seriously damaged, the other European powers smelled blood in the water and formed a Sixth Coalition. On October 16, 1813, a coalition of Russian, Prussian, Austrian and Swedish forces met Napoleon's hastily rebuilt army—which was about half the size of the coalition army—at Leipzig. The subsequent Battle of Leipzig (a.k.a the Battle of the Nations), the largest battle in Europe before World War I, involved 600,000 soldiers and lasted for three days. It ended in a decisive French defeat, forcing Napoleon to abdicate as Emperor of the French not long after, on april 11, 1814.[21]

The victors subsequently exiled their nemesis to the island of Elba, about 15 miles off the Tuscan coast and also not far from Liguria, where his ancestors had been from.[22] Napoleon was given sovereignty over the island and allowed to retain his title of emperor.[23] The first few months he really tried to make something of his rule of Elba, but what was a small island to a man accustomed to play with kingdoms and empires? So, less than a year after his arrival, the Emperor of Elba escaped and sailed for France. And while the nations of Europe were still deliberating the new borders of Europe at the Congress of Vienna, Napoleon landed at the Golfe-Juan, on the Côte d'Azur, on March 1, 1815.

On the road to Paris, he was stopped by the 5th Infantry Regiment, sent to intercept and arrest him. For a moment, it

---

half perished while the other half deserted (Bodart, 127).

21   The French suffered 73,000 casualties and the allies 54,000 at Leipzig (Chandler, 1120). The Germans dubbed the battle *Die Völkerschlacht*, which somehow sounds more honest than the English 'Battle of the Nations'; perhaps because the German word 'Schlacht' can mean battle as well as slaughter.

22   The Buonapartes had emigrated to Corsica in the 16th century.

23   Article III of the Treaty of Fontainebleau (April 11,1814): "*The Isle of Elba, adopted by his majesty the Emperor Napoleon as the place of his residence, shall form, during his life, a separate principality, which shall be possessed by him in all sovereignty and property.*" (qtd. in Kelly, 752).

seemed the comeback of the defeated, deposed and banished Corsican was over before it had begun, but then he demonstrated why he was Napoleon.

"*Here I am. Kill your Emperor, if you wish.*", he said to the soldiers pointing their muskets at him (McLynn, 605). But instead of firing or taking him into custody, they shouted "*Vive L'Empereur!*" and marched to Paris with him (McLynn, 605).

The greatest talent of the man affectionately called '*le petit caporal*' (the little corporal) by his men, was not his sheer limitless energy, impressive intelligence, photographic memory, organizational skill or even his strategic instinct. It was his charismatic personality, creating the kind of loyalty that has men follow their leader to the ends of the world and back, capable of suffering defeat, dead comrades, frozen body parts, starvation and lost honor without wavering in their willingness to pledge their lives to this man on a horse who had fled captivity and was now on his way back to Paris.

With Bonaparte approaching, Louis XVIII, brother of the executed Louis XVI and the new king of France, quickly fled the country. Napoleon was master of the castle once again. But this time, his reign would last only 100 days.

On June 18, 1815, at Waterloo (present-day Belgium), Napoleon fought and lost his last battle against the allied forces of the Seventh Coalition, mainly comprised of soldiers from Great Britain, Prussia and the Netherlands. Talking to British Member of Parliament Thomas Creevey in Brussels just after the battle, the Duke of Wellington, the British commander of the allied forces, called it "*the nearest run thing your ever saw in your life*", but Napoleon had nevertheless lost decisively (Creevey, 236). He was captured within a month and this time exiled to Saint Helena island, in the Atlantic Ocean, far away from any coast, where he died six years later, on May 5, 1821, aged 51.

Napoleon's reign, however short, controversial and full of conflict, has had a profound and lasting influence on France, Europe and many other parts of the world, during as well as long after the fifteen years he ruled, fought and reformed.

His battles and military innovations would be studied at length by all the great commanders of the 19th and 20th century. Even the Duke of Wellington, the hero of Waterloo, when asked by John Le Couteur, Aide-de-camp to Queen Victoria, whom he considered to be the greatest soldier of his age, answered: *"In this age, in past ages, in any age, Napoleon."* (Roberts, "Waterloo", 272).[24]

At the U.S. military academy of West Point, cadets who would later fight as generals during the American Civil War—such as Robert E. Lee, John F. Reynolds and George B. McClellan—all received their military strategy training from professor Dennis Hart Mahan, an American military theorist who was deeply influenced by Napoleon and used the translated writings of Antoine-Henri Jomini—one of Napoleon's former generals, who had sought to systemize Napoleonic warfare—as the main textbooks on military strategy (Chambers, 558).

Napoleon was also largely responsible for the pan-Continental European adoption of the metric system, just as his *Code Napoléon*—the French civil law code—was adopted in many countries occupied by the French during the Napoleonic Wars, including Italy, Spain, Portugal, the Netherlands, Belgium and a large part of Germany. And through colonial ties, Napoleon's Civil Code also influenced the legal systems of several Latin American and African nations, the Canadian province of Quebec and the U.S. state of Louisiana.[25]

---

24 Of course, since Wellington was the one who eventually defeated Napoleon, praising Napoleon for being the greatest soldier ever to have walked the face of the earth made him the soldier who had bested the greatest soldier who had ever walked the face of the earth....

25 As Napoleon correctly predicted to Charles Montholon, one of his former generals who had accompanied him to Saint Helena and stayed with him until

66

With a single stroke of the pen Napoleon also managed to have a lasting effect on the United States, when, in 1803—after deciding to abandon the idea of rebuilding France's New World Empire and instead concentrate on Europe—he sold the entire French claim in North America to the young country that had won its independence from France's archenemy only twenty years earlier. The Louisiana Purchase was by far the largest territorial gain in U.S. history and doubled the size of the country, encompassing (part of) fifteen present-day U.S. states.[26]

As for South America, Napoleon's invasion and subsequent occupation of Spain in 1808 brought *de facto* autonomy to the Spanish colonies there, igniting a spark that would lead to a host of revolutionary wars between 1808–33, through which Argentine, Chile, Peru, Bolivia, Ecuador, Colombia, Venezuela and Mexico all won their independence.

In Europe the old order of things had also been shaken up, most notably in the German and Italian region, where Napoleon had reorganized numerous kingdoms, duchies and principalities into larger entities, thus laying the foundation for a later wave of nationalism from which two new nations would ultimately emerge, one of whom would have a particularly strong influence on some of the most deadly and disturbing events of the turbulent 20th century.

But that's something for another theme park.

---

the end: "*My true glory is not to have won forty battles....Waterloo will erase the memory of so many victories....But what nothing will destroy, what will live forever, is my Civil Code.*" ("Ma gloire n'est pas d'avoir gagné quarante batailles.... Waterloo effacera le souvenir de tant de victoires....Mais ce que rien ne'effacera, ce qui vivra éternellement, c'est mon code civil.") (qtd. in Montholon, 401).

26   The Louisiana Purchase Treaty was signed in Paris on April 30, 1803. Formal ownership was transferred to the United States on March 10, 1804.

4

The Industrial Revolution

"We have not made the Revolution, the Revolution has made us."

Georg Büchner (1813–1837), *Dantons Tod*, Act II. 1835.

O N May 5, 2013, open-source organization Defense Distributed made files for the world's first fully 3D printable gun publicly available. The gun, a .380 single shot pistol aptly named the *Liberator*, was entirely made out of plastic except for the firing pin, and thus undetectable by metal detectors.[1]

The design for the Liberator was downloaded more than 100,000 times in the first two days (Ernesto, "Pirate Bay"). On May 9, the United States Department of State requested Defense Distributed to remove the download links from its site. The organization complied, but by then the files were already available through a host of other online sources, including the notoriously libertarian torrent site The Pirate Bay, which refused to take links to the files down, stating: "*TPB* [The Pirate Bay] *has close to 10 years been operating without taking down one single torrent due to pressure from the outside. And it will never start doing that.*" (qtd. in Ernesto, "Pirate Bay").

The printable gun quickly became world news, introducing many people to the practical applications of 3D printing for

---

1   A 6-ounce steel slug was also added by Defense Distributed, but this only to comply with the Undetectable Firearms Act of 1998; the gun would also work without the slug.

the first time. And with prices of 3D printers having come down sharply—the cheapest 3D printers start at just a few hundred dollars, down from over thousands just a few years ago—many people could now for the first time easily afford to 3D print their own teapots, shoes, jewelry, Star Wars action figures and, well, guns.

The main reason for the huge price drop was the expiration of key patents for one of the more primitive forms of 3D printing, so-called *Fused Deposition Modeling*, in 2009 (Hornick, "3D Printing Patents"). In early 2014, several key patents for a more advanced form of 3D printing also expired, and a few months after that the world's largest 2D printing company, HP, announced the imminent launch of its first 3D printer, which it said would be ten times faster than anything else on the market (Krassenstein, "HP's Multi Jet Fusion").

Something similar happened with the 18th century steam engine, first with the Newcomen steam engine—invented by Thomas Newcomen in 1712—and later also with the famous steam engine of Scottish inventor James Watt, for which the key patents expired at the beginning of the 19th century.

Watt had originally come up with the idea for a better steam engine in 1765, while repairing a small Newcomen steam engine, which he found wasted most of its energy because heating and cooling both took place inside the piston cylinder. Four years later, the patent containing his solution—Patent 913, *A method of lessening the consumption of steam in steam engines through a separate condenser*—was granted (Hills, "James Watt", 13). Through an act of Parliament, Watt then succeeded in extending this patent until the year 1800. In other words, for 30 years no one but James Watt had the right to improve steam engines that used a separate condenser chamber (Osborne, 121–22).

Between 1776, when the first Watt engines were installed, and 1800, when Watt's patent expired, steam engines added about 750 horsepower to the United Kingdom's factories each year. During the 30 years following the patent's expiration this increased to about 4,000 per year (Boldrin, 1). Power and fuel efficiency also rapidly increased in the years after Watt's patent had expired (Boldrin, 1).[2]

Still, Watt's steam engine was a major improvement from the Newcomen engine, providing roughly three times more power with the same amount of fuel (Enys, 449ff.).[3] And it arrived at just the right time too, as the British textile industry was being revolutionized by a handful of game-changing inventions in the 1760s-70s, propelling it from a cottage industry—in which families spun yarn at home and sold it independently to weavers—to one of mass production, where factories filled with automated machines did the work of a thousand manual spinners and weavers.

It was the beginning of the Industrial Revolution.

In 1733, the Englishman John Kay had invented the so-called flying shuttle, a small device that not only enabled weavers to weave twice as fast but also only made the work a lot easier and physically less demanding. Nice for the weavers, but not so much for the spinners, who were already struggling to keep up with the ever increasing demand for yarn. This imbalance between weavers and spinners went on for 30 years, until one James Hargreaves in the 1760s invented the spinning jenny, a spinning frame that used eight spindles instead of one (Espinasse, 324). Hargreaves used the machine to produce yarn himself and also sold some machines to others in Blackburn, where he lived. When, consequently, the price of yarn in the region dropped, angry spinners broke into Hargreaves' house and destroyed his machines (Espinasse, 324). Hargreaves then set up shop in Nottingham, started a

---

2   Boldrin and Levine estimate that the fuel efficiency increased by a factor five between 1810–35. Data for this estimate comes from Nuvolari (2004b).

3   The Newcomen and Watt engines data can be found in Enys, 457–58.

textile business and in 1770 patented a sixteen spindle spinning jenny (Espinasse, 324–25).

He wasn't the only one trying to improve spinning productivity though. In fact, one year earlier, English entrepreneur Richard Arkwright had patented the spinning frame (a.k.a. water frame), which, powered by a waterwheel, could operate automatically and continuously, spinning cotton from multiple spindles into yarn without end. The spinning frame produced stronger yarn than that of a spinning jenny and needed less skilled labor to operate.

And Arkwright did not stop there. In 1771, realizing the potential of the spinning frame, he built a water-powered cotton spinning mill—the world's first—in Cromford, Derbyshire, with the backing of a few other investors (Fitton, 65). Once opened, the mill was in production day and night. Arkwright started with 200 workers, and when he couldn't find enough workers in the local area, he built an entire village around the mill to encourage families to come to Cromford and work for him (Fitton, 97–99). Apart from houses, the village had a church, chapel, inn and a manager's mansion.

By 1776, the Cromford mill employed 500 workers, men, women and children, working twelve-hour shifts (Fitton, 98–99). When Arkwright, sometimes called the 'father of the industrial revolution', died in 1792, aged 59, he was the wealthiest untitled man in England.

After Arkwright's patent had expired, others quickly copied the water frame and opened spinning mills too, further increasing the supply of yarn. Now it was the weavers who had trouble keeping up, clearing the path for Edmund Cartwright's 1785 invention of the power loom, a steam-powered, mechanically operated version of the regular loom. The power loom needed significant improvement by several other inventors in later years, but it did eventually bring back the balance between weavers and spinners. By 1833, there were 100,000 power looms in the UK alone, up from just

2,400 in 1803 (Hills, "Power from Steam", 117). The weavers themselves were less than happy with the introduction of the power loom; fearing loss of work, they allegedly even burned down one of Cartwright's two factories (Strickland, 107–08). But although demand for skilled hand weavers indeed decreased because of the power loom, overall employment actually *increased* over the longer term, as the falling price of cloth continuously increased demand for it.

Meanwhile, the productivity race between weavers and spinners also increased pressure on the cotton industry. Cotton picking was very labor-intensive, because it had to be picked and separated from the seeds by hand. Enter the cotton gin, an inexpensive mechanical device invented by the American Eli Whitney in 1793. The cotton gin was a simple but ingenious contraption, consisting of a spiked wooden cylinder with a roller on top to put pressure on the cotton and pull it through a teethed grid, catching the seeds while forcing the cotton through. An inexpensive little machine, but one that would have enormous consequences.

In the American South, the cotton gin enabled a slave to produce about fifty pounds of cotton lint per day, whereas manual separation netted only about one to two pounds a day (Jacobson, 46). Suddenly, cotton production was a very profitable venture, and with spinning and weaving factories springing up left and right, plantation owners certainly did not have to worry about demand.

Coincidentally, the first waterwheel-powered cotton mill in the United States was also opened in 1793, by the Englishman Samuel Slater. Born in Derbyshire in 1768, not far from where Richard Arkwright would build his cotton mill a few years later, Slater had come to the New World after having learned everything there was to know about weaving and spinning mills as an apprentice of Jedidiah Strutt, a partner of Arkwright (Caranci, 35–37). Fearful of exporting information about designs and processes used in the textile industry to its commercial rivals, Britain had enacted a law that forbade textile workers to emigrate, but disguised as a farm hand Slater had nevertheless made it to America (Caranci, 36).[4]

Needless to say, cotton production exploded throughout the South. Between 1820–50, cotton production in the United States went from 335,000 500-pound bales to 2,136,000 500-pound bales per year ("Statistical Abstract " 1937, 636). By 1860, it was 3,841,000 bales per year. Thus, in just a few decades, the United States became by far the largest supplier of cotton in the world.

With 'King Cotton' making plantation owners richer every year, it is hardly surprising that the number of slave states also increased, from six to fifteen between 1790–1860.[5] The same goes for the number of slaves in the cotton states, which more than tripled between 1820–50, from 632,000 to 1,979,000 (Mann, 53).[6] With these kind of numbers, it is hard to overestimate the impact of Whitney's cotton gin on the economy of the South, the institution of slavery and, ultimately, the outbreak of the American Civil War.

Of course the tremendous increase in cotton production boosted the demand for more cotton spinning, weaving and carding machines as well. Factory owners also began to look for machines with increased durability, ones that used metal instead of wooden parts for instance. This in turn led to a growing demand for all kinds of metalworking (machine) tools, such as the lathe, and an unprecedented increase in demand for iron and smelting furnaces.

---

4   In the United States, Samuel Slater is known as the father of the American Industrial Revolution. By contrast, in the United Kingdom he is known as 'Slater the Traitor' (Caranci, 35).

5   In the years leading up to the American Civil War, the term 'King Cotton' was frequently used in the Southern States to express the economic and political importance of the cotton industry.

6   North-Carolina and Texas are excluded from the data Mann used.

Initially, the furnaces were stoked with charcoal, but by the 1750s coke was replacing charcoal because it was cheaper, easier to make and allowed for larger blast furnaces.[7] During the second part of the 18th century and the early 19th century several improvements to the process of ironmaking further boosted the use of iron in machinery. The rolling mill (1783) greatly increased the speed of production for instance, by rolling instead of hammering iron flat, while the puddling process (1784) improved the quality of iron by stirring it and the hot blast (1828) increased fuel efficiency by preheating the air that was blown into the blast furnace.[8]

Now, to power all those furnaces and steam engines, an awful lot of coal needed to be mined and transported, and the fact that there was so many of it readily available in Great Britain is one of the reasons why the Industrial Revolution not only started there but continued to gain traction. Why so many canals were dug in Britain and why both the inventor of the first locomotive, Richard Trevithick, and the location of the first public railway using steam locomotives, the Stockton & Darlington Railway, were British.[9]

So, where had the revered Renaissance, the smart Scientific Revolution and the eloquent Age of Enlightenment eventually led us, having taught us to focus on the here and now, on making things of beauty, on acquiring and spreading knowledge and education, and on pursuing life, liberty and

---

7   Charcoal is most often made from burning wood slowly, while coke is a by-product from coal.

8   Both puddling and the rolling mill are attributed to Henry Cort (1740–1800), though both methods already existed in rudimentary form before Cort was awarded his patents in 1784. Cort's innovation lay in combining the improvements from these rudimentary methods into a single, new process, not unlike what Gutenberg had done when he combined movable type and block printing into a mechanized process with his printing press (Ashton, 93).

9   In its first successful test run, Trevithick's steam engine carriage, the 'puffing-devil', carried six passengers up Camborne hill on Christmas Eve 1801. The Stockton & Darlington Railway opened in 1825.

happiness? The answer for 19th century socialist philosophers Karl Marx and Friedrich Engels was that it had led to whole families having to work 12-hour shifts in a damp factory for wages that were barely enough to stave of starvation. They foresaw a class struggle between workers and the owners of the means to production (i.e., the 'capitalists'), which they predicted would eventually lead to a revolution in which the workers would take ownership of the factories.[10]

A less pessimistic view is that while factory conditions may have led to a decline in quality of life for those at the lowest rungs of society during the early stages of the Industrial Revolution, real wages, life expectancy and social conditions were all improving in several Western countries by the second part of the 19th century, especially when compared to the malnourished, short, subservient, miserable life that most had been destined to lead before the dawn of the industrial age.

Several studies have shown that the standard of living and real wages hardly increased between 1800 BCE and 1800 CE, because the extra resources won from technological advances always went to an increased population, not to a better life for those already living.[11] This observation—now known as the Malthusian trap—was first made by political economist Thomas Malthus, in 1798. In *An Essay on the Principle of Population*, Malthus observed "*That population does invariably increase when the means of subsistence increase. And, That the superior power of population is repressed, and the actual population kept equal to the means of subsistence, by*

10   The views of Marx and Engels would indeed lead to revolutions in several countries in the 20th century, but none of them would progress the way they had predicted. See also chapter 8, *The Russian Revolution(s)*, chapter 12, *Chinese Civil War Part I & II*, chapter 20, *The Cultural Revolution*, and chapter 21, *The End of Communism*.

11   See for instance Robert C. Allen, *The Great Divergence in European Wages and Prices from the Middle Ages to the First World War*, and Gregory Clark, *A Farewell to Alms: A Brief Economic History of the World*, particularly chapter two.

misery and vice." (Malthus, VII.21). Due to this inescapable relation between the growth of resources and population, Malthus concluded, *"Man cannot live in the midst of plenty."* (Malthus, X.7).[12]

During the Industrial Revolution, however, societies were finally able to escape the Malthusian trap. Malthus had therefore, somewhat ironically, formulated a theory correctly explaining a phenomenon that had existed for millennia—just before it ran out of steam for the first time in history.

The Industrial Revolution certainly made the economic struggle at the bottom more visible though. Families who used to spin or weave days on end in their ill-lit, damp little cottages, were now doing so in Mr. Arkwright's cotton mills, together with hundreds of other families. Wages, work hours, working conditions, child labor, everything was suddenly much more in the open. Factory conditions left much to be desired of course, but it was also because of these factories that for the first time effective labor regulation became even possible. As a result—and a sign of things to come—the first Factory Act was passed in 1802, in Great Britain.[13]

Throughout the 19th and early 20th century, industrialized countries passed several other laws that sought to improve the position of the workers. These laws were one of the reasons why the catastrophe Marx and Engels had predicted never really materialized. Even if their reasoning—that capitalism would inevitably lead to class struggle, followed by its destruction and replacement with socialism—would be correct for a completely free, unregulated market, outcomes were markedly different when the state and/or labor unions stepped in to smooth over the imperfections of the system. Of course, improving the position of the workers also increased

---

12   For a thorough explanation of the Malthusian trap, see *Dynamics and Stagnation in the Malthusian Epoch,* by Quamrul Ashraf and Oded Galor.

13   The *Health and Morals of Apprentices Act 1802.* It regulated the treatment of apprentices (mostly children) by cotton mill owners and set cleanliness requirements for factories.

domestic demand for all those products that were being cranked out day and night by the factories, making factory owners even richer.

Another effect of the Industrial Revolution was a massive urbanization wave. With factories hungry for more workers and people in rural areas hungry for work, cities quickly became magnets for job seekers, startup entrepreneurs and established factory owners alike. And so, while about 6 percent of the world's population lived in cities in 1800, by 2009, for the first time in history, over 50 percent did ("World Urbanization Prospects"; Vries, 71).[14]

Of course the social dynamics of city life are vastly different from those in rural areas. Ideas, unrest and rebellion spread much faster in cities housing millions of people than in a countryside dotted with farms and small villages, which is likely one of the reasons why the 19th and 20th century would see more than their fair share of revolutions, rebellions, civil wars and social movements.

In terms of significance to our economic development and general way of life, the Industrial Revolution certainly ranks at the same level as the Neolithic Revolution that took place some 12,000 years ago. Back then, the paradigm shift in our way of life was going from hunting and gathering to farming; making a home, keeping animals, growing crop. From then on, we built not just on the experiences of our forefathers, but on their achievements as well.

Similarly, the Industrial Revolution put us on an entirely new path of highly specialized labor, ever growing urbanization and global interdependency. Most of us no longer

---

14   De Vries convincingly rejects the frequently cited assertion that only 3 percent of the world's population lived in cities around 1800, asserting that the global urbanization rate at the time was likely more than double that number (Vries, 69ff.). Based on city population numbers, he further estimates that 10 percent of the European population lived in cities of 10,000 and above in 1800, an urbanization rate that climbs to 15 percent when looking at cities of 5,000 and above (Vries, 71–73).

know how to milk a cow or make a table and chairs. Truth be told, in the eyes of Neolithic man, we are utterly helpless and mostly useless. Yet we have more food, more leisure time, more freedom and a higher life expectancy than ever before.

Interestingly enough, 3D printing could mean a high-tech return to the time before the Industrial Revolution. Instead of letting factories stamp out millions of more and the same (only with a different color) we could design and create our own, unique products again, repair stuff instead of having to throw something away because of a broken part that cost only $2.50 to make but is sold for $50. In other words, for the first time in 200 years we could become our own, independent producers again.

Or have we already forgotten how to?

PROVINCE OF CANADA

UNITED STATES

'Border States'

U.S. TERRITORIES

CONFEDERATE STATES

MEXICO

ATLANTIC OCEAN

Lancaster

Pennsylvania

York

☆ Gettysburg (1863)

Cumberland

Hagerstown

Maryland

☆ Antietam (1862)

West Virginia (1863)

U.S.A.

C.S.A.

Winchester

☆ Cedar Creek (1864)

Baltimore

Annapolis

Washington, D.C.

2nd Bull Run (1862) ☆ Alexandria

Harrisonburg

Chancellorsville (1863)

Wilderness (1864) ☆ ☆ ☆ Fredericksburg (1862)
☆
Spotsylvania Court
House (1864)

Charlottesville

Virginia

Chesapeake Bay

Richmond ☆ Cold Harbor (1864)
☆ Seven Pines (1862)
☆ Malvern Hill (1862)

Lynchburg

Petersburg ☆ Petersburg (1864)
☆
3rd Petersburg (1865)

Hampton

Norfolk

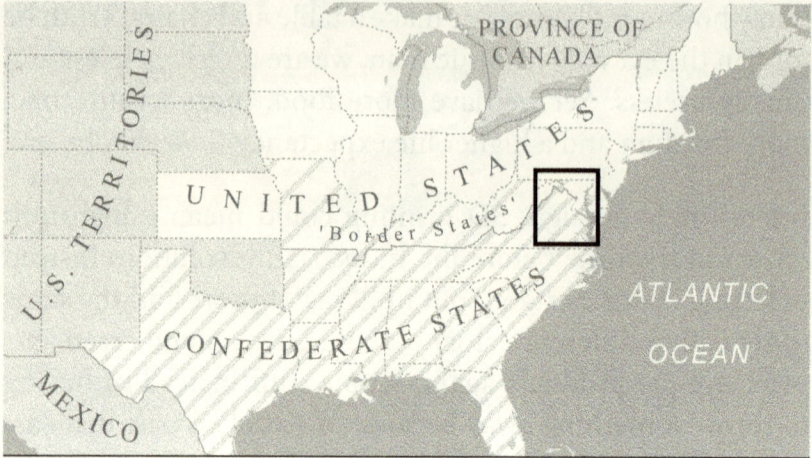

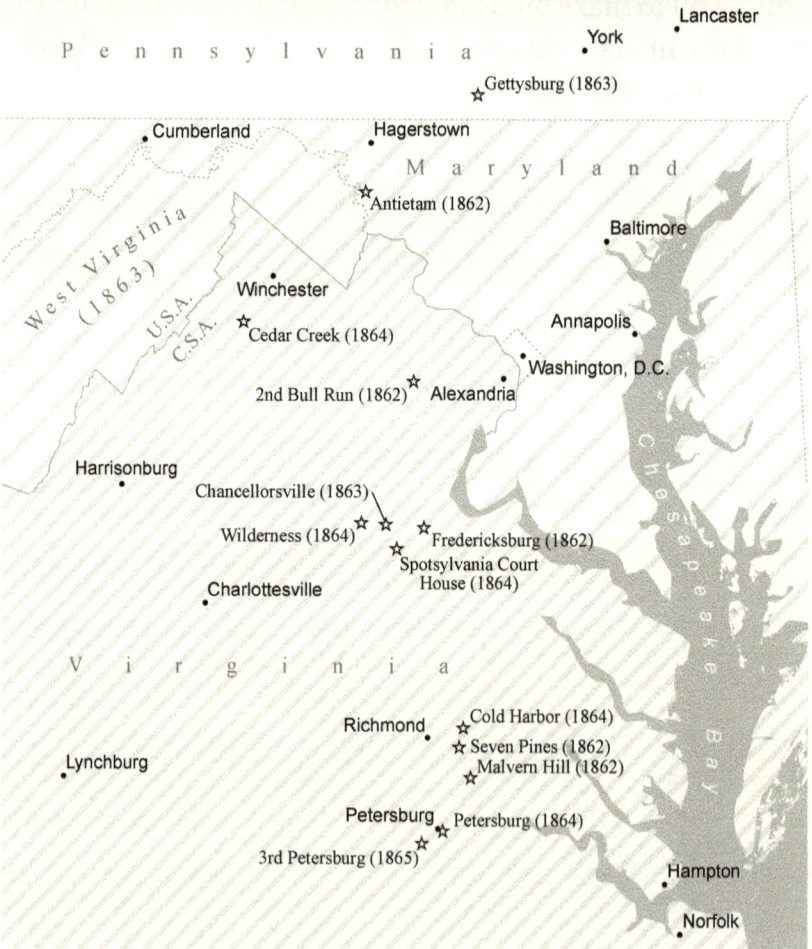

Map 3: The Eastern Theater of the American Civil War, 1861-65

5

A SECOND AMERICAN REVOLUTION

"Fourscore and seven years ago our fathers brought forth on this continent, a new nation, conceived in liberty, and dedicated to the proposition that all men are created equal. Now we are engaged in a great civil war, testing whether that nation, or any nation so conceived and so dedicated, can long endure. We are met on a great battlefield of that war. We have come to dedicate a portion of that field, as a final resting-place for those who here gave their lives that that nation might live. It is altogether fitting and proper that we should do this. But, in a larger sense, we cannot dedicate —we cannot consecrate—we cannot hallow—this ground. The brave men, living and dead, who struggled here, have consecrated it, far above our poor power to add or detract. The world will little note, nor long remember what we say here, but it can never forget what they did here. It is for us the living, rather, to be dedicated here to the unfinished work which they who fought here have thus far so nobly advanced. It is rather for us to be here dedicated to the great task remaining before us—that from these honored dead we take increased devotion to that cause for which they gave the last full measure of devotion—that we here highly resolve that these dead shall not have died in vain, that this nation, under God, shall have a new birth of freedom—and that government of the people, by the people, for the people, shall not perish from the earth."

Abraham Lincoln, Gettysburg Address (Bliss copy),
November 19, 1863

IN 1864, ELIAS BREWSTER HILLARD INTERVIEWED THE last survivor of the American Revolutionary War, which had ended 81 years earlier. Lemuel Cook, born in Litchfield County, Connecticut—back when it was still part of the British Empire—had been only sixteen years old when he joined the 2nd Regiment of Light Dragoons (Hillard, 34).

Cook saw action in several engagements throughout the war and was present at the decisive Battle of Yorktown, where Lord Cornwallis surrendered (Hillard, 36). He also met and spoke a few words with General Washington in the fall of 1776, near White Plains, while the Continental Army was in retreat, and again a couple of years later, when Washington— apparently remembering him—called him by his name and asked him about his horse (Cook, "Lemuel Remembers"). On June 12, 1784, Cook saw Washington one last time, when he received his honorable discharge, signed by the general himself (Hillard, 33; Cook, "Lemuel Remembers").

When Hillard asked him about his thoughts on the *"present war"*, Cook brought down his cane on the floor with force and replied in strong tone: *"It is terrible, but terrible as it is the rebellion must be put down."* (Hillard, 38).[1]

Of course a British centenarian who, as a sixteen-year-old, had supported the Parliamentarian cause during the Glorious Revolution of 1688, would have probably classified the American Revolution of 1776 as a rebellion too. It seems that the longer we live, the easier it is for history to catch up with us.

In any case, for the Southern States that seceded from the union in 1861, secession did not constitute a rebellion but the birth of a new nation, the Confederate States of America.[2] To

---

1   Lemuel Cook lived long enough to see the union preserved, dying on May 20, 1866 in Clarendon, New York ("Lemuel Cook").

2   Seven Southern States seceded from the Union before Abraham Lincoln took office as President on March 4, 1861. The first was South Carolina, on December 20, 1860, followed by Mississippi, Florida, Alabama, Georgia,

them, Abraham Lincoln's victory in the presidential elections on November 6, 1860, had been the final straw. Lincoln had carried only two of the 996 counties in the Southern States, but he still won, because of his strong support in the North and West (Mansch, 61).

Lincoln had run on a moderate anti-slavery platform, objecting to its expansion into new territories but not calling for the end of slavery where it already existed (Jaffa, 74, 79). The expansion of slavery into new territories had been a hotly debated issue between the Northern and Southern States for decades though, for moral, legal, political and economic reasons.

From an economic viewpoint, not allowing slavery in the new territories would make it more difficult for Southern businesses to expand westward, since the South's economy was largely dependent on slavery. Politically, the effect of prohibiting slavery in new states was perhaps even more threatening to the Cotton States in the long run, as it would slowly but certainly erode the South's influence in Washington when new states joined the North in its anti-slavery position, thus swelling the ranks of the abolitionists until the South could no longer prevent Congress from ending slavery completely.

Slavery had been a divisive issue from the beginning. Even at the Constitutional Convention of 1787 slavery had been among the most controversial issues, complicating almost every debate, especially that about representation, with the Southern States wanting to fully include slaves in the population count while the Northern States only wanted to count free persons (Finkelman, 10ff.). The issue was directly linked to the plan of making population the primary criterium for representation in Congress, instead of giving each state one

---

Louisiana and Texas. After the Confederate attack on Unionist Fort Sumter (April 12, 1861) and Lincoln's subsequent call for troops to suppress the nascent rebellion on April 15, Virginia, Arkansas, Tennessee and North Carolina also seceded.

vote, as had been the case with the—ineffective—Articles of Confederation (Finkelman, 11). Eventually the Convention reached a compromise whereby slaves would be counted as three-fifths of a free person.[3]

In the years that followed the differences between North and South only deepened. Eli Whitney's invention of the cotton gin in 1793 made cotton production far more profitable and the need for cheap cotton pickers (i.e., slaves) only greater. Meanwhile, the Northern States, devoid of the easy riches of King Cotton, instead concentrated their economic efforts increasingly on industrialization, with a manufacturing industry based on the British model, fast-growing cities and an expanding network of railroads.

Industrialization was what caused seven out of eight European immigrants to settle in the North, looking for jobs in the many factories, and why many whites from the South moved to the North (McPherson, "Antebellum Southern Exceptionalism", 426–27). Industrialization also caused Northern States to demand higher import tariffs, to protect their businesses against foreign—especially British—competition, something the Southern States were adamantly against, wanting to protect their cotton export to Europe—especially Britain—and fearing British counter-protectionist policies.[4]

In 1820, the pro-slavery and anti-slavery factions had come to the so-called Missouri Compromise, which sought to regulate the expansion of slavery in the western territories by prohibiting it north of the parallel 36°30' north in the former Louisiana Territory, with the exception of the (proposed)

---

3   United States Constitution, Article I, Section 2, Paragraph 3: *Representatives and direct Taxes shall be apportioned among the several States which may be included within this Union, according to their respective Numbers, which shall be determined by adding to the whole Number of free Persons, including those bound to Service for a Term of Years, and excluding Indians not taxed, three fifths of all other Persons.*

4   Between 1830–64, around 70 percent of all U.S. cotton export went to Great Britain and around 20 percent to France (Mann, 57).

state of Missouri. To keep an equal balance between 'slave states' and 'free states', the Northern region of Massachusetts was to be admitted as the free State of Maine. The compromise would indeed ensure a delicate balance between slave states and free states for the coming decades, but Thomas Jefferson, by then a senior citizen of 77 years old, predicted that the compromise line would eventually lead to the destruction of the Union, writing in a letter to John Holmes:

> *"But this momentous question, like a fire bell in the night, awakened and filled me with terror. I considered it at once as the knell of the Union. It is hushed indeed for the moment. but this is a reprieve only, not a final sentence. A geographical line, coinciding with a marked principle, moral and political, once conceived and held up to the angry passions of men, will never be obliterated; and every new irritation will mark it deeper and deeper."* (Jefferson, "John Holmes").[5]

By 1850 another grand bargain had become necessary, to deal with the newly acquired territories resulting from the Mexican-American War (1846–48). The Compromise of 1850 admitted California as a free state in its entirety, instead of dividing it into a northern and southern part as the South had wanted. In exchange, the North agreed that no restrictions on slavery would be placed in the Utah and New Mexico Territory, leaving the question of slavery there to popular sovereignty. Also, slaveholding in Washington D.C. would be preserved but slave trade in the nation's capital was

---

5   Holmes was a supporter of the Missouri Compromise and the first Senator of the State of Maine. Jefferson, a wealthy slave owner himself, had conflicting views on slavery, opposing the institution of slavery and having attempted to legislate slavery emancipation several times, but stopping short of abolishing it in his own household. Describing perhaps his own relationship with slavery as much as the country's, Jefferson wrote to Holmes that *"we have the wolf by the ear, and we can neither hold him, nor safely let him go. justice is in one scale, and self-preservation in the other."* (Jefferson, "John Holmes").

to be prohibited, and Texas surrendered its claims to parts of New Mexico in exchange for federal assumption of its debt.

Lastly, a stronger Fugitive Slave Law was passed, requiring federal judicial officials in all states and territories to actively assist in returning slaves to their masters or be fined $1,000 (Fugitive Slave Act, Sec. 5). Individuals were also strictly prohibited from aiding runaway slaves in any way, or face a prison sentence of up to six months and a fine of up to $1,000 (Fugitive Slave Act, Sec. 7). Many in the North were outraged over the Fugitive Slave Law, especially about the fact that it forced them to basically condone slavery in the North when confronted with runaway slaves from the South.

A few years later, the Supreme Court weighed in on the expansion of slavery in federal territories with its decision in Scott v. Sandford (1857). Dred Scott, an African-American slave, had sued for freedom for himself, his wife and their two daughters on the ground that they had lived with their master in states and territories where slavery was illegal.

But the Supreme Court decided 7–2 against Scott, stating that no person of African ancestry could claim citizenship in the United States and that federal restrictions to slavery in U.S. territories were unconstitutional, because they conflicted with the Fifth Amendment, protecting citizens from being deprived of their property without due process. In other words, slave owners would be deprived of their constitutional right to take certain *"articles of property"* into the territories should Congress be allowed to restrict slavery there (Scott v. Sandford, I.6, IV.3).

In deciding whether African Americans could be considered citizens, Chief Justice Taney harked back to the time of the Declaration of Independence to determine if, at the time, *"the class of persons who had been imported as slaves [or] their descendants, whether they had become free or not, were then acknowledged as a part of the people"* (Scott v. Sandford, 407). Taney held that they were not, stating:

"It is difficult at this day to realize the state of public opinion in regard to that unfortunate race which prevailed in the civilized and enlightened portions of the world at the time of the Declaration of Independence, and when the Constitution of the United States was framed and adopted; but the public history of every European nation displays it in a manner too plain to be mistaken. They had for more than a century before been regarded as beings of an inferior order, and altogether unfit to associate with the white race, either in social or political relations, and so far unfit that they had no rights which the white man was bound to respect." (Scott v. Sandford, 407).

Scott v. Sandford thus nullified the Missouri Compromise (which prohibited slavery north of the parallel 36°30' north in the former Louisiana Territory), enraging the North and bringing the option of civil war as the ultimate way to settle the slavery issue once and for all considerably closer. That is to say, neither the South nor the North wanted war, but both sides had reached the limits of how far they were willing to compromise.

Moderate anti-slavery proponents like Abraham Lincoln thought it a reasonable compromise to let slavery die out over time, to give the South time to adjust. But most Southerners felt no inclination to change at all. They began to realize that staying in the Union would be detrimental to their way of life in the long run, because abolitionists would likely continue to make inroads in Washington.

So when Lincoln was elected in November 1860 without virtually any support in the South, the states of South Carolina, Mississippi, Florida, Alabama, Georgia, Louisiana and Texas saw the writing on the wall and decided to secede from the Union, forming the Confederate States of America (CSA) on February 8, 1861. Federal courthouses, forts and armories in the seceding states were seized left and right, while governors of decidedly pro-union states like New York, Pennsylvania and Massachusetts began to organize militarily as well, preparing for what at this point seemed an inevitable, violent clash between North and South (Keegan, 33; Schouler, 42ff.). Two months later, after President Lincoln called for troops to defend the Union in response to the Confederate attack on Fort Sumter (a union stronghold in Charleston Harbor, Charleston, South Carolina), Virginia, Arkansas, Tennessee and North Carolina seceded from the Union as well and joined the CSA.

The Southern States argued that the Union was a compact that states could abandon without consultation. The Northern states opposed this view, reasoning instead that the Union was perpetual and that abandoning it was not an option.

From a legal point of view, the idea of a 'perpetual union' is of course questionable at best. For one, the United States itself is founded on the principle that a tyrannical government can be a just cause for revolution, as can the absence of representation in government. To the Southern States, the fact that a man could be elected President even when almost the entire South voted against him, must have looked an awful lot like the absence of representation. And if all the new states were to be free states, how long before the abolitionists would have a qualified majority in Congress, allowing them to change the Constitution and end slavery?

Other arguments against the idea of a 'perpetual union' are that it goes against the right of self-determination—implied in John Locke's social contract theory of *government with the consent of the governed* and later also championed by U.S. Presidents Woodrow Wilson and Franklin D. Roosevelt— and that it is too inflexible a concept to deal with fundamental changes in political relations, views and realities.[6]

---

6   President Wilson articulated the right to self-determination for the peoples of Russia and the Ottoman Empire in his Fourteen Points speech of January 8, 1918, and further emphasized its importance in his address to Congress on February 11, 1918, when he said that "*Self-determination' is*

The first shots of the American Civil War were fired on January 9, 1861, when civilian steamship *Star of the West*, hired by the United States government to resupply Fort Sumter, was fired upon by South Carolina forces after passing the mouth of the harbor. The commander of the battery on Morris Island, Major Stevens, fired a shot across her bow, but instead of turning around, the steamship defiantly ran up the United States flag at her foremast a few minutes later (Harris, 23–24). Major Stevens then ordered several more rounds fired, two of which struck the ship, after which the ship did turn. Three more shots were fired from both Morris Island and Fort Moultrie, hitting the ship once more on its way out.

The shots did not mark the official start of the war but they might as well have. What followed was three months of increasing tension, during which the Union soldiers of Fort Sumter rushed to complete the installation of additional guns, while the commander of the Confederate forces in Charleston, General P. G. T. Beauregard, trained an increasing number of guns at the isolated fort.

Unlike his predecessor James Buchanan, Lincoln did not want any more federal forts relinquished to the South. So as soon as he was sworn in, on March 4, 1861, Lincoln ordered Fort Sumter's commander, Major Robert Anderson, to hold until fired upon. This way, if there really was to be civil war, it would be the South who was the aggressor, not the North.

On April 4, Lincoln ordered a relief expedition to supply Fort Sumter, but with provisions only. Two days later, Major Anderson informed South Carolina Governor Francis W. Pickens that *"I am directed by the President of the United States to notify you to expect an attempt will be made to supply Fort Sumter with provisions only, and that if such attempt be*

---

not a mere phrase. It is an imperative principle of actions which statesmen will henceforth ignore at their peril." (Wilson, 106). President Franklin Roosevelt had a strong hand in the Atlantic Charter, a joint British-American declaration made on August 14, 1941, which stated that all peoples have the right to self-determination.

not resisted, no effort to throw in men, arms, or ammunition will be made without further notice, or in case of an attack on the fort." (qtd. in Keegan, 34). It was a very smart move on Lincoln's part, both strategically and tactically. It left the door open for a peaceful resolution without giving anything away, while at the same time putting the ball in the South's court indefinitely, because if—and for as long as—the South allowed the fort to be supplied with provisions only, the garrison could also hold out indefinitely.

But Jefferson Davis, who had just been inaugurated as President of the Confederate States of America (on February 18, 1861) chose door number two, deciding not to allow Fort Sumter to be resupplied in any way. He ordered general Beauregard to demand the Fort's immediate surrender and reduce it if Major Anderson did not comply. When Anderson tried to stall for time, offering to surrender the fort if the supplies had not yet arrived by April 15, Beauregard's aide, Colonel Chesnut, replied to Anderson that this was not good enough and that fire would be opened in one hour lest the fort surrendered immediately (crawford, 424–26). No further communication came from the fort.

On 4.30 a.m, April 12, 1861, the Confederate bombardment commenced. Thirty-four hours and 4,000 Confederate shells later, Anderson surrendered the fort and subsequently evacuated by steamer to New York (Dougherty, 63). The American Civil War had begun.

Of course preparing for a war is very different from actually fighting a war. The mere act of marching in formation, forming a firing line and discharging a weapon, morphs into an entirely different beast when, at a distance of about 100 yards, an equal number of lined up men discharge their weapons in your general direction.[7] Moreover, most officers

---

7   The Journal of the Royal United Service Institution of 1862 dryly noted that, during battle, an infantry soldier was generally not capable of anything more than *"simply raise his rifle to the horizontal, and fire without aiming"* (390).

and soldiers from both sides had no battlefield experience whatsoever.

But many in the Northern States were impatient for results, thinking one swift victory on the battlefield would be enough to put an end to the rebellion. So when General Irvin McDowell, who would soon command the Northern forces in the first large-scale battle of the war, conveyed his reluctance to attack to the President, on account of his men still being very green, Lincoln replied: *"You are green, it is true, but they are green also; you are all green alike."* (qtd. in Eicher, "The Longest Night", 79).

The North's hope for a quick end to Southern sovereignty would soon be crushed though, as it was the Confederate army that won the first major battle, at Bull Run, near Manassas, Virginia (about 30 miles from Washington D.C.) on July 21, 1861, after General Beauregard's men successfully routed McDowell's Army of the Potomac, which had thought to mop up the Confederate army in a surprise flank attack. And less than a month later, on August 10, General Benjamin McCulloch's Confederate forces, aided by the Missouri State Guard, defeated General Nathaniel Lyon's Army of the West at the Battle of Wilson's Creek, near Springfield, Missouri.[8]

So there was to be no double-quick march to the Confederate capital of Richmond, Virginia for the Union army, though the North did not give up either, as many in the South had hoped would happen once the 'yankees' realized Southerners were willing to fight and die for their cause.

In March 1862, General George B. McClellan launched a major spring offensive in southeastern Virginia, with the

---

8   McCulloch could have turned his solid victory into a great one had he opted to pursue the retreating Union forces and destroy the Army of the West entirely, an act that might have given Missouri to the Confederacy. But McCulloch had no faith in the Missouri State Guard, which he called "*undisciplined and led by men who are mere politicians*", and therefore decided not to pursue (qtd. in Piston, 314). The quote is from a letter McCulloch sent to Brigadier General William J. Hardee, on August 24, 1861.

ultimate aim of capturing Richmond. Moving northwest from Fort Monroe (at the southern tip of the Virginia Peninsula) McClellan forced General Joseph E. Johnston and his Army of Northern Virginia to retreat in the direction of Richmond. By the end of May, McClellan's forces were positioned to the northeast of the Confederate capital, straddling the Chickahominy River, with three corps north of the river (II, V and VI) and two corps (III and IV) south of the river.

Johnston was a cautious man and had avoided giving battle during the past weeks, but he could not allow a massive Union army of more than 100,000 men to remain nestled in so close to the capital. On May 31, he launched a large-scale attack against IV Corps, positioned south of the river and closest to Richmond. The plan was to first fully engage and defeat IV Corps, followed by a second attack, this time on III Corps, which by then would be isolated and vulnerable, its back against the river (Luebke, "Seven Pines"). Speed was key, lest III Corps and possibly also the three corps positioned across the river have time to reinforce the embattled IV Corps.

The plan was sound but the execution flawed. Though the front division of IV Corps was pushed back by Confederate forces, it was never fully engaged nor defeated. Moreover, during the day, elements from III Corps and II Corps moved to the front to stop the Confederate advance. Near nightfall, as the fighting petered out, Johnston took a bullet to the shoulder while inspecting the lines (Luebke, "Seven Pines"). Moments later, he was also hit in the chest and thigh by fragments from a Union artillery shell.[9]

The fighting continued the next day, June 1, but after failing to make much headway, the Confederates called it a day before the morning was out. The Union forces settled into their positions as well (Luebke, "Seven Pines"). The Battle of Seven Pines thus ended inconclusively, though it could also

---

9   Johnston's wounds were severe but not lethal. Though he had to relinquish his command of the Army of Northern Virginia, he would return to active duty a few months later and receive another command.

be called a tactical defeat for the Confederates, since they had not succeeded in expelling IV and III Corps. Then again, a few hours after the battle, Confederate President Jefferson Davis appointed General Robert E. Lee as the new commander of the Army of the Northern Virginia, and he would prove to be much more of a menace to the Union Army than Johnston had ever been (or would be).

At 55, Lee had never before led an army in the field. Confederate public opinion was initially against him, fearing 'Granny Lee' would not be aggressive enough, but his early actions quickly showed this to be a fallacy.[10] Before the month was out, Lee had gone on the offensive, driving McClellan away from Richmond and into retreat in a series of six major battles fought within the space of just one week.[11] The son of major general Henry "Light-Horse-Harry" Lee III, who had served under general Washington during the American Revolutionary War, Robert E. Lee proved himself an inspirational commander and brilliant tactician, at a time when Lincoln was struggling to find a military commander capable of taking the initiative in the Eastern Theater.

Still, the biggest threat to the Confederacy was not the Union army but its own fragile economy, its lack of industrialization and resources.[12] And since the South's economy was largely dependent on the cotton export to Europe, the Union blockade of Southern ports established in the summer of 1861 inflicted considerable damage to the Confederate economy.

The South tried to end the blockade of course, most famously during the Battle of Hampton Roads (off the Virginia

---

10   Newspapers had given Lee this nickname for supposedly being timid, a trait that would soon prove to be as fitting a description for Lee as shyness for a wolf (Eicher, "Robert E. Lee", 54).

11   Hence the battles being collectively known as the Seven Days Battles.

12   The Confederate States of America had the fourth highest per capita income in the world in 1860, but after the Union established a naval blockade in the summer of 1861 this quickly changed; cotton export subsequently fell by 95 percent (Bateman, 4).

coast) on March 9, 1862, when the Confederate ironclad CSS
Virginia—having already sunk two wooden Union ships the
day before—got into a deadly battle with the Union ironclad
USS Monitor. The fight raged on for hours, but neither ship
was able to sink the other and the clash ended indecisively,
although strategic victory should perhaps be awarded to the
Union, since the outcome of the battle prevented the South
from ending the blockade.[13]

Another Achilles heel of the South was its lack of resources
relative to the North. In 1860, the North had a population
of 22 million vs. 9 million in the South (of which about 3.5
million were slaves), it counted 22,000 miles of railroad vs.
9,000 miles in the Confederate states, 800,000 draft animals
such as cattle and horses vs. 300,000 in the Confederacy, 93
percent of the nation's pig iron production, 97 percent of its
firearms production and more than 80 percent of the national bank deposits (Gallagher, 37).[14]

All things considered, the only two ways the South could
hope to win its independence was either the North giving up—
for instance because public opinion turned against the war, a
scenario that became more likely as the conflict dragged on
and its death toll increased—or others, most likely the British
or the French, coming to its aid. Both Britain and France
were in fact sympathetic to the Confederate cause, but not so
sympathetic as to risk war with the Union for it, at least not
so long as it appeared the Union might win. In that respect,
the Union victory at Antietam on September 17, 1862—the
bloodiest day in U.S. military history—proved highly important.[15] The battle itself was inconclusive in that General

---

13   Being the first confrontation between ironclads, the battle also received
widespread attention outside the U.S. and led to big changes in navies around
the world. Wooden-hulled ship production was immediately halted in favor of
ironclads, modeled on the USS Monitor (Tucker, "Blue & Gray Navies", 175).

14   For population numbers per state, see the 1860 US census ("Population
of the United States", iv).

15   The combined number of casualties for the twelve hours of fighting on

McClellan only succeeded in halting Lee's advancement in Maryland, while also losing more men than the popular Confederate general even though he outnumbered him two to one, but it was enough of a victory for Lincoln to announce the Emancipation Proclamation five days later, on September 22, 1862.

The Proclamation was an executive order proclaiming the freedom of slaves in the ten states that were still in rebellion, effective January 1, 1863.[16] It made ending slavery a primary and explicit goal for the Union, further dissuading Britain and France from direct involvement on the Confederate side, as they had already abolished slavery and public opinion in both countries was adamantly against it.

In the summer of 1863 the Union dealt the Confederacy two decisive blows on the battlefield. First, at the Battle of Gettysburg (July 1–3), General George Meade's Army of the Potomac defeated Lee's Army of Northern Virginia. The bloodiest battle of the war, with a combined total of more than 45,000 casualties, Gettysburg ended Lee's second invasion of the North, though Meade failed to prevent Lee from retreating with his army over the Potomac, lengthening the war by another two years (Sears, "Gettysburg", 513).

One day later, on July 4, after a siege of six weeks, General John C. Pemberton and his Army of Mississippi surrendered to General Ulysses S. Grant at Vicksburg, an important fortress city that controlled the Confederate section of the Mississippi River. Grant's victory gave the Union

---

September 17, 1862, was 22,719 (Sears, "Landscape Turned Red", 296).

16   The State of Tennessee was by then mostly under Union control and was therefore not named in the Emancipation Proclamation. The Unionist slave-holding states of Missouri, Kentucky, Maryland and Delaware, as well as a number of counties in West Virginia—which would soon be admitted to the Union as the 35th State—were also exempted. Slaves in these states were thus not freed by the Proclamation.

command over the entire Mississippi, effectively splitting the Confederacy in two for the rest of the war.

Because Meade had failed to prevent Lee from retreating, Lincoln replaced him with Grant, who soon decided that since the North had far more resources, the best way to defeat the South was by fighting a war of attrition. Throughout 1864–65 Grant therefore fought several bloody battles with Lee, basically wherever he could force him to fight.

During the Overland Campaign (a.k.a Wilderness Campaign) of May-June 1864, Grant forced Lee into a series of battles in Virginia by threatening to position his Army of the Potomac between Richmond and Lee's Army of Northern Virginia. Union forces suffered more than 50,000 casualties in just 30 days as a result— earning Grant the unflattering nickname "the Butcher" in the North—but Lee's army also suffered more than 32,000 casualties (Bonekemper, 190). And unlike Grant, Lee could not replace his losses. *Granted*, it was not a very sophisticated strategy, but effective nonetheless.

After a series of maneuvers in the direction of the Confederate capital, Grant besieged Richmond and nearby Petersburg, the main supply center for Richmond and the rest of the region. Lee knew he would not be able to hold on to Richmond if Petersburg fell and was therefore forced to defend both. Over the course of several months, Grant constructed 30 miles of trench lines, spanning from Richmond to Petersburg, in an attempt to cut off the railroad supply lines to the Confederate capital. Numerous raids against the Southern railroads in the area put ever greater strain on Lee's dwindling forces.

On March 25, 1865, after nine months of siege warfare, Lee made a last-ditch attempt to break the siege around Petersburg. It failed. Confederate defeat was imminent.

On April 1, Union forces captured the Five Forks road junction (west of Petersburg), key to control of the South Side Railroad, a vital supply line for Petersburg. Upon hearing of the victory, Grant ordered an all-out assault on several points of the Petersburg line to start in the early hours of the next day. At 10:00 pm, Union guns began a massive bombardment that lasted until 2:00 am (Bearss, 516). An eerie calm followed, as the Union infantry waited for the first light of day to start its assault on the Confederate lines.

At 4:40 am, April 2, General Horatio Wright ordered VI Corps to move forward towards the Boydton Plan Road line (Bearss, 534). On its right, IX Corps moved to attack the trenches around Fort Mahone, or as it was called by Union soldiers, "Fort Damnation" (Thompson, "Two Days in April"). The IX Corps assault started off well and several of the fort's batteries were taken, but in the maze of entrenchments within the fort the numerical advantage of the attackers soon disappeared, turning a rolling assault into ferocious and chaotic close quarters combat (Thompson, "Two Days in April"). As one North Carolinian later wrote about the fighting: "*I saw the men of my regiment load their guns behind the traverses, climb to the top, fire down into the ranks of the enemy, roll off and reload and repeat the same.*" (qtd. in Greene, 338).

Wright's VI Corps was more successful. Advancing in a massive wedge formation at the earliest whiff of dawn, the first Union soldiers soon reached the Confederate defenses. Nineteen year old Captain Charles G. Gould of the 5th Vermont Infantry was the first to leap into the enemy trenches (Greene, 222–23). A musket was immediately leveled at him at point-blank range, but misfired. It was a lucky escape, but the next moment he was bayoneted through his cheek and mouth by a North Carolinian, whom he in turn killed with his saber. A third Confederate slashed him with a sword, giving him a nasty head wound. A fourth then bayoneted him in the back, before he was being pulled back over the defensive works and into the ditch by one of his men. Others had followed in Gould's wake though, capturing the battery he had attacked, while the rest of the Vermont Brigade further expanded the breach.[17]

Upon hearing of the breach at Boydton Plank Road, Lee realized he had no choice but to retreat. Just before riding off, he sent a telegram to Confederate Secretary of War John C. Breckenridge, advising him *"that all preparation be made for leaving Richmond tonight."* (qtd. in Thompson, "Two Days in April"). Petersburg and Richmond were occupied by Union forces the next day.

Less than a week later, on April 9, Lee fought his last battle, at Appomattox Court House, some 100 miles west of Petersburg. It was to be a short battle though. Faced with overwhelming numbers of infantry and almost completely surrounded, Lee bowed to the inevitable and surrendered.

One month later, on May 9, 1865, President Andrew Johnson—plucked from Vice Presidential obscurity after Lincoln had been assassinated by Southern sympathizer John Wilkes Booth on April 14—declared that the Civil War was over.[18] It was an anti-climactic end to a war that had cost the lives of more than 620,000 soldiers, roughly the same number as all American deaths in all other wars Americans have ever fought in (McPherson, "Battle Cry of Freedom", 751; Woodward, xix).[19]

---

17   Gould survived his wounds and was later awarded the Medal of Honor, the highest U.S. military decoration. He died in 1916, aged 71, a few months before the U.S. entry into World War I.

18   Lincoln had died nine hours later, on April 15. Johnson's proclamation was published in the New York Times on May 10, 1865, the same day Confederate President Jefferson Davis was captured in Georgia by Union cavalry. The last Confederate general to surrender was Stand Watie (also the only Native American Confederate general), on June 23, 1865.

19   A 2011 analysis of census data by Binghamton University historian J. David Hacker puts the number of dead between 650,000 and 850,000, with 750,000 as the central figure, an estimate McPherson called plausible (Coker 2011).

The South was devastated. A quarter of its white male population of military age had been killed during the war, as had 40 percent of its livestock (McPherson, "Battle Cry of Freedom", 721). Much of the South's wealth had been concentrated in land and slaves, but the four million slaves (of which about 3,5 million were located in the Southern States) had been freed by the Thirteenth Amendment, and with no slaves to work the land, real estate prices plummeted.[20] Banks, railroad companies, plantations, many of them went under, never to resurface. Between 1860 and 1870, income per capita in the South dropped from close to 70 percent to less than 40 percent of that in the North, while its percentage of the national wealth declined from 30 percent to 12 percent (McPherson, "Battle Cry of Freedom", 721).

It would take a century before the former Confederate States were able to somewhat close the wealth gap with the Northern States, although as of 2013 almost all Southern States that fought on the side of the Confederacy still rank below the national average in median per capita income.[21]

The South's political influence in the Union also dissipated. Between 1789–1861, half of the U.S. Presidents had been from the South (serving a total of 49 years), all of them slaveholders, including the first U.S. President, George Washington.[22] After the war it would take a century before another Southerner—Lyndon B. Johnson—was elected President again.[23] Johnson

---

20   The Thirteenth Amendment was passed by the Senate on April 8, 1864, by the House on January 31, 1865 and adopted on December 6, 1865. Its text: *Section 1. Neither slavery nor involuntary servitude, except as a punishment for crime whereof the party shall have been duly convicted, shall exist within the United States, or any place subject to their jurisdiction. Section 2. Congress shall have power to enforce this article by appropriate legislation.*

21   The sole exception being Virginia. Used figures are from the United States Census Bureau. State & County QuickFacts (quickfacts.census.gov).

22   Interestingly, Ulysses S. Grant was the last U.S. President to have owned a slave, though he freed him before the war, in 1859, rather than selling him for a hefty sum, which he certainly could have used at the time (Smith, 94).

23   Woodrow Wilson was from Virginia, but he moved to the North in his

hailed from Stonewall, Texas, established just a few years after the civil war and named after the famous Confederate general Thomas J. 'Stonewall' Jackson.[24]

The Confederate revolution had failed. America would gear up for the most violent century in the history of mankind as one nation, under god, indivisible. It is doubtful whether a Confederate States of America would also have been willing to send millions of troops and armadas full of equipment overseas to influence the outcome of violent conflict between European nations. Twice. If anything, the Confederate States mostly wanted to be left alone by the federal government and had little interest in the old world outside trade interests.[25]

Looking at how the United States fared under the Articles of Confederation—which the Confederacy closely resembled—Confederate States would most likely have retained a large part of their sovereignty, with very little interference from the federal government in taxes, tariffs, banking, infrastructure and everything else that was not absolutely necessary for a central government to deal with. Such a nation could likely scarcely defend itself, let alone influence the outcome of large-scale foreign wars such as World War I and World War II.

As for that other revolution, the emancipation of four million slaves, though it certainly had a profound impact on the South, it would take another 100 years before African Americans would be truly emancipated. That is not to say their position in society did not markedly improve in the

---

twenties. Andrew Johnson and Harry Truman were also from the South, but they only moved up from the Vice-Presidency after their President had died in office. Lyndon B. Johnson became President the same way, but he was also elected President himself, in 1964.

24   Jackson had gotten his legendary nickname after his actions at the First Battle of Bull Run, in July 1861, because he was like a 'stonewall' in the face of the enemy.

25   Even today, many of the States most vigorously opposed to a strong federal government are Southern ones.

decades after the war, because it did—real income, literacy, level of education, all of them rose significantly—but blacks continued to be discriminated. In that sense, the emancipation of minorities would remain an unfinished revolution until at least the African-American Civil Rights Movement of the 1950s and 60s.[26]

In 1956, two years after the U.S. Supreme Court had ruled in Brown v. Board of Education that state laws establishing separate public schools for black and white students were unconstitutional, the last civil war veteran of the Union Army died, aged 109 (New York Times 1956).[27] Albert Henry Woolson had enlisted at age seventeen as a drummer boy in the 1st Minnesota Heavy Artillery Regiment on October 10, 1864, two years after his father had been killed at the Battle of Shiloh.

Upon his death, President Eisenhower said *"The American people have lost the last personal link with the Union Army."* (qtd. in New York Times 1956).

---

26   See also chapter 19 - He Had a Dream.

27   The 1850 census lists Albert Woolson as being only 6 months old, which would make him 106 at the time of his death. This would have no effect on his status as the oldest surviving civil war veteran though.

RUSSIAN EMPIRE

GERMAN

NORTH GERMAN CONFEDERATION

AUSTRIA-HUNGARY

DENMARK

SWEDEN

BALTIC SEA

NORTH SEA

FRANCE

SWITZERLAND

Vilnius

Brest

Warsaw

Königsberg

Danzig

Krakow

Pressburg

Buda-Pest

Vienna

Prague

Dresden

Berlin

Hamburg

Copenhagen

Malmo

Munich

Frankfurt

Zurich

Bern

Amsterdam

The Hague

Brussels

Prussia

1. Oldenburg
2. Schaumburg-Lippe
3. Lippe
4. Waldeck and Pyrmont
5. Upper Hesse
6. Brunswick
7. Schwarzburg-Sondershausen
8. Saxony
9. Anhalt
10. Mecklenburg-Schwerin
11. Mecklenburg-Strelitz
12. Hohenzollern (Prussia)
13. Alsace-Lorraine
14. BAVARIA
15. WÜRTTEMBERG
16. BADEN
17. HESSE
18. LUXEMBOURG
19. NETHERLANDS
20. BELGIUM

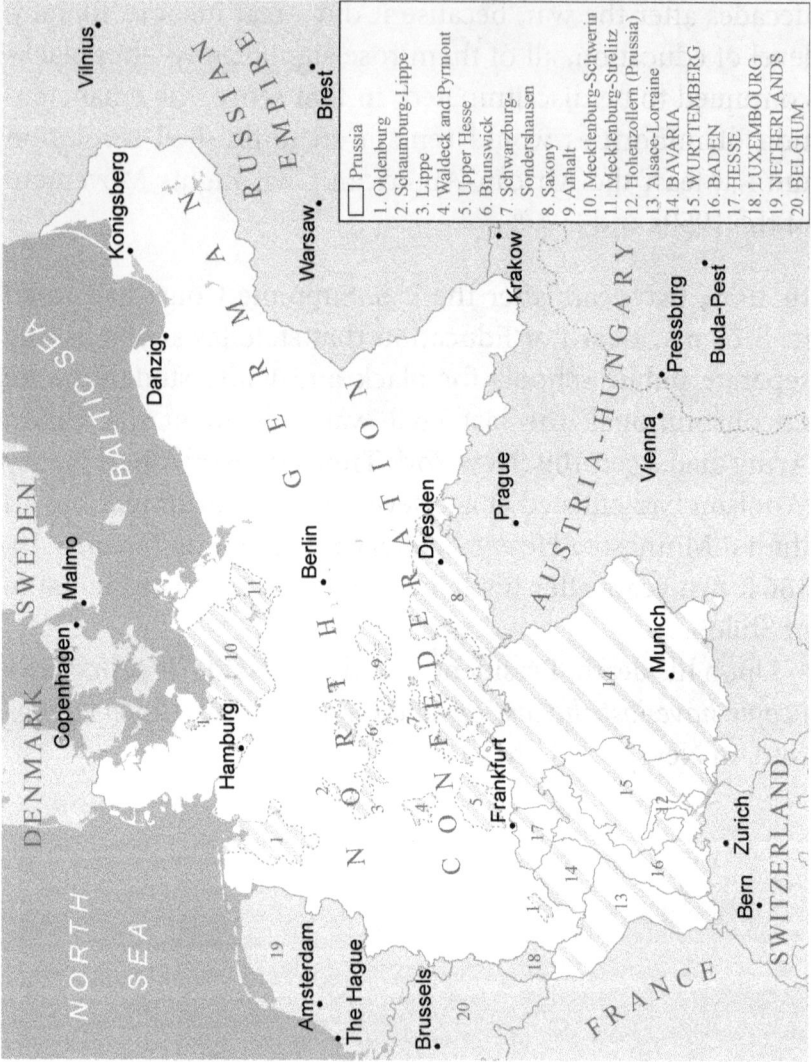

Map 4: The Unification of Germany, c. 1870-71

6

A New Nation in Europe

"The first, original, and truly natural boundaries of States are beyond doubt their internal boundaries. Those who speak the same language are joined to each other by a multitude of invisible bonds by nature herself, long before any human art begins; they understand each other and have the power of continuing to make themselves understood more and more clearly; they belong together and are by nature one and an inseparable whole."[1]

Johann Gottlieb Fichte, Addresses to the German Nation,
1806, French-occupied Berlin

WHAT IS EUROPE? IT IS OBVIOUSLY MORE than just a geographic location, but how much more? Europeans have fought each other ferociously for thousands of years, first as tribes, then as kingdoms, as empires and finally—and most brutally—as modern, civilized nations. Still, all those wars also brought a common religion, a shared legal tradition, shared values, a shared culture and a shared history, i.e., a common heritage, which since the end of the Second World War has helped Europe on a path towards greater co-operation and integration.

But successful as this integration has been, the European sovereign debt crisis that broke out in 2009 exposed a dangerous disconnect between the level of economic integration

---

1   Fichte, 223–24.

and that of political integration within the Eurozone framework.[2] A single market, a shared currency, i.e., monetary union, yes. But no common fiscal, budgetary or economic policy, and certainly no political union. Many have since agreed that further integration is necessary to avoid an eventual breakup of the Eurozone, but most countries are reluctant to hand over more sovereignty to Brussels, especially if that sovereignty would *de facto* end up in Berlin—a very likely scenario.

As the most populous and wealthiest nation of the European Union, Germany has paid more than any other EU member state to stave off the economic meltdown that threatened the Eurozone after the outbreak of the sovereign debt crisis. Simply put, without Germany, there would quite possibly no longer be a Eurozone. Similarly, should Germany, in order to prevent another sovereign debt crisis, want to move towards a more federalized Europe—the way it unified itself almost 150 years ago—it would likely eventually happen. It is simply a matter of *Realpolitik*, as Prussian Chancellor Otto von Bismarck would have said. And he should know, since he was one of the main architects of the German unification of 1871.

That unification was the culmination of a process that had started more than 50 years earlier, around the time Napoleon came back from his disastrous Russian campaign with a decimated, defeated, demoralized army and the Prussians and Austrians smelled blood in the water. The ensuing *Befreiungskriege,* Wars of Liberation, fought in 1813–14, were a joint Austrian, Prussian, Russian and Swedish effort to defeat Napoleon once and for all. The campaign culminated in the Battle of the Nations (October 16–19, 1813), not far from Leipzig, where Napoleon was decisively defeated for the first time and forced to retreat to France, losing control

---

2   As of 2015, there are 28 member states in the European Union (EU). The Eurozone is the economic and monetary union of the 19 EU member states that have so far adopted the euro currency.

over his German territories, which were thus liberated from French occupation.[3]

Ironically, Napoleon had also taken away one of the biggest obstacles on the long road to German unification, when he brought about the dissolution of the Holy Roman Empire after decisively defeating an Austrian-Russian coalition at Austerlitz, on December 2, 1805.

The Holy Roman Empire dated back to at least 962, when German King Otto I was crowned emperor.[4] It was basically a continuation of the Eastern part of the Frankish Kingdom that had been reunited and ruled by Charles Martel and expanded by his grandson, Charlemagne. Unlike France though—the Western part of the Frankish Empire—the Holy Roman Empire had remained a decentralized, limited elective monarchy, with hundreds of territories that were *de facto* independent sovereign nations (albeit tiny nations in most cases).

After Austerlitz, Napoleon formed a Confederation of the Rhine out of sixteen German territories formerly belonging to the Holy Roman Empire, to act as a buffer between France

---

3   The Coalition forces would follow Napoleon into France and force him to abdicate on April 11, 1814, two weeks after capturing Paris.

4   A case could also be made for calling Charlemagne the founder of the Holy Roman Empire. He was, after all, the first ruler in Western Europe since the fall of the Western Roman Empire to be crowned 'Emperor of the Romans', in 800, and had also conquered several key parts of Eastern Francia, the later core of the Holy Roman Empire. But while Charlemagne was part of a number of successive Frankish rulers whose core territories were located in Western Francia—roughly later France—the Holy Roman Empire as it developed through the Middle Ages and the early modern period was a mainly Germanic conglomerate of different states, concentrated in Central Europe. In that respect, the Treaty of Verdun of 843, which split up Charlemagne's empire in a Western, Middle and Eastern part, was an important formative step in the development of the Holy Roman Empire. Like Charlemagne, Otto I, who became King of Germany in 936, greatly expanded his realm during his reign, including the conquest of the Kingdom of Italy. He was also the first German holder of the title of emperor, though the term 'Holy' as connected to the empire was only first used by later emperor Frederick Barbarossa (1122–1190).

and the Russian Empire.[5] At its peak, the Confederation would count 36 German states (though never the two biggest, Austria and Prussia) and be home to a population of about fifteen million people.

In 1814, after Napoleon was defeated and exiled to the island of Elba, the nations of Europe came together at the Congress of Vienna to redraw the map of the continent. More than twenty years of wars had seen many duchies, provinces, cities, states and colonies change hands, and rather than ignite a dozen new wars to settle who owned what, the European powers chose to settle matters in a series of complex negotiations. The Congress was still in session when Napoleon escaped from Elba and enchanted the French one last time into letting slip the dogs of war. The members of the Vienna Congress refused to let themselves be distracted by Napoleon's latest antics though and signed its Final Act nine days before the Battle of Waterloo.

Among many other things, the Congress decided not to restore the Holy Roman Empire but instead create a loose German Confederation of 39 states out of the almost 2,500 independent territories that had been part of the Holy Roman Empire, including (parts of) Austria and Prussia.[6] The German Confederation would be headed by Austria, which, as one of the five great European powers—the others being Great Britain, Russia, Prussia and France— had been given central Europe as its sphere of influence.

Meanwhile, Prussia—the largest, dominant state in the geographic region that would later become Germany—had

---

5   The creation of the Confederation of the Rhine effectively forced Holy Roman Emperor Francis II to abdicate and dissolve the Empire, on August 6, 1806.

6   Of these 2,500 entities, some 2,000 were tiny estates of a few square miles or less that belonged to so-called Imperial Knights. The remaining 400 or so were made up of principalities, ecclesiastical territories and Free or Imperial Cities (Gagliardo, 2).

reinvented itself after its humiliating defeat by Napoleon at the Battle of Jena, in 1806. It had abolished serfdom of its peasants, emancipated the Jews, rearranged the school system and introduced free trade to spur economic growth and industrialization (Clark, 326–37). The army had also been reorganized and in 1813 compulsory military service had been introduced (Clark, 326; Hagemann, 61).[7] As a result Prussia was able to play a decisive role at Waterloo, famously illustrated by the timely arrival on the battlefield of *Generalfeldmarschall* Gebhard von Blücher and his 50,000 Prussians, just in time to save the day.[8]

In 1818, three years after the establishment of the German Confederation, Prussia established an internal customs union throughout its own state and the Hohenzollern territories in southwestern Germany.[9] Before the customs union, there had been over 60 local customs borders, each with its own tariffs, which made transporting goods from one end of Prussia to the other a prohibitive, not to mention tantalizingly slow enterprise (Viner, 120).

The Prussian Customs Union was a great success and several other member states of the German Confederation—which counted a total of 830(!) toll barriers—soon joined.[10] Austria was excluded from joining though, due to internal

---

7   Though the February 9, 1813 'Edict Lifting Previous Exemptions from Cantonal Duties for the Duration of the War' continued to recognize a number of exemptions—such as young men who were the sole breadwinners of their family or who were civil servants of the Prussian state—the Prussian Army still doubled in size in 1813 as compared to 1806 (Hagemann, 61–62).

8   The Prussian army committed for the final battle with Napoleon had originally been 80,000 strong, but had suffered heavy casualties in the Battle of Ligny—Napoleon's last military victory—on June 16, 1815, two days before the battle of Waterloo (Booth, 15; Chesney, 4).

9   Prussia was ruled by the House of Hohenzollern.

10   The high number of toll barriers was caused by most states of the German Confederation having local, i.e., internal tariffs, as Prussia had had before creating its customs union. The situation had been even worse before Napoleon though, with an estimated 1,800 customs frontiers in Germany in 1790 (Henderson, 21–22).

pressure to uphold its own protectionist tariff system, which shielded local manufacturers from foreign competition (Ploeckl, 23).

In 1834, the Prussian Customs Union and several other customs unions that had been formed within the German Confederation merged to form the *Zollverein* (i.e., German Customs Union), further strengthening the Prussian economy while weakening the Austrian economy because of its continued exclusion. The German Customs Union also helped to further advance the idea of a unified Germany.

At the same time, conservative leaders—most notably Austrian Chancellor and Minister of State Klemens von Metternich—sought to suppress liberal movements that were promoting civil rights, democracy and nationalism, ideas that not only threatened the power base of the aristocracy but also the stability of the Austrian Empire itself, which, as a multi-national conglomerate, ran the risk of disintegrating if confronted with a rising tide of nationalism.

As early as 1819, Metternich had taken the initiative for a conference of German Confederation member states in Carlsbad, Bohemia, aimed at curbing civil liberties and crushing reform movements throughout the confederation. The resulting Carlsbad Decrees banned the *Burschenschaften*—student fraternities that were actively advocating nationalist, liberal and democratic ideals—and introduced several restrictions to the freedom of speech for the press and the academic world. University professors and other teachers for instance, should be removed from their positions if they propagated "*harmful doctrines hostile to public order or subversive of existing governmental institutions*" (qtd. in Barnes, 28).

But a decade later, in 1830, a new revolutionary wave swept through Europe, reopening a window of opportunity for nationalists and republicans to bring about regime change. In France, King Charles X was forced to abdicate following the July Revolution of 1830. In the Netherlands, riots broke out in the Southern provinces that had formerly been part of the Austrian Netherlands. They subsequently seceded and founded the new independent nation of Belgium. In Switzerland, the people forced cantonal governments to amend their constitutions. In Poland and Italy uprisings broke out against Russian and Austrian rule, respectively, though both revolutions would be crushed during the spring of 1831. In short, the German Confederation was quite literally surrounded by nations rattled by the turmoil of revolution.

Inspired by these events, German liberal authors, students and intellectuals organized a political festival in May 1832 at Hambach Castle—then part of the Kingdom of Bavaria—called the 'National Festival of the Germans in Hambach'(Sperber, 112). Some 30,000 people showed up, calling for German unity, popular sovereignty and liberty (Sperber, 111–13). The festival proved there was ample popular support for a unified Germany and established the combination of black, red and gold as the symbol of the movement for a democratic and united Germany, the same colors that would later be adopted as the colors of the German flag. Nothing else tangible came out of the gathering though and a year later the Bavarian military tightly controlled the area around Hambach Castle, to make sure no gathering of any kind would take place there again (Sperber, 111–13). The German nationalists had missed their chance and momentum fizzled.

Fifteen years later, the revolutionary year of 1848 gave German revolutionaries one last chance at bringing about a united Germany of the people, by the people and for the people.[11] This time, the revolutionaries successfully pressed

---

11   The German March Revolution was ignited by events in France, where, in late February 1848, the Parisians revolted once again against their king, this time causing the ouster of King Louis-Philippe I, the last king of France (not counting Emperor Napoleon III, who succeeded him), who had succeeded

several state governments into participating in a parliamentary assembly at Frankfurt that would be tasked with
drafting a national constitution (Sperber, 146). In March
1849, the Frankfurt National Assembly had indeed created a
constitution for a united German state, founded on a parliamentary democracy and a constitutional monarchy (Sperber,
149). It would be headed by a hereditary emperor, for which
the Frankfurt Parliament elected Prussian King Friedrich
Wilhelm IV, by a vote of 290 yeas and 248 abstentions.

On April 3, a selected group of deputies, the
Kaiserdeputation, offered Friedrich Wilhelm the crown of
the German Empire. Everything was in place, the yeas had it,
a unified Germany was at the doorstep of history, knocking
impatiently. But then Friedrich Wilhelm surprised everyone
by saying no to the crown. *Nein.* Publicly he said he could not
accept the crown without consensus of the princes and the
free cities within the proposed German Empire, but privately
he said he would not accept a crown that was touched by the
"hussy smell of revolution".[12]

Without the support of the Prussian king, the constitution
of the Frankfurt Assembly was meaningless. The delegates
from Prussia, Austria and several other states were recalled
or left on their own accord, returning to their home states.
A rump parliament was formed in Stuttgart, Württemberg,
but the tide of revolution was turning once again (Kolkey,
75–76). The people longed for order and stability after months
of unrest and increasingly associated the word 'democrat'
with civil unrest and anarchy. In June 1849 the Württemberg

King Charles X in 1830. In Germany, however, the revolution was, as contem-
poraries said, *"stopped at the feet of the thrones"* (qtd. in Sperber, 146).

12   Translated from the German quote *"Ludergeruch der Revolution"*, as
found in *Der lange Weg nach Westen: Deutsche Geschichte vom Ende des Alten
Reiches bis zum Untergang der Weimarer Republik*, Vol. I, 122 (Winkler). It has
also been said Friedrich Wilhelm called it *"a crown from the gutter"* (Sperber,
350; Kolkey, 75).

Army dispersed what remained of the parliament (Kolkey, 75–76). Revolution over.[13]

The failure of the German revolution of 1848–49 had made it clear that the best chance for a unified Germany lay in the so-called *Kleindeutschland* solution—meaning excluding Austria, and under Prussian leadership—and that it would have to be imposed from above, because unification had no chance without the support of the Prussian king.

For a couple of years things remained relatively quiet, until the four most powerful positions within the Prussian establishment were all infused with new blood in the space of just a few years. In 1857, Helmuth von Moltke, one of the greatest military strategists of the second half of the 19th century, became Chief of the Prussian General Staff. Two years later, Albrecht von Roon became Minister of War and set about reorganizing and modernizing the army, greatly increasing its size in the process (Förster, 263–66). Meanwhile, King Friedrich Wilhelm IV had suffered a stroke and was replaced by his brother, Wilhelm I, who would leave the task of governing mostly to his prime minister.

In 1862, Wilhelm appointed Otto von Bismarck to this position, a sly fox who, shortly after being appointed, gave a taste of things to come in his now famous 'Blood and Iron' speech, in which he drove home the point that Prussia's position in Germany did not depend upon its liberalism but upon its power, and that "*Prussia must build up and preserve her strength for the favorable moment, which has already come and gone many times. Her borders under the treaties of Vienna are not favorable for the healthy existence of the state. The great questions of the day will not be settled by speeches and*

---

13   The work of the Frankfurt Parliament would not be completely for nothing though. Its constitution served as the basis for the Weimar Constitution of 1919 and also influenced the 1949 Constitution of the Federal Republic of Germany (Foster, 159).

majority decisions—that was the great mistake of 1848 and 1849—but by blood and iron." (qtd. in Pflanze, 177).

Within four years, Bismarck found an excuse to declare war on Austria, Prussia's main rival for dominance over the German region. It was to be a very short war, with about half of the German Confederation and Austria on one side, and Prussia, Italy (which had just gained its independence from Austria) and about a dozen other German states on the other side.

All in all the war would last seven weeks. On July 3, 1866, the Austrian main army suffered a total defeat in the most important battle, near *Königgrätz* (present-day Czech Republic), partly because the Prussian infantry was equipped with a new type of breech-loading rifle, while the Austrians still had muzzle-loading rifles. This not only enabled Prussian infantry to fire four or five times in the space it took an Austrian soldier to fire just once, but also allowed for loading and firing while lying down instead of standing up (Wawro, "Austro-Prussian War", 22). Military tacticians of the day had initially questioned Moltke's decision to rely on fire tactics rather than shock tactics—soldiers equipped with breech-loading rifles would have to learn to fight and fire more individually and not waste all their ammunition in the first fifteen minutes of the fight—but as the saying goes, the proof of the pudding is in the eating, and Austria's casualties at *Königgrätz* were almost five times higher than Prussia's (Craig, 166).[14]

Though Austria was clearly vulnerable after *Königgrätz*, Bismarck, wanting to prevent France or Russia to join the Austrian side, pushed Wilhelm I to make peace rather than continue the war to gain more territory and concessions. As far as Bismarck was concerned, the goal was not to annihilate or annex Austria but to keep it out of German affairs,

14   For a more in-depth explanation of Moltke's fire tactics and the prevailing military theory of the day that went against it, see Wawro, *The Austro-Prussian War: Austria's War with Prussia and Italy in 1866*, 22–25.

so Prussia could form a German Confederation of its own. This was achieved with the Peace of Prague (August 23, 1866), which abolished the existing German Confederation and permanently excluded Austria from German affairs. Prussia also annexed many of Austria's smaller German allies (mjummy).[15]

A year later, Prussia formed the North German Confederation, which incorporated the 22 German states north of the Main River and had a population of 30 million people.[16] Though the Confederation had the power to deal with many issues, the member states remained independent nations. Complete unification was close though. Only one more thing was needed before a new and powerful nation, comprised of both the Northern and Southern German states, could burst onto the European scene: A common enemy.

That enemy was easily found in France, which already felt threatened in its position as the dominant power of continental Western Europe by its assertive, aggressive neighbor to the East, especially after Prussia had so effortlessly defeated Austria. Of course Bismarck was well aware of this. He would later say: "*I did not doubt that a Franco-German War must take place before the construction of a United Germany could be realised*" (qtd. in Bismarck, 58).

The French simply could not accept Prussian dominance over the Southern German states, located so close to home. Besides, most French generals expected to win a military conflict with Prussia and hoped Austria and perhaps also some of the Southern German states would side with France if it came to that (alas for France, none of them did).

---

15   Among the territories annexed by Prussia were Hanover, Frankfurt, Nassau, Schleswig-Holstein and parts of Hesse-Darmstadt.

16   Of that 30 million, 24 million were Prussian and 2 million were Saxon; the remaining 4 million came from the other 20 member states (Robinson, 126).

Still, even though he needed war with France, Bismarck did not want Prussia to come off as the aggressor. So he waited, for an opportunity to present itself that would either give Prussia a good excuse to go to war or, preferably, goaded the French into declaring war.

Opportunity arose when a diplomatic crisis erupted over the candidacy of a Prussian prince for the vacant Spanish throne. The prince in question, Leopold of Hohenzollern, soon backed down under French pressure and withdrew his consent, but then the French overreached by having their ambassador at the Prussian court, Count Benedetti, more or less ambush King Wilhelm I of Prussia during his morning stroll in the Kurpark at Bad Ems, demanding that he would never again support the candidacy of a Hohenzollern prince for the Spanish throne (Lerman, 148). This Wilhelm I politely but sternly refused. Shortly thereafter, Wilhelm I had his *adjudant* inform Count Benedetti that he had received confirmation from Leopold that he had indeed withdrawn his candidacy, and now considered the matter closed ("Emser Depesche", July 13, 1870).

When Bismarck was informed of this by telegram, he had a slightly altered version of the telegram published in Germany on July 13 and in France—of all days—on July 14 (Bastille Day).

The altered version suggested Wilhelm I had sent the "*Adjudant vom Dienst*" to the French Ambassador, to flatly tell him the king no longer wished to receive him and had nothing further to say on the matter ("Emser Depesche"). That was a bad enough snub already, but what really got the French up in arms was the (untranslated) word 'Adjudant'. In Prussia, an *Adjudant* was a high ranking military official, comparable to the French Aide-de-camp, but in France it was only a non-commissioned officer, comparable to a staff sergeant. Having Count Bernadetti informed by such a low ranking individual was tantamount to a declaration of war in the eyes of even the mildest mannered Frenchman. Needless to say, France took the bait. It declared war on Prussia on July 19, 1870.

Contrary to what the French generals had told their emperor, Napoleon III (nephew of Napoleon I) however, France was not in the best of positions to wage war against Prussia. Not only did the Prussians have the numerical advantage, they were also better trained, better led, better equipped, better organized and more mobile, thanks to an already extensive railroad network.[17] Prussian military superiority would therefore soon make itself apparent to even the most arrogant French generals (which was one military resource France had plenty of).

Sure enough, on September 1, 1870, after a series of victories, the Prussians were able to corner a 120,000 strong French army led by Napoleon III himself, at the Northern French town of Sedan.

Outnumbered, outgunned and unable to retreat, Napoleon III had no choice but to surrender himself and his entire army. The Second French Empire subsequently collapsed, but a hastily formed Government of National Defense (the first government of the newly proclaimed Third Republic) desperately continued the fight, until on January 28, 1871, after a siege of almost five months, Paris fell. Ten days earlier, the German princes and senior military commanders had already proclaimed Wilhelm I German Emperor in the Hall of Mirrors of the Palace of Versailles, just outside of Paris.

Defeated France was forced to pay an indemnity of five billion francs and give up large parts of the Northeastern regions Alsace and Lorraine, the latter containing significant iron ore

---

17   In the summer of 1870, von Moltke was able to transport 400,000 men to the French frontier in just eighteen days thanks to the Prussian railroad network (Mitchell, 66).

reserves.[18] Still, the most important reason for Bismarck and Moltke's insistence that Alsace and Lorraine be transferred to Germany seemed a military one. As Bismarck had told General Félix de Wimpffen, the French negotiator at the for France disastrous Battle of Sedan: *"Over the past 200 years France has declared war on Prussia thirty times and…you will do so again; for that we must be prepared, with…a territorial glacis between you and us."* (qtd. in Wawro, "Franco-Prussian War", 227).

But for France, the loss of what the German Empire now called the *Reichsland Elsass-Lothringen*, the Imperial Territory of Alsace-Lorraine, was positively unbearable, thus assuring a permanent crisis between the two nations until the next war.

The unification of Germany also severely disturbed the balance of power that had been put in place by the Congress of Vienna of 1814–15. A powerful, militaristic, ambitious and confident new nation had emerged smack down in the middle of Europe, dominating both its Austrian-Hungarian neighbor to the south and its French neighbor to the west, the latter a mortal enemy that would howl for *revanche* until it would finally get it. Twice. Peace had been declared, but war was imminent.

The German unification itself was a great success though, with the new nation being the most wealthy and populous country of Europe—as it is today.

As Prussia played a decisive role in the German unification of 1871, so too could modern Germany play a decisive role

---

18   As agreed in the Treaty of Frankfurt on May 10, 1871. Independent observers were alarmed by the huge indemnity Prussia demanded from France, but Bismarck defended the Prussian position, saying *"France being the richest country in Europe, nothing could keep her quiet but effectually to empty her pockets."* (qtd. in Wawro, "Franco-Prussian War", 305). For comparison, the indemnity the Austrians had had to pay only five years earlier, after losing the Austro-Prussian war, had been only one-sixtieth of the French indemnity (Wawro, "Franco-Prussian War", 304).

in the European unification. Question is, with war no longer being an option as a *"continuation of policy by other means"* in Europe, how would Otto von Bismarck go about enlisting French support for a United States of Europe, had he lived today?[19]

---

19   Quote from *On War* (Clausewitz, 87).

7

AGE OF INVENTION

"After the electric light goes into general use, none but the extravagant will burn tallow candles."[1]

Thomas Edison, 1880

"Without high-speed tools and the finer steels which they brought about, there could be nothing of what we call modern industry."[2]

Henry Ford, *Edison as I know him*, 1930

IN SEPTEMBER 2012 THE COMPANY *RETHINK ROBOTICS* introduced Baxter, a highly adaptive general purpose robot that can be equipped with several standard attachments on its arms ("Rethink Robotics").[3] Baxter needs no additional programming to learn new things, a human simply guides its arms through the required motions, which Baxter then memorizes. And all that for the bargain price of just $22,000 ("Rethink Robotics").

And Baxter has many friends. Noodle-slicing robot Chef Cui for instance. Introduced in 2011, quickly adopted by a growing number of Chinese noodle shops and relatively cheap at $1,500 compared to the $4,700 per year a *human* noodle slicer costs in China (Garun 2012). Or the burger robot introduced by San Francisco-based Momentum

---

1   qtd. in "The Electric Light".

2   Ford, "Edison", 33.

3   For an in-depth review of Baxter, see *This Robot Could Transform Manufacturing* (Knight 2012).

Machines in 2013, a robotic assembly line capable of producing 360 hamburgers per hour, complete with freshly
sliced tomatoes, onions and pickles and nicely wrapped up
for serving (Shedlock, "Burger-Flipping Robot"). Combined
with the touchscreen ordering system that McDonald's has
started to implement in its restaurants, customers could soon
find themselves ordering their hamburgers at places that
have completely dispensed with human cashiers, servers and
burger flippers.

And those McJobs will not be the only ones disappearing.
In a 2013 report on disruptive technologies, consultancy
company McKinsey estimated that 15 to 25 percent of industrial worker jobs in developed countries could be automated
by 2025, across occupations such as manufacturing, packing,
construction, maintenance and agriculture (McKinsey, 74).[4]
Meanwhile, robots are getting better (and cheaper) at other
tasks as well; filling out our prescriptions at pharmacies,
driving our cars, cleaning our houses, babysitting our children and, last but not least, fighting our wars. In other words,
the robots are coming.

The robotization of the factory floor did not start yesterday though, in fact it has been going on for decades and is
intimately linked to an innovation introduced by the Ford
Motor Company over a century ago: the assembly line.[5]

In 1913, Ford was having trouble keeping up with the ferocious demand for its legendary Model T automobile,
prompting the introduction of the assembly line, which dras-
tically reduced production time of the Model T from 12.5
man-hours in April 2013 to just 93 man-minutes a year later,
and with less manpower (Hounshell, 254–55). It was so fast

---

4   In developing countries, an estimated 5 to 15 percent of manufacturing
worker tasks could be automated by 2025 (McKinsey, 74).

5   Ford introduced the assembly line in 1913 (Hounshell, 10–11). Source
also discusses the origins and early productivity gains of Ford's assembly line.
See also Ford, My Life and Work, 77–90.

that the drying of the car paint became the bottleneck of the whole production process. And since only black Japan enamel would dry fast enough, black became the only available color for the Model T for a while (Kimes, 52). Ironically, Ford's famous remark that "*any customer can have a car painted any colour that he wants so long as it is black*" was made in 1909, four years before the introduction of the assembly line (Ford, "My Life", 72).[6]

By adding parts in a sequential manner, the production process was divided in small tasks that required little skill. Time waste was also reduced, because workers had to work continuously as long as the assembly line was operational (famously demonstrated by Charlie Chaplin in the epic 'factory work' scene from the 1936 movie *Modern Times*). Needless to say factory workers had no love for the assembly line, but from a production point of view it was a great success and it quickly became ubiquitous in factories throughout the industrialized world.

Although Ford was the first to introduce a *moving* assembly line in a modern factory, the concept of the assembly line itself was not new and had been experimented with since the beginning of the Industrial Revolution, in the late 18th century. In fact, the growing dynamic between production, prices and demand that had been ignited by the Industrial Revolution (increased production pushing prices lower, thus increasing demand, leading to increased production) had spurred several inventions in the 50 years before the introduction of the Model T, making Ford's innovation almost something of a logical necessity.

6   When Ford made this remark, the Model T was in fact available in different colors. He was merely talking about how in the future Ford Motor Company would build all Model T's exactly the same, to further cut cost and production time. At the time his autobiography *My Life and Work* was first published, in 1922, the statement was true though.

One key invention in the second half of the 19th century was the Bessemer process—named after its inventor, Henry Bessemer—which revolutionized steel manufacturing, greatly increasing scale and speed of production while significantly lowering its cost from $160 per long ton in 1867 to $42 per long ton in 1887 (Misa, 31–32). Being much stronger than iron, steel could be used to make stronger, more durable metal parts, bigger, high-pressure boilers in steam engines—greatly increasing power output—and larger, stronger ships, tanks and guns (which would revolutionize warfare in the 20th century).

Electrification was another key industrial development originating in the second half of the 19th century. Not only did it bring Thomas Edison's light bulb into homes and factories, it also paved the way for electric motors, which required less maintenance and were much more efficient and flexible (needing only an electrical cord between engine and power outlet) than small steam engines. Electrification thus enabled modern mass production, automating many processes that had previously been done slower, less efficient and more expensive with steam- and or manpower.

Just as with the Industrial Revolution a century earlier, machines and improved production processes were replacing or diminishing a host of manual labor tasks, only this time things were unfolding much faster. You could say that the period between 1860–1914 was the Industrial Revolution on *speed*. Inventions like the steam engine and the railroad came to full maturity, while a flurry of new inventions impacted the already radically changing Western economies. Between 1861–1900, more than 1,000,000 patents were issued for new inventions in the U.S. alone, almost 15 times more than had been issued in the previous 70 years ("Statistical Abstract 1942", 952).

Railroad mileage tripled between 1860–80 in the U.S., and again by 1920 ("Statistical Abstract 1942", 478). And since transportation was much cheaper by rail than by road, overall transportation cost fell significantly during this period, as did delivery times. In 1869 for example, delivery time from the East Coast to San Francisco, California was reduced to just six days when the first transcontinental railroad opened.[7] And after automobile development and manufacturing accelerated following the invention of the gasoline-fueled internal combustion engine, goods could be delivered fast and cheap even to remote locations.

Another invention originating in the Industrial Revolution era, the telegraph, had developed into a worldwide communication network by the 1890s, connecting major cities around the world and increasing both speed and frequency of international commerce, diplomatic relations and information about newsworthy events.[8] The invention of the telephone in 1876 made communication even easier, since people could now talk directly and interactively to each other over great distances—instead of being limited to the beep-beep-beeps of morse code—and in 1901 Italian inventor Guglielmo Marconi brought communication to a whole new level when he succeeded in wirelessly transmitting and receiving a transatlantic morse code radio signal.[9]

All these inventions, innovations and developments greatly accelerated the economic transformation that had been underway since the Industrial Revolution. Factories grew ever bigger and more complex, while the job of the average worker became ever smaller and simpler. A growing army

---

7   The more dangerous and more expensive stagecoach took 28 days to get to California, and that was when starting from Missouri.

8   The first commercially viable electromagnetic telegraphs had been introduced in the 1830s.

9   There was and still is doubt, though, about whether Marconi really did succeed in wirelessly transmitting the letter 'S' in Morse code (dit-dit-dit) from Cornwall, England to Newfoundland, Canada, on December 12, 1901 (Sarkar, 387–94). Source gives an in-depth explanation of Marconi's first transatlantic experiment.

of managers was hired to increase control, oversight and organizational efficiency of the production process and the work force, in turn stimulating the development of the data processing industry, which brought inventions such as the electronic tabulating machine, the punchcard and the time clock (all three developed by companies that would later merge into International Business Machines, IBM).

One important side effect of the growing importance of communication and business administration was the increasing participation of women in the labor process, who were hired en masse as stenographers, typists and switchboard operators. The number of American women working in clerical and similar occupations for instance, rose from less than 11,000 in 1870 to more than 1,900,000 in 1920 (Hill, 40).

The new sense of independence women gained through these jobs would play a major role in fueling the Women's Rights Movement of the late 19th and early 20th century. It was but one of the many revolutionary effects of the unprecedented advances in factory productivity in the period 1860–1914.

Meanwhile, huge fortunes were also won and lost with speculative investments in rapidly developing industries from which some companies emerged as big winners but many others did not. In the 1870s for instance, a railroad investment bubble formed in the U.S. after government land grants and subsidies had attracted enormous investments in—and abnormal growth of—the railroad construction industry (at the time the country's second largest employer, after agriculture) and its supporting facilities. Many of these investments offered no early returns outside of their speculative value though—not unlike the dotcom bubble of 2000—and when the Jay Cooke & Company bank failed because it couldn't unload the millions of dollars in Northern Pacific Railway bonds it owned, panic ensued (Wicker, 19–21).

The failure of Jay Cooke on September 18, 1873, set off a chain reaction of bank failures and the closing of the New York Stock Exchange for a full ten days (Kindleberger, 321). In the two months that followed, 55 U.S. railroad companies failed and another 60 in the nine months after that. 18,000 businesses went belly up between 1873–75, causing unemployment to rise to a peak of 8.25 percent in 1878 (Vernon 1994, 710). At the time, the period between 1873–79 was called the Great Depression, until that moniker was given to the more severe depression of the 1930s and the period of 1873–1879 was retroactively renamed the Long Depression (Swarup, 212).

Real Net National Product in the U.S. actually grew at a clip of 6.8 percent per year between 1869–79 though and the implied rate of growth of real per capita income during this period was 4.5 percent, so most people were actually better off at the end of the Long "Depression" than they had been before it (Friedman, 37).[10] There was panic and a general feeling of malaise, yes, but in reality the economy kept pushing forward.

In general, quality of life in the West greatly improved during the 50 years leading up to World War I. Famines disappeared for the first time in history—the last famine in the West unrelated to war occurred in 1880—real income rose considerably, work-hours declined (albeit slowly), infant mortality rates declined by as much as 50 percent and life expectancy rose from less than 40 to more than 50 years (Roser, "Life Expectancy"; "Child Mortality").[11] The scientific proof for the germ theory of disease in the 1860s and 70s had

---

10   The fact that real GNP grew by 6.8 percent per year between 1869–79, real income per capita increased by 4.5 percent per year and the total money supply grew by 2.7 percent per year between 1873–78, led libertarian economist Murray Rothbard to dub the 'Great Depression' of the 1870s a myth (Rothbard, 154).

11   The last famine in the Western world unrelated to war occurred at St. Lawrence Island, Alaska, between 1878–80. The last Irish famine was in 1879.

an especially big impact in this respect. Increased sanitation, proper cooking, cleaning and preservation subsequently caused a sharp decline in mortality rates.[12]

But however positive and revolutionary these advances in life expectancy and prosperity were, a different—though equally revolutionary—side of the age of invention would soon manifest itself after the European empires declared war on each other in August 1914 and wasted no time using their extensive railroad networks to quickly transport an unprecedented number of soldiers, ammunition and artillery to the battle grounds, where 19th century warfare would brutally clash with 20th century technology.

Artillery firing 1760-pound (800 kg) shells over a distance of 9 miles (15 km), guided to target with the help of field telephones, machine guns mowing down charging infantry by the hundreds, flamethrowers, modern hand grenades, poison gas (which made over one million casualties, including over 80,000 deaths), aircraft and aerial bombardments, barbed wire, tanks, submarines, they would all be deployed on a large scale for the first time in World War I. When it was over, 8.5 million soldiers and between 6–9 million civilians had been killed in just four short years.[13]

Unabashed, detached and amoral, technology had shown its dark side, or rather—though equally disturbing—its neutral side, yielding without hesitation to whoever was in control.

As the robots do.

At least until they decide not to.

---

12   Groundbreaking work in the field of epidemiology was done, i.a., by John Snow, who discovered the source of a cholera outbreak in London in 1854, and Louis Pasteur, who discovered the principles of vaccination.

13   As reported by the U.S. War Department, February 1924. U.S. casualties amended by the Statistical Services Center, Office of the Secretary of Defense, November 7, 1957 (see also table in Hosch, 219).

Tromso

Murmansk

Trondheim

SWEDEN

Oslo

Helsinki

Stockholm

Kronstadt

Reval

St. Petersburg

Yekaterinburg

RUSSIAN EMPIRE

Riga

Vilnius

Minsk

Moscow

Warsaw

1917

1916

1914

Kiev

1918

Budapest

Chisinau

Belgrade

Bucharest

Odessa

Constanta

Feodosia

Sofia

Sevastapol

Black Sea

Istanbul

Salonica

Ankara

Athens

OTTOMAN EMPIRE

1. NORWAY
2. GERMANY
3. AUSTRIA-HUNGARY
4. RUMANIA
5. BULGARIA
6. SERBIA
7. GREECE

Map 5: The Russian Front of the First World War, 1914-18

8

The Russian Revolution(s)

"Sire: We, the workers and inhabitants of St. Petersburg, of various estates, our wives, our children, and our aged, helpless parents, come to Thee, O Sire, to seek justice and protection. We are impoverished; we are oppressed, overburdened with excessive toil, contemptuously treated. We are not even recognized as human beings, but are treated like slaves who must suffer their bitter fate in silence and without complaint. And we have suffered, but even so we are being further (and further) pushed into the slough of poverty, arbitrariness, and ignorance. We are suffocating in despotism and lawlessness. O Sire, we have no strength left, and our endurance is at an end. We have reached that frightful moment when death is better than the prolongation of our unbearable sufferings."[1]

Petition carried by protesters on Bloody Sunday, January 22, 1905

EVERY EIGHTEEN MONTHS, ONE OF THE MOST influential people of the 20th century gets a month-long bath (Yurchak, 141). Only instead of water an embalming solution is used, because the reason for the long soak has more to do with preserving than with cleaning. And preserve it does, seeing as for the past 90 years the embalmed body of Vladimir Lenin, founder of the Soviet Union, has been on display at the mausoleum in Red Square, in the center of Moscow, looking like he died only yesterday.

To keep the body in mint condition, an embalming compound was developed that replaced all the water in Lenin's

---

1   qtd. in Ascher, 87.

skin. As long as the temperature is 16 degrees Celsius and relative humidity is 70 percent, the compound neither absorbs water nor evaporates (Schmemann 1991). Multiple sensors therefore constantly monitor temperature and humidity around the body.

Preserving Lenin requires more than just monitoring though. Apart from the month-long immersion in a bath of embalming fluid once every eighteen months, Lenin's head and hands get a fresh daub of embalming compound every week, and every four or five years the body is thoroughly inspected by a commission of senior scientists (Schmemann 1991).

Comrade Joseph Stalin was preserved the same way after his death in 1953, but one night in 1961 his body went from hallowed sarcophagus to common coffin and was buried next to the Kremlin wall without pomp and circumstance.

Not Lenin though. Even decades after the fall of the Soviet Union, the iconic revolutionary remains on display in his mausoleum. But while the appearance of his body, sickly and fragile in life, has been preserved intact, his brain, once home to an energetic and virile mind, has been sliced into 30,000 pieces, to study the source of his genius (Neumeyer 2014).

Still more ironic (some might say tragic) is that Lenin's feeble bodily remains managed to outlive his crowning achievement, the Union of Soviet Socialist Republics, one of the most dominant and defining nations of the 20th century. And that while its hard-fought founding had so proudly carried the promise of that rarest of things: the beginning of a completely new world.

That new world was to be a socialist state, in which property and resources would be owned and shared by all. A promise that resounded especially strong in a country where roughly 35 percent of the population had been a serf before serfdom was finally abolished in Tsarist Russia in 1861 (Moon, 3).[2] Very little had changed for the ex-serfs in the decades that followed though. Land, money and other resources still remained firmly in the hands of the ruling class.

Because landowners had for so long been able to count on serfs, Russia was late to industrialize.[3] When it finally did, industrialization progressed faster than in most parts of the West, resulting in fewer but bigger factories, massive urban overcrowding and deplorable conditions for the workers. By 1912, 43 percent of Russian industrial laborers worked in factories employing more than 1,000 workers, up from 27 percent in 1866; in the U.S., it was only 18 percent (Wolf, 74–75; Carmichael, 8).

Because of this high concentration of workers, protests could suddenly ignite and spread much faster than when most people were still living in rural areas. As a result, average annual strikes increased from 33 between 1886–94, to 176 between 1895–1904 (Ascher, 23).

Meanwhile, Tsar Nicholas II didn't make it any easier for the people after he came to power in 1894 at the age of 26, though in his defense, his father, Tsar Alexander III, had not made it any easier for the people either.[4] Like his father, Nicholas II concerned himself little with the common people. In his mind, enlightenment ideas like the social contract and 'government with consent of the governed' had no place in the Russian Empire. Nicholas II firmly believed that his power to rule was granted by Divine Right, i.e., not derived from the people but directly from God himself.

---

2   The same year serfdom was abolished in Russia, fundamental disagreement about the future of slavery also prompted the outbreak of civil war in the United States, that other dominant and defining country of the 20th century.

3   Not unlike the antebellum Southern United States and its reliance on slavery.

4   Vladimir Lenin's older brother Aleksandr had been involved in a plot to kill Tsar Alexander III. It failed, and Aleksandr was executed.

So, when a deputation of peasants and workers from various local assemblies came to the Winter Palace shortly after Nicholas II had ascended to the throne, with proposals aimed at improving the political and economic life of the peasantry, such as land reform and a constitutional monarchy, Nicholas II told them angrily that *"I want everyone to know that I will devote all my strength to maintain, for the good of the whole nation, the principle of absolute autocracy, as firmly and as strongly as did my late lamented father."* (qtd. in Ferro, 39).

A few years later, on Sunday January 22, 1905 (January 9, O.S.), another delegation of peaceful protesters wanted to present a petition to Nicholas II at the Winter Palace in St.Petersburg.[5] The leader of the procession, the Russian Orthodox priest George Gapon, had informed the government of the upcoming procession, after which the ministers had advised Nicholas II to leave the city, which he did.

The protest was not in any way directed against the Tsar himself though. In fact, the protesters were singing the imperial anthem 'God Save the Tsar' and carried portraits of Nicholas II, Russian flags, religious banners and icons on their way to the Winter Palace.

But as the processions—which had started from six different points—converged on the palace, the marchers found their routes blocked by soldiers at strategic points in the city. At some of these points soldiers told the marchers to turn back, while at others no such warning was given. Authorities had apparently not issued clear instructions to the soldiers as to what to do when confronted with advancing crowds, a recipe for disaster when deploying the military for crowd control (Ascher, 91–92).

---

5   The notation O.S. refers to the Julian calendar, a.k.a. Old Style, which remained in use in Russia until 1918, when it switched to the Gregorian calendar, a.k.a. New Style (N.S.).

When a large crowd including George Gapon arrived at Narva Gate, in the middle of the expansive Narva Square, they were met by determined infantry units that had positioned themselves as if the square were a battlefield.

Soon it would be.

A single bugle was blown, serving simultaneously as apparent warning to the protesters and signal for the soldiers to take aim and fire into the crowd (Ascher, 91–92). Moments later dozens of protesters lay dead in the square. At several other points in the city soldiers also opened fire on the protesters and whoever else happened to be there. According to most estimates, at least hundreds of people were killed or seriously wounded.[6]

The massacre that would come to be known as Bloody Sunday put Russia on a much more serious trajectory to real revolution. Initially, the protesters had just wanted the Tsar to help them improve their living conditions, but in the wake of Bloody Sunday the demands became much more political, with growing calls for freedom of speech, an elected parliament and the right to form political parties. And even though the Tsar had not ordered the shooting and was in fact appalled by it, the blame was still placed squarely on his shoulders.

In the words of the U.S Consul in Odessa: "*All classes condemn the authorities and more particularly the Emperor. The present ruler has lost absolutely the affection of the Russian people, and whatever the future may have in store for the dynasty, the present Tsar will never again be safe in the midst of his people.*" (qtd. in Ascher, 92–93).

---

6   The exact figure is unknown. The official records report 130 people killed and 299 seriously wounded (Ascher, 91–92; Sablinsky, 266). Various other estimates are much higher though and talk about thousands of deaths. For a discussion of various estimates, see Sablinsky, *The Road to Bloody Sunday* (261–68).

Shortly after Bloody Sunday the first Soviet (council of workers' delegates) was created in St. Petersburg, to coordinate worker strike activities there.[7] Throughout the rest of the winter and spring of 1905, massive strikes and peasant uprisings also erupted in other parts of the empire.

Even more alarming to the Tsarist regime was the mutiny that erupted on June 14 (June 27, O.S.) on the brand-new battleship *Potemkin*—the pride and joy of the imperial Black Sea fleet—after the ship's captain had tried to force the crew to eat borscht made from rotten, maggot-infested meat (Bell, 12). The government's concern was understandable. With a water displacement of 12,582 tons, a crew of 800, a top speed of 16 knots and the capability to hold 10,000 rounds of various calibers of ammunition, the *Potemkin* was certainly more of a threat than a bunch of poor peasants carrying icons and singing hymns, not to mention the danger of the mutiny spreading to other ships, or even throughout the entire armed forces (Bell, 11).

The mutineers decided to make for Odessa harbor (arriving there late at night the same day), to give one of their fallen comrades a public burial, take in fresh water and coal and see if they could drum up support from the local soldiers and revolutionaries there. Some of the more radical sailors also wanted to try and take Odessa itself, but this was rejected by the Commission that had been elected to be in charge of the

---

7   The Russian revolutionary Voline describes the birth of the first Soviet, in St. Petersburg, only a few days after Bloody Sunday, in his book *The Unknown Revolution, 1917–1921* (89ff.). According to Voline, the first meeting took place in his own apartment and was meant to organize the distribution of funds from affluent supporters among the many workers on strike (97–98). Another prominent Russian revolutionary however, Leon Trotsky, writes in *his* book, *1905*, that the first Soviet was organized months later, on October 13, 1905 (chapter 22). According to Violine, Trotsky did this for political reasons, namely to give a bigger founding role to the Russian Social Democratic Labour Party, which created this later Soviet.

ship, which wanted to wait for an already planned fleet-wide mutiny to break out (Bell, 14).

The next day, thousands of people came out to the harbor to see the mighty battleship with their own eyes, pay their respect to the fallen sailor and express their support for the sailors' cause (Bell, 14). Later that day though, Tsarist land forces bent on restoring order fired directly into the crowd, killing at least 1,000 people.

The *Potemkin* was relatively helpless against the operations of the Tsarist soldiers in the city, lacking the necessary precision to be effective without causing too much collateral damage. A few shells were fired on the Tsarist forces' headquarters in the city, but when they overshot and hit a nearby residence, actions were quickly halted (Bell, 15).

On day three of the mutiny the *Potemkin* left Odessa harbor to confront a squadron of ships that had been sent to force its surrender (Bell, 15). Twice the *Potemkin* steamed right through the task force, its powerful guns aimed and ready but silent, as were those of the other ships. When the task force retreated, some sailors proposed to make use of the momentum, pursue the ships and pressure their crews into joining the mutiny, but this was rejected by the ship's Commission (Bell, 15). Instead it was decided to set course for the Romanian harbor of Constanța, on the western coast of the Black Sea, to take in provisions (Bell, 16).

When the Romanians refused to supply them, the mutineers tried the Crimean harbor of Feodosia, but city officials there too refused to help (Bell, 16). The mutineers threatened to bombard the city, but when their ultimatum expired and the city had not given in to their demand, they decided to return to Constanța and on June 25 surrendered the battleship to the Romanian authorities, eleven days after the mutiny had begun (Bell, 17).

And so the *Potemkin* mutiny petered out. Momentum for a successful fleet-wide mutiny and a country-wide revolution had come and gone. Radical revolutionaries would come to view the eleven-day mutiny as an iconic but nevertheless wasted opportunity, drawing lessons from it that would serve them well twelve years later, when they got a second chance at radical change.

Then again, although the mutiny of the *Potemkin* itself had failed, it did show—in the words of Ivan Lychev, one of the members of the ship's Commission, who later wrote an account of his experience aboard the ship—*"the nation and the entire world that the revolutionary rumblings penetrated into the most secure pillars of the tsarist throne - the navy and the army."* (qtd. in Bell, 20).

In the fall of 1905, uprisings broke out at the naval bases of Kronstadt, Vladivostok, even at Black Sea Fleet headquarters in Sevastopol. Though put down by (other) government forces, the uprisings indeed showed that the problem ran far deeper than a few disgruntled workers and peasants.

Meanwhile, Count Sergey Witte, who as the Tsar's plenipotentiary had just successfully concluded peace negotiations with Japan—with whom Russia had been entangled in a disastrous war since 1904—impressed upon Nicholas II that he had only two options in dealing with the growing strikes and uprisings: using force, or implementing reforms (Harcave, 169).[8]

Choosing door number two, the Tsar asked Witte to write an imperial manifesto to satisfy the more moderate participants in the nascent revolution. Witte subsequently drafted

---

8   Nicholas II did not like Witte—a tireless industrial reformer who wanted to modernize Russia and bring it on par with the Western powers—and had in fact at first declined the proposal of his Secretary of State to even add Witte to the delegation charged with negotiating with Japan, writing *"anyone but Witte"* on the note with the proposal (Harcave, 143). Only after several others had declined did the Tsar reluctantly agree with Witte as his plenipotentiary (Harcave, 144). Witte was unexpectedly able to secure very favorable terms from Japan though, which undoubtedly increased his influence with Nicholas II (Harcave, 152–53).

the so-called October Manifesto, which promised a constitutional monarchy, a parliament with popularly elected members and the power to veto every law (the Duma), and guaranteed civil liberties such as freedom of speech, freedom of religion and the right of association and assembly.

In short, everything Nicholas II hated. For days he stalled, hesitated and pondered on alternatives, before finally, grudgingly, signing the Manifesto on October 30 / October 17, O.S., 1905 (Harcave, 173). The effects of the Manifesto were immediate, all strikes and demonstrations ended within days of its signing. The moderates were satisfied, but the more radical revolutionaries argued that since the Duma could not pass any laws without the Tsar's approval, most power still lay in the hands of the Tsar, not the people.

The government had also offered political amnesty for passed transgressions, but at the same time made clear it would crush continued rebellion with an iron fist. When the Bolsheviks, Mensheviks and Socialist Revolutionaries nevertheless called a general strike in Moscow in early December, the government showed it meant business by sending a full regiment to quell the unrest.[9] Arriving in the city on December 4, Admiral Fyodor Dubasov, the newly appointed Governor-General of Moscow, did not waste any time either and declared a state of emergency on December 7 (Engelstein, 197).

Three days later, government troops bombarded a school where workers and students had barricaded themselves (Engelstein, 203–04). Elsewhere in the city, dragoons attacked

---

9   The Bolsheviks and Mensheviks had both been part of the Russian Social Democratic Labor Party (RSDLP), until splitting up over disagreement as to what should be expected from a party member, with Vladimir Lenin aiming for a party of professional revolutionaries, while his principal opponent in the matter, Julius Martov, wanted a less stringent membership policy. Lenin and his supporters were called Bolsheviks (*Bol'shinstvo*, meaning 'majority') while those who sided with Martov were known as Mensheviks (*Men'shinstvo*, meaning 'minority'). Lenin's faction was actually the minority at the time of the split though; the naming of the factions stemmed from an earlier vote.

a crowd of 5,000 workers (Engelstein, 205). Even when most armed resistance had subsided after a couple of days, government troops kept up their urban warfare tactics, shelling factories and setting fire to buildings where striking workers had entrenched themselves (Engelstein, 220). By the time the workers' parties ordered an end to the strike, on December 19, about 700 revolutionaries and civilians had been killed and some 2,000 wounded (Engelstein, 220–21).

On April 23, 1906, a few days before the first Duma would convene, Nicholas signed the *Fundamental State Laws of the Russian Empire*, the first Russian Constitution.[10] But although it recognized limitations to the power of the Tsar for the first time, it did not go as far as had been promised by the October Manifesto. For one, the Duma could not alter the Constitution unless it was initiated by the Tsar, who could also dismiss the Duma at any time, a self-given right that would not remain idle in the hands of Nicholas II ("Russian Fundamental Laws", I.8, X.104–05). Chapter I, article 4 of the Fundamental State Laws furthermore declared that the emperor possessed "*Supreme Sovereign Power*" and that "*Obedience to His authority, not only out of fear, but in good conscience, is ordained by God Himself*".

So what happens when a Duma bent on change confronts an Emperor bent on conservation? Chaos and political mayhem is what happened. Although the first Duma was boycotted by the most radical left parties—the Bolsheviks, Mensheviks and Socialist Revolutionaries—that did not prevent it to come up with all kinds of radical reforms, including electoral and land reform, both equally horrible to Nicholas II, who dissolved the Duma within three months.

The second Duma lasted a whole four months (which could perhaps be called progress by the staunchest of optimists) but turned out to be even more radical than the first, after the

10   The Constitution of 1906 was a major revision of the *Set of Laws of the Russian Empire* of 1832.

Bolsheviks and Mensheviks—having decided to participate in the election this time—won a significant number of seats. For some of the nobles, having to deal with peasants and workers on equal footing simply proved too much. Count Fredericks, Minister of the Court, at one point commented in disgust: "*The Deputies, they give one the impression of a gang of criminals who are only waiting for the signal to throw themselves upon the ministers and cut their throats. What wicked faces! I will never again set foot among those people.*" (qtd. in Massie, 219).

After dissolving the second Duma, Nicholas unilaterally changed the electoral law to give greater electoral value to the propertied class (thus violating the Constitution of 1906). Consequently, the third Duma—derisively called 'The Duma of Lords and Lackeys'—was a lot more cooperative and served out the full five year term, as did the fourth and final Duma, which lasted until 1917 (Milyukov, 159, 164).[11] By then though, three disastrous war years had run out the clock on the path of slow, gradual change that was followed by the largely ineffective Russian parliament.

Russian losses during World War I were staggeringly high. In the first year alone, the Russian Army suffered 2.4 million casualties, plus another 1 million of its soldiers taken prisoner, while German losses on the Eastern front probably did not exceed 300,000, with only a few thousand taken prisoner (Sondhaus, 150). The German army was simply better prepared, better trained, better supplied and better led. Many Russian soldiers lacked shoes, munitions and food. Hard to fight under such deplorable conditions. And the soldiers weren't the only ones starving, factory workers also suffered from a dearth of food and basic supplies.

In October 1916, the secret police of St. Petersburg warned against the threat of riots by "*the lower classes of the empire*

---

11   Pavel Milyukov was the founder and leader of the Constitutional Democratic Party, a.k.a the Kadets.

enraged by the burdens of daily existence." (qtd. in Steinberg, 51). The Duma also urged the Tsar to commit to constitutional reform, lest things should get terribly out of hand. Of course they already had.

The position of Nicholas II was like that of the Titanic just after it hit the iceberg, the hull perforated all along the side. Still deemed unsinkable but with a mortal wound already inflicted below the waterline, the supposedly watertight compartments quickly filling with ice-cold water.

One of those compartments represented the worsening living conditions of the people—peasants, workers and soldiers alike. Another compartment represented the burden of a losing war with unprecedented casualty numbers, a third one Nicholas II taking direct command of the army in 1915 (though ill-prepared for such a task), making him the main person responsible for the disastrous course of the war.

And then there was his wife Alexandra, the Tsarina, whom he had left in charge of the government in his absence and who had fallen under the influence of the Russian mystic Grigori Rasputin, a man who was unpopular with both the Russian nobility and the common people. Alexandra herself was thoroughly disliked as well, not just because she was of German descent and scores of Russians were being slaughtered by the Germans, but also because she was *"an unbalanced character, a nervous, hysterical woman, who, through her very love for her husband and the persistence with which she advised him to cling to an order that had already served its purpose, proved his undoing."* (Radziwill, 173).

On March 7, 1917 (February 22, O.S.), workers at the Putilov plant, St. Petersburg's largest industrial plant, began to strike (Service, 32). Three days later almost all the factories of St. Petersburg had shut down. Nicholas II ordered the army to put down the riots with force but the soldiers refused to shoot at the demonstrators, handing their rifles to them instead, if not simply joining in on the protests outright (Service, 32).

Anarchy ruled in St. Petersburg and when the Tsar returned to the city on March 14 (March 1, O.S.), his Army Chiefs and the ministers who had not yet fled the capital urged him to abdicate, which Nicholas II did the next day. A couple of days later, the ex-tsar and his family were placed under house arrest at Alexander Palace—Nicholas' favorite residence—about 16 miles (26 km) from St. Petersburg.

The people were thrilled with their major victory, having forced the tsar's abdication in just eight days. But although the tsar was now gone, the revolution was only beginning. A provisional government was formed, comprised mostly of members of the liberal Constitutional Democratic Party (a.k.a. the Kadets) and the leftist Socialist-Revolutionary Party. The even more radical leftists, i.e., the Bolsheviks and Mensheviks, opted out of the provisional government though, focusing their efforts instead on organizing the workers and soldiers in the Petrograd Soviet, a citywide council they had formed a few days before the tsar's abdication.

The Petrograd Soviet wanted to ensure that the Provisional Government fulfilled the promise of creating a democratic republic with guaranteed civil rights and electoral reform. To keep the pressure on, they even met in the same building as the government, the Tauride Palace.

But social, economic and electoral reform—as opposed to political revolution—does not happen in a week. The Provisional Government was led by capable people but they could not work miracles. Food and supplies remained scarce, the war raged on and Russia remained on the losing side of it. Most Russians wanted to end the war, but the Provisional Government was loath to sue for peace on unfavorable terms. Soon, soldiers, peasants and workers blamed the Provisional Government for all the things they had blamed the tsar for only weeks earlier.

And then Lenin returned. He had been living in exile in Switzerland, but with the tsar gone he believed now was the time for a real, marxist revolution. For a Russian national to travel from Switzerland to Russia while there was a war on with Germany seemed next to impossible, but fortunately the Germans were kind enough to help the radical-revolutionary-who-wanted-to-end-war-with-Germany-at-all-cost safely reach St. Petersburg (Fitzpatrick, 50).

Lenin arrived in the Russian capital in April 1917. In the months that followed, his party, the Bolsheviks, grew into the largest political movement in Russia's two most important cities, Moscow and St. Petersburg, by promising the masses that once in power, the Bolsheviks would deliver peace, bread and land to the peasants and power to the people (Service, 48).

Meanwhile, the position of the Provisional Government continued to weaken and on November 7, 1917 (October 25, O.S.), the Bolsheviks ousted the Provisional Government from the Winter Palace in a rather undramatic fashion, belying the later, far more heroic depiction of events by the Soviets (Fitzpatrick, 64).[12]

Making good on his promise, Lenin soon thereafter opened peace negotiations with Germany. On March 3, 1918, the new Bolshevik government signed the Treaty of Brest-Litovsk, committing Russia to a highly unfavorable, humiliating peace, by renouncing Russia's claims to Finland, Estonia, Latvia, Belarus, Ukraine and Lithuania, territory that included important industries and was called home by a quarter of its population ("Treaty of Brest-Litovsk", art. 6).

Still, Lenin had good reasons for wanting to come to terms with the Germans quickly, because almost immediately after the Bolsheviks had seized power, civil war broke out between

---

12   As Russia was still using the Julian, i.e., Old Style calendar at this time, the events are known as the October Revolution. Russia switched to the Gregorian calendar early 1918.

the communists and a colorful coalition of those seeking to remove them from power, including militarists, monarchists, foreign nations (such as Great-Britain, France and Japan) and various independence movements.

In April 1918, the Romanov family was moved deeper into Russia, to Yekaterinburg, to prevent the ex-tsar from falling into the hands of the anti-bolshevik coalition. The Bolsheviks wanted to bring Nicholas to trial, but when elements of the anti-communist Czech Legion advanced to within a day of Yekaterinburg (though unaware that the Romanov family was being held there), the communists panicked.

And so, on July 17, 1918, they executed the Romanovs in the basement of the house where they were held, Nicholas and his wife Alexandra, their four daughters Olga, Tatiana, Maria and Anastasia, and their thirteen-year-old son Alexei, as well as the court physician, a maid, a footman and a cook, servants who had remained with the Romanov family voluntarily.[13]

But the war between the Red Army and the White Army (as the collective opposition was known) did not end with the execution of the Romanov family. It raged on for another five years, in all claiming the lives of roughly one million soldiers and an additional one million civilians (White, 357).[14] In the end, the Red Army was victorious in Russia, thus securing the establishment of the Soviet Union, while pro-independence movements won independence for Finland, Estonia, Latvia, Lithuania and Poland.

---

13   In *Nicholas II: Last of the Tsars*, the execution of the Romanov family and their four servants is described in detail by eyewitness Pavel Medvedev, a member of the squad of soldiers guarding the royal family (Ferro, 246–49). Medvedev said he did not take part in the actual shooting though, as he had been sent outside to check if anybody was on the street and whether the shots could be heard there.

14   If Russian famine and epidemic disease deaths between 1918–20 are included, the total death toll of the Russian Civil War would rise to a staggering nine million though (White, 357).

Lenin had his socialist state, but he would not be around for long to enjoy it, or shape it for that matter. Between 1922–23 the father of the Russian revolution suffered a series of strokes, rendering him partly paralyzed, mute and bed-ridden until his death in 1924, at the age of 53.

In his political testament, Lenin warned against the General Secretary of the newly created Soviet Union, Joseph Stalin, who had *"unlimited authority concentrated in his hands, and I am not sure whether he will always be capable of using that authority with sufficient caution."* (Lenin, "Letter to Congress", II). In a postscript written shortly thereafter, Lenin even recommended Stalin's removal from his position, because he is *"too rude"* (Lenin, "Letter to Congress", Addition). Instead, someone had to be found who was *"more tolerant, more loyal, more polite and more considerate to the comrades"*.

Unfortunately, Lenin turned out to be all too right in his premonition. In the years after his death, Stalin would rise to the most prominent position in the Soviet government, and during his regime hundreds of thousands—if not millions— were killed.[15] Considering this, one wonders why Stalin's body was kept on display in the mausoleum next to Lenin at all, let alone for eight years.

On the other hand, unlike Lenin had done in 1918, Stalin did not seek peace at any price against Germany in 1941. On the contrary, he threw everything but the kitchen sink at Soviet Russia's epic fight against the Nazis, thus providing invaluable reprieve to his Western Allies and playing a decisive role in the defeat of the Axis powers during the Second World War.

---

15   In "Victims of the Soviet Penal System in the Pre-war Years", Getty, Rittersporn and Zemskov show there is hard evidence for a total of slightly more than 840,000 camp deaths and executions between 1937–38—the worst years of Stalinist repression—which, though extremely high, is still much lower than the millions frequently mentioned in accounts of the Great Purge (1022, table 1).

Cooperation between the Soviet Union and the West proved to be short-lived though, as what would become a decades-long Cold War between East and West had already begun to emerge even before the end of WW II, pitting Russia and Eastern Europe versus the United States and Western Europe. During the second half of the 20th century, aside from competing against each other in a nuclear arms race and a space race, the U.S.S.R and the U.S. would also fight hot proxy wars in Korea, Vietnam and Afghanistan and narrowly avert nuclear war in Cuba.[16]

Just like Tsar Nicholas II, the Soviet Union promised but failed to deliver on democracy, guaranteed civil rights and prosperity. And just like Tsarist Russia, Marxist-Leninist Russia ultimately collapsed, in 1991. Russia has since adopted capitalism with considerable success, but democracy and civil rights remain underdeveloped.

Speculation about the removal of Lenin's body from the mausoleum at Red Square began almost immediately after the fall of the Soviet Union. In January 2011, Vladimir Putin's United Russia Party organized an online poll where visitors could vote for or against burial of Lenin (Osborn 2011). More than two-thirds voted in support of interment. A result that was confirmed in another poll, held in April 2014.[17]

He's still there though.

---

16 See also chapter 17—The Space Race—and chapter 18—How Vasili Arkhipov Saved the World.

17 This poll was organized by the Public Opinion Foundation on April 22, 2014, Lenin's 144th birthday. It confirmed that a broad majority of Russians want Lenin to be buried ("Majority of Russians").

PART II
WAR

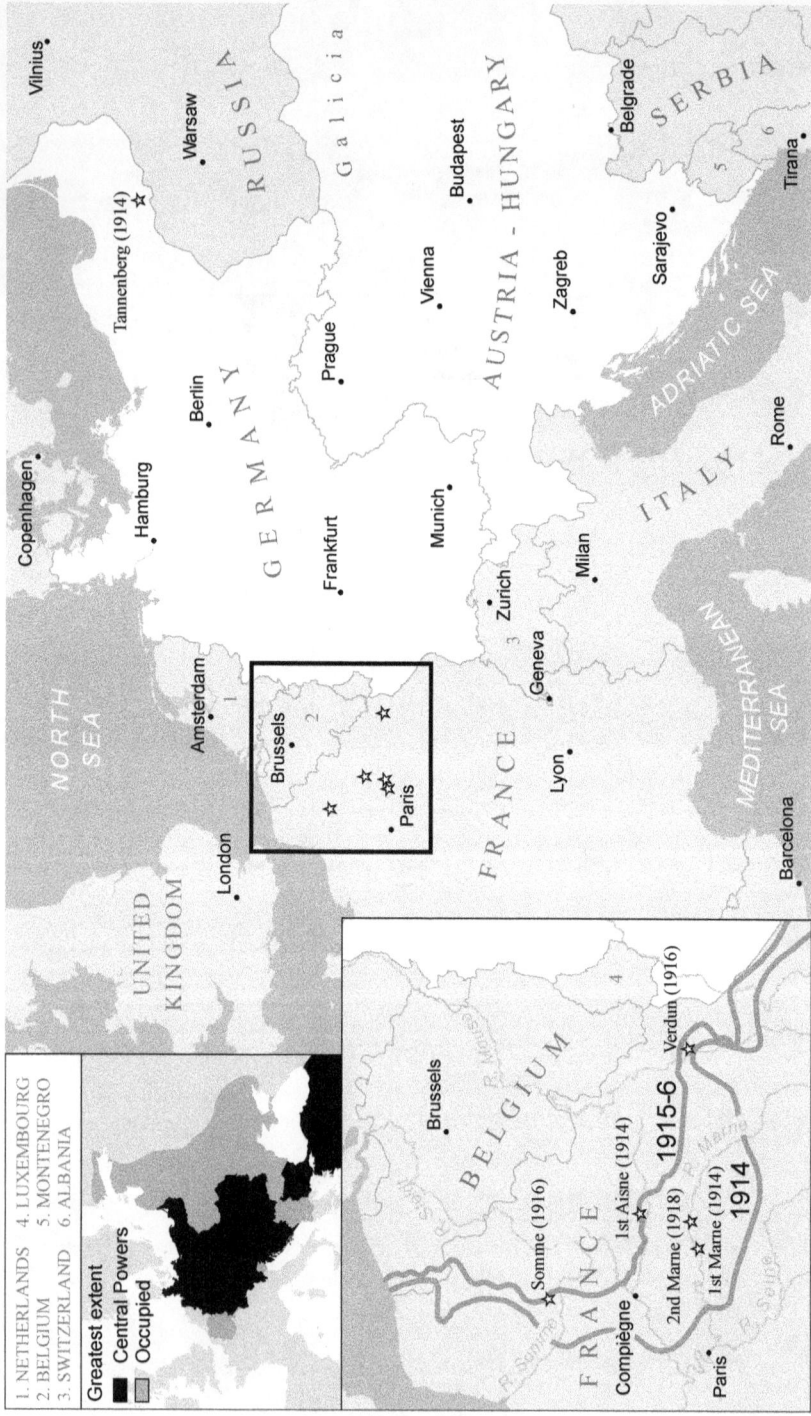

Map 6: The Central Powers in the First World War, 1914-18

9

THE GREAT WAR

"Humanity is mad. It must be mad to do what it is doing. What a massacre! What scenes of horror and carnage! I cannot find words to translate my impressions. Hell cannot be so terrible. Men are mad!"[1]

Second Lieutenant Alfred Joubaire,
May 23, 1916, diary, last entry

ON NOVEMBER 11, 1918, AT 10:59 A.M, in the village of Chaumont-devant-Damvillers, North-Eastern France, Private Henry Gunther rose up and started running through the fog, towards the German roadblock guarded by machine guns.[2] 29 minutes earlier, Gunther and the other members of his company had learned that the war would end at 11:00 a.m, exactly six hours after the signing of the armistice in the forest of Compiègne.

His comrades shouted for him to stop, but Gunther kept storming on. The German soldiers at the roadblock joined in, shouting at him to go back, that the war was over ("History of the Seventy-ninth", 505). Only it wasn't. Not yet.

Gunther kept charging and fired a couple of shots in the direction of the roadblock. When he got close, too close, one of the machine guns fired back, killing Henry Gunther on

---

1   Qtd. in Freedman, 101.

2   Gunther had recently been demoted to private from the rank of supply sergeant and was determined to "make good" before the war was over ("History of the Seventy-ninth", 505).

the spot ("History of the Seventy-ninth", 505). Seconds later, the clock struck 11:00 a.m. The First World War was over.

Of course it wasn't called the First World War back then, simply The Great War. U.S. President Woodrow Wilson had even optimistically called it *"the war to end all wars"*, in an effort to rally pacifist groups behind the cause of the Allied Powers against the Central Powers.[3]

As early as September 1914, the German philosopher Ernst Haeckel had called the quickly spreading European war a "First World War", but most people were not in the mood to philosophize about whether or not this particular global carnage would be the start of a series.[4]

It had started with only two shots, fired in Sarajevo, Bosnia-Herzegovina, by 19-year-old Bosnian Serb Gavrilo Princip, at Archduke Franz Ferdinand of Austria—heir presumptive to the Austro-Hungarian throne—and his wife Sophie, on June 28, 1914, at 10:45 a.m.

Princip was a Yugoslav nationalist and member of an organization called Young Bosnia, which wanted to dislodge Bosnia and Herzegovina from the Austro-Hungarian empire and either unite it with the Kingdom of Serbia or unite all the south Slavs—Bosniaks, Croats and Serbs—in a united Yugoslavia.[5] He had drawn his inspiration from another

3   Though Wilson made the phrase famous, it is actually contributed to H.G. Wells, who, in October 1914, published the book 'The War That Will End War'.

4   In the Indianapolis Star of Sept. 20, 1914, Haeckel was quoted as saying that *"There is no doubt that the course and character of the feared "European War"...will become the first world war in the full sense of the word."* (qtd. in Shapiro, 329). He would not be around long enough to be proved right though, dying in August 1919 at the ripe old age of 85.

5   Some (Bosnian Serbian) members of Young Bosnia wanted to separate Bosnia and Herzegovina from Austria-Hungary only so it could be annexed by Serbia, but this was not Gavrilo Princip's primary aim. As he said during his trial: *"I am a Yugoslav nationalist, aiming for the unification of all Yugoslavs, and I do not care what form of state, but it must be free from Austria."* (qtd. in Butcher, 248).

young Bosnian, Bogdan Žerajić, a law student who had attempted to assassinate the Austro-Hungarian appointed Governor of Bosnia and Herzegovina, General Marijan Varešanin, in 1910.[6]

Austria-Hungary blamed the Kingdom of Serbia for the assassination and issued a ten-point ultimatum, with the intention of either eliminating Serbia as a threat to Austrian-Hungarian control of the Northern Balkans or—which would be even better—provoking it into a war.[7] Consequently, the terms of the ultimatum were intentionally harsh, making it next to impossible for Serbia to comply, lest it was willing to lose all its dignity as a sovereign state.

During the weeks that followed, Serbia's allies Russia and France, feeling ill-prepared to go to war—especially against Austria's mighty ally, Germany— nevertheless exerted pressure on Serbia to accept the terms of the ultimatum. The German Empire, meanwhile, was eager for *Krieg*, at least the military and governmental elite were, reasoning that Germany was currently better prepared for war than France and Russia, but that that advantage would likely dissipate over the course of the next few years. In other words, if ever there was a good moment for a successful 'preventive war', it was now (Mombauer, 107–09).[8]

---

6   Žerajić had fired five bullets at Varešanin, all of which missed. The sixth and last bullet, which he used for himself, did not miss. At his trial, Princip, talking about his admiration for Žerajić and the many visits to his grave, said: "*I often spent whole nights there, thinking about our situation, about our miserable conditions and about him. So I resolved to carry out the assassination.*" (Preston 2014).

7   It later became clear that Serbian military intelligence had indeed been involved in the assassination on several levels (Maurer, 51–52).

8   According to Mombauer, 'preventive' war in this particular context did not mean preemptive—as in taking action to prevent being attacked—but rather to forestall a situation where Germany would no longer be able to take the initiative itself and was forced in a defensive position by stronger enemies (Mombauer, 108, note 6).

So the German Ambassador to Vienna, Heinrich von Tschirschky, was instructed by German Emperor Wilhelm II *"to emphatically press the point that Berlin expected action be taken against Serbia, and that Germany would not understand it when this opportunity to deal a blow was wasted"*, a message Tschirschky faithfully carried over to the Austro-Hungarian Secretary of State, Count Leopold Berchtold, on July 8.[9]

Meanwhile, several other countries weighed in on the diplomatic front, including Great-Britain, which proposed a mediation effort led by Britain, France, Germany and Italy, to solve the dispute between Austria-Hungary and Serbia (Martel, 196ff.). Of course Britain was unaware that Germany actually *wanted* to go to war and was strengthening Austro-Hungarian resolve to deal with Serbia once and for all.

However serious the situation though, most countries still believed they would be able to stay out of any war that might result from the Austrian-Serbian crisis.[10] They failed to fully realize that war between Austria-Hungary and Serbia would push a complex network of political and military alliances into action, like a finger flicking over the first domino. That those alliances would involve not only the great powers and their allies but also their many colonies and protectorates, essentially committing—apart from Europe—the entire African continent, the Middle East, India, Canada, New-Zealand and Australia to the conflict.

---

9   Translated from German: *"Hier mit allem Nachdruck zu erklären, dass man in Berlin eine Aktion gegen Serbien erwarte und dass es in Deutschland nicht verstanden würde, wenn wir die gegebene Gelegenheit vorüber gehen ließen, ohne einen Schlag zu führen."* The quote was relayed in a letter sent by Count Leopold Berchtold to the Hungarian Prime Minister, Count István Tisza, on July 8, after concluding his meeting with Von Tschirschky.

10   A key exception was Russia, which had already decided it could never accept Austro-Hungarian dominance of the Balkans and would in any case go to war should the Austrian-Hungarian Empire attack Serbia, even if it could only count on the support of France—which it certainly could, as the French Ambassador assuredly told the Russian Secretary of State, Sergei Sazonov—and Britain stayed out of the conflict entirely (Martel, 196).

And war had changed. The silent marriage between the concept of total warfare—introduced by revolutionary France a little over a century earlier—and technology—responsible for mass production, cheap steel and a host of new weapons—would produce an outpouring of men, machines and munitions such as the world had never seen.

This time, there would be machine guns, barbed wire, airplanes, submarines, powerful artillery, poison gas and flame throwers. No more heroic cavalry charges gloriously winning the day, no more civilized day-time only battles on green fields, fought by neatly positioned infantry units in colorful uniforms. This time there would be mud, trenches, incessant bombardments, poison gas, almost suicidal attacks and counter-attacks and most of all dead bodies; dead bodies morning, afternoon and night.

And then there was the Schlieffen plan, or rather the Moltke plan, the German attack plan (Fromkin, 35).[11] In the early 1900s, Alfred Graf von Schlieffen, then Chief of the Imperial German General Staff, had envisioned defeating France by marching the German right wing through the Southern Netherlands, Belgium and Luxembourg in a wheel-like motion, thus involving not only those three countries but almost certainly also Great Britain (and with it the rest of the

---

11   New documents about Schlieffen's plans have come to light after the fall of the Berlin Wall in 1989. Since then, a heated debate has emerged in the academic community about whether or not the Schlieffen Plan really existed as a ready-made attack plan for a two-front war, complete with railroad timetable allowing 42 days for victory in France before the bulk of the army had to be moved East to deal with Russia, as typical textbooks on the subject have for decades stated. Based on the new sources, military historian Terence Zuber has argued there was not, at least not in the clear-cut form historians have presented it in since the 1920s. I decided to include some of Zuber's evidence, while still emphasizing that the core of Schlieffen's deployment plans for war with France—a fast, strong, right-wing attack through Belgium and Northern France—remained intact in Moltke's plan.

British Commonwealth) because the British had guaranteed Belgian neutrality in the Treaty of London of 1839.[12]

In 1906, Helmuth von Moltke the Younger (so-called to distinguish him from his uncle, Helmuth von Moltke the Elder, the Prussian / Imperial German Chief of the General Staff between 1857–88) succeeded Count Schlieffen as Chief of the General Staff. Moltke based his own attack plan on a possible two-front war with France in the West and Russia in the East, taking much of his inspiration from two deployment plans Schlieffen had worked on shortly before his retirement in 1906, known as *Aufmarsch I*—which concentrated German forces largely in the West—and *Aufmarsch II*, with a heavier focus on the East (Zuber 2011, 13–14).

Aufmarsch I was based on an isolated war between Germany and France, with a numerical superior Germany army outflanking the French forces by marching through Holland, Belgium, Luxembourg and Northern France, to attack the French forces from the flank and the rear. In view of the German numerical superiority, a French attack in Lorraine seemed unlikely in this scenario, though Schlieffen—who believed a counter-attack strategy was key for Germany in the event of a two-front war—certainly would have welcomed it (Zuber 2002, 46; Zuber 2011, 8, 22).[13]

Aufmarsch II was based on a two-front war with Russia and France and diverted more divisions to East Prussia, to

---

12   Germany seriously doubted the English would really make good on their promise to protect Belgium when push came to shove though. On the night Britain formally declared war on Germany, Chancellor Theobald von Bethman Hollweg infamously asked his friend Sir Edward Goschen, the British Ambassador to Germany, how Britain could go to war over a *"scrap of paper"*, i.e., the 1839 Treaty of London (qtd. in Zuckerman, 20).

13   In the 1905/06 *Aufmarsch I* plan, the entire German Army—seventy-two active and reserve divisions, eleven cavalry divisions and twenty-six and a half Landwehr brigades, possibly further supplemented by ten Italian divisions— were employed in the west, against fifty-five French ones (Zuber 2011, 46–48). With this in mind, it is not difficult to understand that in this particular scenario Schlieffen would have considered a French attack into Lorraine a *"Liebesdienst"* (qtd. in Zuber 2002, 46).

defend against a Russian attack before mounting a count-er-attack (Zuber 2011, 46).

Moltke based his own operational plan on Schlieffen's two-front war scenario of *Aufmarsch II*, but used Schlieffen's overall strategy of the single-front war of *Aufmarsch I* for his attack on France (Holmes 2014). There were however two fundamental differences between Schlieffen's last wargame scenarios and Moltke's final, actual war plan.

The first was that Schlieffen did not factor in war with Russia in *Aufmarsch I* and thus positioned only a few divisions in East Prussia, using the rest for the Western front. Considering the fact that in 1905 the Russian Empire was mired in revolution and war with Japan, this was not an altogether unreasonable presumption. Secondly, Schlieffen used more divisions than were actually at his disposal. In his 1905 scenario for war with France for instance, Schlieffen employed ninety-six divisions, twenty-four more than actually existed (Zuber 2011, 7).[14]

In other words, Moltke based the overall strategy for the Western part of his two-front war plan on a one-front war plan in which twenty-four extra, non-existent divisions (two entire armies) had been added to the equation. One could therefore argue that, in the eyes of Count Schlieffen at least, Moltke's attack plan was doomed to fail from the start, simply because it lacked the necessary military strength.[15]

---

14   It is important to note that Schlieffen did not add the extra, non-existent divisions to the Germany Army because he was overly optimistic or bad at losing, but because he strongly believed the army had to be enlarged if Germany was to be prepared for every eventuality. Like Moltke, Schlieffen was a strong proponent of universal conscription after French example, something that did not exist in the German Empire at the time.

15   This point is made by Terence Holmes in his article "Absolute Numbers: The Schlieffen Plan as a Critique of German Strategy in 1914" (2014). Holmes writes that Schlieffen concluded that the German army would need at least 48.5 corps to succeed in a French attack through Belgium, while Moltke planned this attack with 'only' 34 corps at his disposal.

To make matters even worse, Moltke sent three more corps and a cavalry division to the East during the first weeks of the war—thus further weakening the right wing on the Western front—when it became clear that Russia was mobilizing much faster than had been anticipated (Marshall, 106).

As it turned out, those troops were still in transit when General von Hindenburg's Eighth Army delivered a crushing defeat to the Russians at the Battle of Tannenberg (Aug. 26–30, 1914). At the same time they were dearly missed at the Western front though, where the Germans came very close to breaking the French lines at the First Battle of the Marne (Sep. 5–12) but were ultimately defeated by a last ditch effort from the French, who threw everything they had in the fight. At one point the French authorities even commandeered 1,200 Parisian taxicabs to transport 6,000 French reserves to the battlefield (Tyng, 239–40).

On September 9, after the German Army had started its retreat to the Aisne River, Moltke reportedly told the German emperor „*Majestät, wir haben den Krieg verloren!*", Your Majesty, we have lost the war! (Schüddekopf, 18–19).

The German Army was pushed back some 30 miles, where it entrenched itself in a defensive position. In subsequent months, the Allied (French, British, Belgian) and German forces constantly tried to outflank each other, resulting in the so-called 'race to the sea' through Northern France. When they finally couldn't go any further, the Western front span from the French-Swiss border in the East up to the North Sea Coast in the West. Thus, by November 1914, the fast-paced mobile war of the first months had morphed into a static trench war that would last for years.

Though both sides continued to try and gain the upper hand, the front line would hardly change. At the Battle of Verdun for instance (Feb. 21-Dec. 18, 1916, the longest continuous battle in history) the Germans attacked the French for months, before being driven back again by massive French counter-offensives.

The new Chief of the German General Staff, Erich von Falkenhayn, who had succeeded Moltke after the lost Battle of the Marne, had chosen the city of Verdun as the best place to rupture the French front, and possibly also because it had been an important French bastion for centuries and he believed the French would be seriously demoralized if the Germans succeeded in capturing it.[16] Several forts protecting Verdun—such as Fort Douaumont and Fort Vaux—were captured and recaptured over the course of the battle, against staggering losses on both sides. In all, the Battle of Verdun caused more than 700,000 casualties, including 305,000 dead (Strachan, 188).

Meanwhile, at the Battle of the Somme (July 1- Nov. 18, 1916), it was the British and the French who were on the offensive. Part of a simultaneous offensive with the Italians at the Italian front and the Russians on the Eastern front, the original tactical objective of the Somme Offensive was to deny the Central Powers the possibility of moving troops between front lines during quiet periods at one of the other fronts.[17]

In the words of French Commander-in-Chief Joseph Joffre, who had successfully pushed for coordinated Allied

16   This at least seemed the contention of legendary French General and President of the Fifth Republic Charles de Gaulle, when he spoke about the German objectives at Verdun 50 years later, before the Ossuary at Douaumont, the memorial for the soldiers who died during the battle (Jankowski, 46). Shortly after the war, Erich von Falkenhayn had advanced the theory of *Ausblutung* as his leitmotiv for the brutal slaughter at Verdun, basically to bleed the French army to death by using Germany's superior artillery (Jankowski, 44). In the 1990s, historians debunked this theory as an excuse for a failed offensive (Jankowski, 46).

17   The location of the battle was chosen because it was where the French and British armies met. The first day of the Battle of the Somme, July 1st, 1916, remains the bloodiest day in British military history, with the British Expeditionary Force suffering 57,470 casualties, including 19,240 dead (Strachan, 192).

offensives at the second Allied military conference at Chantilly (24 miles north of Paris) on December 6, 1915, with his 'Plan of Action Proposed by France to the Coalition': *"Suppose, on the other hand, that there is no co-ordination of effort. In the present situation the Germans are able to add 10 divisions, no longer required in Serbia, to their forces in reserve--about 12 divisions--on the French front. Combined with the troops which could with safety be withdrawn from the Russian front, a mass of 25 to 30 divisions could be assembled. If the enemy is permitted to carry out these movements, he will employ this force, acting on interior lines, on each front in succession."* (Joffre 1915).

After the start of the German attack at Verdun, the direct objectives of the Somme Offensive became to relieve pressure on the French forces at Verdun and to inflict as many losses on the enemy as possible (Philpott, 120–22).

The Battle of the Somme was even deadlier than that of Verdun, with well over a million casualties in just a few months (Ellis, 272).[18] Friedrich Steinbrecher, a German officer who was there, at one point wrote in desperation: *"Somme. The whole history of the world cannot contain a more ghastly word!"* (qtd. in Witkop, 322).[19]

When major operations at the Somme were halted in November due to poor weather conditions, the Allies had advanced about eight miles into German-occupied territory, or 14,080 yards. With a grand total of 693,000 Allied casualties, that comes to some 49 casualties per yard.

Though the British public was aghast with the high number of casualties and placed the blame for the high losses squarely on the shoulders of the British Expeditionary Force (BEF)

---

18   Ellis and Cox arrive at 498,000 BEF casualties, 195,000 French and 420,000 German casualties (Ellis, 272). As with other battles, historians' estimates vary, but most are above one million total casualties.

19   Witkop and Winter accidentally date Steinbrecher's letter to April 12th, 1916. The correct date is August 12, 1916. Friedrich Steinbrecher was killed April 19th, 1917, near Moronvillers (Witkop, 320).

commander General Sir Douglas Haig, he had had very little choice in the matter. The Somme Offensive had been vital in denying the German Army reinforcements at Verdun, and with the French heavily occupied with the Germans there, responsibility for the Somme Offensive inevitably fell to the British.

Besides, what other course was open to the Allies but to fight an unrelenting war of attrition? Like General Ulysses S. Grant during the American Civil War, 50 years earlier, British and French generals concluded that the best strategy against a determined, well-trained, but outnumbered enemy was to fight large, deadly battles until he simply could not go on anymore. In this regard, the battles at Verdun and the Somme certainly did the job.

On the Eastern front the Germans were more successful. In August 1914, the Russians had invaded East Prussia and, more to the south, the Austro-Hungarian province of Galicia (part of present-day Poland and Ukraine), but a couple of weeks later they were badly defeated at the Battle of Tannenberg, in East Prussia (present-day Poland). The Russian Second Army was almost completely destroyed and not long after the Russian First Army suffered a similar fate. After the battle, General Alexander Samsonov, commander of the destroyed Russian Second Army, put a revolver to his head and killed himself (Marshall, 108).

The German Army was simply better equipped, better trained, better led and much more mobile than the Russian Army, with large numbers of troops being rapidly transported by rail, thus achieving a better concentration of fighting forces where needed.

The Russian Army did enjoy some success against the Austro-Hungarian Army, but after the Western front solidified in late 1914, the German High Command decided to concentrate its main effort on the Eastern front. During May-June 1915, the German Gorlice–Tarnów Offensive pushed the Russians back hundreds of miles, completely eliminating any threat of a Russian invasion of Germany or Austria-Hungary.

In the Summer of 1916, the Russians launched the Brusilov Offensive (named after General Aleksei Brusilov, who had conceived it), in line with the agreed upon strategy of co-ordinated Allied attacks. The offensive concentrated on the Austro-Hungarian province of Galicia. The main objectives were to provide relief to the French forces fighting at Verdun and the Italian forces fighting at Asiago, and to possibly knock the Austrian-Hungarian Empire out of the war. The offensive was very successful, diminishing Austria-Hungary as an independent fighting force and forcing the Germans to halt their attack at Verdun. It was Russia's finest hour of the war, but it would still be too little too late to turn the tide for Tsar Nicholas II.

Following the Russian October Revolution of 1917, the Bolsheviks sued for peace with the Central Powers to deliver on their promise to end the war, and also because they needed the army to fight in the civil war that was fast emerging between the communists and their opponents (basically everybody else).

On March 3, 1918, the Bolshevik government signed the Treaty of Brest-Litovsk, giving up Russian territorial claims in Finland, Estonia, Latvia, Belarus, Poland, Ukraine and Lithuania and ceding the cities of Kars, Ardahan and Batum (all three close to the present-day Turkish-Georgian border) to the Ottoman Empire. The communists thus signed away a total of one million square miles, containing a third of Russia's population, a third of its agricultural land, 85 percent of its beet-sugar land, more than half of its industry and nine-tenth of its coal mines (Grenville, 79–84; Wheeler-Bennett, 269). A heavy price for peace indeed, but perhaps not too heavy to stay in power and save the revolution.

The Ottomans had joined the Central Powers in August 1914 partly to recover Kars, Ardahan and Batum, which they had lost in the Russo-Turkish War of 1877–78. But while Germany threw the Ottoman Empire a bone in the Treaty of Brest-Litovsk by having those territories ceded back to it, its decision to enter the war on the side of the Central Powers would still cost it dearly.

Over the course of the war, the 'sick man of Europe', as the Ottoman Empire was called, lost all of its territory in the Middle East to the British and the French.[20] And it didn't stop there. Following the Ottoman Empire's surrender in October 1918, the Allies occupied Constantinople and divided most of the Anatolian heartland of the empire amongst themselves, thus effectively ending the more than 600-year-old Ottoman Empire in all but name. Turkish nationalists led by General Mustafa Kemal Pasha then started a war of independence, leading to the (official) dissolution of the Ottoman Empire but also the establishment of the modern-day Republic of Turkey, in 1923.

While the Ottoman Empire was a declining superpower that chose the wrong side, the United States was a rising superpower that preferred to choose no side, not least because public opinion was very much against American involvement in what was deemed a European affair. But opinions can change.

In May 1915, a German U-boat sank the British Ocean liner RMS Lusitania off the Southern Coast of Ireland, killing 1,195 passengers, 128 of them Americans.[21] U.S. President

---

20   France and Great-Britain subsequently divided the Middle-Eastern territories amongst themselves along the lines of the secret Sykes-Picot Agreement of 1916. The Russian Empire had been a minor party to that agreement as well, but in November 1917 the Bolshevik Government exposed the agreement to the general public.

21   In February 1915, Germany had declared the seas around the British Isles a war zone, giving itself license to sink all Allied ships in the area without warning. The New York German community wanted to run an ad in 50

Woodrow Wilson demanded that Germany stop attacking passenger ships and Berlin complied, but early 1917 it resumed its unrestricted submarine warfare, in an effort to starve Britain out of the war. Germany had to do something and the High Command had calculated that if the U-boats could attack all commercial ships headed for Britain, it would be possible to sink 600,000 British shipping tons every month, forcing the British to sue for peace in five months (Halpern, 337–38).

Of course the generals knew full well that unrestricted U-boat warfare would most likely mean war with the United States, but they figured they would be able to broker a favorable peace before U.S. troops could make any real difference.

But, alas for the German High Command, reality would not play along—at least not long enough—as is so often the case with the best laid plans of mice and men.

To be sure, the new strategy of unrestricted U-boat warfare was a great success during the first few months of 1917. In both February and March about 500,000 tons of shipping were sunk (in January it had been only 110,000) climbing to 860,000 tons in April, 600,000 in May and 700,000 in June, while only nine U-boats were lost between February-April (Morrow, 202).

But after the British started deploying convoy tactics— large numbers of ships sailing together, escorted by destroyers and long-range aircraft—the volume of tonnage sunk fell dramatically.[22] Convoys not only narrowed the area where

American newspapers, warning passengers of the risks of embarking on a ship bound for Great Britain, but the ad was initially blocked by the U.S. State Department, until the person responsible for placing the ad pointed out that the Lusitania would not just be carrying passengers but also six million rounds of ammunition. U.S. Secretary of State William Bryan then cleared the advertisement, which ran on the morning the ship sailed (Simpson 1972).

22 In April 1917, at the peak of the German submarine offensive, 226 Allied ships were sunk. In September, the number had decreased to 87 ships (Abbatiello, 107). During the entire unrestricted submarine warfare campaign, a total of 1,757 ships were sunk, 1,500 of whom were sailing independently,

U-boats could strike effectively, it also made hunting merchant and troop ships a much more dangerous affair, as the
convoys were generally well-defended by destroyers, while
the use of observation aircraft robbed the submarines of their
chief advantage, the element of surprise (Abbatiello, 111).

Meanwhile, after years of remaining on the sidelines,
Germany's (renewed) unrestricted U-boat warfare swayed
American public opinion—and pacifist U.S. President
Woodrow Wilson—towards entering the war on the Allied
side, not least because most of the torpedoed American ships
in March and early April—such as the *Vigilancia*, the *Illinois*,
the *Healdton* and the *Aztec*— had been attacked without
warning (Doenecke, 278–85).[23]

On April 6, 1917, Congress voted to declare war on
Germany. By July 1st of the next year, more than one million
men had embarked from the United States for France
(Pershing, 184).[24]

In the spring of 1918, the Germans tried to force a break on
the Western front one last time, before the by now continuous stream of fresh U.S. troops to the battlefields of France
would permanently tip the balance in favor of the Allies. And
also because 500,000 German troops had just arrived from
the Eastern front, thanks to the Treaty of Brest-Litovsk with
Russia (Gray, 7).

according to Abbatiello.

23   Another incident that helped turn American public opinion against
Germany was the publication of the Zimmerman telegram, on February 28.
It revealed the content of a message Arthur Zimmerman, the German Foreign
Secretary, had sent to the German Ambassador to Mexico in January, in which
he instructed him to propose a military alliance to the Mexican government
should the United States enter the war on the Allied side. Germany would
in that case provide Mexico with ample funding for it to mount an offensive
against the U.S. and reclaim the territories it had lost in Texas, New Mexico and
Arizona. The telegram was intercepted and decoded by British intelligence.

24   General John J. Pershing was the commander of the American
Expeditionary Forces in World War I.

To prevent a repetition of Verdun, where massive frontal assaults preceded by heavy artillery bombardments had gained little ground, Chief of Staff General Ludendorff instead opted for the same tactic the Russians had deployed with so much success during the Brusilov Offensive two years earlier, using light, fast stormtroopers to penetrate weak points in the enemy front line after a short bombardment.[25] Once a breach was made, heavier armed infantry would follow and advance.

The German spring offensive was very successful at first, gaining more ground than either side had been able to capture since the front lines had solidified late 1914. A series of attacks was launched from separate points, one of them bringing the Germans to within 75 miles (120 km) of Paris. There, they deployed the so-called Paris Gun, a monster measuring 118 feet (36 m), weighing 318,000 pounds (159 short tons) and firing 264 pound (120 kg) shells over a distance of 80 miles / 130 kilometer (Miller, "Railway Artillery", 732–45).

The first shell hit Paris on March 23, 1918, at 7:15 a.m (Miller, 723). Twenty others would follow that same day. The main objective of the Paris Gun was not to destroy the French capital, but rather to demoralize the Parisians by attacking their sense of security—knowing they could now be targeted by artillery. This objective was not achieved, partly because the Parisians didn't realize they were being attacked by long-range artillery and also because the bombardments did not do much damage. A total of 303 shells were fired, killing 256 people and wounding 620 others (Miller, 729–31).[26] The gun itself was never captured by the Allies.

---

25   Ludendorff's official title was *Erster Generalquartiermeister* (first quarter-master) but in effect he was the Chief of Staff of Field Marshal Paul Hindenburg, who had been appointed head of the Supreme Command in August 1916 (Chickering, 74).

26   Harry W. Miller writes he was in the city himself several times during the period of the bombardments ("Railway Artillery", 727).

Ultimately the German spring offensive failed, mainly because of logistical problems but also because it lacked a clear strategical goal beyond advancing and breaking the enemy. Perhaps Ludendorff's decision to stage a massive offensive at this stage of the war without a clear objective can best be explained by looking at the alternatives, which were: 1—trying to hold a defensive position in enemy France with more American troops arriving there every day, or 2— retreating back to Germany and hoping the Allies would not follow. Seen from that perspective, launching a final, all-out offensive to break the back of the enemy no doubt seemed a much more attractive option.

But the gamble failed and eight months and one massive Allied offensive later Germany surrendered, signing the Armistice in the early hours of November 11, 1918.

In the ensuing peace negotiations, Britain and the United States urged France to refrain from setting all too harsh conditions for peace with Germany, but the country that had lost so many of its sons at the Marne, the Somme and Verdun was adamant in its demands that adequate measures be taken to ensure its old foe would never again pose a threat to the French people. In the words of French Prime Minister Georges Clemenceau, describing France's position to President Wilson: "*America is far away, protected by the ocean. Not even Napoleon himself could touch England. You are both sheltered; we are not.*" (qtd. in Keylor, 43).

To satisfy the French, Germany was thus forced to acknowledge the 'Alleinschuld', the sole responsibility for all the losses and damages the Allies had suffered during the war. [27] In addition to paying hefty reparations, Germany also had to cede a significant amount of its territory to France (Alsace-Lorraine), Poland (parts of East Prussia), Denmark

---

27   Voiced in Part VIII, Article 231, of the Treaty of Versailles, a.k.a. the War Guild Clause ("Versailles Treaty").

(Northern Schleswig) and Belgium (Eupen-Malmedy), and give up its colonies in Africa and the Pacific.

Not all the French agreed with their government's crushing demands though. Following the finalization of the Treaty of Versailles—signed on June 28, 1919, exactly five years after the assassination of Archduke Franz Ferdinand and his wife in Sarajevo—French Marshal Ferdinand Foch declared: *"This is not peace. It is an Armistice for twenty years."* (qtd. in Adamthwaite, 28).

The German Empire had fallen. Emperor Wilhelm II fled to the Netherlands, where he would live out the remainder of his life peacefully, dying there in 1941 at the age of 82 (in what was by then German-occupied Holland).

Germany itself was transformed into a democracy at the worst possible time for such an open form of government, never giving the so-called Weimar Republic a fighting chance. Between 1919–33, socialists, communists, democrats and national-socialists fought each other inside and outside the *Reichstag*, until Adolf Hitler's National Socialist Party came to power democratically and then quickly consolidated that power undemocratically.

The Austro-Hungarian Empire had fallen as well, giving rise to several new states, such as Austria, Hungary, Czechoslovakia and Yugoslavia. Other countries in Central and Eastern Europe whose birth was intimately linked to the First World War were Finland, Poland, Estonia, Latvia and Lithuania.

The former Middle-Eastern possessions of the soon-to-be former Ottoman Empire were mostly divided among Great-Britain and France, with Mesopotamia, Palestine and Transjordan going to the British and Syria and Lebanon going to the French. Through the Balfour Declaration of 1917, the British government had promised the Zionist movement its support in establishing a Jewish state in Palestine, but although Great-Britain did allow mass immigration into

British-controlled Palestine in the 1920s and 30s, the Jews would have to wait until after the Second World War before the British promise would materialize in a country of their own.[28]

The war also had a significant and lasting social impact, especially on the position of women. With their men fighting at the front, many young women had suddenly had to learn to fend for themselves, answering the call to contribute to the war effort by filling the positions left open by laborers who had been called up. Consequently, when the men that had survived the war returned, they found skilled, independent-minded women working at their old jobs. Needless to say this not only contributed to radical socio-economic changes but also boosted the feminist movement and its drive for equal rights and universal suffrage.

Approximately 8.5 million soldiers were killed during the First World War, 21 million were wounded and almost 8 million were reported as prisoner or missing.[29] The war thus counted almost 37.5 million military casualties, over 57 percent of all mobilized forces (Hosch, 219). Civilian deaths are not as well-documented and estimates among historians vary considerably, but most arrive at a figure somewhere between 6–9 million.

Although American Private Henry Gunther was the last soldier to have fallen, he was not the only casualty in the six hours between the signing of the Armistice and it going into effect. In fact, 10,944 casualties were recorded in those six hours, 2,738 of which were deaths, more than the average daily casualty rate throughout the war and more than the

---

28   Between 1920–48, Palestine was administered by Britain as a mandate on behalf of the League of Nations and the League's post-World War II successor, the United Nations.

29   As reported by the U.S. War Department, February 1924. U.S. casualties amended by the Statistical Services Center, Office of the Secretary of Defense, November 7, 1957 (see also table in Hosch, 219).

number of Allied casualties on D-Day, June 6, 1944, when Allied forces landed on the heavily defended beaches of Normandy—to end the next World War (Persico, 378).

10

Deeds, not Words

"If I were a man and I said to you, 'I come from a country which professes to have representative institutions and yet denies me, a taxpayer, an inhabitant of the country, representative rights,' you would at once understand that that human being, being a man, was justified in the adoption of revolutionary methods to get representative institutions. But since I am a woman it is necessary in the twentieth century to explain why women have adopted revolutionary methods in order to win the rights of citizenship."[1]

Emmeline Pankhurst, Freedom or Death speech,
November 13, 1913

IN SEPTEMBER 2013, A GERMAN COURT OF appeal ruled that a thirteen-year-old Muslim girl was not allowed to opt out of mixed swimming lessons at her school, which she had been doing since she was eleven (Bartsch, "Integration Case"). The girl's parents, who were from Morocco, had filed a law suit to obtain legal dispensation to either skip the swimming lessons, or be given special instruction on her own (Hall, "Muslim girl").

The girl, or rather her parents, argued that wearing a 'burkini'—a swimming costume that covers the entire body—was not sufficient, because the Quran not only forbade a girl from showing herself to boys but also from seeing shirtless boys. The court rejected this argument, saying that "*the plaintiff has not made sufficiently clear that taking part in co-educational*

---

1   Pankhurst 1913.

swimming lessons with a burkini breaches Muslim rules on clothing", adding that *"the social reality of life in Germany comes above her religious beliefs"* (qtd. in Hall, "Muslim girl").

That social reality is that girls and boys in Germany are educated together, play sports together, and participate in society together. Of course it wasn't always so. In fact, less than 100 years ago women couldn't even vote in Germany, let alone enjoy the same rights as men to a higher education or a career.

The fight for women's right to vote—which militant suffragettes like Emmeline Pankhurst compared to fighting a civil war—had been slowly gaining momentum in the West since the 1850s, urged on by a small group of educated, resourceful and highly dedicated women, such as Susan B. Anthony (United States), Millicent Fawcett (United Kingdom), Kate Sheppard (New Zealand), Signe Bergman (Sweden) and Clara Zetkin (Germany).[2]

Women's suffrage was—and in some countries still is—part of a larger movement for freedom, democracy and equality regardless of race, sex, religion, sexual orientation or station in life, a movement that has been underway since the English Civil Wars of the 17th century, when King Charles I of England refused to yield to the demands of Parliament and was subsequently beheaded, in 1649.[3]

---

2   Anthony died in 1906, fourteen years before ratification of the Nineteenth Amendment (a.k.a the 'Anthony Amendment'), which prohibits denying the right to vote based on sex. Fawcett, born in 1847, would live just long enough to see women's suffrage fully implemented in the United Kingdom, in 1928; she died the following year, aged 82. Bergman, Sheppard and Zetkin all lived to see the full implementation of the women's right to vote in their respective countries.

3   It could also be argued the roots of this movement go back to the late 16th century Low Countries, when the Dutch successfully rebelled against the Spanish Empire because of high taxes and religious oppression, subsequently founding the independent Dutch Republic, the first modern nation to guarantee religious freedom to its citizens (Union of Utrecht Treaty of 1579, article XIII). The Dutch Revolt was more focused on religious freedom than on securing

Before that time, inequality—between nobility and commoners, black and white, women and men, Muslims and Christians, Catholics and Protestants—had always been regarded as normal. But during the Age of Enlightenment, philosophers such as John Locke, Baruch Spinoza, Jean-Jacques Rousseau and Montesquieu helped popularize and solidify legal theories that turned this long accepted reality on its head. And in the second half of the 18th and the first half of the 19th century, these theories—such as government with consent of the governed, equality before the law and the separation of church and state—would help ignite revolutions in the Thirteen Colonies, France, a string of colonies in South America, France again, Belgium, France again, the German states, the Italian states, and several other European regions.

Of course, with the acknowledgement that the nobleman was equal to the peasant—at least philosophically and before the law—the cat was out of the bag. Because the same basic argument that made the peasant equal to the nobleman (their both being human) would prove just as potent an argument against slavery and discrimination based on sex, race or religion.

Another reason for the gradually changing view on women's suffrage in the 19th century was the changing role of women in society, spurred by the Industrial Revolution, which saw large numbers of women enter the professional workforce for the first time. In the textile town of Lowell, Massachusetts, for instance, 28 textile mills employed 8,000 workers by the late 1830s, the great majority of these women coming from the New England countryside (Montrie, 20). And this certainly was not the only place where women found employ.

The effect of women earning their own income was twofold: their economic value grew—both in the family and in society

political rights though, whereas the English Civil Wars, while fought partly against the backdrop of religious differences, were much more of a political power struggle between the King and Parliament.

as a whole—and their independence increased. For the first time women did not necessarily need a man to support them.

The educational level of women also rose in the 19th century, especially in the second half, aided by a growing number of colleges founded exclusively for the education of young women. Such as Wheaton Female Seminary, established in Norton, Massachusetts, in 1834, with the help of noted women's educator Mary Lyon, who also created the first curriculum for the school, with the specific goal of making it equal in quality to those at men's colleges (Helmreich, 40–42). Three years later, Lyon also founded Mount Holyoke Female Seminary, in South Hadley, Massachusetts. In 1848, Queen's College, an independent school for girls, was established in London. This was also the first institution to award academic qualifications to women. Girton College, the first Cambridge college to admit women, followed in 1869, two years before Newham College, the second Cambridge college for women, to name just a few of the dozens of women's colleges established between 1830 and 1900.

Considering the growing number of smart, talented, mostly upper class young women finding their way into first-rate colleges to receive academic training and the significant number of young working class women earning their own income for the first time, it can hardly be called a coincidence that the women's movement gained so much traction in the second half of the 19th century.

In 1893, New Zealand became the first country in the world to give women the right to vote on a national level, while in 1907 the autonomous Grand Duchy of Finland (then still part of the Russian Empire) became the first European territory to adopt full women's suffrage.[4] The United Kingdom permitted women some voting rights in local elections through

---

4   The Parliament of the Grand Duchy of Finland was also the first in the world to have female MPs, following the 1907 elections.

the Local Government Act of 1894, but nothing on a national level.

For some women, especially in the United Kingdom, progress was not going fast enough. They argued that the strategy of peaceful debate and gentle persuasion was not working. In 1903, Emmeline Pankhurst and her daughter Christabel therefore founded the militant Women's Social and Political Union (WSPU). To underscore that this movement would not just sit and drink tea, the founders gave the WSPU the motto 'Deeds, not words' (Bartley, 126).

To Emmeline Pankhurst and her followers, soon called suffragettes, the fight for equal rights for women was not a fight in the figurative sense, but a literal, actual fight, a war even. Pankhurst said WSPU members should see themselves as guerrilla fighters engaged in a civil war (Smith, 55).

Like revolutionaries before them (and after them), WSPU members felt they had no other option left but violence to achieve democratic participation. So they slashed paintings at museums, cut telegraph wires, burned empty country houses, tea houses, churches—because the Church of England was against woman suffrage—even a school; they smashed windows of government buildings, firebombed politician's houses and attacked politicians as they went to work (Smith, 51; Stillion Southard, 61).

Never before had women made their case so forcefully, so violently, and many people thought the suffragettes went much too far in their zeal for equal voting rights.[5] Then again, women had already been making their case peacefully for more than 50 years, and men in the same situation had rebelled against their governments and fought wars not so long ago in the United States, France, Great Britain and many other countries.

---

5   Among them leading English feminist Milicent Fawcett, who wrote to a friend in 1909: "*It seems to me that there is only a slight distinction between their* [WSPU] *recent actions and positive crime.*" (qtd. in Holton, 47).

In the United States, meanwhile, things did not take quite so violent a turn as in Britain, but there too the women's movement began adopting a more visible approach. On March 3, 1913, for instance—one day before President Woodrow Wilson's inauguration—8,000 women marched down Pennsylvania Avenue in Washington D.C, gaining widespread attention for their cause (Barber, 66).[6] Women's movements in other countries adopted similar tactics.

At the outbreak of World War I the suffragettes halted all of their activities, calling on women to replace male workers who had gone off to the front. As the war progressed, women proved to be an indispensable part of the war effort, working en masse in factories to keep the economy going and to produce shells, uniforms, guns and bullets. WW I thus acted as a powerful catalyst for the women's movement.

In 1918, Germany, Austria, Russia and Poland gave women the right to vote, while the United Kingdom expanded suffrage to all women over 30 and all men over 21. Canada granted women the right to vote in most provinces, but it would take until 1929 before women could also stand for election for all offices. The Netherlands, Luxembourg and Belgium granted full suffrage in 1919, Czechoslovakia followed in 1920, as did the United States, through ratification of the Nineteenth Amendment.

On July 2, 1928, the United Kingdom granted women equal voting rights. Emmeline Pankhurst had died less than a month earlier, on June 14, aged 69.

---

6   The number of marchers could have been even bigger if black women had been encouraged to participate, but the National American Woman Suffrage Association (NWSA) was not interested in this and even discouraged it. Alice Paul, the lead organizer of the march, said at one point that "*we must have a white procession, or a negro procession, or no procession at all*." (Barber, 62). A rare lack of vision for someone so passionately fighting for equal rights. Ultimately, 42 black women participated in the march. Alice Paul lived to the ripe old age of 92, dying in 1977, fourteen years after the 'March on Washington for Jobs and Freedom' and thirteen years after the passage of the Civil Rights Act of 1964.

In December 2015—122 years after New Zealand became the first country to grant women the right to vote—women in Saudi Arabia participated in municipal elections for the first time since the now deceased King Abdullah in 2011 granted women the right to vote in future municipal elections (MacFarquhar 2011; Giacomo 2015).[7] Since then, Vatican City has held the dubious honor of being the last remaining bastion of the all-male democracy.

Of course the path to full equality does not end with equal voting rights. Equal employment rights, equal pay for equal work, reproductive rights, adoption rights, custody rights, property rights, the right not to be treated as the weaker sex; full equality for every citizen regardless of sex, race, religion or sexual orientation remains a work in progress in most countries (if not all).

And although gender discrimination has been greatly reduced in the West in the 20th century, in some other regions women are still a long way away from being treated even remotely equal, just as some women are a long way away from considering themselves as such.

With that in mind, one wonders what Emmeline Pankhurst would have said to the thirteen-year-old Muslim girl who wouldn't swim with boys.

---

7   Municipal elections are also the only elections in Saudi Arabia, which functions as an absolute monarchy on all other levels. The first municipal elections were held in 2005.

11

THE GREAT DEPRESSION

"Many people in America seem to be more concerned about the present situation than the Federal Reserve System is. If unsound credit practices have developed, these practices will in time correct themselves, and if some of the overindulgent get 'burnt' during the period of correction, they will have to shoulder the blame themselves and not attempt to shift it to someone else." [1]

Roy A. Young, chairman of the Federal Reserve Board,
September 20, 1928

ON MARCH 9, 2009, THE DOW JONES Industrial Average (DJIA) closed at its lowest point in twelve years. By then, the Dow had lost 52.5 percent of its value since reaching its record high of 14,279 points seventeen months earlier, on October 11, 2007. Market strategists and financial journalists eerily observed that the current rate of decline was closely mimicking that of the Dow during the Great Depression. Back then, the DJIA had hit its high mark on September 3, 1929, at 381 points. But seventeen months and a Black Thursday, Monday, and Tuesday later, the Dow had been deflated to 172 points, 54.7 percent lower than its 1929 high. And there were other similarities with that gloomy, despondent era commonly associated with bank runs, massive unemployment, tent cities and long bread lines. Both the Great Recession—as the financial crisis that started late 2007

---

1   Young 1928.

has come to be known—and its infamous sibling, the Great Depression, were preceded by years of cheap credit and the accumulation of consumer debt, followed by a flood of individual bankruptcies and very public collapses of big banks, rising unemployment and the freezing up of credit markets.

Some of the panic at the beginning of both crises no doubt also felt the same. In September/October 2008, daily news bombardments about the collapse of investment bank Lehman Brothers, bank runs, hastily concocted bank takeovers and the high-powered Troubled Asset Relief Program (TARP) instilled people with fear that the whole financial system was crumbling down. In October 1929, the panic was caused by the uncontrollable crash of a stock market that many had been playing with borrowed money.

After having reached an all-time high on September 3, 1929, trading on the New York Stock Exchange had become increasingly volatile in the weeks that followed, with stock prices trending downward unevenly. At first, the downturn was seen as a healthy correction of an overheated market and buyers stepped in at every trough, trying to get in cheap. But that all changed on October 23, when, at the end of the trading day, everyone suddenly seemed to want to offload their stock at the same time and 2.6 million shares—roughly the trading volume for an entire day—changed hands in just one hour (Blumenthal, 13). The Dow Jones Industrial Average ended the day almost 7 percent lower.

Now investors and speculators most definitely *were* panicking. The next day, October 24—Black Thursday—the Dow quickly lost eleven percent after the opening bell. Around midmorning, a group of leading Wall Street bankers met to discuss how to calm markets and stop the bleeding (Geisst, 191).[2] The solution they came up with was a classic one: to

2   Among them Thomas Lamont of Morgan, Albert Wiggin of Chase National and Charles Mitchell and George F. Baker Jr. of National City Bank (now Citibank).

commit a serious amount of money to buying up a large block of key stocks like US Steel, AT&T, Anaconda Copper and General Electric.[3]

It worked. 12,894,650 million shares were sold on Black Thursday, but at the closing bell the Dow was down only 2 percent, a modest loss compared to the 11 percent it had been at the beginning of the day or the 7 percent the Dow had lost the day before (Wigmore, 7). The next day, the Dow even closed higher.

But it soon became clear that the market had only been pushed into the eye of the storm, a storm that grew even stronger over the weekend. On Monday the Dow took another nosedive, shedding 13 percent of its value, and this time the bankers did not intervene. On Tuesday, October 29—Black Tuesday—more than 16 million shares changed hands while the Dow fell another 11 percent.

The next day, Albert Wiggin, president of Chase National Bank lamented : "*We are reaping the natural fruit of the orgy of speculation in which millions of people have indulged. It was inevitable, because of the tremendous increase in the number of stockholders in recent years, that the number of sellers would be greater than ever when the boom ended and selling took the place of buying.*"[4] (qtd. in "Second Crash").

Of course in hindsight we are all wise men, but he was right nevertheless. In the years leading up to the crash of October 1929, many people had borrowed money to buy into the stock market, believing stocks would continue to rise in perpetuity. It was the same kind of thinking that had helped create the Dutch tulip mania of the 1630s, at the height of which a

---

3   The same kind of rescue operation had also been successfully performed during the Panic of 1907, when financiers J.P. Morgan, John D. Rockefeller and other key figures from the New York banking scene had committed their own funds to stop a banking panic and calm down the stock market.

4   In 1930, Chase National Bank would acquire the Equitable Trust Company of New York, making it the world's largest bank.

single tulip bulb sometimes changed hands for as much as fl. 1,200, about $20,000 in 2014 money (Goldgar, 238).[5] The same kind of thinking, also, that helped create the dot-com bubble of the late 1990s, and the same kind of thinking that created the real estate bubble of subprime mortgages in the early 2000s, which helped ignite the Great Recession in 2007.

Then again, the Dow Jones Industrial Average had risen close to a staggering *500 percent* in the period 1921–29.[6] The war was over, the economy was booming and everybody was getting richer. Investing in the stock market had always been the exclusive playground of professional traders and the very wealthy, but in the 1920s brokers started attracting small investors as well, offering loans that sometimes financed up to 90 percent of the face value of stocks being bought. It promised to be a fast track to the American dream for millions of ordinary Americans and was hard to resist in a trading climate that was booming year after year. So when the Dow peaked on September 3, 1929, roughly $8.5 billion of the invested money was out on loan, almost double the entire amount of currency in circulation in the United States at the time (Lambert 2008).

Seven weeks later, when the bubble finally burst—as bubbles tend to do—all those small investors were quickly wiped out, pulling their brokers down with them. But large investors were hit hard too, as were many businesses and commercial banks that had invested part of their capital in the stock market.

---

5   One such bulb was an Admirael van der Eyck, sold on January 18, 1637 for fl. 1,205. (Goldgar, 238). In her introduction, Goldgar aptly summarizes the main themes of the tulipmania by quoting two phrases from a conversation at the time, during which one man showed another a precious bulb: "*That must have cost you*", and "*it still isn't paid for*" ("Tulipmania", Introduction, i). The purchasing power of the Dutch florijn in today's money was calculated at iisg. nl/hpw/calculate2.php.

6   The Dow's low of 1921 was 64, the high of September 3, 1929 was 381, i.e., up 317 points compared to the low (Gann, 17).

Banks played a key role in the Great Depression, just as they would in the Great Recession some 80 years later. Many commercial banks had invested part of their customer's savings in stocks, which seriously hurt their solvency after the markets crashed. On top of that, a growing number of debtors—small investors, businesses suffering from weakening demand, farmers hit hard by falling prices and falling exports—started defaulting on their loans. As a result, several banks had to close their doors, causing many people to panic and attempt to withdraw their savings. These bank runs then led to more bank failures, further eroding trust in the financial system, leading to still more bank runs and more bank failures. In all, some 9,000 banks—a third of U.S. banks—thus went under during the Great Depression (Guttmann, 6).

Meanwhile, with sagging demand and frozen credit markets, other businesses were in a bind as well. Acquiring funding through the stock or bond market was obviously out and banks were also unwilling and/or unable to issue any new loans, as they were desperately trying to improve their own capital ratio to survive. With the capital markets quickly drying up, businesses began to cut back on investments, supplies, wages, working hours, everything to cut cost. Needless to say many businesses still went belly-up, defaulting on their debts and adding to the already rising unemployment.[7]

Before long, tens of thousands of workers were being laid off. By 1932, Gross Domestic Product was only half that of 1929, industrial production was down 46 percent, unemployment had risen to 36 percent and the average hourly pay in manufacturing had dropped more than 20 percent compared to 1929 (Wigmore, 315–16, 418).

Now, during the Global Financial Crisis of 2008, governments and central banks swooped in to save the day. The U.S.Treasury alone bought more than $400 billion in bad

---

7   A total of 86,462 businesses went bankrupt between 1930–32 (Wigmore, 132, 230, 315).

debt from banks and other financial institutions through the Troubled Asset Relief Program (TARP), and implemented two stimulus packages totaling almost $1 trillion.[8]-[9] At the same time, the Federal Reserve embarked upon the largest monetary policy action in history, buying up Treasury notes and mortgage-backed securities from banks to increase the money supply, a practice known as quantitative easing. The Federal Reserve, the European Central Bank, the Bank of England and other central banks also quickly lowered interest rates, to make borrowing cheaper for commercial banks and halt the credit crunch that had so devastated businesses in the 1930s.

But in 1929, there was no such swooping in. The government was not prepared to bail out failed banks or businesses and the Federal Reserve could not unfreeze the credit markets by increasing the money supply, because the U.S. was on the gold standard and the Federal Reserve Act required that all credit issued by the Federal Reserve should be backed by gold for at least 40 percent (Bernanke, 126). In fact, the money supply actually shrunk by a third between 1929–33, making money even more expensive (Friedman, 299). Nobel laureate economist Milton Friedman has argued that this is one of the main reasons why the recession of the early 1930s became the Great Depression, while Ben Bernanke, former Chairman of the Federal Reserve, has noted that there is strong evidence

---

8   The U.S. Treasury took on $466 billion of obligations under the TARP program, which included the AIG rescue. A total of $418 billion was actually disbursed ("Troubled Asset Relief Program", 3, fig.1). As of January 2013, $344 billion has been repaid. Together with other income—such as dividend and interest—the total cashback was $405 billion.

9   The first stimulus package, the Economic Stimulus Act of 2008, valued at $152 billion, was enacted in February 2008 to avert an impending recession. The second stimulus package, the American Recovery and Reinvestment Act (ARRA) of 2009, with an estimated cost of $831 billion between 2009–19, was enacted in February 2009 to deal with the Great Recession. ("Estimated Impact",1) The Congressional Budget Office has estimated that more than 90 percent of ARRA's impact was realized by the end of 2011.

that countries that left the gold standard recovered more quickly from the Great Depression than those that stuck with it (Friedman, 299–301; Bernanke, 8).

Meanwhile, one of the measures Washington did take in the early days of the Great Depression—passing the Smoot-Hawley Tariff Act in May 1930—proved to be hugely counter-productive (Bernanke 2013). Smoot-Hawley was aimed at protecting domestic businesses from foreign competition by raising the average tariff on imported goods by some 20 percent. In a last-ditch effort to prevent the bill from becoming law, more than 1,000 economists signed a petition asking President Hoover to veto it, writing: "*Countries cannot permanently buy from us unless they are permitted to sell to us, and the more we restrict the importation of goods from them by means of ever higher tariffs, the more we reduce the possibility of our exporting to them* (qtd. in New York Times 1930). But although Hoover himself was against the legislation, in the end he yielded to pressure from within the Republican party and signed the bill.

This naturally led to retaliatory policies in countries whose economies were adversely affected by the increased tariffs, most notably in Europe, where a decline in U.S. exports from $1,334 million in 1929 to $390 million in 1932 was answered with a decline in U.S. imports from $2,341 million to $784 million in the same period, thus deepening and lengthening the global Depression (Lawrence 2009).

All industrialized countries suffered during the Great Depression, but the vicious circle of rising unemployment and falling demand was particularly steep in the United States, which at the time was the only industrialized country without unemployment insurance and pension system. The purchasing power of Americans out of work therefore declined much more than that of the unemployed in many European countries. When President Franklin Delano Roosevelt came into office in March 1933, he sought to remedy this with an extensive social program he called "*a new deal for the American people*."[10]

It was quite literally a new deal. The 'old deal', so to speak, had been that government interfered as little as possible with people's lives but at the same time also did very little to help them. Before Roosevelt, the U.S. government was a night-watchman state in every sense: it provided the people with protection against assault, theft, breach of contract and fraud and was charged with defending the nation in times of war, but that was about it. Low taxation, very little rules and regulations and no social security whatsoever; capitalism in its purest form possible.

When a modern society is in its early stages, this kind of laissez-faire approach makes a lot of sense. Agriculture, industry, commerce, trade, infrastructure, security, much of it still has to be developed, and the quickest way to do that is by providing citizens as much incentive as possible to work as hard as possible. Social security is a negative incentive in this phase, as it makes it easier for people to remain on the sidelines while others do the heavy lifting. But as society progresses and people's lives improve they also have more to lose, as does society.

What Roosevelt proposed was to change the social contract between the state and the people from a night-watchman state to a welfare state, from a laissez faire government to one that intervened in the economy to counter the less desirable effects of pure capitalism.

---

10   Roosevelt had already announced his intention to enact large-scale social reform the year before, saying in his speech accepting the Democratic Party's Presidential Nomination: "*Throughout the Nation, men and women, forgotten in the political philosophy of the Government of the last years look to us here for guidance and for more equitable opportunity to share in the distribution of national wealth.(..) I pledge you, I pledge myself, to a new deal for the American people. Let us all here assembled constitute ourselves prophets of a new order of competence and of courage. This is more than a political campaign; it is a call to arms.*" (Roosevelt 1932).

And intervene it did. Through the Federal Emergency Relief Administration (FERA) of 1933 for instance, which provided funds to states and cities for relief operations and the employment of people in a wide range of public jobs. In 1935 FERA was replaced by the Works Progress Administration, which at its peak in 1938 employed more than three million people in public works projects such as constructing parks, bridges, roads and schools (Odekon, 661). The Farm Security Administration (1935) aimed to improve the conditions for sharecroppers, tenants and small landowning farmers by providing credit when banks would not.[11] The National Labor Relations Act (1935) guaranteed workers the right to collective bargaining through unions and the Fair Labor Standards Act of 1938 set minimum wages and maximum working hours.

But the signature piece of the New Deal was the Social Security Act of 1935, which finally established a national system of unemployment insurance, welfare benefits for the handicapped and universal retirement pensions. It was paid for by a payroll tax, thus effectively institutionalizing solidarity among workers. More than any other New Deal legislation, the Social Security Act laid the foundation of the American welfare system. It still exists today.[12]

The New Deal was not just about social legislation though, it also sought to prevent future depressions through financial regulation and intervention. The Emergency Banking Act (1933) made it possible to place banks under Treasury supervision—keeping them afloat with federal loans if necessary—while the Glass-Steagall Act (1933) separated commercial banking from investment banking and protected savings accounts from being used by banks to speculate on

---

11   The FSA was originally called the Resettlement Administration but was renamed in 1937.

12   Today it is part of U.S. Code: Title 42 - The Public Health and Welfare, chapter 7 - Social Security.

the stock market.[13] To prevent future bank runs the Federal Deposit Insurance Corporation (1933) was established, for the first time federally insuring bank deposits, up to $2,500.

To increase the money supply and thus stimulate inflation and investment, the Roosevelt administration sought to increase the gold supply and devalue the dollar relative to gold. The Gold Reserve Act of 1934 therefore concentrated all U.S. gold coin and gold bullion held by the Federal Reserve in the hands of the U.S. Treasury and forced all U.S. citizens and institutions to sell their gold to the Treasury as well, while section 12 of the act gave the President the power to establish the gold value of the dollar by proclamation.[14] Roosevelt did so the day after signing the act, devaluing the dollar from $20.67 to $35 per troy ounce.[15]

It worked. As Milton Friedman and Anna Schwartz wrote in 'A Monetary History of the United States, 1867–1960': "*the money stock grew at a rapid rate in the three successive years from June 1933 to June 1936—at continuous annual rates of 9.5 percent, 14.0 percent, and 13.0 percent. The rapid rise was a consequence of the gold inflow produced by the revaluation of gold plus the flight of capital to the United States....And the*

13   Glass-Steagall was repealed in 1999. Some economists have argued that the repeal contributed to the financial crisis of 2007–08, among them Nobel Laureate Joseph Stiglitz, Robert Kuttner and Richard D. Wolff (Stiglitz 2009; Kuttner 2011; Wolff, 75).

14   Roosevelt had already criminalized the possession of gold by Executive Order on April 5, 1933, a month and a day after taking office (Exec. Order 6102). The authority to do so he derived from an amendment of the Trading With the Enemy Act of 1917, which extended the scope of the act to any declared national emergency, not just one declared during times of war. The Gold Reserve Act ratified this Executive Order, among other things. In 1935, the constitutionality of the federal government's restrictions on the private ownership of gold was upheld by the Supreme Court in a series of rulings—known as the gold clause cases—by a narrow 5–4 majority.

15   By seizing the Federal Reserve's gold reserves and giving the President the power to unilaterally determine the value of the dollar, the Gold Reserve Act deprived the Federal Reserve of its primary function as independent monetary policy authority, a function it would not regain until the Treasury-Federal Reserve Accord of 1951.

rapid rate of rise in the money stock certainly promoted and facilitated the concurrent economic expansion." (544).

Needless to say, many Republicans were dead set against what they deemed a shameless attack on the free market economy, infringing on the very freedoms the country was built on with this buffet of measures that amounted to nothing less than blatant socialism. But since an overwhelming majority of the people agreed with Roosevelt, they were powerless to stop it.

The New Deal certainly eased the pain for millions of Americans and it is probable that it also helped end the Great Depression, though the final nail in the coffin of the economic depression of the 1930s would be the outbreak of World War II.

Europe had already been rearming in the years leading up to the war—contributing to falling unemployment there—but when it comes to battling unemployment, nothing beats fighting a total war.

In 1939, a short 21 years after the end of the Great War, the next generation of young men was drafted by the millions and peace-time economies were once again transformed into war-time economies, cranking out more heavy machinery than ever, hundreds of thousands of tanks, trucks, artillery and aircraft, hundreds of destroyers and submarines, dozens of aircraft carriers and battleships.

More than any other war before it, the Second World War would be an industrialized, mechanized, technological and total war of attrition, flattening cities and villages and killing people in the tens of millions. No economic depression could ever be great enough to withstand such willingness to waste.

Ironically, the Great Depression was not only ended by the Second World War but had also been one of its main causes, as it had hit one of the main instigators particularly hard.

Germany had been forced to pay hefty reparations after losing WW I, crippling its economy. The Dawes Plan of

1924 (named after the American banker who devised it) had reduced the yearly reparation payments to a more manageable amount and established a loan program from American investment banks, but after the crash in 1929 those loans had stopped and the German economy quickly collapsed.

Politically speaking, radical parties like the Communist Party and the Nazi Party benefitted the most from the ensuing chaos, poverty and unemployment in the fragile, young democracy that was the Weimar Republic. After the Nazi Party had been voted into power in 1933, it quickly banned the Communist Party and ensured passage of the Enabling Act, which gave the government—i.e., Reich Chancellor Adolf Hitler—the power to legislate without the approval of the *Reichstag,* the German Parliament. This effectively ended the Weimar Republic and set Germany on the path to war (once more).

The impact of the Great Depression did not end with WW II, but has reverberated even into our own time, through its most lasting effect, the establishment of a new social contract between the state and the people. A contract demanding more responsibility for people's well-being from the state, in exchange for more taxes, more regulation and less individual freedom.

A paradigm shift that is still being debated today, or perhaps especially today, with the memory of that hard decade safely tucked away in the long long ago.

188

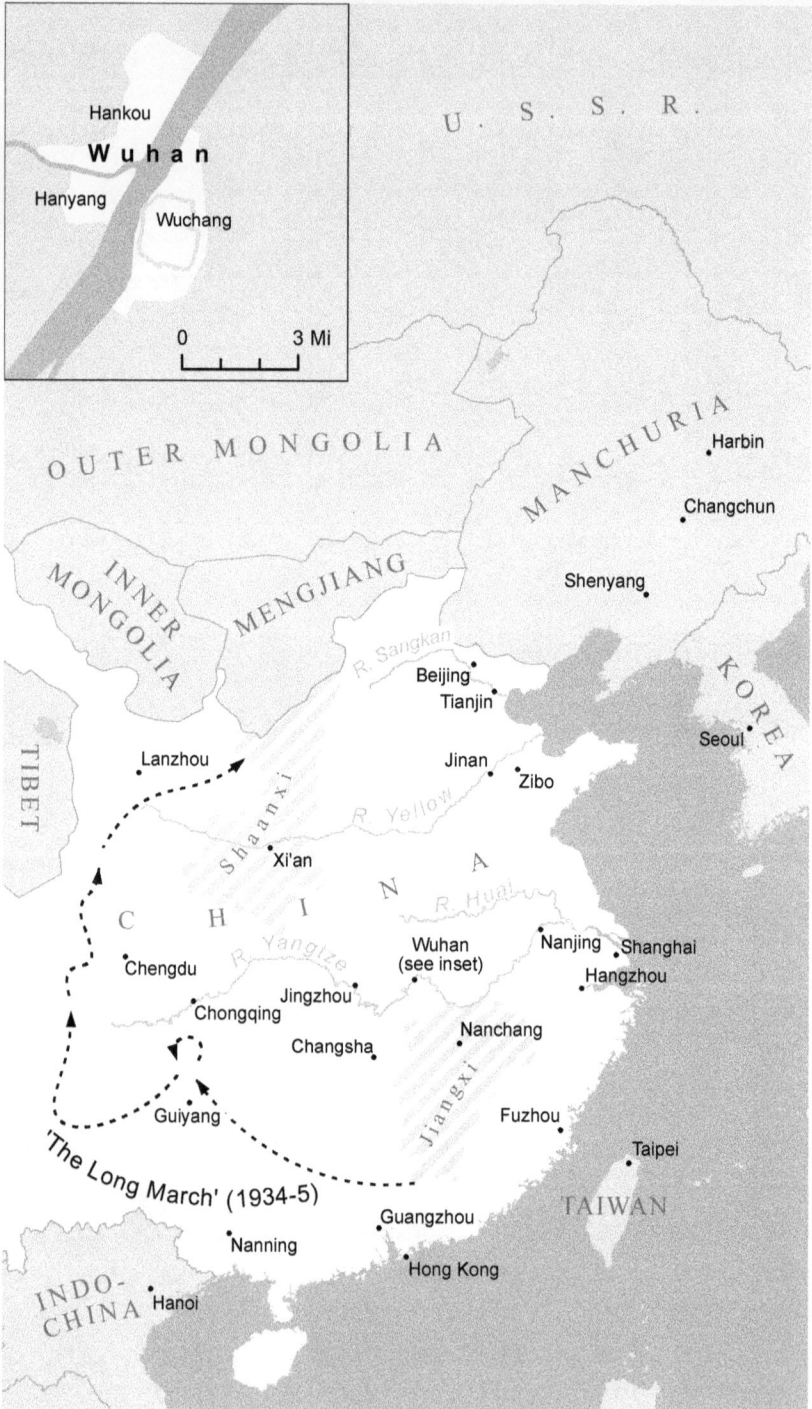

Map 7: The Communist Insurgency in China, 1927-37

12

CHINESE CIVIL WAR PART I & II

"Every Communist must grasp the truth, "Political power grows out of the barrel of a gun." Our principle is that the Party commands the gun, and the gun must never be allowed to command the Party."[1]

Mao Zedong, Problems of War and Strategy, 1938

IN A COUNTRY WITH A POPULATION OF over 1.3 billion, an organized protest of a mere 200 people might not seem worth mentioning.[2] Except that in this particular country, protests are frowned upon (as in forbidden) and protesters are frequently escorted to a place where they can quietly rethink their behavior (as in jailed). So, when, on February 20, 2011, 200 Chinese actually showed up in front of the McDonald's in Wangfujing—a famous shopping street in Beijing—in response to an online call to express displeasure about the lack of reforms and the widespread corruption in the one-party state, it was indeed taken very seriously by the Chinese authorities (Branigan 2011).

Inspired by and in reference to the Tunisian Revolution—which had led to the ousting of Tunisian President Zine El Abidine Ben Ali just a month before—the organizers called the protests the start of a 'Jasmine Revolution' (Branigan 2011). The police showed up in full force. Dozens were detained, some by security officers in plain-clothes. Several of

---

1   Qtd. in Zedong, "Selected Works", 224.
2   Population estimate as of September 2013.

those arrested seemed nothing more than curious onlookers, some were shouting "*why are you arresting me, I haven't done anything wrong.*" as they were roughly dragged away from the site (qtd. in "China police").

Their objection to being arrested was not entirely unfounded—even if they were demonstrating —since the Chinese Constitution states that "*citizens of the People's Republic of China enjoy freedom of speech, of the press, of assembly, of association, of procession, and of demonstration.*" ("Constitution People's Republic", II.35). Then again, it also states that "*The Chinese people must fight against those forces and elements, both at home and abroad, that are hostile to China's socialist system and try to undermine it*" ("Constitution People's Republic", preamble). That is because the ultimate function of the Chinese Constitution is not to protect the people, but the state. So it makes perfect sense that the general rule with regards to freedom of expression in China is that you can say, print and paint whatever you want, until the government says you cannot.

Of course the Communist Party of China, which has ruled China since 1949, certainly knows a thing or two about how to undermine the system and ultimately overthrow the government through protests, strikes, rebellion and revolution, seeing as it had for decades fought several rival factions in a number of uprisings and civil wars, before finally being able to proclaim the People's Republic of China. A long march indeed.

It had all started 50 years earlier, in 1899, with the Boxer Rebellion. After China had lost the Opium Wars of the mid-19th century, the British and French had forced the Middle Kingdom to open up its ports to trade with the West, legalize the import of opium, permit the establishment of diplomatic missions in Beijing and allow Christian missionary activity. Growing opposition against this forced foreign presence gave rise to a sectarian movement in rural areas, soon referred to as a 'Militia United in Righteousness' by its followers and called 'Boxers' in the West (Esherick, 68–69, 154–55; Harrington, 12). Simply put, the Boxers wanted to protect traditional values and throw the foreigners out, something the ruling Qing dynasty was clearly unable to do.[3]

On June 10, 1900, with the Boxers threatening the legations (diplomatic posts) in Beijing, the Western powers and Japan sent troops to protect the Legation Quarter (Xiang, 244–45).[4] Meanwhile, with the Boxer movement quickly gaining momentum, Empress Dowager Cixi finally decided to throw in the support of the Imperial army with the rebellion. On June 19, an ultimatum was sent to the Legations, ordering all diplomats and foreigners to leave Beijing and proceed to Tianjin within 24 hours (Xiang, 318). On June 21, China formally declared war on all foreign powers.

During an emergency meeting at the Spanish Legation, the diplomats from the various foreign nations decided that leaving Beijing without the support of the relief force would be tantamount to suicide (unbeknownst to the diplomats the relief force had already been defeated though). Instead, it was decided to play for time and wait for the troops (Xiang, 319–23).

German diplomat Baron von Ketteler emphatically disagreed with this decision however and decided to leave Beijing that same day. When he was killed in the streets by a Manchu soldier shortly after leaving, the other foreigners were all the more convinced that the only thing they could do was stay and defend the Legation Quarter until help arrived (Xiang, 333–34).

---

3   The Boxers were not out to unseat the Qing dynasty though, as their most common slogan was 'Fu-Qing mie-yang', 'Support the Qing, destroy the foreign' (Esherick, 68).

4   The expeditionary force, led by British Vice-Admiral Edward Seymour, totaled over 2,000, with about 1,000 British troops and another 1,000 from various other nations (Xiang, 258). They were defeated by a combined force of some 3,000 Imperial troops and 2,000 boxers (Xiang, 263–66).

When the Chinese army and the Boxers subsequently besieged the quarter, about 475 civilians and 450 soldiers from the United Kingdom, France, Germany, Italy, Austria-Hungary, Belgium, Russia, Japan, the Netherlands, Spain and the United States, together with around 3,000 Chinese Christians, defended the quarter and held out for 55 days, until an Eight-Nation alliance landed in China, defeated the Imperial Army and occupied Beijing on August 14, 1900 (Fairbank, "New History", 231).

On September 7, 1901, China was forced to sign the so-called Boxer protocol, a humiliating peace treaty. The Legation Quarter was to be enlarged, fortified and garrisoned with a permanent contingent of foreign troops, some 25 Qing forts were to be destroyed and the Imperial government had to pay an indemnity of $333 million over a period of 40 years, at an interest that would more than double that amount (Fairbank, "New History", 231–32).

During the next few years, several uprisings unsuccessfully tried to overthrow the unpopular Qing dynasty. But revolutions cannot be rushed. Like many violent eruptions, it often takes years, if not decades of antagonizing frustration without relief, before they have gathered enough strength to explode out in the open and destroy the old.

It was coming though.

In May 1911, the Imperial government decided to nationalize local railway development ventures and hand them over to foreign powers, as part of the indemnity owed. Many Chinese were livid over this illegal confiscation and popular outcry soon escalated into another full-blown uprising.

On October 10, the Tongmenghui, or 'United League', an underground resistance movement made up of several revolutionary groups, launched a revolt in the city of Wuchang (in Hubei Province, South Central China), together with mutinying soldiers. After the revolutionaries had succeeded in taking the city, uprisings also broke out in several other, mostly southern provinces, some of whom subsequently declared their independence from the Qing government.

Of course, all revolutionary enthusiasm and solemn independence declaring aside, there was also still an emperor, an Imperial government and—most important of all—an Imperial Army. Acknowledging the seriousness of the situation, the Qing government recalled Yuan Shikai, former commander of the powerful Beiyang Army, from retirement, to suppress the revolutionaries.[5]

Fighting between loyalist and revolutionary forces soon concentrated on the two cities of Hankou and Hanyang, on the north bank of the Yangtze River, opposite to Wuchang, where the uprising had started. After 41 days of hard fighting, Yuan Shikai succeeded in retaking Hankou and Hanyang. But then, in a surprise move, he opted for a ceasefire and negotiating with the revolutionaries, rather than pushing on to Wuchang and finish them.

A shrewd strategist, Yuan realized that after crushing the rebellion, the Qing government would most likely thank him for his services and send him back into retirement again, whereas the revolutionaries could help him achieve much more. After some back and forth, a political compromise was reached between Yuan Shikai and Sun Yat-sen, the leader of the Tongmenghui, whereby Yuan would help force the emperor to abdicate and establish a unified Chinese Republic, in return for the support of the southern provinces in electing him as the first President of the new republic. On January 1, 1912, representatives of the seceded provinces thus proclaimed the Republic of China.[6]

---

5   Yuan Shikai had been commander of the Beiyang army from 1901 until 1908, when he was forced into retirement following the death of Empress Dowager Cixi. He still commanded the loyalty of most of the officers in 1911.

6   Sun Yat-sen became the first provisional President of the Republic of China in January 1912, but he was succeeded by Yuan Shikai just a few months

In the run up to the first Parliamentary elections, the Tongmenghui merged with several smaller pro-revolutionary groups to form the Kuomintang, the Chinese Nationalist Party (Goldman, 58–59). After winning the 1913 elections by a landslide, the Kuomintang (KMT) quickly moved to increase the independence of Parliament and curtail the power of the President by mandating open presidential elections. Yuan, determined to protect his position, reacted by clamping down on the KMT, removing its leaders from key positions and dissolving the KMT-dominated Parliament (Dillon, 150–51). The KMT called for a 'Second Revolution', but every hint of uprising was immediately crushed by Yuan's forces.

In December 1915, Yuan, apparently not satisfied with ruling as presidential dictator, declared himself emperor. The nascent republic thus seemed on the fast-track back to becoming the Middle Kingdom again, but widespread opposition quickly surfaced, with military leaders and governors of several provinces declaring their independence.

Yuan started backpedaling and renounced his imperial aspirations three months later, but the damage was already done. Another three months later he was dead (of natural causes), leaving behind a country in disarray. Regional warlords soon rose to power, establishing the kind of feudal rule reminiscent of medieval Europe, when local lords frequently ruled as absolute kings.

To the north, in Beijing, a military regime was established, dominated by whatever general was in control of the Beiyang Army (hence its nickname, 'Beiyang government'), while Sun Yat-sen and his Kuomintang set up a rival government in the south, in Guangzhou. Aside from fighting each other, both governments were also beset by internal conflict, rife with power grabs, intrigue and shifting alliances.

---

later.

In 1923, the Kuomintang joined forces with the Chinese Communist Party (CCP), which had been established two years earlier, to form the First United Front. The Soviet Union had actively championed cooperation between the CCP and the KMT, telling the mostly reluctant CCP it was necessary to form a bloc within the much larger KMT so it could be taken over from the inside, while at the same time luring the KMT with the promise of more (financial) support (Saich, 8–10).[7]

The first few years the alliance was a success. With Russian help, the KMT and CCP successfully fought the warlords and formed a disciplined, well-trained National Revolutionary Army. But after the death of Kuomintang founder Sun Yat-sen in 1925, the alliance began to weaken. A power struggle also emerged within the KMT, between the left-leaning Wang Jingwei and the right-leaning Chiang Kai-shek.

In 1926, with internal tension already building up, Chiang launched the Northern Expedition, a military campaign aimed at finally defeating the warlords and reunify China under one government. Regional warlords had plagued China for a decade but now their number was up; the National Revolutionary Army was better motivated, better trained and better equipped than the warlord armies and picked them off one by one. Several warlords did not even let it come to a fight but instead defected and joined the Nationalists (Zarrow, 233–44).

Meanwhile, tensions between the KMT's left and right wing reached new heights after Wang Jingwei moved the seat of government from Guangzhou to Wuhan, in January 1927. Chiang responded by setting up a rival government in Nanjing a few months later (Taylor, 68).

---

7   Notably, the Soviets financed the establishment of and provided the necessary support for Whampoa Military Academy, which helped profes-sionalize the newly formed National Revolutionary Army. Soviet officers also taught at the Academy. Its first commandant was the later Kuomintang leader Chiang-Kai-shek.

Events took a surprising turn in March though, when the workers' movement in Shanghai took up arms against the Zhili warlord regime there and succeeded in taking control of the city when the local garrison commander defected (Taylor, 64–65). The Communist Party quickly set up a provisional government and organized the masses. When the Northern Expedition Army—which had been advancing on the city—entered Shanghai a few days later it found a city of armed civilian militias, a thriving communist organization and a concerned business community. It was then that Chiang Kai-shek (who arrived a few days after the army) and other right-wing leaders of the KMT decided it was time to purge the party of the communists (Zhao, 94).

On April 12, Chiang ordered the disarming of the workers' militias in Shanghai and declared the provisional government, labor unions and all other communist organizations dissolved. When some of them resisted, a bloodbath ensued (Zhao, 94; Taylor, 66–68). It would mark the start of a bitter, 22-year-long civil war between the Kuomintang and the Chinese Communist Party.

In July, the left-wing Kuomintang government in Wuhan followed suit and started purging the Communists from its ranks as well, after finding out that Stalin had instructed the Communists to recruit their own army and overthrow the Kuomintang government (Gray, 224). A couple of months later, the left and right wing of the Kuomintang reunited under leadership of Chiang Kai-shek.

The Communists were off to a bad start in the civil war. Already weakened by the purge, they nevertheless launched several uprisings in the second half of 1927, all of which failed. Among them an action organized by 33-year-old Mao Zedong, one of the founding members of the CCP, who in September led a small army of peasants against the KMT in Hunan province but was quickly defeated, forcing him to retreat into the mountains.[8] Two months later the Communists took over the city of Guangzhou in the south (less than 100 miles from Hong Kong), but the KMT crushed the uprising within 48 hours, leaving 5,000 Communists dead. The Guangzhou uprising made it painfully clear that the CCP lacked the muscle to fight the Kuomintang in open combat. The Communists therefore decided to retreat to the countryside, where they began building a loyal base of followers among the peasants.

In 1930 another civil war broke out within the ranks of the Kuomintang. This time, four warlords who had previously aligned themselves with Chiang Kai-shek revolted, because of Chiang's ongoing effort to strengthen the central government at the expense of regional—meaning *their*—power bases (Taylor, 89). Several other warlords soon joined the anti-Chiang coalition, swelling its numbers to an impressive 600,000 men. Chiang himself had 1 million troops under this command, but a significant portion of these were on garrison and could not be sent on campaign (Taylor, 89).

The so-called Central Plains War would be short-lived but intense. By November 1930, Chiang had subdued the warlords, but at the considerable cost of a total of 240,000 casualties (Taylor, 89). The war also bought the CCP valuable time and seriously weakened the defenses in Manchuria, in Northeast China, which attributed to the Japanese invasion there the following year—yet another headache for Chiang.

Having emerged as the undisputed leader of the Kuomintang after the Central Plains War, Chiang set out to destroy the CCP's Red Army and launched a series of encirclement campaigns. At first these were not very successful, but in October 1934 the KMT succeeded in surrounding the First Red Front Army in Jiangxi province, where the CCP had established the so-called Chinese Soviet Republic.

---

8   Mao had been one of only twelve delegates to attend the First National Congress of the Communist Party of China, in July 1921, in Shanghai (Uhalley, 17).

Faced with the threat of total annihilation, the First Army's commanders—Mao Zedong, Zhu De and Zhou Enlai—decided to try and break through the KMT lines and retreat. It worked, and 90,000 soldiers escaped the trap and embarked on what would come to be known as the Long March, a year-long march over a distance of 6,000 miles from Southeast to Northwest China (Snow, 36).[9] Of the 90,000 soldiers, about 7,000 would make it to the Northwestern Shaanxi province in October 1935 (Snow, 432–34).

Although the Long March came at a high cost, it provided the CCP with an isolated region where it could regroup and rebuild its numbers. It also made heroes out of the survivors in the eyes of many peasants and cemented the Red Army's reputation of being fiercely dedicated and determined. Retreat and defeat were thus turned around and beautified with a hopeful smile of achievable victory.

Together with the irresistible carrot of land reform, promising land to all those poor farmers working in the fields of rich landlords, the Long March contributed greatly to the growing popularity of the CCP in the countryside, while also solidifying the position of Mao Zedong as the undisputed leader of the Chinese Communist Party.

Meanwhile, Japan, which had invaded Manchuria (Northeast China) in 1931, continued to steadily expand its control over the region, bringing local Chinese warlords under its sphere of influence and forcing the Kuomintang into agreements that weakened it militarily in the north.[10] KMT generals increas-

---

9   Edgar Snow interviewed Mao and other Communist leaders between June-September 1936, a year after the Long March. The estimated distance Snow gives of the Long March is from Mao himself. In recent years some controversy has emerged about this estimate, after two British researchers who retraced the route arrived at a distance of 3,700 miles (Jocelyn, 288).

10   Notably through the Tanggu Truce of May 31,1933, and the He-Umezu Agreement of June 10, 1935. The Tanggue Truce forced the KMT to recognize the puppet state of Manchukuo in Northeast China and consent to a large demilitarized zone extending 100 kilometers (62 mi) south of a Japanese-controlled

ingly pressured Chiang Kai-shek to focus his military efforts on fighting Japan instead of the CCP, but Chiang wanted to defeat the Communists first, saying *"the Japanese are like a disease of the skin, but the Communists are like a disease of the heart"* (qtd. in Eastman, 33). He also believed only a united China would be able to repel the Japanese invaders.

In December 1936, realizing Chiang would rather let half of China fall to the Empire of Japan before abandoning his mission to destroy the Communists, two disgruntled KMT generals decided to kidnap Chiang Kai-shek in Xi'an (the capital of Shaanxi province, Northwest China) and force him to negotiate a truce with the Communists.[11] At first, most CCP leaders, including Mao, said they would rather execute Chiang for his communist purges than negotiate any kind of truce with him. But after Stalin urged Mao to negotiate with Chiang—seeing as the death of Chiang at this stage would benefit neither Chinese resistance to Japan nor Russian interests in the East—Mao acquiesced to talks with the KMT, which subsequently led to an uneasy truce between the two belligerents on December 24, 1936 (Taylor, 129–30).

Though conflict intensity between the KMT and the CCP was toned down during the Second Sino-Japanese War (1937–45), there was hardly any real cooperation between the two sides, either.[12] The Communists engaged the Japanese mostly in

---

Great Wall, with KMT forces having no access to the zone while Japanese patrol and reconnaissance forces would be allowed there. The He-Umezu Agreement gave Japan political and military control over the province of Hebei, surrounding the Beijing region.

11   One of these generals was Zhang Xueliang, who had been the ruling warlord of Manchuria before the Japanese invasion of 1931. After the Xi'an incident—as the kidnapping of Chiang Kai-shek to force him to negotiate with the Communists is often called—Zhang was placed under house arrest by Chiang for forty years, first in mainland China, later in Taiwan, until Chiang's death in 1975. Zhang Xueliang himself died in 2001, aged 100.

12   The First Sino-Japanese War had been fought between 1894–95 over supremacy in Korea, which had long been a Chinese client state. The war was decisively won by the Empire of Japan, establishing it as the dominant power in

guerrilla warfare while the KMT predominantly fought open battles. The Communists also continued to build popular support in rural areas, while skirmishes between the KMT and CCP continued in regions isolated from the war, known as "Free China".

In January 1941, what little cooperation that had been left between the two sides ended, after KMT forces surrounded and subsequently attacked the Communist New Fourth Army (N4A), which suffered an estimated 9,000 casualties as a result (Fairbank, "Republican China", 666–69). According to the KMT, the New Fourth Army Incident was caused by the N4A's refusal to move out of southern Anhwei and Jiangsu by December 31, as had been ordered by Chiang Kai-shek, but an angry CCP called it a second 'anti-Communist upsurge' (Fairbank, "Republican China", 666–69). Whatever the case, after the New Fourth Army Incident the truce between the CPC and the KMT existed in name only.

After the unconditional surrender of Japan on August 14, 1945, a renewed effort was made by the Kuomintang and the Communists to come to a peaceful solution. Subsequent talks attended by Chiang Kai-shek, Mao Zedong and U.S. Ambassador to China Patrick J. Hurley, led to the Double Tenth Agreement of October 10 (10/10), in which both sides agreed on basic principles for peaceful reconstruction. But for all the talk, heavy fighting between both sides had continued during almost the entire time of the peace conference (Fairbank, "Republican China", 726).

The United States, for its part, preferred a peaceful solution, but at the same time it was also determined to prevent a communist takeover in China, just as much as the Soviet Union was determined to make it happen. To help the Kuomintang, the U.S. provided it with hundreds of millions of dollars in loans, military equipment and training (Blum, 23). It even transported some 500,000 KMT troops over sea and air to

Asia for the first time, after China had dominated the region for millennia.

Central and Northern China, after the Russians refused to let the KMT pass through Soviet-occupied Manchuria (Fairbank, "Republican China", 726). As early as September 30, with the peace talks still going on in Chongqing, the U.S. sent 53,000 troops to Northern China in support of the Chinese Nationalists.

In the summer of 1946, Chiang Kai-shek launched a large-scale invasion of communist territory in Eastern and Northern China. Mao ordered the People's Liberation Army (PLA, the new name for the Eighth Route Army and New Fourth Army) to avoid open battle and instead engage in mobile warfare (Zedong, "War of Self-Defense", 3). Cities and other places were not to be defended at all costs, as that would only play into the hands of the KMT, whose strength lay in conventional warfare. Instead, Mao wanted to wear down the invasion force, attacking it where it was weak while avoiding battle in all other circumstances. At the same time, he urged party members to continue to win over the peasants by promising them land reform (Zedong, "War of Self-Defense", 4). The strategy proved successful, with the KMT suffering heavy casualties without making serious gains.

In the summer of 1947 the CCP counter-attacked in Northeast China. Over the course of a year, the Communists gradually pushed back the KMT, capturing cities and towns in the north while also inflicting heavy casualties on Chiang's forces (Fairbank, "Republican China", 765–72).[13] The CCP suffered heavy casualties as well, but because of their widespread support in the countryside they had less trouble replenishing their ranks. The balance of power began to shift in favor of the People's Liberation Army.

In September 1948, the PLA launched the first of three decisive counter-offensives. During the Liaoshen Campaign, the

---

13   Mao calculated that at the end of the summer of 1947 Chiang Kai-shek had lost 780,000 men, while CCP losses were about 300,000 (Fairbank, "Republican China", 770).

PLA concentrated on Northeast China (a.k.a. Manchuria), particularly the areas around the cities of Shenyang, Changchun and Jingzhou, where the KMT troops were stationed. In six weeks time, the Communists captured all three cities—and with it the whole of Manchuria—inflicting 472,000 casualties on the Nationalist forces (including defections and prisoners of war) at a cost of 65,000 PLA casualties (Lew, "Historical", 121–22).

According to contemporary U.S. military analysts, causes of the Nationalist defeat in Manchuria lay mainly in the over-extension of its forces and the ineptitude of its leadership (Fairbank, "Republican China", 766). Also, what the Communists lacked in training and equipment, they more than made up for in zeal, a sense of common purpose and a knack for strategic and tactical warfare.

Though not fatal right away, the Liaoshen Campaign had struck a wound from which the KMT would not recover. Four days after its conclusion, on November 6, the Communists launched a second counter-offensive, the Huaihai Campaign. This time fighting concentrated at the Huai River basin, between the Yellow River and the Yangtze River, with the destruction of the KMT forces there the main objective (Lew, "Historical", 88–89). By the end of November the KMT's 7th Army had been destroyed, and two weeks of hard fighting later the 12th and 16th Army had also been wiped out (Lew, "Analysis", 120).

The last phase of the Huaihai Campaign started on January 6, 1949, with the Communist forces attacking the remaining Nationalist troops north of the Huai River, the 13th, 6th and 8th Army. By January 10, the 13th Army was no more, while the severely weakened 6th and 8th Army had retreated south of the Huai River. In just two months, the KMT had lost over half a million soldiers when including the troops that surrendered (Lew, "Analysis", 122–23). It was an astounding success for the Communists, and before the month was out they dealt a third and final blow to the Kuomintang with the capture of the cities of Tianjin and Beijing and the integration into the PLA of the half a million strong KMT army that had been charged with defending the two cities (Lew "Historical", 185–186).[14]

In the months that followed the remnants of the Kuomintang Army kept retreating southward, until finally fleeing to the island of Taiwan in December 1949, two months after Mao had proclaimed the People's Republic of China (PRC) in Beijing, on October 1.

Following the outbreak of the Korean War, in June 1950, President Truman sent the U.S. Seventh Fleet to the Taiwan Strait, to prevent the Communists from invading and over-running Taiwan, thus effectively placing the island under American protection.[15-16] Ongoing tension between Taiwan and mainland China led to several small-scale military engagements in the 1950s, but in later years tensions would subside.

---

14 The third and last of the three major campaigns was called Pingjin, a reference to Beiping—the old name for Beijing—and Tianjin.

15 North Korea had been occupied by the Soviet Union north of the 38th parallel since August 1945, as agreed with the U.S, which had subsequently occupied South Korea. On June 25, 1950, North Korean forces, aided by the U.S.S.R and China, invaded the South.

16 Truman's stated reason for sending in the 7th Fleet: "*The attack upon Korea makes it plain beyond all doubt that communism has passed beyond the use of subversion to conquer independent nations and will now use armed invasion and war. It has defied the orders of the Security Council of the United Nations issued to preserve international peace and security. In these circumstances the occupation of Formosa* [an earlier name for Taiwan] *by Communist forces would be a direct threat to the security of the Pacific area and to United States forces performing their lawful and necessary functions in that area. Accordingly, I have ordered the 7th Fleet to prevent any attack on Formosa. As a corollary of this action, I am calling upon the Chinese Government on Formosa to cease all air and sea operations against the mainland. The 7th Fleet will see that this is done. The determination of the future status of Formosa must await the restoration of security in the Pacific, a peace settlement with Japan, or consideration by the United Nations.*" (Truman, "Statement").

With the proclamation of the People's Republic of China, the decades-long power struggle between the Communists and Nationalists had at last come to a clear end. After centuries of weak imperial government and foreign imperialism, followed by the chaos of the Warlord Era and the dictatorship of Chiang Kai-shek, it was now time for the Communists to take a crack at it, with Mao Zedong —the undisputed hero of the civil war—as the undisputed political leader. Unfortunately for the Chinese, Chairman Mao would prove to be a lot less successful than Commander Mao.[17]

Through the Great Leap Forward (1958–61) and the Cultural Revolution (1966–76), Mao would try to bring about a real communist state, free of private ownership and all forms of capitalism. Free also of all traditional and cultural elements of Chinese society, a formidable challenge in and of itself in a country whose civilization is among the oldest in the world. Both programs would prove miserable failures. The Great Leap led to the Great Chinese Famine, causing tens of millions of Chinese to die of starvation, while the Cultural Revolution led to widespread persecution, political paralysis and a failing economy.

In 1976, two years after Mao's death, much needed economic reforms were at long last pushed through, reintroducing capitalist principles and turning the Chinese economy into one of the world's fastest growing. Who knows what will happen once China reforms its political system as well and starts allowing people to say, print and paint whatever they want, whenever they want.

17   See chapter 20—The Cultural Revolution.

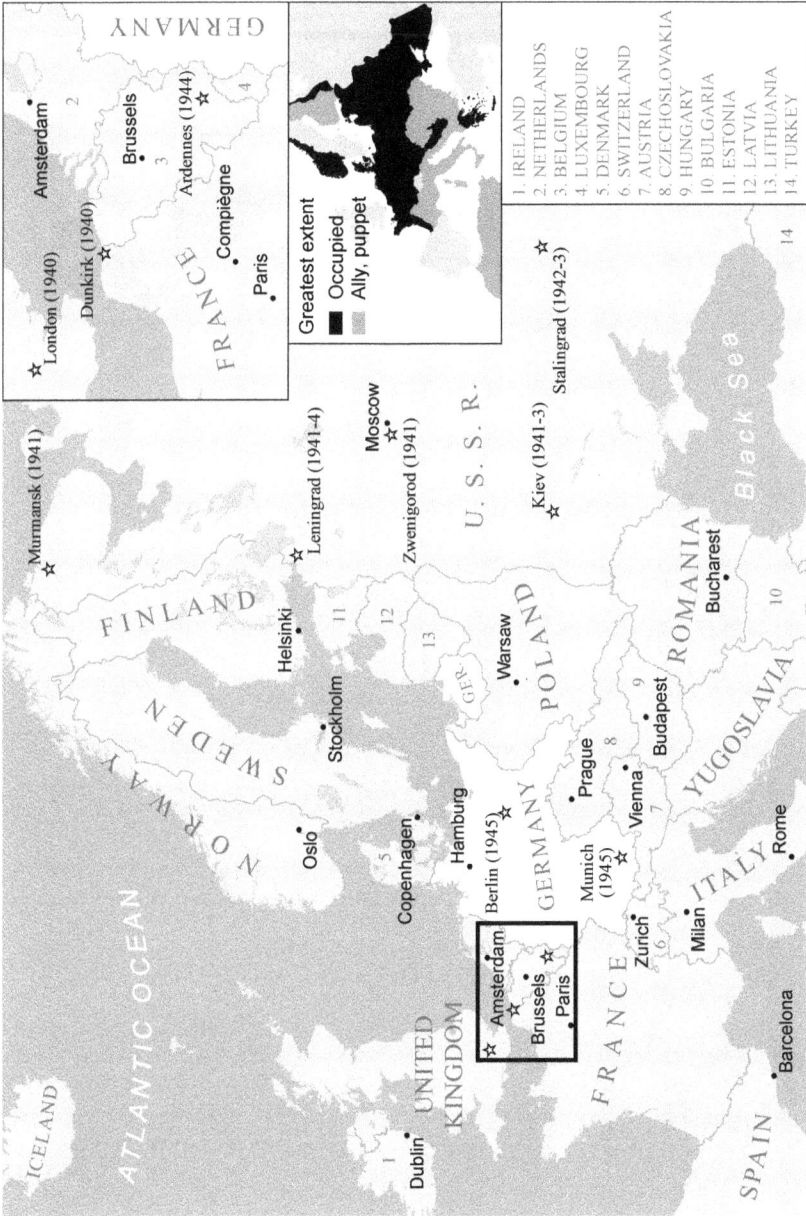

Map 8: The European Theater of the Second World War, 1939-45

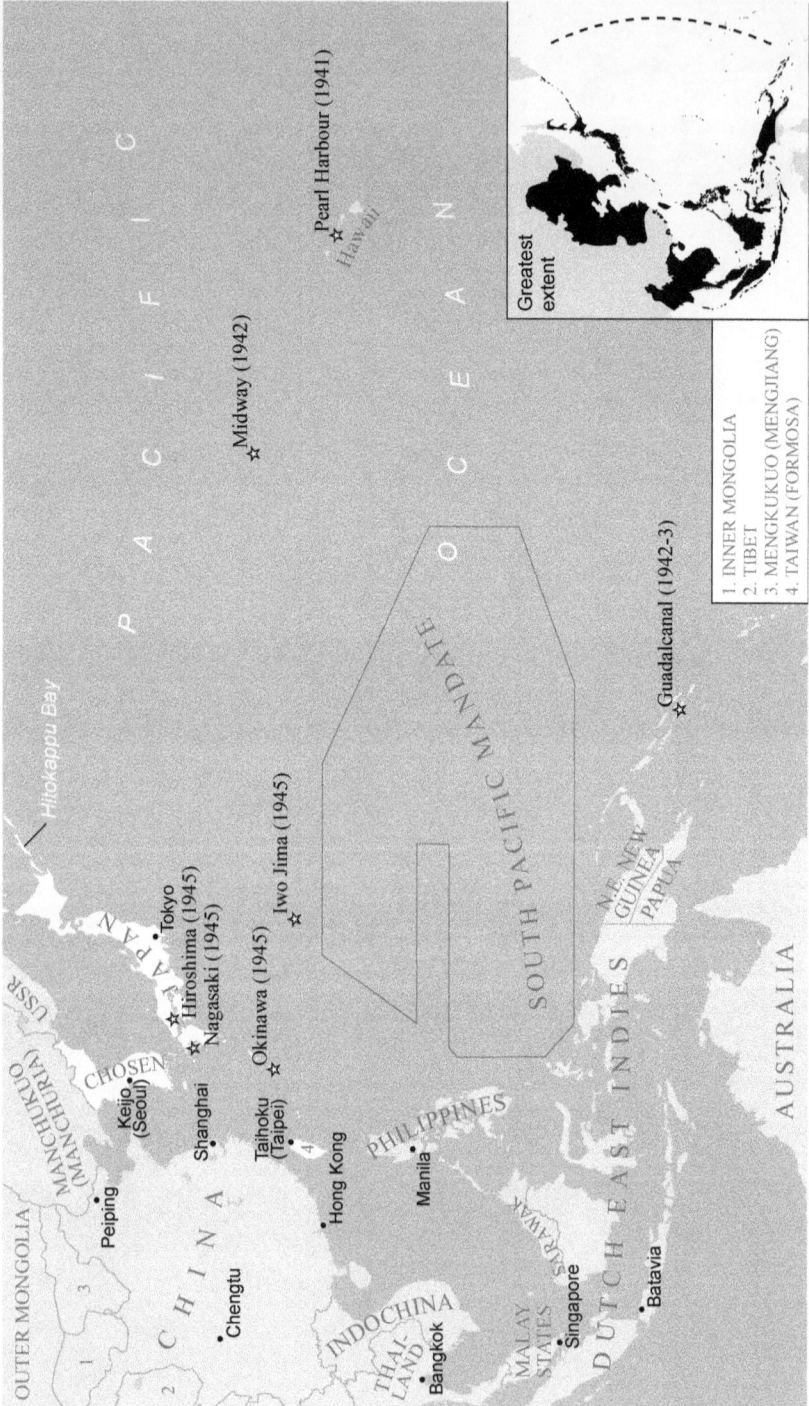

Map 9: The Pacific Theater of the Second World War, 1941-45

13

WW 2.0

"This war, like the next war, is a war to end war."[1]

David Lloyd George, British Prime Minister, 1916

"After the 'war to end war', they seem to have been pretty successful in Paris at making a 'peace to end peace.'"[2]

Brig. general Archibald Wavell,
on the results of the Paris Peace Conference, 1919

O N MAY 1, 1945, DEEP INSIDE THE *Führerbunker* underneath the Reichstag, Rochus Misch, Hitler's telephone operator and personal bodyguard, went to Joseph Goebbels and asked him if there was anything left for him to do (Schnoor, "last survivor"). Their boss had committed suicide the day before, the same day the Reichstag had been captured by the Russians. But even though the end of the Third Reich seemed a matter of hours, Misch did not just want to pick up and leave, as most of the others had done. He wanted to end his service to the "*Führer, people and fatherland*" in the proper manner (qtd. in Schnoor, "last survivor"). So he went to the man whom Hitler had appointed the new Reich Chancellor in his last will and asked for instructions.

The former German Minister of Propaganda answered "*We have understood how to live, we will also understand how to die.*" (qtd. in Schnoor, "last survivor"). Later that day, Dr. Goebbels put on his hat, coat and gloves, took his wife's arm

---

1   Qtd. in Billington, 365.

2   Qtd. in Fromkin, "Peace", frontispiece quote.

and went upstairs to the garden. There, he shot his wife, and then himself. Shortly before, Magda Goebbels had already ended the lives of their six children by crushing an ampoule of cyanide in each of their mouths (Fox, "Rochus Misch").

Misch, however, decided not to shoot himself but escape instead. He was one of the last to leave the *Führerbunker*— alive at least. As a member of the elite SS unit *Leibstandarte SS Adolf Hitler*, Misch had also been there at the beginning of the war, six years earlier, in September 1939, when Germany had invaded Poland.[3] In fact, his actions on the Polish front and the serious wound to the chest he sustained there had been one of the reasons for his promotion to the Führer's personal protection unit, the *Führerbegleitkommando* (Misch, 4).

The German invasion of Poland marked the beginning of the Second World War, as it prompted England, France and the Commonwealth nations of Canada, Australia, New-Zealand and South Africa to declare war on Germany. That declaration of war was a direct consequence of a British pledge, six months earlier, to lend Poland *"all support in their power"* in the event its independence was threatened.[4] The pledge, in turn, was a direct consequence of the German invasion of Czechoslovakia in March 1939, despite previous guarantees of German Reich Chancellor Adolf Hitler not to do so.

The reason Hitler had decided to attack Poland anyway was not because he wanted to go to war with England and France, but because he thought he wouldn't have to. And not without reason. After all, they hadn't undertaken any action after his earlier transgressions either, having opted for the political strategy of appeasement instead, i.e., trying to prevent war by giving in to most of his demands.

---

3   Misch had enlisted voluntarily with the *SS-Verfügungstruppe*, a predecessor of the *Waffen-SS*, in 1937. He was called to the elite SS unit *Leibstandarte-SS Adolf Hitler* that same year (Misch, 4,19–20).

4   Said by British Prime Minister Neville Chamberlain in a statement in the House of Commons, on March 31, 1939 (Chamberlain, "Statement").

Since coming to power in 1933, Hitler had started a German rearmament campaign and remilitarized the Rhineland, both in violation of the Treaty of Versailles of 1919.[5] He had also annexed Austria in March 1938 (euphemistically dubbed the '*Anschluss*') and Czechoslovakia in March 1939, the latter in clear violation of the Munich Agreement.

The Munich Agreement of September 1938 had already been a major concession from England and France to Germany, allowing it to annex a large part of Czechoslovakia known as Sudetenland, simply because it was mainly inhabited by German-speaking people who wanted to be part of Germany.

Czechoslovakia was one of the new nations that had been created after World War I from parts of the former empires of Germany, Austria-Hungary and Russia. When the Third Reich annexed German-speaking Austria in March 1938 and then hungrily eyed German-speaking Sudetenland, the British and French convinced themselves that Hitler's demand wasn't all that unreasonable.[6-7] So, at a hastily organized conference in Munich, Germany, late September that same year, England and France, eager—perhaps too eager—to keep the peace, agreed to German occupation of Sudetenland, as long as the rest of Czechoslovakia would be left alone (incidentally, Czechoslovakia itself had not even been invited to the conference).

Hitler happily agreed and a relieved British Prime Minister Neville Chamberlain flew back to London, where he showed

---

5   Articles 42, 43 and 44 of Section III of the Versailles Treaty forbade Germany to maintain and assemble armed forces or construct any fortifications, a violation of which was said to "*disturb the peace of the world*", according to article 44 ("Versailles Treaty"). For clauses on German armed forces, see section V of the treaty, Military, Naval and Air Clauses, articles 159–213.

6   Other European nations (re)established after WW I were Austria, Hungary, Yugoslavia, Poland, Finland, Estonia, Latvia and Lithuania.

7   The term 'Third Reich' meant to designate Nazi Germany as the third German Empire, after the Holy Roman Empire and the German Empire of 1870–1918.

the piece of paper with Hitler's signature on it and declared it meant *"peace for our time"*.[8] Six months later Hitler invaded the rest of Czechoslovakia.

Of course it was more than a little astonishing that Germany was able to basically dictate terms to Britain and France just twenty years after losing a devastating war that had left it at the mercy of those same countries, one of which had shown particularly little leniency in imposing and enforcing harsh sanctions to ensure its neighbor to the East would never again pose a threat.[9]

And they hadn't been exactly easy years either. The Versailles Treaty of 1919 had stripped Germany of a large part of its territory, forced it to acknowledge that it alone had been guilty of the war (*Alleinschuld*) and charged it with paying hefty reparations to the victors. When it could no longer keep up those payments a few years later, French and Belgian soldiers had occupied the Ruhr, the heart of Germany's industrial area, causing its economy to collapse.[10]

In 1929, just when the German economy was getting back on its feet again thanks in part to American loans, stock markets crashed and the Great Depression started, causing U.S. investors to pull out and the economy to collapse again. Under those trying circumstances it was hardly surprising that in 1933, the fragile democracy of the newly formed German Republic (a.k.a. Weimar Republic) gave way to the totalitarian rule of Adolf Hitler and his National-Socialist Party.

---

8   In a statement made in front of #10 Downing Street, London, on September 30, 1938 (Chamberlain, "Peace").

9   See chapter 9—The Great War.

10   Germany could pay off the reparations in cash or in kind, for instance with deliveries of coal, timber and other commodities. From the start, it frequently missed payments and goods deliveries. Some historians have argued that Germany could have paid more easily and in fact actively sabotaged an economically feasible repayment plan. (Boemeke, 402–04). In *"The Treaty of Versailles: A reassessment after 75 Years"*, Boemeke et al. discuss several historians who have been critical of Germany's inability to pay the WWI reparations.

Six years and a string of appeasement offerings later, Hitler gambled that he could annex Poland just as he had annexed Austria and Czechoslovakia, without any meaningful counter-action from the English or the French.

Still, mindful of the mistakes Germany had made in the Great War— a war he had fought in himself as a young corporal—Hitler took out an insurance policy against a possible two-front war, signing a secret non-aggression pact with the Soviet Union just days before the attack on Poland. Although the fascists and communists were sworn enemies, Hitler correctly assumed that fellow dictator Joseph Stalin would be willing to strike a deal on Poland and the "*territorial and political rearrangement*" of other Eastern European countries (i.e., divvy them up between the two of them), especially with Japan biting at Russia's heels in the Far East and the Russian Army still reeling from the loss of many of its best officers during the Great Purge of 1936–39.[11-12]

The British and French declaration of war—while morally supportive—did nothing to save Poland from being overrun by two mighty armies in September 1939. First, German tanks and storm troopers quickly occupied the 'German half' of Poland, after which the Russians invaded the beleaguered Eastern European nation from the other side on September 17, one day after a ceasefire with Japan had gone into effect, following the battle of Khalkin Gol.[13]

---

11   The quote is from Article 1 and 2 from the secret additional protocol— not published at the time—of the Molotov-Ribbentrop Pact, signed on August 23, 1939, in Moscow (Molotov 1939). The pact was named after Soviet Foreign Minister Vyacheslav Molotov and German Foreign Minister Joachim von Ribbentrop.

12   According to declassified Soviet archives, 681,692 people were shot for "*anti-Soviet activities*" between 1937–38 alone (Pipes, 66–67). Of the Red Army's five marshals, three were killed, of its fifteen generals, thirteen did not survive the 'Great Terror' and of the nine navy admirals only one survived.

13   Fought near the Eastern border of Mongolia and Japanese-occupied Manchuria, the battle of Khalkin Gol was a decisive Russian and Mongolian victory that would lead Japan to concentrate its efforts of world conquest

After Poland had been devoured, nothing much happened in Europe for six months, leading some to call this second world war a 'phoney war' (the Germans preferred the term *sitzkrieg*, as opposed to the *blitzkrieg* conquest of Poland).[14] But those who had seen it all before knew the only thing phony was the ominous calm hanging over Europe.

In the spring of 1940, the German war machine sprang into action again, invading Denmark and Norway in April, followed by a simultaneous attack on France, the Netherlands, Belgium and Luxembourg on May 10. That same day Neville Chamberlain resigned as British Prime Minister and was succeeded by Winston Churchill, an old war-horse who had fighting experience, commanding experience and decades of political and government experience.

Meanwhile, the French felt they were well-prepared for another defensive war against the Germans. After World War I they had constructed a massive, seemingly impenetrable line of defense in Northern France, the so-called Maginot Line. Stretching from Switzerland to Luxembourg, it was made up of 44 large works (*Gross ouvrages*), 58 small works (*Petits ouvrages*), 81 troop shelters —each capable of housing 250 soldiers—360 artillery, machine gun and anti-tank gun emplacements (casemates), 17 observation posts, numerous other supporting structures and extended anti-tank defenses (Allcorn, 12). But, as the saying goes, generals always prepare

---

southward, towards China and the European colonies in Southeast Asia.

14   Several German generals would later declare at the Nuremberg Trials that had the French and the British attacked in the West during the German invasion of Poland, the German Army would have been powerless to stop their numerically vastly superior forces. General Alfred Jodl, for instance, said during his testimony at the Nuremberg Trials: *"we were never, either in 1938 or 1939, actually in a position to withstand a concentrated attack by these states [France, Poland and Czechoslovakia] together. And if we did not collapse already in the year 1939 that was due only to the fact that during the Polish campaign, the approximately 110 French and British divisions in the West were held completely inactive against the 23 German divisions."* (qtd. in "Trial of the Major War Criminals", Vol. 15, 350).

for the last war, something especially true for the French generals of the interwar period. Because while the French were busy pouring concrete into Northern France to prepare for another trench war, the Germans were busy pouring steel into the Ruhr to produce tanks and airplanes, preparing for a new form of highly mobile warfare that would soon earn the well-deserved moniker *blitzkrieg.*

No doubt the Maginot Line would have done a wonderful job in World War I, but sadly for the French, the Germans did not even engage them there this time around. German tanks first raced through the Ardennes forest in Southeast Belgium to cut off the Allied forces that had advanced into Belgium, subsequently pushing them towards the coast.[15] Soon, the British Expeditionary Force, the remains of the Belgian forces and three French armies (1st, 7th and 9th) were surrounded by the Germans in an area along the Northern coast of France.

To save them, the British sent every ship capable of staying afloat to the French harbor of Dunkirk. Destroyers, trawlers, yachts, personnel ships, naval motor boats, tugboats, minesweepers, almost 700 ships in total. The French, Dutch and Belgians provided an additional 168 ships, for a grand total hodgepodge collection of 861 ships (Churchill, "Their Finest Hour", 90). In nine days some 338,000 troops were thus evacuated to England, 100,000 of whom French. The successful evacuation almost felt like a victory to the British, but Churchill reminded the country that *"Wars are not won by evacuations."*[16]

---

15   This was *Fall Gelb* (Plan Yellow), a.k.a the Manstein Plan, after General Erich von Manstein, who had conceived it and convinced Hitler of adopting it during a personal meeting (May, 236–39).

16   The quote is from the legendary *"We Shall Fight on the Beaches"* speech, delivered by Winston Churchill before the House of Commons on June 4, 1940. In the same speech, Churchill voiced his aim of victory whatever the cost, speaking the famous words: *"We shall go on to the end, we shall fight in France, we shall fight on the seas and oceans, we shall fight with growing confidence and growing strength in the air, we shall defend our Island, whatever the cost may be,*

Meanwhile, the German forces pushed deep into France, outflanking the Maginot Line and arriving in an undefended Paris on June 14.[17] With the capital lost, the French forces at the Maginot Line isolated and the Luftwaffe reigning supreme over the French skies, Marshal Philippe Pétain—who had just succeeded Paul Reynaud as Prime Minister—asked Germany for terms.

France signed the armistice on June 22. Hitler was thrilled with the victory, which in his eyes wiped out the humiliating defeat of 1918. Eager to emphasize this, and ever mindful of the power of historic symbolism, the Führer had therefore not only arranged for the French surrender to be signed in the same railway car Germany had signed the armistice in on November 11, 1918, but even had it placed at the exact same spot in the forest of Compiègne where that signing had taken place; the railway carriage was removed from the museum especially for the occasion (LIFE, "Defeat").[18]

Two weeks later the Battle of Britain began. Knowing that an invasion of the island could not be successful without commanding the skies over the channel, Hitler had charged Hermann Göring, the commander of the Luftwaffe, with annihilating the British Royal Air force (RAF) first.

For months, the two air forces were locked in an all-out, deadly struggle for air superiority. Daily waves of Messerschmitt Bf 109s crossed the channel to meet and engage the RAF's Hawker Hurricanes and Supermarine Spitfires protecting the English coast. Göring also launched a bomber campaign to destroy British airfields, aircraft

---

we shall fight on the beaches, we shall fight on the landing grounds, we shall fight in the fields and in the streets, we shall fight in the hills; we shall never surrender (..)."

17   Paris had been declared an 'open city' on June 10 by General Maxime Weygand, meaning it would not be defended (Risser, 92).

18   The railroad car was later taken to Berlin and destroyed by the Germans in 1945 (Sciolino, "North of Paris").

factories and radar stations. As the campaign intensified, the Luftwaffe attacks went increasingly further inland, at one point reaching the London perimeter airfields.

But the achilles heel of the RAF was not its lack of aircraft or airstrips, it was its lack of pilots (Richards, 190–93). In his seminal work on the history of the RAF, British historian Denis Richards wrote that the number of pilots was "*distressingly less at the beginning of September* [1940] *than at the beginning of August*", a fact that was only aggravated by the fact that the new pilots, though being "*of course, magnificent material*", did not yet have the technical competence of those they replaced (Richards, 192).

The RAF nevertheless held on, if only by the skin of its teeth. In the end, a total of 2,936 RAF pilots—596 of them foreigners from Poland, New Zealand, Canada, Czechoslovakia and Australia, among other countries—successfully held the mighty Luftwaffe at bay ("Roll of Honour"). On August 20, two days after what would become known as The Hardest Day—when the Luftwaffe had thrown everything but the kitchen sink at the RAF and was still beaten back—Churchill thanked the pilots by saying that "*Never in the field of human conflict was so much owed by so many to so few.*" (Churchill, "The Few").

Saving Britain from Nazi occupation was all the more important because it allowed Britain to build up its military strength and serve as the base from where the Western Allies could launch their main assault on Nazi-occupied Europe, later in the war. For this reason, the Battle of Britain could be considered an early turning point of the war.

Late October 1940, around the same time the Battle of Britain ended, Germany's ally Italy invaded Greece.[19] Italian dictator Benito Mussolini had grand dreams of establishing a New

---

19 Germany and its allies are collectively known as the Axis powers. Germany's main allies were Italy and Japan, but Hungary, Romania and Bulgaria were also part of the Axis alliance.

Roman Empire and conquering Greece seemed like a solid step in that direction. The ancient Romans had done it too after all, in 146 BCE.[20] Of course the Roman legions of Lucius Mummius had not needed any help from the Germans, contrary to Mussolini's forces, who were soon stopped and then pushed back by the Greeks in a counter-offensive between late 1940 early 1941. After the 'New Roman Empire' had fought itself to a stalemate, Hitler reluctantly came to Il Duce's aid, invading Greece on April 6, 1941, and forcing its surrender two and a half weeks later. Italy would pose no further threat to anyone in the war—if it ever had.[21]

With most of Western Europe under his boot, Hitler now looked to the East. On June 22, 1941, Germany invaded the Soviet Union with almost 4 million soldiers, 3,350 tanks, 2,770 aircraft and 7,200 artillery pieces, along a front of 1,080 miles/1,800 km (Glantz, ch.1).[22] The Red Army had about 4.5 million troops in Western Russia, about 3 million of them

---

20   146 BCE had been a particularly good year for the Roman Republic, as it achieved total and definitive victory over both the Carthaginian Empire and the Achaean League, making it the sole superpower of the Mediterranean. The cities of Carthage (located in present-day Tunisia) and Corinth (in present-day southern Greece) were both utterly destroyed, its male citizens put to the sword, its women and children sold into slavery.

21   Italy had in fact conquered Abyssinia (present-day Ethiopia) in 1936, but even though most Abyssinian soldiers had been ill-trained and equipped with antiquated rifles or less—think spears and bow and arrow—and the Abyssinian air force counted only a handful of planes and even fewer pilots, it had still taken Mussolini eight months to subdue the proud nation.

22   Russian sources cited by David Glantz in chapter 1, note 3 of *Operation Barbarossa: Hitler's Invasion of Russia 1941*, give somewhat higher estimates of soldiers, tanks and combat aircraft. Oscar Pinkus gives a figure of 3.4 million German men in his work *The War Aims and Strategies of Adolf Hitler*, but since there were also about 30 divisions of Finnish and Romanian troops involved in Barbarossa, an estimate of a grand total of almost 4 million (Axis) soldiers seems fair enough (Pinkus, 188). Pinkus also mentions the German Army had some 600,000 motor vehicles and 650,000 horses at its disposal for artillery and supplies.

being close enough to be deployed on the front at the beginning of the invasion (Pinkus, 188).

Operation Barbarossa, the German codename for the invasion, was the largest invasion in history and the precursor to some of the deadliest, most brutal battles ever fought, not least because both sides were commanded by ruthless dictators who had no regard whatsoever for human lives and would stop at nothing to achieve total victory.

It was also more than 'just' an invasion aimed at conquering and occupying new territory. For Hitler and the Nazi party, the drive East was part of a perceived destiny that saw Germany expand into Central and Eastern Europe, deporting and/or enslaving and/or killing the Slavic peoples living there, so as to create more *lebensraum* ('living space') for the German people. *Generalplan Ost*, the secret Nazi plan outlining German colonization of Eastern Europe, thus categorized 31 million out of the 45 million people living in occupied Poland, Lithuania, Latvia, Estonia, Russia, Belarus and Ukraine as 'racially undesirable' (Schmuhl, 348–49).

Operation Barbarossa caught the Soviet Union completely by surprise. All three prongs of the attack—Army Group North (AGN), Army Group Center (AGC) and Army Group South (AGS)—achieved significant advances during the early stages of the campaign. Army Group Center, for example, advanced 360 miles (600 km) in the first eighteen days of combat, inflicting more than 400,000 casualties on the Red Army, including 341,000 dead (Glantz, ch.2). The Russians also lost almost 5,000 tanks, 9,400 guns and mortars and more than 1,700 combat aircraft.

But however total the initial shock and awe of this new, audacious German blitzkrieg was, the Red Army—though seriously bleeding from several wounds—was not yet defeated, and over the course of the next month, the German advance was repeatedly bogged down by fierce Russian resistance. It became clear to the German generals they had underestimated the strength of the Soviet forces. The length-ening supply lines were also starting to become a problem, forcing the Army Groups to slow down as they waited to be resupplied.

By the end of August, only AGC had achieved its objec-tives, coming within 200 miles of the Kremlin and taking 800,000 prisoners in the process (Pinkus, 203). But Army Group North had so far failed to take Leningrad and link up with the Finns to the North, who in turn had yet to succeed in taking their own main objective, the port city of Murmansk. Army Group South, meanwhile, had met heavy resistance around Kiev and had not yet succeeded in taking the city, let alone advance further into southern Russia, to take control of the oil fields in the Caucasus.

In light of the situation, the generals argued that all three Army Groups should be redeployed in a single, spearheaded attack on Moscow (Pinkus, 205). Not only was the bulk of the Russian Army concentrated around the city—making an enveloping maneuver and a total, decisive victory in one battle possible— it was also a major center of arms produc-tion and an important transportation hub. And of course capturing the capital would also deal a huge blow to Russian morale, while simultaneously boosting the German one. Hitler decided against it though, because he did not want to abandon the goal of annihilating Leningrad (present-day Saint Petersburg) and linking up with the Finnish forces to the North.

On August 21, the Führer issued a directive for a dual offensive on the wings, to take Leningrad in the North and Kiev in the South (Pinkus, 224). While these operations were still underway, preparations for an offensive in the center— code named Typhoon—also began, requiring additional Infantry and Panzer divisions from both Army Group North and Army Group South, to participate in a drive for Moscow, starting on October 2 (Pinkus, 227–28).

Two weeks later, the 4th Panzer Army of General Erich Hoepner breached the Mozhaisk defense line, coming within 50 miles northeast of Moscow (Pinkus, 230). Soviet defeat seemed imminent and a matter of a few weeks at most. But then the weather joined in on the side of Mother Russia, raining (or rather, snowing) down on the infantry and turning the unpaved roads into squishy mud.

The advance was slowed down to a crawl and keeping the—already stretched—supply lines intact became next to impossible. The German High Command had no choice but to order a halt to the entire operation, so the Army Groups could reorganize and supply lines could catch up. Of course the Russians made good use of this very welcome pause, transporting troops from the Far East as fast as they could, taking the calculated (and correct) risk that the Japanese would not attack them again in the Manchurian border area (Pinkus, 234–35).[23]

Mid-November, with the roads hardened again at the onset of winter, the Germans renewed their advance, but soon after the harsh Russian winter arrived in full force, freezing tanks in the mud and soldiers in their summer uniforms. On November 21, General Heinz Guderian, commander of the Second Panzer Army, wrote in his diary: "*The icy cold, the lack of shelter, the shortage of clothing, the heavy losses of men and equipment, the wretched state of our fuel supplies, all this makes the duties of a Commander a misery and the longer it goes on the more I am crushed by the enormous responsibility which I have to bear (..)*" (Guderian, 251).

Late November, Hoepner's 4th Panzer Army reached Zwenigorod, about 20 miles northeast from Moscow. It was the closest the Germans would come to the Soviet capital (Pinkus, 238).

---

23   Pinkus mentions the transfer of 29 infantry divisions and 9 armored brigades from the Far East to the Russian Western front, all equipped for winter warfare, unlike the German troops.

Tantalizingly close as it was, the 4th Panzer could in all honestly no longer be called a fighting force. As Hoepner wrote in a report on December 3: "*Physical and spiritual over-exertion no longer endurable. In the view of the commanding generals troops no longer have any fighting capacity. The High Command is to decide about a withdrawal.*" (qtd. in Pinkus, 238).[24]

On December 5 the Russians launched a counter-offensive, driving the exhausted, half-frozen German forces back some 100–200 miles (160–320 km) over a broad front (Roberts, "Stalin's Wars", 112). Unlike Napoleon Bonaparte's *Grande Armée* of 1812 though, Hitler's Wehrmacht and Waffen-SS would be back for another round in Russia, testing the resolve of the Red Army beyond all reason and rationality.

But before that second, decisive battle on the European Eastern Front, the main theater of the Second World War would first shift to the Pacific, where, on December 7, 1941, just two days after the Russians had started their counter-offensive against the Germans, the Empire of Japan launched a surprise attack on the U.S. naval base Pearl Harbor at Oahu island, Hawaii.

The attack on Pearl Harbor—home to the U.S. Pacific Fleet—was a logical decision for Japan, after negotiations with the Americans about imposed trade sanctions had faltered.

In July 1941, the United States, Great Britain and the Netherlands—whose Dutch East Indies colony (present-day Indonesia) was rich in oil—had imposed an oil embargo on Japan, in an effort to stop Japanese involvement in China and

---

24   A few days later Hoepner ordered the retreat of his forces, going against Hitler's orders. A month after that he was relieved of his command. In 1944 Hoepner participated in the failed 20 July plot to assassinate Hitler. He was arrested, sentenced to death and hanged on August 8 of that same year.

its further expansion into Southeast Asia.[25]-[26] The U.S. and Japan had subsequently opened negotiations in an effort to find a way out of the rapidly deteriorating relationship, but no progress was made.

On November 20 Japan made its final offer, to withdraw its troops from southern French Indochina to northern French Indochina (to Tonkin, present-day North Vietnam), thus removing the immediate threat of an invasion of the Dutch East Indies, in exchange for U.S. cooperation with *"securing the acquisition of those goods and commodities which the two countries need in Netherlands East Indies"* (the Dutch much have loved that part), supply Japan with all the oil it required and refrain from interfering in China (qtd. in United States Government, "Peace and War", 801–02). In other words, the Empire of the Rising Sun was willing to make do with China as its sole area of expansion, as long as the oil would flow again.

On November 26, the Americans rejected this offer in the best of fashions: by way of a counterproposal that was the complete opposite of the Japanese proposal. The U.S. proposed Japan withdraw from both China and Indochina and refrain from supporting any other Chinese government than the National Government of the Republic of China (i.e., the government of Chiang Kai-shek), in exchange for the mutual unfreezing of funds and the opening of trade negotiations (United States Government, "Peace and War", 810–12).

---

25 On July 26, 1941, President Roosevelt froze all Japanese assets in the United States by Executive Order, bringing *"all financial and import and export trade transactions in which Japanese interests are involved under the control of the Government (..)."* (qtd. in United States Government, "Peace and War", 704).

26 For several years, the U.S. had continued its oil exports to an increasingly aggressive Japan, to prevent it from attacking the Dutch East Indies for its oil supplies, which would in turn have forced the British to come to their aid, creating a war in the Pacific that would be squarely against U.S. interests. That equation changed when Japan invaded French Indochina, in September 1940, in an effort to cut off exports from there to China, with which it was already at war.

A day earlier, Vice-Admiral Chuichi Nagumo had already left Hitokappu Bay, Japan, though, embarking on a 3,300 mile journey across the Pacific Ocean with a task force of 6 aircraft carriers, 2 battleships, 2 heavy cruisers, 1 light cruiser, 9 destroyers, 3 submarines and 8 tankers (Dull, 11).[27] He reached his destination, about 275 miles north of Oahu island, in the early hours of December 7 (Dull, 14).

At 6:00 a.m. the carriers launched the first wave of torpedo bombers, dive bombers, horizontal bombers and fighters—183 in total—which reached the U.S. Naval Station at Pearl Harbor shortly before 8:00 a.m. (Dull, 16). The two-pronged attack hit the military airfields and harbor at the same time. In the harbor, more than 90 ships—among them 8 battleships, 8 cruisers, 29 destroyers and 5 submarines—lay neatly side by side, ripe for the picking. The battleships had been designated as primary targets, along with the air bases, to prevent U.S. aircraft from repelling the attack. Shortly after the assault had begun, an armor-piercing bomb exploded in the forward ammunition magazine of the battleship USS Arizona, costing the lives of 1,177 crewmen, about half of all Americans killed during the attack (Dull, 17; Madsen, 173). Three other battleships were also sunk, the other four were damaged but stayed afloat.

A second wave of 167 planes was sent in at 7:15 a.m., with the same objectives as the first wave (Dull, 18). Around 10:00 a.m. all Japanese planes returned to their carriers, and less than four hours later the Imperial fleet was on its way home again. In all, 21 U.S. ships had been either sunk or damaged, 188 aircraft had been destroyed, an additional 159 aircraft had been damaged, 2,403 U.S. servicemen had been killed, and 1,178 wounded (Dull, 19).

It was bad, but it could have been even worse. A planned third wave, directed against important onshore harbor

---

27   Hitokappu Bay (present-day Kasatka Bay) is located on the eastern shore of Iturup, the largest of the Kuril Islands, northeast of Japan. Soviet forces occupied the Kurils in 1945. The islands are still controlled by Russia today.

facilities—fuel depots, navy repair yards and submarine docks—was canceled by Nagumo, who feared another run might expose his fleet to an attack by the Pacific Fleet's carriers, whose whereabouts were still unknown (Dull, 19–20). Admiral Chester Nimitz, who took command of the Pacific Fleet shortly after the attack on Pearl Harbor, later said the war would have been prolonged by two years had the Japanese succeeded in destroying the fuel depots, as they carried the oil supplies for the entire fleet (Miller, 16–17).

The fact that the three aircraft carriers of the Pacific Fleet, *Enterprise*, *Saratoga* and *Lexington*, had not been at Pearl Harbor at the time, meant the U.S. could still get into the war in the Pacific fairly quickly. Had they been destroyed, the Pacific Fleet would have likely been unable to conduct any large-scale offensive operations for more than a year. The damage to the Pacific Fleet's battleships was extensive, yes, but it would be aircraft carriers and submarines, not the relatively slow battleships, that would prove to be of vital importance in the war in the Pacific.

Of course the attack instantly silenced the non-interventionists in the United States, who had previously made the case for staying out of the war. Following President Roosevelt's famous 'Infamy Speech', on December 8, Congress needed just 33 minutes to declare War on Japan, with only one Representative, the pacifist Jeannette Rankin, voting against the declaration.[28]

Three days later, Germany and Italy, honoring the Tripartite Pact with Japan, declared war on the United States. The U.S. responded in kind. The British also declared war on Japan, but Russia decided to keep its neutrality pact with Japan in

---

28   The 'Infamy Speech'—Roosevelt's Address to Congress of December 8, 1941—contained the famous words: "*December 7, 1941—a date which will live in infamy—the United States of America was suddenly and deliberately attacked by naval and air forces of the empire of Japan.*" Jeanette Rankin's no vote was met with "*boos and hisses*", according to an article in the New York Times at the time (Kluckhohn, "U.S. Declares War"; Roosevelt, "Day of Infamy").

place, careful not to get drawn into a two-front war with Japan attacking from the East.[29]

It was a smart move on Stalin's part, because in the summer of 1942 Germany launched a second massive offensive on Soviet territory, code-named *Fall Blau* (Case Blue). The primary objective was to capture the Caucasus oil fields in the South, the main Russian source of oil (Fritz, 231–32). To protect the left flank of the advance into the Caucasus, the city of Stalingrad (present-day Volgograd) had to be captured as well—or at least neutralized. It was also where Stalin decided to make his last stand.

One month into the German offensive, Stalin issued the (in)famous Order No. 227, a.k.a. the 'Not one step back' order. Signed by *"the national commissar for defense: J. Stalin"*, the order was not meant to simply boost morale or instill fear of insubordination in the troops, but sought to actually root out all unauthorized retreats, whatever the circumstances, using harsh but effective measures (Stalin, Order 227). Officers that allowed unauthorized retreats would be unconditionally removed from command and sent to court martial. Each army was also to set up 'penal companies', where those *"guilty of a breach of discipline due to cowardice or bewilderment will be sent, and put…on more difficult sectors of the front to give them an opportunity to redeem by blood their crimes against the Motherland"* (Stalin, Order 227). Furthermore, 'defensive squads' would be placed behind 'unstable divisions', to *"shoot in place panic-mongers and cowards and thus help the honest soldiers of the division execute their duty to the Motherland"*.

With one army thus determined to conquer at all cost and the other to defend at all cost, the epic struggle for Stalingrad began.

---

29   The Soviet-Japanese Neutrality Pact had been signed on April 13, 1941, just two months before Germany launched Operation Barbarossa against the Soviet Union. The pact would remain in place until April 5, 1945, when the Soviet Union denounced it.

Between August 23, 1942-February 2, 1943, the unfortunate city was reduced to little more than a vast field of ruins, a cemetery for the hundreds of thousands—if not more than a million—of soldiers and civilians that perished there.[30]

Mid-November 1942, the Germans were tantalizingly close to victory, holding more than 90 percent of the city, but when winter set in they still had not broken the back of the 62nd Army, which, charged with holding Stalingrad at all cost and commanded by General Vasily Chuikov, had been able to entrench itself in a 16-mile strip in the city, alongside the Volga's west bank (Roberts, "Victory at Stalingrad", 85).

Chuikov developed several urban war tactics during the battle for Stalingrad, such as instructing his commanders to fight with small groups wielding machine guns, grenades and Molotov Cocktails, instead of committing whole companies and battalions at a time (Chuikov, 150). He also found a way to decrease the effectiveness of the German Luftwaffe, by reducing *"the no-man's land as much as possible - to the throw of a grenade"*, making it much harder for the Luftwaffe to bomb Soviet frontline positions (Chuikov, 84). As Chuikov later wrote: *"City fighting is a special kind of fighting. Things are settled here not by strength, but by skill, resourcefulness and swiftness."* (Chuikov, 146).

Two other fundamental problems for the Germans were logistics and the lack of reserves. Equipment, fuel, food, ammunition, medicine, it was all much harder to come by for the Germans, who were fighting far away from home, than for the Russians, who were fighting for their home. At several critical moments of the months-long battle, General Chuikov's forces were replenished by the timely arrival of

---

30   In *Enemy at the Gates: The Battle for Stalingrad*, William Craig estimates the total casualties for both sides at 1,520,000, of which 750,000 Soviet soldiers, 400,000 Germans, 130,000 Italians, 120,000 Romanians and 120,000 Hungarians (Craig, xiv). Richard Overy mentions 500,000 Russian and 147,000 German dead in *Russia's War: A History of the Soviet War Effort: 1941–1945*, (Overy, 185). The total number of civilian casualties remains unknown.

reinforcements, while those of his main adversary, General Friedrich Paulus, Commander of the German 6th Army, were not (Roberts, "Victory at Stalingrad", 90–91).

When, late November, the 6th Army was encircled during a Russian counter-offensive, Paulus requested permission to try and break out, but Hitler refused, ordering him to hold his position (Jukes, 107–08). Paulus complied, but two months later—the situation of his army by then utterly desperate and destitute—he sent another message to Hitler, asking for the permission to surrender. The Führer refused again, shooting back: "*Surrender is out of the question. The troops will defend themselves to the last.*" (qtd. in Roberts, "Victory at Stalingrad", 132).

On January 31, 1943, the 6th Army nevertheless surrendered, although Paulus left the actual surrendering to someone else and also refused to sign or issue orders for his men to surrender (Roberts, "Victory at Stalingrad", 133). Two days later, On February 2, the remaining German forces in Stalingrad also surrendered.

One of the deadliest battles in history, Stalingrad would prove to be the turning point of the war in Europe. Germany never really regained the initiative on the Eastern front after it, but instead began its long retreat back to the *Heimat*.[31]

In September 1943, a couple of months after the British had defeated the Axis forces in North Africa, the Western Allies invaded the Italian mainland. With the subsequent Allied invasion in Normandy less than a year later, on June 6, 1944 (D-Day), the Western Allies delivered on their promise to Stalin to open up a second front, though the Soviet dictator

---

31   The Germans did mount another offensive in July 1943, code-named *Unternehmen Zitadelle* (Operation Citadel), but it was successfully countered by the Red Army before achieving any significant breakthrough. The failure of *Zitadelle* was at least partly caused by British intelligence on German preparations for the offensive finding its way to Stalin—both officially and unofficially, as the Soviets had a spy inside the British code-breaking center at Bletchley Park—two months before it was launched (Copeland, 4–6).

never stopped believing the Americans and British had deliberately delayed their invasion to let the Soviet Union suffer the brunt of the German onslaught.

The turning point of the War in the Pacific, meanwhile, came a few months before Stalingrad, at the Battle of Midway (June 4–7, 1942), when the Japanese Navy lost four aircraft carriers while sinking only one U.S. carrier. It also lost some 270 aircraft and—much worse—125 experienced pilots, more than half of the Japanese pilots who had entered the battle (Isom, 229–36).[32] The defeat seriously crippled the offensive capabilities of the Japanese fleet and increasingly forced it on the defensive.

Following the emboldening victory at Midway, the Allies decided to invade the Japanese-occupied island of Guadalcanal (part of the present-day Solomon Islands), east of New Guinea. The main reason for the attack was to prevent the Japanese Navy from using the island as a base from where supply routes between Australia and the U.S. could be threatened.

In February 1943, after six months of heavy fighting, the Japanese finally surrendered the island to the Allied forces. Over the next two years, several other Japanese-held islands would follow in similar fashion, as the Americans slowly but certainly advanced towards mainland Japan by way of their *island-hopping* strategy.

Back in Europe, no hopping was necessary to advance towards Germany. After a last failed German offensive in the Ardennes (December 16, 1944-January 25, 1945) Western Allied forces crossed the Rhine in March 1945 and fanned out across Germany. By then the Red Army had already advanced into Germany from the East, and on April 25 American and Russian forces linked up at the Elbe river. Five

---

32   Dallas Isom writes in *Midway Inquest* that the loss of the experienced pilots hurt the Japanese Navy more than that of the four carriers; the pilots were never replaced and the remaining attack carriers could no longer be provided with a full contingent of first-line pilots (Isom, 236).

days later Hitler committed suicide in his bunker and two days after that Berlin fell. On May 8, shortly before midnight, the German Supreme Command of the Armed Forces surrendered unconditionally in Berlin. [33]

After the defeat of Germany, the U.S. started preparations for their invasion of the Japanese mainland (code-named *Operation Downfall*). Given their experience against the Japanese Army in several brutal island battles such as Guadalcanal, Iwo Jima and Okinawa, estimates about American casualties in the event of an invasion of Japan ranged from approximately 200,000 to as high as 4 million.[34] Staggering figures that are still used as the principal justification for the subsequent atomic bombings of the Japanese cities of Hiroshima and Nagasaki on August 6 and 9, 1945, respectively, meant to compel Japan to surrender without having to invade it first. The two bombs likely killed upwards of 250,000 people (Holdstock, 2). Six days later Japan surrendered unconditionally.[35]

---

33 The German Instrument of Surrender had actually already been signed in Reims, on May 7, but the Soviet Union had formally protested that the signed document was not the same as the draft that had been prepared earlier and that the Soviet Representative in Reims, General Susloparov, had not been been authorized to sign the document of surrender. The Soviets also considered Berlin a far more suitable location for the ceremonial surrender of Nazi Germany than Reims, hence the second, official surrender in Berlin on May 8 (Pinkus, 501–03).

34 Of course nobody could predict casualty rates with any certainty. All estimates looked at previous campaigns and tried to account for the likely level of participation from the Japanese civilian population. Thus, General Curtis LeMay arrived at 500,000 casualties, while a study by the Joint Chiefs of Staff estimated around 456,000 casualties—including 109,000 dead or missing—for the first part of the campaign, climbing to a total of 1,200,000 casualties of which 267,000 fatalities for the second part. Another study, done for the Secretary of War, estimated that conquering Japan in its entirety in case of large-scale participation by civilians could cost as much as 1.7–4 million American casualties.

35 The formal signing of the Japanese Instrument of Surrender took place in Tokyo Bay, aboard the USS Missouri, on September 2, 1945.

The war was over, but the world would never be the same.[36]

The center of geopolitical power had shifted from Europe to the United States and the Soviet Union, two countries that would soon find themselves on opposing sides in everything except for a shared, basic understanding that mankind might not survive another world war.

In the decades that followed, the world would be largely divided into an American/Western/capitalist sphere of influence and a Russian/Eastern/communist sphere of influence. So too in Europe, with democracy restored and far-reaching economic and military cooperation established between Western Europe and the U.S., while Eastern Europe, liberated by the Red Army, would remain under Soviet influence, frequently enforced heavy-handedly.

And then there was the Bomb. For a few years, the U.S. remained the only country that had it, but on August 29, 1949, the U.S.S.R successfully tested an atomic weapon of its own, thus ushering in the era of Mutually Assured Destruction (MAD).[37] Fortunately for all of us, despite a dark dalliance with nuclear war in 1962, the East-West conflict would largely remain a 'Cold War', although several proxy wars were fought—in Greece, China, Korea, Vietnam, Afghanistan, to name a few—to keep things interesting.[38]

WW II also spelled the end for the European colonial empires, with decolonization waves rolling through Africa, Asia and the Middle East in the 1940s, 1950s and 1960s. They

36   World War II casualty estimates mostly range between 40–75 million, but as Matthew White points out in his excellent work about the 100 deadliest episodes in human history, a majority of historians—among them John Haywood, John Keegan, Charles Messenger and J.M Roberts—arrive at a total of 50 million military and civilian deaths (White, 605). The likely high number of civilian deaths combined with the general lack of reliable population data is the reason there is so much variation between the different estimates.

37   See chapter 15—A Bomb.

38   For the 1962 Cuban Missile Crisis, see chapter 18—How Vasili Arkhipov Saved the World.

would bring independence, but also instability and in many cases (civil) war.

Another independent nation owing its existence to the Second World War finally gave the Jews a home of their own again, but the creation of the state of Israel, in 1948, would come at the cost of great instability in the Middle East, which lasts to this day.

Still, after all the carnage, cruelty and destruction there was also hope, in the form of a burgeoning understanding that all human life is precious and that war should no longer be accepted as a means to an end in a modern world. On this shared conviction—however fragile, imperfect and at times ambiguous—the United Nations and the Universal Declaration of Human Rights were created.

Rochus Misch, one of the last to leave the *Führerbunker* alive on May 2, 1945, was captured by the Russians shortly after his escape. He spent the next nine years as a Soviet prisoner, before returning to Berlin in 1953, where he lived out the remainder of his life just two miles from the location of Hitler's last hideout (Schnoor, "last survivor"). The last survivor of the *Führerbunker*, Misch died on September 5, 2013. He remained loyal to his Führer until the end.

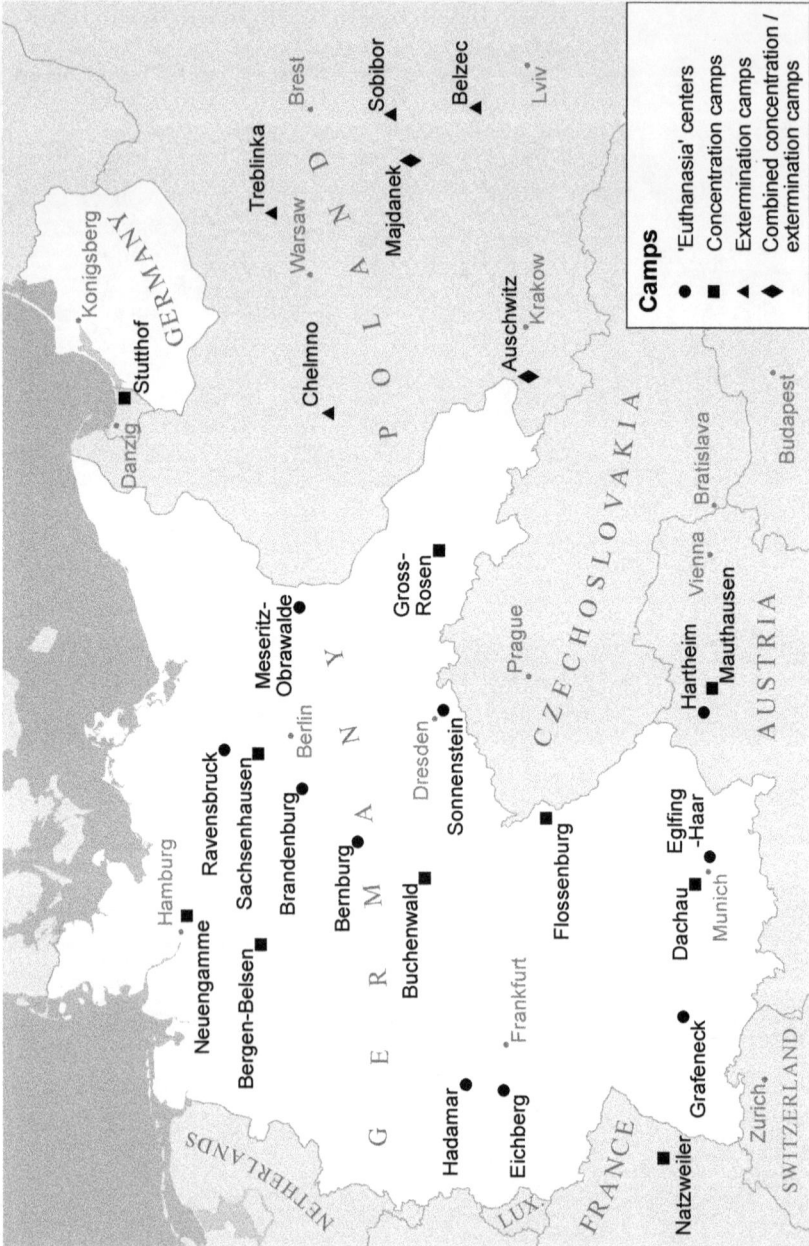

Map 10: Nazi Camps, 1933-45

14

How to Kill an Entire People

"Technically? That wasn't so hard—it would not have been hard to exterminate even greater numbers (..) The killing itself took the least time. You could dispose of 2,000 head in a half hour, but it was the burning that took all the time. The killing was easy; you didn't even need guards to drive them into the chambers; they just went in expecting to take showers and, instead of water, we turned on poison gas. The whole thing went very quickly."[1]

Rudolf Höss, Commandant of Auschwitz, 1946

IN 2008, SEVENTEEN-YEAR-OLD ELI SAGIR GOT A tattoo after returning from a high school trip to Poland. Nothing too elaborate or complicated, just a number. 157622 (Rudoren, "Proudly Bearing"). When she showed it to her grandfather, he bent his head and kissed it, because he had the same number, in the same spot. Only he hadn't gotten his at a hip tattoo parlor but at Auschwitz concentration camp, nearly 70 years ago.

Several other young descendants of Auschwitz survivors have done the same. They view the number as part of their family history, an heirloom almost. They want to remember. They want others to remember. Not surprisingly, the young, numbered forearms trigger reactions far and wide. Some are disgusted, shocked, even angry. Others find it a beautiful gesture (Rudoren, "Proudly Bearing").

---

1   Qtd. in Gilbert, 249–50.

It is not all that different from how Auschwitz survivors treated their own tattoo. Some rushed to the plastic surgeon after the war to have the numbers removed, others viewed it as a scar that nevertheless needed to be preserved. Still others viewed it with pride, because it proved they survived. Everything.

For some of the few that remain, surviving started almost immediately after the *Nationalsozialistische Deutsche Arbeiterpartei* (NSDAP, a.k.a the Nazi Party) came to power in Germany, in 1933. NSDAP leader Adolf Hitler had never made a secret of his hatred for the Jewish people (or many other people for that matter), a hatred emphatically shared by the Nazi Party electorate and even by many who had not voted for the Nazis in 1933.[2] In fact, Jews had been subject to hatred, discrimination and violence for centuries throughout Europe. They were used to it. But this time, in this country, it would be different.

The Nazi ideology was centered around the belief in the superiority of the Aryan race, the German *Volk* (people) and German culture. To fulfill its perceived destiny of world domination, Germany needed to have a strong state, a strong leader and a strong people. The state should therefore be given the means to control and legislate every aspect of society and its citizens, and the leader should be given the means to control every aspect of the state—the so-called *Führerprinzip* (Bendersky, 41–42).[3] The people, for their part, should be

---

2   In his autobiographical manifesto *Mein Kampf* (My Struggle) Hitler writes: "*If one considers how much he has sinned against the masses in the course of the centuries, how again and again he squeezed and extorted without mercy, if one considers further how the people gradually learned to hate him for this and finally saw in his existence really nothing but a punishment of Heaven, then one can understand how hard this change must be for the Jew.*" (Hitler, 431). And: "*Therefore, I believe today that I am acting in the sense of the Almighty Creator: By warding off the Jews I am fighting for the Lord's work.*" (Hitler, 84).

3   In chapter three of *A History of Nazi Germany: 1919–1945*, Bendersky also discusses the historical roots of Nazi ideology.

pure of blood and purpose, willing to sacrifice everything for the good of the state.

Everybody who disagreed with this view was to be considered a disruptive force to the strength of the state and therefore a danger to the security of the state. Everybody who was impure of blood or weak in any other way could not be part of the New Order and should either be reeducated (if only weak) or permanently expelled (if impure).[4] These *Unerwünschten* (undesirables) included Jews, Slavs, Gypsies, blacks, communists, homosexuals, the mentally ill, the disabled, Jehovah's Witnesses and Freemasons.

But above all, the Jews.

Still, although getting rid of the Jews stood front and center of the Nazi ideology, actually getting it done posed various practical challenges. It is one thing to shout all manner of things in speeches at beer cellars and backrooms, but quite another to turn those rants into actual policy. An estimated 530,000 Jews lived in Germany alone in 1933 (Nicosia, 4). They served in the military, taught at universities, sat on judge's benches, worked as doctors, lawyers, in factories, owned shops, stocks, bonds, houses, employed people, married, had children. Whatever their perceived undesirability, their lives were entwined with all aspects of German society.

Historians still debate whether Hitler had already decided to exterminate all the Jews even before he came to power, but

---

4   That the National Socialists meant business regarding the 'purification' of the German *Volksgemeinschaft* became clear just a couple of months after they came to power, when Wilhelm Frick, the newly appointed Reich Minister of the Interior, implemented the 'Law for the Prevention of Genetically Diseased Offspring' (*Gesetz zur Verhütung erbkranken Nachwuchses*), in July 1933. This law provided the state with the power to forcibly sterilize those suffering from a hereditary disease. Around 400,000 people would subsequently be sterilized over the next decade and thus in many cases be permanently expelled from the gene pool (Crew 113–14).

given the different solutions to the 'Jewish Question' the Nazis tried out between 1933–41 it seems unlikely he had, even if only for practical reasons. After all, the Germany of 1933 was very different from that of 1941. For one thing, Germany was not at war with anybody in 1933, nor was it ready for war. Its armed forces were relatively small compared to countries like France and Great Britain. What would these countries have done if the Nazis had started exterminating the Jews then and there? And what would the German people have done if their Jewish officers, teachers, professors and colleagues had been dragged away in the middle of the night? In hindsight, the answer to both questions is: probably nothing. But in 1933, this seemed far from certain.

Hitler therefore initially opted for a strategy of isolation and emigration. By isolating the Jews, their entanglement with German society would diminish, making it easier to remove them altogether later on. It would also create jobs for *Volksgenossen* (compatriots; only Germans of pure blood could be a *Volksgenosse*), an advantage not to be discarded in times of economic depression.[5]

The first major law aimed directly at pushing Jewish German citizens out of society was the *Law for the Restoration of the Professional Service*. It was adopted on April 7, 1933, just two weeks after the Reichstag had passed the *Enabling Act*, which gave Hitler dictatorial powers.[6] The law exclud-

---

5   Point 4 of the National Socialist Program stated: *"Only those who are our fellow countrymen can become citizens. Only those who have German blood, regardless of creed, can be our countrymen. Hence no Jew can be a countryman."* ("Program").

6   The Enabling Act of 1933 gave the cabinet the right to enact laws without the consent of the Reichstag (by passing this law the Reichstag thus made itself superfluous). To get the necessary majority, the government had arrested all the Communist (KPD) Reichstag members and several Social Democrat (SPD) Reichstag members under cover of the Reichstag Fire Decree, a law that suspended several constitutionally guaranteed rights 'until further notice', following the alleged arson of the Reichstag by communists. With the KPD and several SPD members gone and the Center Party bullied into voting for

ed all those of non-Aryan descent—as well as opponents of the Nazi regime—from working as civil servants. It meant Jews could no longer serve as teachers, judges or professors. Not long after that, a similar law was passed forbidding Jews to work as lawyers, doctors, notaries or tax consultants, while another restricted the number of Jewish students at schools and universities, later excluding them from educational institutions altogether.

In enforcing these laws, however, a new problem surfaced. One that hadn't been given much consideration before, perhaps because it didn't make for very sexy anti-Semitic election rhetoric. Now that anti-Semitic rhetoric had become government policy though, it needed to be addressed. The problem lay in determining who exactly counted as a Jew. Was it everybody who had a Jewish ancestor? But how far back? And was one enough or should there be multiple Jewish ancestors? And what if none of the Jewish ancestors were female? After all, according to the Jewish faith, only those born from a Jewish woman are considered Jewish by birth. And what about converts? Since one could become Jewish by conversion, should that mean one could also stop being Jewish, for instance by converting to Christianity?

The need to answer these questions became especially acute when, in September 1935, the Reich Ministry of the Interior wanted to introduce new laws to further isolate the Jews from German society. These Nuremberg Laws—so named because they were introduced at the annual Nazi Party rally in Nuremberg—stripped Jews of their citizenship and forbade marriage and sexual relations between Jews and Germans.[7]

---

the measure with the Nazi Party, the enabling act was passed 444 in favor, 94 against.

7   The Nuremberg Laws adopted at the Nazi Party rally were the 'Reich Citizenship Law' and the 'Law for the Protection of German Blood and German Honor' (Steinweis, "Law in Nazi Germany", 47–48).

After much debate, it was determined that a person who had at least three Jewish grandparents was to be considered *Volljude* (a full Jew), regardless of religious affiliation (Steinweis, "Studying the Jew", 42). A person who had two Jewish grandparents was considered a *Mischling* (crossbreed) in the first degree. With one Jewish grandparent one was considered a *Mischling* in the second degree. However, there were certain circumstances that could render a *Mischling* legally Jewish, making such a person a so-called *Geltungsjude*. Being a member of a Jewish congregation for instance, or being married to a Jew.

Having settled the legal definition of Jewishness, existing anti-Jewish legislation could now also be better enforced. Following the Nuremberg Laws, a host of national and local new anti-Jewish legislation was introduced, isolating the Jews ever further.

Under these circumstances it was hardly surprising that many Jews wanted to quit Germany altogether. Between 1933–38, 140,000 Jews thus emigrated from Germany, for the most part to neighboring countries like Denmark, the Netherlands, Belgium and France, countries that would unfortunately prove to be only a temporary safe haven from Nazi persecution (Nicosia, 7).[8]

After the first wave of Jewish emigration in 1933, when 37,000 left, the numbers declined again—to 23,000 in 1934 and 21,000 in 1935—partly because the situation in Germany stabilized somewhat, but also because most countries did not want them (Longerich, 67). It prompted Zionist leader (and later first President of Israel) Chaim Weizmann to lament: *"The world seemed to be divided into two parts - those places*

---

8   Anne Frank was one of them. Having emigrated from Germany to the Netherlands early 1934, the Frank family went into hiding after Germany invaded and occupied Holland. In August 1944 they were nevertheless arrested by the *Sicherheitsdienst* and put on transport. Anne and her sister Margot died in concentration camp Bergen-Belsen in March 1945, a few weeks before the camp was liberated by the British.

*where the Jews could not live, and those where they could not
enter."* (qtd. in Sherman, 112).

To find a solution for the increasing number of Jewish refugees from Nazi Germany, an international conference was
organized in Evian-Les-Bains, France, in July 1938. A few
months earlier, at a speech in Königsberg, Hitler had already
made it clear he would welcome any initiative in this direction, saying: *"I can only hope and expect that the other world,
which has such deep sympathy for these criminals, will at least
be generous enough to convert this sympathy into practical aid.
We, on our part, are ready to put all these criminals at the
disposal of these countries, for all I care, even on luxury ships"*
(qtd. in New York Times, "Hitler").[9] 32 countries attended
the conference, but the Netherlands and Denmark were the
only European countries willing to accept a limited increase
in the number of refugees (Landau, 138).

A couple of months later, in the night of November 9–10,
1938, thousands of Jewish homes, hospitals, schools, syna-
gogues and businesses were destroyed, 20,000 Jews were
arrested—most of whom were sent to concentration camps,
of which there were six at the time, mainly meant for political
dissidents—and 91 people were killed (Sherman, 166–67).

Kristallnacht, so called because of the large number of
shattered windows, brought Jewish persecution in Germany
to a whole new level. Whoever had still been fooling himself
thinking Jews might have some kind of future in Nazi
Germany, could do so no longer. By June 1939, 309,000
German, Austrian and Czech Jews had applied for the 27,000
places available in the U.S. quota. By the time the war broke
out, in September 1939, some 95,000 had managed to emigrate to the United States, 60,000 had emigrated to Palestine,

---

9   Distasteful as the comment is, it also clearly shows Hitler was not yet
committed to the destruction of the Jewish race.

40,000 to Great Britain and about 75,000 to Central and South America ("German Jewish Refugees").[10]

Apart from terrorizing the Jews to stimulate emigration, the Nazis also floated several state sanctioned 'total emigration' plans. There was the *Schacht plan*—named after Hjalmar Schacht, President of the Reichsbank, who conceived it—which called for World Jewry to establish a fund that would finance the resettlement of a total of 150,000 able-bodied German and Austrian Jews, who would later be joined by 250,000 dependents (Yahil, 117). Another fund was to be established out of the emigrants' property and used to pay for maintaining those Jews who were unable to emigrate. Progress was made in subsequent negotiations with the United States and Britain, but before a version of the plan could be implemented the war broke out (Yahil, 118).

Another idea was the *Nisko Plan*, concocted in September 1939 and meant as a Jewish Reservation of sorts in occupied Poland. It resulted in the first deportations East, but a host of practical problems and bad international press as to the treatment of the deportees—at a time foreign public opinion still mattered somewhat to the Nazis—caused the plan to be shelved (Yahil, 138–40, 160–61).

The *Madagascar Plan*, which (re)surfaced in the summer of 1940, after the defeat of France, envisioned shipping the entire German Jewish population to the island of Madagascar, a French colony (Yahil, 253–54).[11] It was seriously considered by Hitler, but abandoned after Germany lost the Battle

---

10   This was out of a total of 282,000 Jews (from the initial 530,000 in 1933) that made it out of Germany between 1933–39 and 117,000 Jews that emigrated from annexed Austria ("German Jewish Refugees").

11   The idea to resettle European Jews on Madagascar was not a German one, the French and the Poles had also considered it in the late 1930s (Yahil, 254; Browning, 81–82). The Poles had even sent a small investigating team to the island, with consent of the French, as part of a feasibility study (Browning, 81–82). It concluded that a maximum of 5,000–7,000 families could be settled there.

of Britain. One plan that did come to fruition was the *Transfer (a.k.a. Haavara) Agreement*, which facilitated the emigration of around 51,000 German Jews to Palestine between 1933–39 (Yahil, 100–04).[12]

The outbreak of the war made emigration of the remaining Jews practically impossible. Not only did it make foreign countries even less susceptible to accepting Jewish refugees, German conquests also dramatically increased the number of Jews living in the Third Reich.[13] And the fact that almost half of the German Jewish population was still living in Germany even after having been subjugated to the harshest anti-Semitic laws, made it clear that wartime emigration of three million Polish Jews just wasn't going to happen. It was time for a different answer to the 'Jewish Question'.

On September 21, 1939, SS-*Gruppenführer* Reinhard Heydrich—whom Hitler called The Man with the Iron Heart—sent a memo to the chiefs of all the *Einsatzgruppen* of the *Sicherheitspolizei* (Security Police), concerning the "*Judenfrage im besetzten Gebiete*", the Jewish Question in Occupied Territory (Arad, "Documents", 173–78).[14] The *Einsatzgruppen*, formed in the summer of 1939, leading up to the invasion of Poland, were SS death squads, operating in the wake of the regular army with instructions to eliminate "*all anti-German elements in hostile country behind the troops in combat.*" (Browning, 16).[15]

---

12   Under the agreement, Jewish emigrants to Palestine had to pay 1,000 pounds sterling into a trust company in Germany, which used the funds to buy German goods and sell them to the Haavara company, which in turn sold them in Palestine, thus stimulating German export ("Encyclopedia Judaica: Haavara"). The proceeds went to the emigrants living in Palestine.

13   Poland alone, invaded in September 1939, was home to an estimated three million Jews (Yahil, 187).

14   Source includes the complete memo.

15   The *Einsatzgruppen* were controlled by the powerful SS-*Reichssicherheitshauptamt*, the Reich Main Security Office, which had been created on September 27, 1939, to bring the *Sicherheitspolizei* and

In the memo, Heydrich instructed the chiefs to start round-ing up the Jews and put them in "*concentration centers*" (Arad, "Documents", 173–78). These ghettos, he wrote, should be located near a railroad junction or at least on a railway, to accommodate transportation of the Jews at a later date.

Jewish enterprises, factories, farms and land were to be "*aryanized*" (i.e., confiscated), though Heydrich pointed out that a transition period might be necessary in some cases, so as not to hurt German economic interests (Arad, "Documents", 173–78). The memo also talked about how "*the final aim*" (*Endziel*) of the measures "*will require extended periods of time*", and that all the "*planned total measures are to be kept strictly secret*". It therefore seems that, by September 1939, at the very least Reinhard Heydrich had made up his mind as to the faith of the Jewish population in the Reich.

Between October 1939-July 1942, more than 1,100 Jewish ghettos were created in Nazi-occupied Eastern Europe (Michman, 8). The allotted space for the ghettos was far too small for the number of Jews forced to live there. The result-ing overcrowding, as well as the absence of even the most basic sanitation services, caused diseases like typhus, dys-entery and diphtheria to spread fast and freely (Friedman, 122). Malnutrition was another serious problem. It was in-tentionally caused, by keeping food deliveries far below even the bare minimum. In the Warsaw ghetto, for instance, Jews were forced to subsist on 180 calories per day—a quarter of what was given to Poles—while also being forbidden, on pain of death, to leave the ghetto and trade for food and other essentials (Friedman, 122). Hundreds of thousands thus died

---

the *Sicherheitsdienst* under the same roof. It was run by Heydrich. The *Einsatzgruppen* were responsible for numerous mass shootings between 1941–45, killing an estimated two million civilians, including 1.3 million Jews (Headland, 98–106). In *Messages of Murder*, Headland includes detailed killing statistics from the various *Einsatzgruppen*, before concurring with Raul Hilberg's oft-cited estimate from *The Destruction of the European Jews* that 1,300,000 Jews were killed in the East by the *Einsatzgruppen*, other SS agencies and collaborators (Headland, 106).

of starvation, exhaustion and disease before the ghettos were liquidated in 1942–43.

The number of forced labor camps also rapidly expanded after the outbreak of the war, eventually numbering more than 30,000 including subcamps, most of them in Germany and Poland.[16] Jews, Slavs, Russian prisoners of war, Gypsies, gays and political dissidents, millions were forced to work in the camps, providing ultra cheap labor for the German industry. To sustain this economic system it needed to be fed with a continuous stream of new workers, as most prisoners succumbed within a few months to the grueling conditions. At concentration camp Buchenwald, for example, the average life expectancy of a prisoner working in the factories was nine months (Fleischman, 71).[17]

Following the German invasion of Russia (Operation Barbarossa) in June 1941, Heydrich's boss, *Reichsführer* Heinrich Himmler, instructed the *Einsatzgruppen* to regard all Jews as partisans and to shoot all male Jews of military age (Longerich, 198). From August, the *Einsatzgruppen* began to execute women, children and the elderly as well (Longerich, 207).

---

16   Research by Geoffrey P. Megargee et al. about the full extent of Nazi camps has concluded that, contrary to what was previously believed, the total number of camps between 1933–45 was 42,500, of which 30,000 slave labor camps (including subcamps), 1,150 Jewish ghettos, 1,000 prisoner-of-war camps and 980 concentration camps. Dr. Megargee is the lead researcher of a team working on a multivolume encyclopedia that aims to document all the camps. As of 2014, the first two of an expected total of seven volumes of the *Encyclopedia of Camps and Ghettos, 1933–1945*, have been published (Lichtblau 2013).

17   According to an income statement from Buchenwald, total net revenue for a prisoner was 1,631 Reichsmark, of which 1,431 Reichsmark was made during a total expected life span of nine months—6 RM per day minus 70 cents for food and clothes, times 30 (days) times 9 (months)—and another 200 Reichsmark was made after the prisoner's death, from his corpse, his clothing and valuable items he sometimes left behind (Fleischman, 71–73). According to Holocaust historian Raul Hilberg, life expectancy of a Jewish inmate at the I.G. Farben plant near Auschwitz was three to four months and at the outlying coal mines about one month (Hilberg, 996).

244 — WORLD 2.0

By then, Heydrich had already been instructed by *Reichsmarschall* Hermann Göring—whom Hitler had appointed as his first successor—to submit "*an overall plan of the preliminary organizational, practical and financial measures for the execution of the intended final solution* [Endlösung] *of the Jewish question*" (Arad, "Documents", 233).

Around the same time, *SS-Sturmbannführer* Rudolf Höss was ordered by Himmler to establish extermination facilities at the concentration camp where he was commander, Auschwitz.[18] Thus, after isolation, emigration and concentration, the final solution to the Jewish Question would be extermination.

Hundreds of thousands of Jews had already been shot by the *Einsatzgruppen,* died of exhaustion from doing hard labor or from starvation or disease in the camps and ghettos, but mid-1941 the total annihilation of the Jews was made a primary goal for the first time. Because it would be highly counter-productive to the German war industry—which relied heavily on Jewish slave labor—there was some opposition from upper Nazi echelons against killing the Jews outright instead of simply working them to death, but the real decision had already been made.

On January 20, 1942, following up on Göring's order, Heydrich organized a conference for senior officials from several government ministries, in the Berlin suburb of

---

18   At the Nuremberg trial after the war, Höss was questioned about this meeting with Himmler:

DR. KAUFFMANN: *Is it true that in 1941 you were ordered to Berlin to see Himmler? Please state briefly what was discussed.*

HOESS: *Yes. In the summer of 1941 I was summoned to Berlin to Reichsführer SS Himmler to receive personal orders. He told me something to the effect—I do not remember the exact words— that the Führer had given the order for a final solution of the Jewish question. We, the SS, must carry out that order. If it is not carried out now then the Jews will later on destroy the German people. He had chosen Auschwitz on account of its easy access by rail and also because the extensive site offered space for measures ensuring isolation.*" (qtd. in "Trial of the Major War Criminals", Vol. XI, 398).

Wannsee. For Heydrich, the main goals of the conference were to secure the cooperation of the various departments and to make sure that the implementation of the *Endlösung* would be regarded as an internal matter of the SS (Longerich, 310). A secondary goal was to determine who would be regarded as Jewish in the sense of the Final Solution and what to do with the *Mischlinge.*

In all, Heydrich invited fourteen people, among them officials from the Justice department, State department, Economics department and Ministry of the Interior, as well as representatives of administrations in charge of occupied territories in Eastern Europe. Seven of the fifteen attendants (including Heydrich) held an SS rank, eight had earned a doctorate, six of which were in law.

The whole conference took no more than 90 minutes, after which Heydrich had secured the full cooperation of the various departments.

SS-Obersturmbannführer Adolf Eichmann was charged with the task of organizing the transports from all over German-occupied Europe to the six designated death camps, Auschwitz-Birkenau, Chelmno, Majdanek, Belzec, Sobibor and Treblinka.

Of these, Auschwitz was the most efficient. One reason for this was that Auschwitz Commandant Höss had made several improvements to the extermination process he had witnessed at Treblinka. For instance, instead of gas chambers capable of holding 200 people, like in Treblinka, he had gas chambers built that could hold 2,000 ("Trials of the Major War Criminals", Vol. XI, 417). For the gassing itself, Höss opted for Zyklon B, a crystallized prussic acid, instead of the monoxide gas used at Treblinka, because it worked faster ("Trials of the Major War Criminals", Vol. XI, 416). In his memoirs, Höss recalled:

> "The gassing was carried out in the detention cells of Block 11. Protected by a gas mask, I watched the killing myself. In the crowded cells, death came instantaneously the moment the Zyklon B was thrown in. A short, almost smothered cry, and it was all over... I must even admit that this gassing set my mind at rest, for the mass extermination of the Jews was to start soon, and at that time neither Eichmann nor I was certain as to how these mass killings were to be carried out. It would be by gas, but we did not know which gas and how it was to be used. Now we had the gas, and we had established a procedure." (Hoss, 92–95).

Höss also went to great lengths to fool victims into thinking they were being deloused rather than gassed. Numbered coat hangers were put in the outer chamber for prisoners to hang their clothes on as they undressed. Meanwhile Jewish prisoners from the *Sonderkommando*—a special work detail forced to aid the SS with the extermination process—walked around, instructing victims to remember their coat hanger number so they could come back for their clothes after the delousing shower. The gas chamber itself was disguised as a shower room, with clean, whitewashed walls and shower heads hanging from the ceiling.

The gassing itself was handled by the SS, but the subsequent disposal and cleaning process was carried out by the prisoners of the *Sonderkommando* (Greif, 2–6).[19] Selected on their arrival in the extermination camp and given the choice to join the *Sonderkommando* or die, most prisoners decided to join. Their living conditions were markedly better than those of regular camp prisoners. They had their own barracks, received better food and had access to liquor, cigarettes and medicines (Greif, 145, 234, 246, 374). They also

---

19   Greif also describes how the *Sonderkommando* came into existence, evolving out of specific kommandos such as the *Krematoriums-Kommando* and the *Begrabungskommando* with the emergence of the policy to systematically exterminate all the Jews (Greif, 3–6).

did not have to fear to be killed at random like the other prisoners. In exchange, they did the dirty work.

After the gassing, the *Sonderkommando* removed the bodies from the gas chamber and brought them to a nearby room, where they were checked for valuables. Eyeglasses were lifted, rings slid of fingers, mouths checked for gold teeth, bridges and crowns, breaking them out if found (Greif, 321).[20] If a spot check by the SS revealed that gold had been missed, the prisoner responsible would be lucky to get away with a severe beating (Greif, 301).[21] Other body orifices were checked as well for hidden valuables. After this, hair from female victims was shaved off. The teeth gold was melted into gold bars and transported to Berlin. The hair was sold to felt factories that used them in mattresses.

Meanwhile, prisoners from the *Kanada Kommando* collected the belongings from the gassed—suitcases, shoes, clothing, jewelry, photographs etc.—and brought them to a warehouse they called Canada (German: *Kanada*), a country that symbolized wealth in their eyes (Berg, 301). At the warehouse, everything was sorted and from there transported back to Germany at regular intervals.

Having checked the corpses, the *Sonderkommando* took the bodies to the crematorium, where they were put on metal stretchers and pushed into the furnace. In times of high volume, open-air pits were used together with the Crematoria. The remaining ashes were dumped in a lake nearby (Greif, 18, 95, 157, 251). While the corpses were incinerated, another detail of the *Sonderkommando* cleaned the gas chamber, washing away the blood, vomit, urine and

---

20 Höss also mentions this in his testimony at Nuremberg ("Trial of the Major War Criminals", Vol. XI, 416).

21 Greif got this information from Leon Cohen, whose exclusive job in the *Sonderkommando* was to pull gold teeth from the gassed corpses. Cohen said that during his twelve-hour shifts new corpses would arrive every half-hour and each time he had ten minutes to pull out the gold teeth of some sixty to seventy-five corpses (Greif, 300–01).

excrement, and whitewashing the walls. Making everything ready for processing of the next group. Following this procedure 20,000 people could be disposed of within 24 hours at Auschwitz (Piper, 173–74). But that was at peak operation.

To prevent the inner workings of the extermination process to travel beyond the Crematoria, the SS replaced each *Sonderkommando* every four months or so. Of the thousands of prisoners active in one of the *Sonderkommandos* in Auschwitz-Birkenau between 1941–45, only about 80 lived to tell (Greif, 83). But even if none of them would have survived their story would have, as several of them wrote it down and buried it in the grounds of the Crematoria, right in the heart of darkness (Czech, 372). The documents were discovered years after the war.

Early 1942, when it became clear that Germany might not be able to hold on to all of its previously conquered territory in the East, on account of the failure of Operation Barbarossa (June-December 1941) and the subsequent Soviet counter-offensive, Heydrich met with *SS-Standartenführer* Paul Blobel to discuss the need to erase all traces of the mass executions (Arad, "Operation Reinhard", 170).

Heydrich was subsequently assassinated in Prague, before he could officially appoint Blobel, but not long after Gestapo chief *SS-Gruppenführer* Heinrich Müller put Blobel in charge of the secret operation, code-named *Sonderaktion 1005*, whose objective it was to cover up remaining evidence of the mass murders by exhuming all the bodies from mass graves and burn them (Arad, "Operation Reinhard", 170–71).[22] The *Sonderkommandos* charged with exhuming and burning the bodies were killed after their work was done.

On October 7, 1944, the Auschwitz *Sonderkommando* of Crematorium IV revolted after a rumor they would soon

22   Blobel had been the commanding officer of Sonderkommando 4a of Einsatzgruppe C, which had, among other things, carried out the massacres at Babi Yar (in Kiev, Ukraine) on September 29–30, 1941. He was sentenced to death by the Nuremberg Tribunal and hanged in 1951.

be 'transferred to another camp', SS-speak for extermination (Henry, 58). Before the revolt was suppressed, the *Sonderkommando* had succeeded in blowing up Crematorium IV, damaging it beyond repair. It was never used again. 250 *Sonderkommando* members lost their lives during the revolt, 200 others were shot by the SS as a reprisal and disposed of by the next *Sonderkommando* (Henry, 58). One month later, Himmler ordered the destruction of the remaining Crematoria.

On January 18, 1945, shortly before the Russians reached the camp, the SS marched the remaining 60,000 prisoners out of Auschwitz to Wodzislaw, 35 miles (56 km) away, from where they were put on freight trains to other camps (Rozett, 183). At least 15,000 of them died or were killed during this death march. Those who had been too weak or too sick to walk had been left behind at the camp. When the Russians liberated Auschwitz a few days later, on January 27, about 7,000 of them were still alive (Stone, 41).

All told, approximately 6 million Jews were killed by the Nazis—about two thirds of the entire European Jewish population—4 million in extermination camps and another 2 million through mass shootings from the *Einsatzgruppen*, starvation, disease and exhaustion.[23] 3.3 million Soviet POWs also perished at the hands of the Germans, as did nearly 3 million non-Jewish Poles, between 220,000–1,500,000 Gypsies, 200,000 disabled, and between 3,000 and 10,000 homosexuals.[24]

---

23   At Nuremberg, the Austrian SS officer (and historian) Wilhelm Höttl testified about a conversation he had had with Adolf Eichmann, late August 1944, during which the latter had confided that, *"Approximately 4 million Jews had been killed in the various concentration camps, while an additional 2 million met death in other ways, the major part of which were shot by operational squads of the Security Police during the campaign against Russia."*(qtd. in "Trial of the Major War Criminals", Vol. III, 569).

24   In his *History of the Holocaust*, Jonathan Friedman notes that estimates about the number of Gypsies killed vary greatly, with the figure of 1.5 million

An estimated 1.1 million Jews were exterminated in Auschwitz between September 1941-November 1944 (Gutman, 71).[25]

Auschwitz was also the only camp where prisoners were tattooed with a serial number—the ones who were given prisoner status that is—405,000 in total (Marrus, 1131). Of those, 261,000 died or were killed in Auschwitz. How many of the rest perished in other camps or died on death marches is unknown.

Working as a cashier at a mini-market in the heart of Jerusalem, Ms. Sagir says she is asked about the number on her forearm about ten times a day. One time, a police officer said *"God creates the forgetfulness so we can forget."*, to which she responded *"Because of people like you who want to forget this, we will have it again."*[26]

---

at the high end, but the estimates he quotes in a subsequent note (44) are all around 200,000 (Friedman, 381, 384). The estimate of the number of mentally and physically disabled killed is more certain (Friedman, 138). On the number of homosexuals killed, Friedman notes that of the estimated 5,000–15,000 that ended up in concentration camps, two thirds died (395). The estimate on the number of non-Jewish Poles killed is from Kwiet and Matthaus (Kwiet, 258). Concerning the murder of Soviet POWs, Hannes Heer and Klaus Naumann write, in *War of Extermination: The German Military in World War II 1941-1944*: *"Between 22 June 1941 and the end of the war, roughly 5.7 million members of the Red Army fell into German hands. In January 1945, 930,000 were still in German camps. A million at most had been released, most of whom were so-called "volunteers" (Hilfswillige) for (often compulsory) auxiliary service in the Wehrmacht. Another 500,000, as estimated by the Army High Command, had either fled or been liberated. The remaining 3,300,000 (57.5 percent of the total) had perished."* (Heer, 80–81).

25   Gutman and Berenbaum note that this number is regarded as a minimum estimate.

26   Qtd. in Rudoren, "Proudly Bearing".

15

A BOMB

"My God, what have we done?"[1]

Captain Robert Lewis, co-pilot of B-29 bomber Enola Gay,
writing in the official log after dropping the atomic bomb
'Little Boy' on Hiroshima, August 6, 1945

O N SEPTEMBER 20, 2009, IRAN'S SUPREME LEADER,
Ayatollah Ali Khamenei declared: *"We fundamentally
reject nuclear weapons and prohibit the use and production
of nuclear weapons."* (qtd. in Erdbrink, "Iran Denies"). When
newly elected Iranian President Hassan Rouhani visited the
U.N. General Assembly in New York four years later, he con-
curred that Iran would never *"seek weapons of mass destruction, including nuclear weapons."* (qtd. in Erdbrink, "Iran's
Leaders").

Soothing words. Of course the main question in the West,
including Israel—especially Israel—is whether they are true.
Ever since an Iranian political opposition group in 2002
revealed that Iran had a nuclear program that included a
uranium enrichment plant in the vicinity of the city of Natanz
and a heavy water production plant at the city of Arak, the
developed world has stepped up its efforts to prevent Iran
from ever getting the bomb.[2]

---

1   Qtd. in MacPherson 2015.

2   On August 14, 2002, Alireza Jafarzadeh, spokesman for the National
Council of Resistance of Iran, presented new evidence about the existence of
secret nuclear facilities in the cities of Natanz and Arak ("Iran and Nuclear
Weapons").

One of the main aims of the so-called P5+1 nations, the five permanent members of the U.N. Security Council—the United States, Russia, China, Britain and France—plus Germany, has been to prevent Iran from enriching uranium to the point where building a nuclear weapon would only be a matter of months. To that end, the P5+1 have followed a dual-track strategy since 2006, combining negotiations with U.N. Security Council resolutions demanding the country to halt uranium enrichment and imposing sanctions to force it to comply.[3]-[4] Incidentally (or perhaps rather *not* incidentally), the P5 nations are also the first five nations that acquired the bomb for themselves.

Britain was the first country to take a serious stab at building a nuclear bomb, in 1941. A few years earlier, on December 17, 1938, the German chemist Otto Hahn and his assistant Fritz Strassman had discovered nuclear fission of the heavy element uranium—i.e., the splitting of its nucleus—after bombarding it with neutrons, causing the release of a great amount of energy in the process.

A couple of months later, physicists Enrico Fermi, Leó Szilárd and Herbert Anderson proved that bombarding uranium with neutrons resulted in significant neutron multiplication, thus setting off a self-propagating chain reaction capable of releasing massive amounts of energy (Anderson,

---

3   A possible third track is the frustration of Iran's nuclear program through covert means, e.g., cyber warfare. An example is the computer worm Stuxnet, discovered in 2010, which was inserted in Iran's nuclear facility at Natanz and reportedly destroyed a fifth of Iran's nuclear centrifuges. It has been speculated (though not proven) that the worm was created by the United States and/or Israel.

4   United Nations Security Council Resolution 1696, adopted on July 31, 2006, demanded Iran suspend its uranium enrichment program "*or face possible economic, diplomatic sanctions*". After the country failed to do so, United Nations Security Council Resolution 1737 was passed on December 23 that same year, imposing the first sanctions. Between 2007–10, these sanctions were subsequently expanded through resolutions 1747, 1803 and 1929 ("Security Council Committee").

"Neutron Production"). They immediately realized their discovery could lead to the development of a nuclear bomb. Szilárd later said: "*that night* [March 3, 1939, after the definitive experiment] *there was very little doubt in my mind that the world was headed for grief.*" (qtd. in Rhodes, 292).

Initially, it was believed that several tons of uranium were needed to achieve the 'critical mass' necessary for a sustained nuclear chain reaction.[5] Though possible, it would hardly be practical. Still, the estimated destructive capability of a nuclear bomb would be so great that it prompted Szilárd to write a concerned letter to U.S. President Franklin Roosevelt on August 2, 1939, less than a month before Hitler invaded Poland. The letter was signed by Albert Einstein, who had readily agreed to lend his signature after Szilárd told him about the concept of sustained nuclear chain reaction and his experiment proving it. "*Daran habe ich gar nicht gedacht!*" ("I never even thought of that!") Einstein famously replied after Szilárd's explanation (qtd. in Rhodes, 305). In the letter to Roosevelt, Szilárd theorized that a nuclear bomb "*carried by boat and exploded in a port, might very well destroy the whole port together with some of the surrounding territory. However, such bombs might very well prove to be too heavy for transportation by air.*" (Einstein 1939)..

But in March 1940, physicists Otto Frisch and Rudolf Peierls, both working at Birmingham University, calculated that only about one pound of pure uranium-235 (U-235) would be needed to produce a nuclear bomb with an explosive force equivalent to "*1,000 tons of dynamite*" (Frisch, "Memorandum"). They wrote a memo explaining the science that supported their conclusions and outlining the implications of their calculations—small bombs capable of massive

---

5   The German-Jewish physicist Rudolf Peierls, who had remained in England after Hitler came to power in 1933, initially calculated that the needed critical mass was "*of the order of tons*" (qtd. in Rhodes, 321). The theoretical physicist Werner Heisenberg, who would be part of the German nuclear weapon project, believed it was about one ton (Bernstein, 129).

destruction, large numbers of civilian casualties, including from nuclear radiation, and the urgency of getting the bomb before Germany.

It would later turn out that their calculations were incorrect (the minimum amount of U-235 needed for a sustained nuclear reaction is 115 pounds, not one) but the memorandum was a definite wake up call for the British, who soon established a committee, code-named M.A.U.D., to conduct a feasibility study on the production of a nuclear weapon (Rhodes, 340–41).

One year later, in the summer of 1941, as German tanks rolled into Russia during Operation Barbarossa, the M.A.U.D. committee reported that it would be possible to produce a nuclear bomb with a critical mass of about 25 lb (11,5 kg) of active material, that this bomb could be ready by the end of 1943 and that a plant capable of producing three such bombs per month would cost approximately 5 million pounds (M.A.U.D., "Report"). All of these statements would later prove incorrect, but the British war cabinet was sold. Churchill dryly commented: "*Although personally I am quite content with the existing explosives, I feel we must not stand in the path of improvement.*" (qtd. in Rhodes, 372).

One of the main reasons for the British effort was fear the Nazis would get the bomb. Germany had been at the vanguard of some early discoveries in the field of nuclear physics and had produced several prominent physicists, though a good deal of them had quit the country after 1933—many because they were Jewish—among them Albert Einstein, Leó Szilárd, Max Born, Otto Frisch, Rudolf Peierls, Lise Meitner, Edward Teller and Hans Bethe, to name a few.[6-7]

---

6   Enrico Fermi emigrated from Benito Mussolini's fascist Italy to the United States in the late 1930s, because of new Italian racial laws affecting his Jewish wife.

7   Several of the emigrated scientists had already made key discoveries in nuclear physics and would come to play an important role in the American effort to develop a nuclear bomb, the Manhattan Project. Who knows what

The British had also been alarmed by German efforts to produce greater quantities of heavy water at the Norwegian Hydrogen plant Norsk Hydro (Bernstein, 27). Heavy water, as had been recently discovered, could be used to produce plutonium, another element besides uranium capable of sustaining a nuclear chain reaction. German interest in heavy water therefore indicated they had made strong advances in nuclear research and might be attempting to produce enough fissile material for a bomb.

Later in the war it would become clear that around the same time the Americans decided to pull out all the stops in developing the bomb, the Nazis decided not to, chiefly because the scientists involved had reported that the development of a nuclear weapon would take too long to make a difference in the war.[8]-[9]

Of course the British did not know exactly how far the Germans had progressed, and fear can be a powerful motivator. Therefore, aside from pouring resources into their own project, code-named *Tube Alloys,* they also sent Australian physicist and member of the M.A.U.D. Committee Dr. Mark Oliphant to the United States, to try and persuade

---

would have happened if Hitler had been just a warmonger, instead of being equally hell-bent on the destruction of the Jews.

8   They were partially right, since Germany had indeed already been defeated by the time the Americans acquired the bomb. Then again, with the atomic bomb being such a game changer, any German military victory would have been rendered meaningless the moment one of its (still undefeated) enemies acquired it.

9   In *Hitler's Uranium Club: The Secret Recordings at Farm Hall*, Jeremy Bernstein publishes a fascinating discussion—held on August 6, 1945, just after the announcement that an atomic bomb had been dropped—between some of the most important German scientists who the Allies believed had worked on Nazi Germany's nuclear program (115–25). In an operation code-named 'Epsilon', meant to uncover how close Germany had come to a nuclear bomb, the scientists, who were detained by the Allies after the defeat of Germany, among them Otto Hahn and Werner Heisenberg, were interned at Farm Hall, a bugged house in Godmanchester, England. During the discussion, they express disbelief about the American success of developing and deploying a nuclear weapon and contemplate why the German effort was unsuccessful.

the Americans to step up their efforts into nuclear weapons research. It worked, because in October 1941 President Roosevelt approved the atomic program, though it would be the Japanese attack on Pearl Harbor a few months later that really ignited American enthusiasm for the project.[10]

Unlike the Germans, who were too impatient and had scared away one too many brilliant scientist, or the British, who were too optimistic about the cost, or the Russians, who were simply too busy fighting for their lives, the Americans had plenty of brilliant scientists (several of whom were coming from Germany), plenty of money, plenty of resources and a highly supportive government. Between 1942–45, the U.S. would spend a total of $1.9 billion on its nuclear program, known as the *Manhattan Project*, the equivalent of $25 billion in 2014 (Schwartz, 58).

The Manhattan Project was a huge undertaking, employing some 130,000 people at its peak, the vast majority construction workers working on the various nuclear reactors (Jones, 344). But despite the magnitude of the workforce, very few people knew the full extent of what was actually going on. They erected accommodations, constructed roads, put up fences, pushed buttons, operated levers and watched meters, but they did not know what for.

One woman who worked in the laundry at the Monsanto Chemical Company, explained: "*The uniforms were first washed, then ironed, all new buttons sewed on and passed to me. I'd hold the uniform up to a special instrument and if I heard a clicking noise - I'd throw it back in to be done all over again. That's all I did - all day long.*" (qtd. in Atomic Energy Commission, "Script", 7).

_____

10   After the war, Leó Szilárd said: "*If Congress knew the true history of the atomic energy project, I have no doubt but that it would create a special medal to be given to meddling foreigners for distinguished services, and Dr. Oliphant would be the first to receive one.*" (qtd. in Rhodes, 372).

Another, working at the Carbide and Carbon Chemical Company Plant, said: "*I stood in front of a panel board with a dial. When the hand moved from zero to 100 I would turn a valve. The hand would fall back to zero. I turn another valve and the hand would go back to 100. All day long. Watch a hand go from zero to 100 then turn a valve. It got so I was doing it in my sleep.*"(qtd. in Atomic Energy Commission, "Script", 8).

Some only found out years later they had worked at a place that had been part of the Manhattan Project, others never did. Of course there were also those, working at the project's principal laboratory in Los Alamos, New Mexico, who realized what they had been working on right after the Trinity Test, on July 16, 1945, when the first nuclear device was detonated at the Alamogordo Bombing and Gunnery Range (present-day White Sands Missile Range), some 200 miles from Los Alamos.

No more than a handful of people knew what was going on before that day, and even the few scientists present at the test didn't fully know what to expect. Would it work? Were they standing at a safe enough distance? What would it look like?

Before the test, Edward Teller, one of the theoretical physicists, had raised the possibility of the explosion igniting the atmosphere, which could perhaps cause a chain reaction eliminating all life on the planet (Rhodes, 418). Teller himself and fellow physicist Hans Bethe had subsequently calculated that such a self-propagating chain reaction was highly unlikely to occur, but did the calculation also prevent Teller from imagining—if only for a moment—a burning atmosphere consuming all in its path and ending life as we know it, as he was watching 'the gadget' (as it was called) fall from the bomb tower in Alamogordo? Indeed, did it prevent the others from thinking they might be at the verge of unleashing forces they still knew so little about? Especially since the evening before the explosion, Enrico Fermi, in an attempt to alleviate the nervous waiting, had offered to take bets from the other scientists on whether or not the bomb would ignite the atmosphere, and if so, whether it would destroy just New Mexico or the entire world (Rhodes, 664).

Fortunately, life as we know it was not eliminated, though the gadget did explode with a force equivalent to about 20,000 tons of TNT, big enough to completely evaporate the center of a city. There was a bright light that could be seen up to 180 miles away, a thundering shockwave traveling a 100 miles in each direction—even breaking a window 125 miles away—and a great mushroom cloud rising up 41,000 feet from the epicenter of the explosion (Groves, 1–2). Some called it beautiful.

Even before the Trinity Test Leó Szilárd had started circulating a petition among scientists working at the Manhattan Project, that sought to discourage President Harry S. Truman—who had succeeded to the presidency just a few months earlier, when Roosevelt died in office—from using the bomb against Japan. Szilárd suggested to first make public the terms of surrender to Japan and give the country a chance to lay down its arms, before resorting to the use of atomic bombs.

He also warned that using the bomb might "[open] *the door to an era of devastation on an unimaginable scale.*" (Szilard, "Petition"). And that, if *"rival powers"* would be permitted *"to be in uncontrolled possession of these new means of destruction, the cities of the United States as well as the cities of other nations will be in continuous danger of sudden annihilation.".*

The petition was signed by 69 other scientists but never made it through to the President.

An advisory scientific panel, consisting of Robert Oppenheimer, Enrico Fermi and others, found itself fundamentally divided as well, as became clear from its June 16 'Recommendations on the Immediate Use of Nuclear Weapons', with some favoring a *"military application best designed to induce surrender"*, and others proposing a *"purely technical demonstration"* (Cantelon, 47–48).

But there was still a war on and many in the government and the military saw the atom bomb as a quick way to end it, without further loss of American lives. No one knew for sure how many American soldiers would be killed in an all-out assault on an all-out resistant Japan, but it was clear the price would likely be very high, with official estimates running from 200,000 to as high as 4 million casualties.[11] On the other hand, key people in the government and the military also realized at this point that the surrender of Japan was only a matter of months, three to six at the most. In other words, an invasion might not even be necessary.

Still, there were other reasons for wanting to actually use the bomb and drop it on a populated city instead of an uninhabited island somewhere in the Pacific. For one, a demonstration could go wrong. The prospect of telling the whole world about a $2 billion super bomb that had been worked on for three years, only to see it fail miserably at a test in front of the enemy (present and future ones) was not particularly alluring to military strategists. Dropping the bomb unannounced would give away far less in case of failure and insulate the U.S. from a potentially highly embarrassing incident.

And then there were the Russians, who everybody knew would be allies only for as long as the war lasted. Trying to wait out the Japanese would see a bigger piece of the Asian pie going to the Soviet Union, all the more so because the war in Europe had ended, freeing up Soviet forces to be redeployed in Asia. Also, in terms of containment, what better message could be sent to an overbearing, aggressive dictator like Joseph Stalin than dropping a nuclear weapon on an enemy city? Not only would it prove to him the U.S. really had the bomb, but also that it wasn't afraid to use it, thus effectively killing two birds with one atomic bomb.

So they dropped it.

---

11   See chapter 13, WW 2.0, note 34.

Twice.

The uranium-based atomic bomb *Little Boy* was detonated over Hiroshima on August 6, 1945, at 08:15 local time, with a force equivalent to 16 kilotons of TNT, destroying 4.4 square miles. (Young, 42–61; McRaney, 4). Between 70,000–80,000 people were killed by the blast and subsequent firestorm, with an equal number of people injured (United States Government, "U.S. Strategic Bombing Survey", 16).[12] Three days later, on August 9, the plutonium-based atomic bomb *Fat Man* was detonated over Nagasaki, at 11:01 local time, with a force equivalent to 21 kilotons of TNT (Young, 42–61). An estimated 35,000–40,000 people died instantly, with about the same number of injured (United States Government, "U.S. Strategic Bombing Survey", 4).[13] The Empire of Japan surrendered six days later, on August 15.[14]

As Leó Szilárd had predicted, the use of the A-bomb on Japan immediately triggered an international nuclear arms race. On August 29, 1949, only four years after Hiroshima and Nagasaki, the Russians conducted their own first successful nuclear weapons test, code-named *First Lightning*.

The Soviet atomic bomb project benefitted greatly from captured German facilities, resources, research and scientific personnel. The Russians also acquired valuable information

---

12　The survey acknowledges that accurate figures are impossible to give, since many people had already left because of declining activity in the cities, the constant threat of incendiary raids and government evacuation programs (United States Government, "U.S. Strategic Bombing Survey", 16).

13　In Hiroshima, a surging fire storm increased the devastation caused by the bomb, as did the flat terrain of the city. As the U.S. Strategic Bombing Survey states: *"In Nagasaki, no such fire storm arose, and the uneven terrain of the city confined the maximum intensity of the damage to the valley over which the bomb exploded. The area of nearly complete devastation was thus much smaller; only about 1.8 square miles."* (United States Government, "U.S. Strategic Bombing Survey", 4).

14　The official Japanese instrument of surrender was signed on September 2, 1945.

from atomic spy Klaus Fuchs, a German-born physicist who had worked with Rudolf Peierls on the Tube Alloys project and under Hans Bethe at the Los Alamos Laboratory.[15]

When the United States refused to share nuclear technology with the United Kingdom after the war—even though the U.K. had shared its knowledge with the U.S.—the British restarted their own nuclear program, successfully detonating their first atomic weapon on October 3, 1952, in the lagoon between the Montebello Islands, in Western Australia.

Realizing it had to join the atomic club if it wanted to remain a global power (and it most definitely did), France started a nuclear weapons program of its own in 1956. The French conducted their first successful test on February 13, 1960, in the Algerian Sahara desert.

China started a nuclear weapons program around the same time as France, but it took the Chinese a few years longer to get to their first successful test, on October 16, 1964. Since then, several other countries have joined the atomic club, India in 1974, Pakistan in 1998 and North Korea in 2006; Israel is also believed to possess nuclear weapons, although it has never publicly confirmed this.[16]

While the nuclear arsenals of Britain, France and China never exceeded the hundreds, the U.S. and the U.S.S.R went out of their way to achieve Mutually Assured Destruction (MAD) many times over, building up arsenals of tens of thousands of nuclear warheads, keeping strategic nuclear bombers in the air, nuclear submarines at sea and equipping

---

15   Fuchs had fled Nazi Germany in 1933 because of his communist beliefs and was granted British citizenship in 1942. He gave the Soviets valuable information on the required atomic mass and the method of detonation, among other things (Trenear-Harvey, 78–79). Early 1950, Fuchs was arrested, tried and convicted to fourteen years imprisonment. After his release, he was allowed to emigrate to East Germany, where he continued his scientific career. He died in 1988, one year before the fall of the Berlin Wall.

16   Though these countries are known or believed to possess nuclear weapons, they are not recognized by the Non-Proliferation Treaty as 'nuclear-weapons states'. Only the first five are.

underground missile silos with land-based intercontinental ballistic missiles (ICBMs), so nuclear retaliation was assured in any event.[17]

During the Cuban missile crisis of October 1962, all this aggressive-defensive posturing would bring both countries—and their allies—on the verge of assuring each other's destruction beyond the theoretical, but at the last moment saner heads prevailed.[18]

Since the 1980s, the two nuclear superpowers have worked together in reducing their gargantuan nuclear stockpiles. As of 2014, Russia still possesses an estimated 8,000 nuclear weapons though, while the U.S. is not far behind with some 7,300 nuclear weapons (Kristensen, 97).

Since they both still have so many, perhaps they could lease a couple to Iran on the condition it won't develop a nuclear weapon of its own.

---

17   As of 2014, the British nuclear weapons inventory counts an estimated 225 nuclear warheads, with a peak of some 500 in the 1970s (Kristensen, 97). For France, the total arsenal is estimated to be around 300, while China is believed to possess approximately 250 nuclear weapons, according to Hans Kristensen in "Worldwide deployments of nuclear weapons, 2014". Estimates of between 2,000–3,000 Chinese nuclear warheads have also surfaced, but these appear to be based on unsubstantiated rumors.

18   See chapter 18—How Vasili Arkhipov Saved the World.

PART III
WORLD 2.0

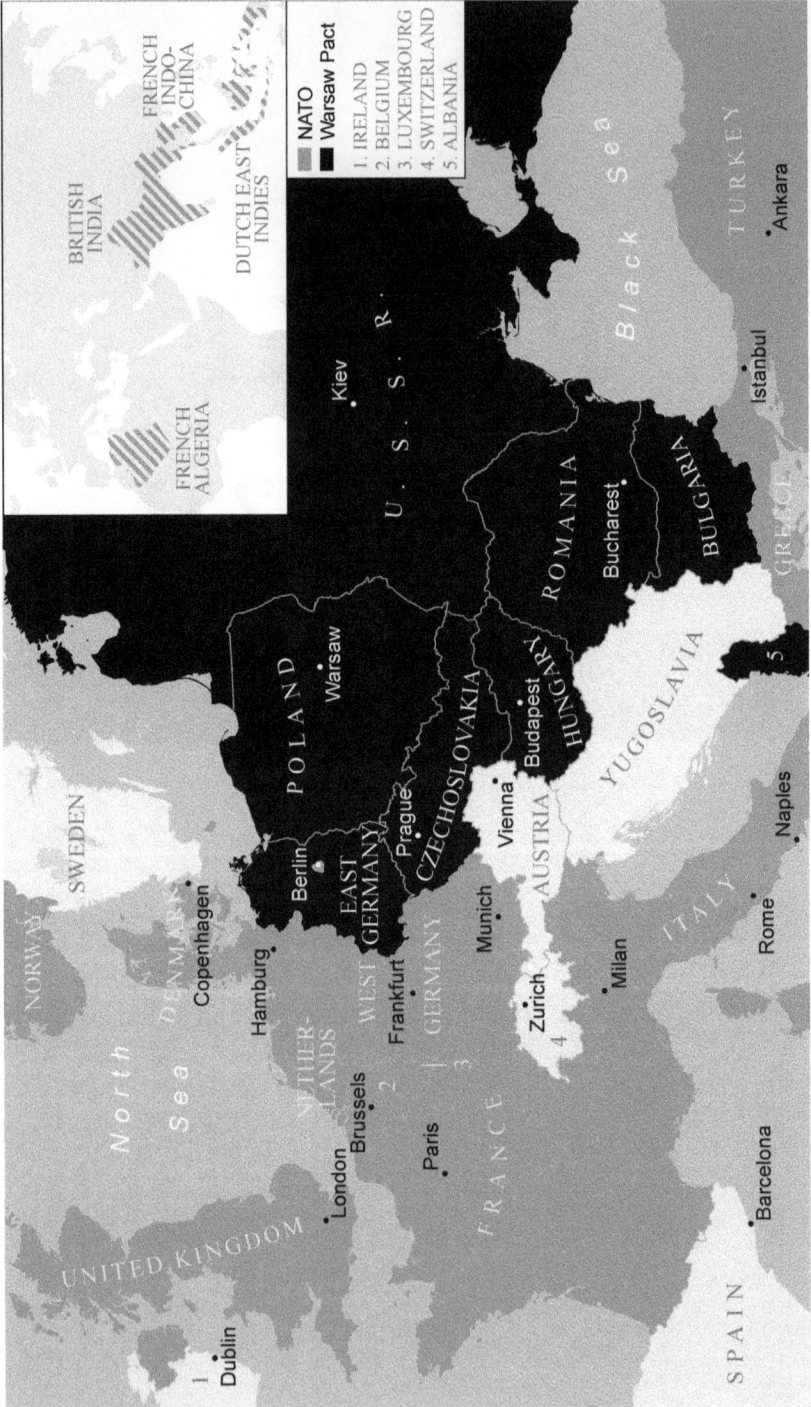

Map 11: NATO and the Warsaw Pact, c. 1955-66

NATO
Warsaw Pact

1. IRELAND
2. BELGIUM
3. LUXEMBOURG
4. SWITZERLAND
5. ALBANIA

BRITISH INDIA

FRENCH INDO-CHINA

DUTCH EAST INDIES

FRENCH ALGERIA

U. S. S. R.

Kiev

ROMANIA

Bucharest

BULGARIA

TURKEY

Ankara

Istanbul

Black Sea

GREECE

POLAND

Warsaw

HUNGARY

Budapest

YUGOSLAVIA

5

CZECHOSLOVAKIA

Prague

Vienna

AUSTRIA

Naples

Rome

ITALY

Berlin

EAST GERMANY

Munich

WEST GERMANY

Frankfurt

Zurich

Milan

4

SWEDEN

NORWAY

DENMARK

Copenhagen

Hamburg

NETHER-LANDS

Brussels

2

3

Paris

FRANCE

North Sea

London

UNITED KINGDOM

Dublin

1

Barcelona

SPAIN

16

A NEW WORLD ORDER

"Out of this conflict have come powerful military nations, now fully trained and equipped for war. But they have no right to dominate the world. It is rather the duty of these powerful nations to assume the responsibility for leadership toward a world of peace. That is why we have here resolved that power and strength shall be used not to wage war, but to keep the world at peace, and free from the fear of war."[1]

President Harry S. Truman,
address in San Francisco at the closing session
of the United Nations Conference, June 26, 1945

ON THE EVENING OF OCTOBER 9, 1944, British Prime Minister Winston Churchill decided to talk realpolitik with Russian leader Joseph Stalin. Meeting in the Soviet dictator's rather gloomy office in the Kremlin, Churchill said: *"Let us settle about our affairs in the Balkans. Your armies are in Romania and Bulgaria. We have interests, missions, and agents there. Don't let us get at cross-purposes in small ways. So far as Britain and Russia are concerned, how would it do for you to have ninety percent predominance in Romania, for us to have ninety percent of the say in Greece, and go fifty-fifty about Yugoslavia?"* (Churchill, "Triumph and Tragedy", 227).

While his words were being translated, Churchill produced a scrap of paper and wrote down the names of Romania, Greece, Yugoslavia, Hungary and Bulgaria, adding the percentages he had just proposed.

---

1   Truman, "Address in San Francisco".

He then pushed the paper across the table to Stalin, who looked at it for a moment and took a thoughtful drag from his pipe. *"Then he took his blue pencil and made a large tick upon it, and passed it back to us. It was all settled in no more time than it takes to set down...After this there was a long silence. The pencilled paper lay in the centre of the table. At length I said, "Might it not be thought rather cynical if it seemed we had disposed of these issues so fateful to millions of people, in such an offhand manner? Let us burn the paper." "No, you keep it.", said Stalin."* (Churchill, "Triumph and Tragedy", 227–28).[2]

Poland was conspicuously left out of the 'naughty document', as it would come to be known.[3] The Red Army had already advanced deep into Poland and Churchill knew Stalin would never agree to relinquish it and let the Poles have free elections. On the contrary, the Soviet leader intended to annex Poland and use it as a buffer zone between Russia and Western Europe.

Churchill did make a few half-hearted attempts to persuade Stalin to restore Poland's sovereignty after the war, but both men knew that Russia held all the cards; the Red Army was already in control of most of Eastern Europe, while the British could only play second fiddle to the Americans on the Western front. And judging from America's quick departure from Europe after World War I, chances were U.S. troops would not linger this time either. In other words, weakened and financially exhausted Britain and France would probably have to keep the Russians at bay themselves in Western Europe, while at the same time trying to preserve their colonies. Not an easy task.

Churchill had therefore already written off Eastern Europe entirely before even stepping into Stalin's office that October evening. He had only one goal: to make sure Stalin would

2   Churchill did keep the piece of paper. The handwritten document is preserved in Britain's Public Record Office, PREM 3/66/7, available on request.

3   The use of the epithet 'naughty document' seems to have originated with Churchill himself (Blake, 320).

stay out of Greece. A free and democratic Greece was of vital importance to the British because of its strategic position in the Mediterranean, close to Egypt, Britain's gateway to Asia and its most important oversees colony, British India.

Stalin did indeed stay out of Greece after the war, but when it came to Eastern Europe the only percentage acceptable to the Russian leader turned out to be 100. And who was going to stop him? The exhausted British? The French, who had just gotten their country back and now had to deal with a serious uprising in French Indochina? The Poles, who were still reeling from five years of brutal occupation and extermination? The Americans, who were so eager to go home?

A new geopolitical reality was thus fast emerging in the second half of the 1940s, one in which the old European powers proved to be frighteningly powerless and two new, ideologically opposed superpowers emerged as the real victors of the Second World War. Driving through the rubble and ruins of once proud and industrious German cities, it did not take the Americans long to realize that this time—contrary to the end of the First World War—there would be no rapid return to political isolationism. This time, they would have to stay.

Even if the U.S. had the bomb and the Soviet Union did not, everybody knew it would likely take the Russians no more than a couple of years to follow suit now that the nuclear cat was out of the bag, and what would become of Western Europe then? A contingency plan prepared by the U.S. military in the late 1940s, code-named *Operation Dropshot*, expected a Soviet takeover of Western Europe around 1957 (Mastny, 146–49). The plan called for the use of tactical nuclear weapons in the eventuality of war with the Russians in Europe.[4] But of course prevention was better.

---

4   Declassified in 1977, Operation Dropshot stated that: "*An important element in blunting Soviet offensives would be the use of atomic weapons and conventional bombs against LOCs* [lines of communication], *supply bases, and troop concentrations in the USSR, in the satellites, and in overrun countries which*

To contain Stalin, the U.S. therefore opted for the three-pronged strategy of rebuild, defend and unite in Western Europe. This included West Germany, not just because of its strategic geographic location—it shared a border with Soviet-controlled East Germany and Czechoslovakia—but also because it was clear that economic recovery in Europe would not be possible without the reconstruction of the German industrial base (Leffler, 155–57).[5]

In April 1948 the United States launched the European Recovery Program, to help rebuild Europe. Better known as the Marshall Plan—after Secretary of State George C. Marshall, who had announced the plan a year earlier—it would disburse a little over $12 billion (the equivalent of about $115 billion in 2014) in economic recovery funds in Western Europe during the four years it was active, which were mostly used for the import of fuel, food, feed, fertilizers, raw materials, semi-manufactured products, machines, vehicles and equipment (Hogan, 414–15).

Stalin initially welcomed the plan, until he realized the funds would be disbursed on the condition of economic cooperation under the supervision of the United States,

---

directly support Soviet advances. The use of atomic bombs against satellite and overrun areas, however, should be confined as far as possible to those targets the destruction of which would not involve large masses of population (...) it is considered that a reasonable requirement for atomic bombs on target for this purpose might be on the order of an additional **one hundred atomic bombs** [boldface added] of a type not now available but which are considered capable of development and production in sufficient quantity by 1957" (United States, "Dropshot", 4.a.2.b). Note that this would be on top of the 75–100 atomic bombs necessary for attacks on "atomic-assembly facilities, storage points, and heavy-bomber airfields" (United States, "Dropshot", 4.a.2.a).

5   At the Potsdam Conference (July 17-August 2, 1945), the United States, the Soviet Union and the United Kingdom had agreed to divide Germany into four military occupation zones, with the United states in charge in the south, France in the southwest, Britain in the northwest and the Soviet Union in the east. In 1949, the three zones occupied by the Western powers were rejoined in the newly formed Federal Republic of Germany. The Soviet-occupied zone became the German Democratic Republic that same year.

thus increasing U.S. influence in recipient countries, at the expense of Soviet influence (Wettig, 138–39). Even worse in the eyes of Stalin, or at least just as worse, was that Germany, which had been defeated only a few years ago at a staggering price in Russian lives, was to be included as a recipient of the Marshall funds. Stalin therefore discouraged (i.e., forbade) the Eastern European countries under his control from taking part in the program (Wettig, 138–39).

Of course for the United States, investing in the economic recovery of Europe was not simply an act of altruism from a generous victor. Apart from wanting to prevent a weak Europe from becoming an easy prey for the Soviet Union—which by now spanned from the Bering Strait to Berlin—the U.S. also had a more direct, economic interest in a strong European recovery. With the war industry winding down and many soldiers returning home to civilian life and looking for work, the U.S. economy was running the risk of entering a recession. U.S. export needed to grow and for that European economies needed to be restored to their pre-war levels (Davidson, 186–87).

Another important pillar in countering the Soviet threat in Europe was European unification, something that could also help to permanently contain Germany. To this end, the American Committee on United Europe (ACUE) was founded in 1948, which before long began to covertly funnel monies to several European federalist movements (Scott-Smith, 46–47).[6] The early leadership of the ACUE read as a who's who of U.S. central intelligence chiefs; its first chairman was the wartime head of the OSS (the precursor of the CIA), William Joseph Donovan, its first vice-chairman was Allen Dulles, who would succeed Walter Bedell Smith—another board member of the ACUE—as director of the CIA in 1953.

---

6   For a more detailed explanation of the ACUE, also see *OSS, CIA and European Unity: The American Committee on United Europe, 1948- 60*, by Richard Aldrich.

In May 1948, 713 delegates from all over Europe—political leaders, philosophers, lawyers, historians, journalists, entrepreneurs, professors—met in The Hague, the Netherlands, to talk about political, economic and monetary unification of Europe (Laffan, 37–38). The Hague Congress led to the establishment of several pan-European organizations, such as the Council of Europe, the College of Europe and the European Movement, a federalist movement striving for a United States of Europe.[7]

One of the first Presidents of the European Movement was former French Prime Minister and Foreign Minister Robert Schuman. He was the first to propose a supranational European organization for the creation and regulation of a common market for coal and steel, on May 9, 1950.[8] Two years later, the European Coal and Steel Community (ECSC) was established by West Germany, France, Italy, the Netherlands, Belgium and Luxembourg. Its success spurred the subsequent creation of the European Economic Community, in 1957, which would later become part of the European Union (in 2009).

Meanwhile, despite growing tensions between the Soviet Union and the United States during the second half of the 1940s, there was also some global institutional progress. Realizing that mankind might not survive another world war—especially in light of the arrival of the atomic bomb—that advances in technology were making the world ever smaller and that a better permanent forum for the international community was badly needed, the United Nations was established on October 24, 1945.

---

7   The European Movement was heavily financed by the ACUE in the 1950s (Aldrich, 184–85).

8   In the EU, May 9 is still celebrated as Europe Day, in commemoration to the historical significance of the Schuman Declaration. Schuman, who was also the first President of the European Parliament, is considered one of the Founding Fathers of the European Union.

Three years later, in a bid to prevent atrocities such as had been committed by Nazi Germany and the Empire of Japan from ever happening again, the United Nations General Assembly took a first step towards universal protection of fundamental human rights when it adopted the Universal Declaration of Human Rights (UDHR) on December 10, 1948, acknowledging in its preamble that "*recognition of the inherent dignity and of the equal and inalienable rights of all members of the human family is the foundation of freedom, justice and peace in the world*" (United Nations, "Declaration").[9]

Though the UDHR was not meant to be legally binding as such, the fundamental rights enunciated in articles two to twenty-one quickly became part of international customary law, not least because of their extensive use in national constitutions, international legislation and decisions by national and international courts (Humphrey, 28–29).[10]

But however noble and hopeful these early post-WW II era dreams of a new world were, the claims and agreements of the real world—divided along the same old lines of national interest—quickly caught up with them, giving the noble dreamers a rude wake-up call. Because not only did the Soviet Union still move in to secure control of Poland, Bulgaria, Hungary, Czechoslovakia, Romania, Albania and East Germany, several European powers also took steps to retain their colonies, just as they had done after the First World War.

Germany and Italy were forced to give up their colonies by the victors, but France sent troops to Indochina early 1946, to deal with communist revolutionary Ho Chi Minh and his Viet Minh, which sought Vietnamese independence from

---

9   While there were no votes against the Universal Declaration, eight members of the United Nations General Assembly abstained from voting, among them the Soviet Union.

10   John Peters Humphrey wrote the first draft of the Universal Declaration.

French rule. Around the same time, the Netherlands also sent a fighting force to Southeast Asia, to suppress a nationalist revolution in the Dutch East Indies. Both colonial powers used a significant part of the funds they received from the U.S. Marshall Plan to finance their expeditionary forces.

By the end of 1948 the Dutch had amassed some 140,000 troops in the East Indies, but international pressure for a cease fire mounted, including from the U.S., which threatened to stop its financial aid to the Netherlands and even exclude it from the pending North Atlantic Treaty (Groen, 32–35). Out of options, the Dutch had no choice but to give in to the pressure and recognize the independence of Indonesia in 1949.

Meanwhile, the British took a different tack in dealing with their own most prized Asian colony, India. During the war, the British Empire had suppressed Indian independence movements, but now that the Axis had finally been defeated, Britain found itself in dire financial straits, leading it to quickly reconcile itself with the prospect of Indian independence (Knight, 152–53).[11] British India thus became independent in 1947, when it was partitioned into two independent states, India, predominantly Hindu, and Pakistan, predominantly Muslim.[12]

By that time France was already knee-deep in violent conflict in Indochina. Between 1946–54, the French—with

---

11   Of course there were also other factors at play that nudged the British government towards the decision to quit India. For one, Indian nationalism had grown during the war years, increasing the likelihood of having to send extra troops to suppress nationalist movements if the colony was to be retained, a prospect the cabinet certainly wanted to avoid, especially in light of the recent difficulties the French and the Dutch had encountered in this respect. Another factor was that the British public was more focused on the problems at home than on retaining India.

12   In 1971, civil war broke out between (West) Pakistan and its province East Pakistan, located in the Bengal region (east of India), after the Pakistani government answered the latter's demand for more autonomy with a campaign of military terror. East Pakistan subsequently declared itself the independent state of Bangladesh. When India joined the war on the side of Bangladesh a few months later, Pakistan was quickly forced to surrender.

increasing financial support from the United States—fought the communist forces of Ho Chi Minh—supported by Red China and Soviet Russia—until finally deciding to pull out after losing big at the battle of Dien Bien Phu (March-May 1954).[13] Soon after the Americans moved in, first with military advisors and financial aid, later with active combat troops, to prevent a communist takeover of South Vietnam.[14] They too would fail though against Ho Chi Minh and his most prominent General, Vo Nguyen Giap.[15]

Just a few months after the end of the First Indochina War another French colonial war started, this time in French Algeria, North Africa. Determined not to let another colony slip away, the French military went all out to push back the Algerian fighters of the National Liberation Front (FLN). They succeeded, but only through the use of brutal measures such as torture and bombings targeting civilians. In 1958, the French Fourth Republic, already unstable and utterly incapable of dealing with the political tensions the war created, collapsed. General Charles de Gaulle, hero of the French

---

13   According to the so-called 'Pentagon Papers', an internal study on U.S. involvement in Vietnam between 1945–67, done by the U.S. Defense department between 1967–69, the decision to provide support to the French was taken "*in spite of the U.S. desire to avoid direct involvement in a colonial war*" (United States, "Pentagon Papers", IV. A. 2., i). The reason the United States nevertheless chose the side of the colonial power rather than that of the independence movement (as it had done with the Dutch East Indies, for instance) had everything to do with the "*broader considerations of U.S. policy for the containment of communism in Europe and Asia.*" (United States, "Pentagon Papers", II. A. 1–2). The Pentagon Papers were partially leaked to the press in 1971. In 2011, the entire study was declassified and publicly released.

14   Between 1954–60, Vietnam was the third largest non-NATO recipient of U.S. economic and military assistance (United States, "Pentagon Papers", IV. A. 4., 1.1). The Joint Chiefs of Staff nevertheless determined in 1960 that despite these efforts, the Vietnamese National Army was still inadequately trained (United States, "Pentagon Papers", 1.1ff.). For information on the buildup of U.S. combat troops, see Part IV. C. 4–5 of the Pentagon Papers.

15   Vo Nguyen Giap died on October 4, 2013, at the age of 102.

resistance in WW II, was subsequently asked to come out of retirement and create order out of chaos.[16]

De Gaulle initially seemed to favor resolving the conflict by offering French Algeria more autonomy, albeit in close association with France.[17] He also quickly initiated a financial aid program for Algeria, to the tune of about $200 million a year, to show the benefits of staying in a close relationship with France (Kolodziej, 457). At the same time he continued the war against the insurgents.

But when the military campaign failed to defeat the insurgents and public opinion—both at home and abroad—turned against the ongoing war, de Gaulle gave in and announced France would accept a political solution for the war, based on the right to self-determination.[18] In a subsequent referendum, held in January 1961, both the French and Algerian population voted overwhelmingly in favor of the French government submitting a bill for Algerian self-determination (Kolodziej, 460). In the Algerian independence referendum

---

16   The order De Gaulle created was the establishment of the Fifth Republic, a presidential constitutional republic, as opposed to the parliamentary republic of the Fourth Republic, which, ineffective and politically unstable, had counted no less than twenty-six governments in the twelve years years of its existence (Wakeman, 73).

17   In his book *Mémoires d'Espoir* (Memoirs of Hope), de Gaulle wrote that "*there was in my opinion no other solution than that of Algerian self-determination*" (qtd. in Berstein, 28). French historian Serge Bernstein writes in *The Republic of de Gaulle 1958–1969*, however, that there is no proof this really was de Gaulle's plan from the outset, but that on the contrary it appears de Gaulle had no clear idea yet as to how to resolve the conflict when he returned to power in 1958 (Berstein, 28–30).

18   De Gaulle's decision to withdraw from Algeria met with strong resistance from parts of the French Army, who subsequently organized themselves in the *Organization de l'Armée Secrète* (Organization of the Secret Army, OAS). The OAS launched a bombing campaign to stop the political process of withdrawal from Algeria. In 1962, the group even attempted to assassinate President de Gaulle in the Paris suburb of Petit-Clamart. De Gaulle's car was hit with fourteen bullets, but miraculously nobody was hurt. The mastermind behind the attack, French Air Force lieutenant-colonel Jean-Marie Bastien-Thiry, was sentenced to death and executed by firing squad on March 11, 1963.

held on July 1 of the following year, 99 percent of the votes were in favor of independence (Berstein, 56). Of course by then most of the French and Algerians loyal to France had already left Algeria.

During the final stages of the Algerian War, a flurry of other African colonies—most of them French or British—also declared themselves independent. Cameroon, Chad, Republic of the Congo, Cote d'Ivoire, Gabon, Mali, Senegal, Mauritania, Niger, Togo, Central African Republic, Madagascar, Nigeria, Somaliland and Belgian Congo all in 1960, Tanzania, Sierra Leone and British Cameroon in 1961 and Uganda in 1962. Within 20 years after the end of the Second World War, the right to self-determination as recognized in Chapter 1, Article 1 of the United Nations Charter, thus became reality for dozens of former European colonies in Asia, Africa and the Middle East.

Colonialism was out, ideological imperialism was in. From the mid-1940s until the collapse of the U.S.S.R in 1991, much of the world would be divided between East and West, the former dominated by the Soviet Union, the latter by the United States.

In 1949, Western countries united themselves militarily in the North Atlantic Treaty Organization (NATO), in an effort to better coordinate their defenses. Six years later, on May 14, 1955—five days after Germany was admitted to NATO—the U.S.S.R and its Eastern European satellite states founded their own mutual defense organization, the Warsaw Pact.

For the next four decades, the United States and Russia would keep themselves and their allies in a continuous state of political and military tension. A 'cold war', relying on rational minds, strict rules of engagement and Mutual Assured Destruction (MAD) to prevent it from going hot—and nuclear. Apart from direct military confrontation and the use of nuclear weapons pretty much everything was allowed to gain an edge, including spying, sabotage, propaganda and of course the fighting or financing (or both) of proxy wars, such as in Korea, Vietnam and Afghanistan.

In short, for the first time in 500 years, the naughty documents were no longer being produced by Europe.

17

THE SPACE RACE

"We choose to go to the moon. We choose to go to the moon in this decade and do the other things, not because they are easy, but because they are hard, because that goal will serve to organize and measure the best of our energies and skills, because that challenge is one that we are willing to accept, one we are unwilling to postpone, and one which we intend to win, and the others, too."[1]

President John F. Kennedy, September 12, 1962

ON AUGUST 25, 2012, SPACE PROBE VOYAGER 1 became the first manmade object ever to leave the solar system and enter interstellar space (Barnes 2013). Launched on September 5, 1977, its primary mission was to study the outer planets in our solar system, a mission it completed in 1980.

After that it just kept going, traveling at a velocity relative to the sun of 17 km/s. As of July 2014, it was about 19.2 billion km/11.9 billion mi from the Sun, about 130 times farther than the distance from the Earth to the Sun (NASA, "Voyager"). Voyager mission control was still sending and/or receiving data to/from the probe every day, which, traveling at the speed of light, took about seventeen hours to reach its destination.

Packed with scientific instruments—a handful of them still working as of 2014, thirty-seven years after the start of the mission—Voyager 1 was meant to give us new insights about

---

1   Kennedy, "Rice University".

278 — WORLD 2.0

our solar system. A rather lofty goal, especially considering the more down-to-earth military objectives that initially propelled mankind into space.

The Space Age began on October 3, 1942, in Nazi Germany, when rocket scientist Wernher von Braun and his team succeeded in launching an A-4 rocket—better known as the V-2—that reached outer space (Neufeld, 164).[2] The world's first ballistic missile, it could travel at 5,760 kph/3,580 mph and had a range of 320 km/200 mi. In all, close to 6,000 V-2s were produced, of which approximately 3,200 were launched against Allied targets, most of them targeting Antwerp and London (Neufeld, 263–64). The last one was fired on March 27, 1945. There was virtually no defense against them.

The V-2 ballistic missile was incredibly advanced for its time and none of the Allies was even close to achieving something similar, which explains why they went out of their way to secure V-2 components, schematics and above all nazi scientists as they penetrated deeper and deeper into the heartland of the Third Reich.

Many of the V-2 scientists, including von Braun, had worked at the research center at Peenemünde, on the Baltic Sea coast, northeast Germany, for most of the war. But in February 1945, with the Russians closing in on Peenemünde, von Braun and his team, together with their equipment, were relocated to the V-2 Mittelwerk factory in Central Germany (Neufeld, 256–58). There, prisoners from the Mittelbau-Dora concentration camp were working at fever pitch to produce V-2 rockets.[3] Early April, when the Americans were close

---

2   The A-4, the fourth rocket design in the Aggregat series, was renamed V-2 (V for *Vergeltungswaffe*, weapon of vengeance) by German Minister of Propaganda Joseph Goebbels (King, 2).

3   An estimated 20,000 forced laborers from the camp died from exhaustion, disease, starvation, or were executed. In *The Rocket and the Reich*, Michael Neufeld estimates that approximately half of these deaths can be linked to V-2 production, while the total death toll of all V-2 attacks on Allied targets was about 5,000 (Neufeld, 264). Apart from its unique technological capabilities,

to capturing the Mittelwerk factory, the SS moved von Braun and some five hundred other 'Peenemünders' to the Bavarian Alps (Neufeld, 263). The factory was captured by the U.S. Army shortly thereafter.

In the weeks that followed, the Americans did their best to move as many V-2 components and research from the Mittelwerk factory as possible, as it was located in what was to become the Soviet Zone of occupation.[4] The loot from Mittelwerk was quickly transported by rail to the harbor of Antwerp, Belgium, where it filled sixteen Liberty ships (Adams, 71). And when von Braun and his team surrendered to elements of the U.S. 44th Infantry Division on May 3, 1945, the Americans were really in business (Ward, 56).

The Office of Strategic Services (OSS, predecessor of the CIA) had initially only wanted to interrogate the scientists, but soon realized it would be far more sensible to recruit them outright and move them to the United States (Piszkiewicz, 225–26).[5] One problem with this was that President Truman had expressly ordered to exclude from recruitment all scientists who had been a member of the Nazi Party (Piszkiewicz, 225–26; Neufeld, 270). Since that was the case with most of the top scientists, including von Braun, a way was devised to….work around the President's directive, by creating false employment histories and biographies from which all nazi affiliation had been expunged (i.e., by lying).

---

the V-2 was thus also the only World War II weapon that was twice as deadly inside the factory as it was outside.

4   The post-war occupation zones for Germany had been agreed upon by Churchill, Roosevelt and Stalin at the Yalta Conference in February 1945.

5   Initially code-named 'Operation Overcast', the effort was renamed 'Project Paperclip' when it went from simply interrogating scientists to outright recruiting and relocating them to the United States. The Joint Intelligence Objectives Agency (JIOA), a subcommittee of the Joint Intelligence Committee (JIC), the intelligence arm of the Joint Chiefs of Staff, was directly responsible for Operation Paperclip. Its files on 1,500+ German and other foreign scientists brought to the U.S. under Operation Paperclip and similar programs are accessible through the National Archives ("Foreign Scientist Case Files") .

And so, in September 1945, von Braun and 118 members of his team arrived in the United States, ready to continue their game-changing work, albeit in service of new masters (Adams, 71). Hundreds more would follow.

Meanwhile the Soviets had released Sergei Korolev—their top rocket scientist—from the slave labor camp they had sent him to in 1939, during Stalin's Great Purge. His ordeal had included a stint at Kolyma, the most notorious Gulag labor camp, located in northeast Siberia—where it was winter for twelve months and summer for the rest of the year—during which he had lost fourteen of his teeth to scurvy, among other unpleasantries (Siddiqi, 188).[6] But when the Soviets discovered scores of V-2 rocket components in Peenemünde and Mittelwerk, they needed Korolev to make sense of it all, and thus, in a remarkable reversal of fortune, Korolev was made a colonel in the Red Army and sent to Germany to study the V-2 guidance system, turbo-pump, engine and fuel mixture (Osiander, 220). The Russians also managed to recruit some 150 German scientists, though most of them had been involved with the mass production of the V-2 at Mittelwerk and had not directly worked with von Braun.[7]

Of course the successful atomic bombings of Hiroshima and Nagasaki in August 1945 gave a whole new sense of urgency to the development of a reliable ballistic missile, something that only increased after the Russians successfully tested their own nuclear bomb in 1949, and with the outbreak of the Korean war, a year after that. Whoever would be the first to develop a rocket that could carry a nuclear

---

6   Korolev had been sentenced to ten years hard labor after having been falsely denounced by coworkers for sabotage and admitting under torture— which involved breaking both his upper and lower jaw—that he had been a member of an "*anti-Soviet*" organization (Siddiqi, 177). He had initially been sentenced to death, but for reasons still unclear, his sentence was at the last minute commuted to ten years imprisonment (Siddiqi, 177–78).

7   An exception was Helmut Gröttrup, a German electrical engineer who had worked as an assistant of von Braun.

warhead and be guided fairly accurately to a target a couple of thousand miles away, would be able to annihilate the other before he could retaliate.

Both in the U.S. and the U.S.S.R., the first advances in rocketry were made based on the V-2 design. On May 10, 1946, the Americans sent up a modified V-2 for the first scientific exploration of space (a cosmic radiation experiment), and another one a few months later, on October 24, to take the first pictures of earth from an altitude of 65 mi/105 km. Though grainy black and white, the images nevertheless clearly showed Earth against the blackness of space. A few months after that, in February 1947, the first animals, a couple of fruit flies, were launched into space with a U.S. modified V-2, reaching an altitude of 68 mi/109 km before plunging back to earth. The fearless fruit flies were retrieved alive.

In the early 1950s both sides started with the development of an intercontinental ballistic missile (ICBM), capable of traveling at least 3,400 mi/5,500 km, which was a whole different ball game than the V-2, with its 200 mi/320 km range. In the U.S., the Army, Navy and Air Force each set up their own program, leading to considerable duplication of effort, whereas in the U.S.S.R., ICBM research—headed by Sergei Korolev—was more centrally organized, although several groups worked on different designs and competed with each other for funding (Burns, 165–73).

Quietly, the Russians took the lead, and on August 21, 1957, they successfully launched an R-7 rocket that traveled some 4,000 miles, making it the world's first ICBM (Hardesty, 67). Although the R-7 was developed to carry a nuclear payload to another continent, it could also carry a different kind of payload, into space. Not everybody in the Soviet military agreed with using the R-7 for anything other than carrying a nuclear warhead, but Korolev nevertheless succeeded in obtaining permission from the all powerful Central Committee and the Council of Ministers to launch a satellite into space, by arguing that there was not just a nuclear arms race going on with the United States but also a burgeoning space race, which, of course, the Soviet Union had to win (Hall, 60).

Because the R-7 was such a powerful rocket, Korolev initially planned to send up a satellite weighing a massive 1,200 kg/2,645 lb (Hall, 60).[8] Dubbed 'Object D', the satellite would be stuffed chockablock with scientific goodies.[9] But when Object D ran into complex design and manufacturing problems, Korolev decided to launch a much smaller satellite into orbit instead, with the main purpose of beating the Americans to it.

This would be Sputnik 1, a science-fiction-like silver-colored sphere, with four long antennas, weighing a measly 83.6 kg/182 lb (Logsdon, "Sputnik", 60). Its scientific capabilities were far less ambitious than those of Object D had been, but it would still be able to send out a radio signal and help measure the density of the upper atmosphere.

On October 4, 1957, Sputnik 1 was successfully put into orbit and began transmitting its "beep-beep-beep" signal at specific frequencies, which could be picked up by ham radio operators around the world.[10] It was a huge success for Korolev and his team and a huge surprise to everybody else, especially the Americans.

Less than two months later, on December 6, the U.S. attempted to launch a satellite of its own into orbit with a Vanguard rocket. After the booster was ignited the rocket began to lift off, but a few seconds later, having risen just a

---

8   For comparison, Voyager 1 weighed 815 kg / 1797 lb at launch.

9   The rather cryptic designation 'Object D', was meant to differentiate it from A, B, V and G payloads for the R-7, which were all nuclear warheads (Logsdon, "Sputnik", 54).

10   The official designation of Sputnik was PS-1. Russian media reporting the historic achievement a day after the launch did not ascribe a specific name to the satellite though, but simply referred to it as 'Sputnik', the Russian word for satellite (Logsdon, "Sputnik", 66).

little over one meter, it fell back again and exploded in a sea of flames. It was a big flop and newspapers outdid themselves in looking for that one word that best summed up the humiliating event, coming up with such finds as "Flopnik", "Dudnik", "Oopsnik" "Kaputnik" and "pfft-nik", to name a few (qtd. in TIME, "Vanguard's Aftermath").

All joking aside though, Sputnik's success and Vanguard's failure also spread fear in the West. Shocked and awestruck, the public suddenly realized the United States was significantly lagging the Soviet Union in space age technology and that the Russians now had missiles capable of targeting American cities with hydrogen bombs, while the United States did not (Dickson, 2–7).

The events led to a real 'Sputnik crisis', to which Washington responded with a range of measures aimed at closing the 'missile gap' and the (perceived) 'technology gap'.[11] In February 1958, the Advanced Research Projects Agency (ARPA) was created, which was to be responsible for the development of technologies with potential military applications.[12] ARPA would be involved in several groundbreaking inventions and innovations, including ARPANET, the progenitor of the internet.[13]

Just a few months after the creation of ARPA, on July 29, the National Aeronautics and Space Act came into effect, creating the National Aeronautics and Space Administration (NASA), the agency responsible for the U.S. civilian space

---

11   The fear of a missile gap was happily fueled by Soviet leader Nikita Khrushchev, who claimed in the late 1950s that the Soviet Union was producing ICBMs *"like sausages"*, though in reality the Russians only had a handful of R-7 ICBMs at the time (qtd. in Hardesty, 107). After the U.S. started launching its Corona reconnaissance satellites—the first successful launch and recovery of which was in August 1960—it quickly became clear there was no missile gap, at least not one in which the Soviet Union was in the lead (Burns, 278).

12   The Advanced Research Projects Agency was renamed Defense Advanced Research Projects Agency (DARPA) in 1972. It was changed back to ARPA in 1993, before being changed yet again in 1996, to DARPA.

13   See also chapter 22—The Second Greatest Invention of the Millennium.

program and for aeronautics and aerospace research, and a few months after that the National Defense Education Act (NDEA) was signed into law, pouring hundreds of millions of dollars in additional funding into educational institutions on all levels.[14]

In short, it was on.

On January 31, 1958, less than four months after Sputnik 1 and not two months after 'Kaputnik', the U.S. had also succeeded in putting a satellite of its own in orbit, the Explorer 1, but in this kind of race there was no silver medal for finishing second. And although the United States had now firmly picked up the gauntlet to become the leading space power, it would finish second several more times.

Between 1959–61 the Russians were reaping victory after victory, being the first to impact the moon with a man-made object (September 13, 1959), the first to take photographs of the far side of the moon (October 4, 1959) and the first to launch mammals into earth orbit—the dogs Belka and Strelka—and retrieve them alive (August 19, 1960).[15]

But the biggest blow to U.S. prestige came on April 12, 1961, when Yuri Alekseyevich Gagarin became the first man in space. Gagarin, a fighter pilot in the Soviet Air Force, had been carefully selected for the Soviet space program with nineteen others and was subsequently picked to be the first in space because he was highly intelligent, very likable, came from humble beginnings—his parents worked on a collective farm—and measured only 1.57 meters, the latter being

---

14   Among other things, the NDEA also introduced federal loans to American students, causing the number of students who borrowed from college student-loan funds to jump from 80,000 in 1957—the year before the NDEA was passed—to 115,000 in 1961. In all, some 1.5 million students used an NDEA loan to go to college between 1959 and 1969 (Loss, 159).

15   When Strelka had a litter of puppies a year later, Khrushchev sent one of them to the First Family as a gift.

important because room in the Vostok space capsule was limited (Burgess, 145–47).[16]

Gagarin's flight in the Vostok 1 lasted 108 minutes, enough for a single earth orbit. The capsule subsequently reentered the atmosphere and ejected Gagarin at a height of 4.3 mi/7 km (Burgess, 161). A few minutes later the world's first cosmonaut landed safely on the ground.

It was a monumental achievement, and not just for the people of the Soviet Union. All mankind was united in awe, just sixteen years after the end of the most devastating war the world had ever seen. And since Russia had arguably suffered the most during that war—losing over 25 million of its citizens and much of its industrial infrastructure—the achievement was all the more remarkable.

Of course, in the West, joy and awe quickly mixed with fear. Gagarin's successful flight proved the Soviets were still ahead in the Space Race, and if their space program was already advanced enough to put people into orbit, perhaps they could also put platforms into orbit equipped with nuclear weapons, for a surprise attack on the United States and Europe.

The deep, mutual sense of distrust between East and West, so typical of the Cold War, thus clouded every scientific achievement of the early Space Age. It was understandable enough though, especially since the competition between the two superpowers was far less scientific in Korea and Vietnam, or Germany for that matter, where tensions had been rising due to massive emigration from East Germany to the West.[17]

---

16   Gagarin had been in close competition with Gherman Stepanovich Titov for the top spot. Both men were obviously excellent candidates, equally capable of piloting the Vostok capsule. Exactly why Gagarin was eventually chosen over Titov remains unclear. According to Titov, it was Gagarin's likable personality that was the deciding factor in him being selected. As Titov later said: "*Yura turned out to be the man everyone loved. Me they couldn't love. They loved Yura. I'm telling you, they were right to choose Yura.*" (qtd. in Burgess, 147).

17   Emigration from East to West Germany had risen from 166,000 in 1951 to 182,000 in 1952 and 226,000 in just the first six months of 1953 (Dale, 17). The border between East and West Germany was subsequently closed by East

This exodus was abruptly halted on August 13, 1961—four months after Gagarin's flight—when the East German Army closed the border between East and West Berlin with barbed wire and started construction of a miles-long concrete wall a few days later. And so, if Yuri Gagarin's historic flight and broad smile had made people in the West realize they were all humans inhabiting the same small planet, the Berlin Wall made them remember their insurmountable differences again.

Though the U.S. was behind in the Space Race, the gap wasn't all that big. On May 5, 1961, just 23 days after Gagarin had forever etched his name into the great book of human history, Alan Shepard was launched into space with his Freedom 7 capsule, fixed atop a Mercury-Redstone rocket. The mission was to reach outer space and then come back down safely. The entire flight lasted only fifteen minutes, but the rocket reached an altitude of 116.5 miles, enough to make Shepard the first American and the second man in space (Hardesty, 125). Less than a year later, on February 20, 1962, John Glenn became the first American to orbit earth.[18]

That same year the world would also came to the brink of nuclear war, after the Soviet Union deployed nuclear missiles in Cuba.[19] The Kennedy administration initially considered taking out the missiles with air strikes or even a full-scale invasion of Cuba, before deciding to first try the less invasive military measure of the naval blockade, followed by

Germany, except in Berlin, which then became the primary escape route for East Germans wanting to leave the German Democratic Republic. And leave they did; between 1945–61, an estimated 3.5 million people emigrated from East to West Germany (Dale, 68).

18   With the death of Scott Carpenter, in October 2013, John Glenn became the last surviving member of the Mercury Seven, the seven original astronauts selected by NASA in April 1959.

19   The U.S. had deployed nuclear missiles in Turkey the previous April.

back-channel diplomacy aimed at finding a mutually satis-factory way out of the maze.[20]

After President Kennedy and Russian leader Khrushchev had somehow managed to avoid blowing up the planet, Kennedy tried to usher in an era of détente, proposing in a speech before the United Nations General Assembly on September 20, 1963, that the United States and the Soviet Union join forces and try to reach the moon together (Hamilton, "Joint Moon Flight"). Khrushchev initially reject-ed the proposal, but his thinking apparently evolved during the weeks that followed, because on November 1 he expressed clear interest in Kennedy's proposal, saying at a reception at the Kremlin that he considered it would be "*useful if the U.S.S.R and the U.S. pooled their efforts in exploring space for scientific purposes, specifically for arranging a joint flight to the moon. Would it not be fine if a Soviet man and an American or Soviet cosmonaut and an American woman flew to the moon? Of course it would.*" (qtd. in Logsdon, "Moon", 191).

It would have been, but just a few weeks later, on November 22, President Kennedy was shot in Dallas, Texas. His propos-al for a joint moon program did not survive either.

During the second half of the 1960s the Russians initially continued their streak of firsts, while the Americans worked on closing the gap and taking the ultimate prize—also televi-sion event of the century—landing a man on the moon. On March 18, 1965, cosmonaut Alexey Leonov became the first person to exit his capsule in space and perform extra-vehic-ular activity (EVA), on February 3, 1966, the Russian Luna 9 was the first spacecraft to achieve a soft landing on the moon and a few months later, on April 3, the Luna 10 became the first artificial satellite of the moon. The Russians seemed poised to attempt a manned lunar landing next.

---

20   See also chapter 18—How Vasili Arkhipov Saved the World.

But the untimely death, early 1966, of Sergei Korolev, the mastermind of the Soviet space program, significantly delayed the Russian lunar landing program at a time the U.S. was blasting full speed ahead. During 1965–66, the astronauts perfected working outside a spacecraft (EVA) and piloting a space capsule for rendezvous and docking purposes.

On December 24, 1968, the United States took the indisputable lead in the Space Race for the first time, when Frank Borman, Jim Lovell and William Anders became the first to orbit the moon and actually see Earth as a whole planet. Five months later, on May 18, 1969, in a final 'dress rehearsal', Apollo 10 was launched with the specific mission to fly the Lunar Module around the moon, without landing it. The manned Lunar Module came within 8.4 nm/15.6 km of the lunar surface, the closest humans had ever been (Godwin, 152).

Just two months later, on July 16, Apollo 11 was launched from the Kennedy Space Center in Florida. On board: Neil Armstrong, Michael Collins, Edwin 'Buzz' Aldrin and one Lunar Module. Destination: the moon again, but this time the Lunar Module would do more than just orbit.

On July 20, Armstrong and Aldrin piloted the Lunar Module to the surface of the moon, touching down at 20:18 UTC. A couple of hours later, on July 21, 02:56 UTC, Neil Armstrong became the first human to step on the lunar surface, claiming the moment for all humanity with the immortal words "*That's one small step for* (a) *man, one giant leap for mankind*".[21]

It was indeed a high point of human achievement. But after a couple of more trips to the moon the American public quickly lost interest in space travel and Congress started cutting NASA's funding.[22] The Russians, for their part,

---

21 Though the 'a' is not audible in the recordings, Armstrong later said he had intended to say 'one small step for a man' and also believed he had done so (Jones, "Apollo 11").

22 In the mid 1960s, NASA's budget as a percentage of total U.S. federal

having no desire to claim that non-existent silver medal, lost interest in the moon as well, deciding instead to focus their efforts on space stations, like Salyut 1 and Mir.[23]

The Space Race was over.

Then again, perhaps it had only just begun. After all, the final frontier is vast and we have only barely scratched the (lunar) surface. As of 2015, no manned spacecraft has ever orbited any of the other planets in our solar system, let alone set foot on them. Put differently, where are this generation's Yuri Gagarin, Alexey Leonov, Jim Lovell, Neil Armstrong and Buzz Aldrin? Where is the next giant leap for mankind?

Aboard Voyager 1 is a golden phonograph record with sounds and images to explain to possible extraterrestrial civilizations something about the diversity of life and culture on earth. It holds 116 images showing humans, animals, chemical compositions, DNA, Earth, Jupiter and the location of our solar system, among other things, as well as a variety of sounds, including sounds of nature, musical selections and spoken greetings in 55 languages. There is also an official

---

spending rose to 4.41 percent, but by 1971 it had declined to 1.61 percent. After 1975 the percentage remained under 1 percent, with the exception of 1993, when it was 1.01 percent. Since 2009, it has been around 0.50 percent (Rogers, "Nasa budgets"). When corrected for inflation, the 1965 budget would have been the equivalent of almost $40 billion in 2010; the actual NASA budget in 2010 was $18.9 billion.

23   There has been considerable debate about why Russia lost the moon race. Technological failure of the N1 rocket—the Russian counterpart of the Saturn V rocket that was used for the Apollo missions—is often mentioned as the primary reason, but so are managerial incompetence, underinvestment and insufficient commitment to a lunar landing, politically as well as militarily and scientifically. In Russia in Space: The Failed Frontier?, Brian Harvey writes that the Russians were late to realize there even was a race, that the involvement of no less than 26(!) government departments indeed caused considerable managerial complexity and that there was a significant lack of funding (Harvey, 13). Interestingly enough, Soviet engineers told visiting American aerospace engineers from MIT in November 1989—the same month the Berlin Wall fell—that it was problems with the N1 booster that had held up the Russian lunar landing mission, which was otherwise 'ready to go' in 1968. (Wilford 1989).

message of President Jimmy Carter, which ends: *"We are attempting to survive our time so we may live into yours. We hope some day, having solved the problems we face, to join a community of galactic civilizations. This record represents our hope and our determination, and our goodwill in a vast and awesome universe."* (Carter, "Voyager Spacecraft Statement").

Let's hope we will have solved our problems by the time they pay us a visit.

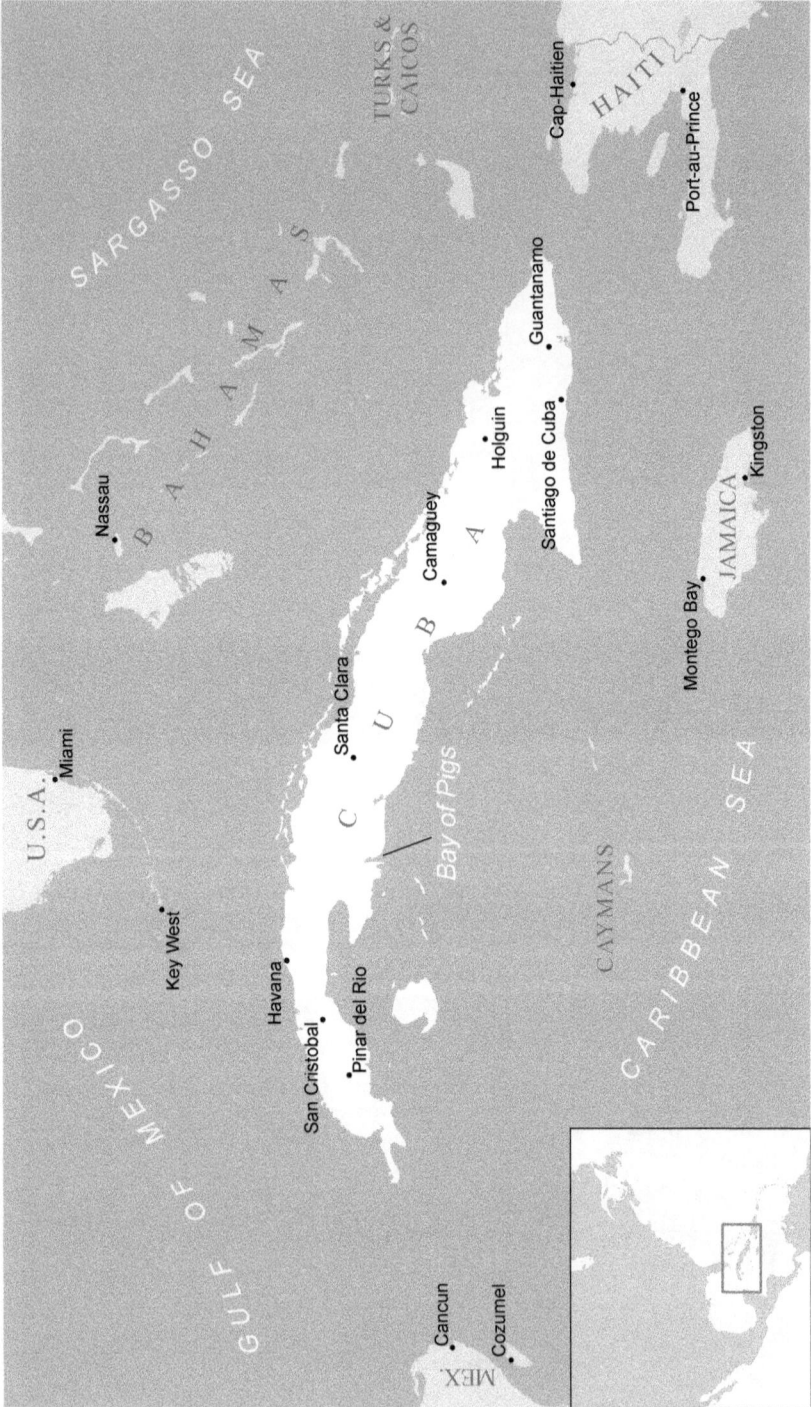

Map 12: Cuba and its Surrounding Waters

18

How Vasili Arkhipov Saved the World

"I want to say, and this is very important: at the end we lucked out. It was luck that prevented nuclear war. We came that close to nuclear war at the end. Rational individuals: Kennedy was rational; Khrushchev was rational; Castro was rational. Rational individuals came that close to total destruction of their societies. And that danger exists today."

Robert S. McNamara,
Secretary of Defense 1961–68,
in *The Fog of War* (2003)

"Maybe the war has already started up there, while we are doing summersaults here! We're going to blast them now! We will die, but we will sink them all - We will not disgrace our Navy!"[1]

Captain Valentin Savitsky,
commander of the nuclear armed Russian submarine B-59,
in the Caribbean near Cuba, October 27, 1962

On October 11, 2002, in Havana, Cuba, the participants at the historic 40th anniversary conference on the Cuban missile crisis learned for the first time that the world had come even closer to nuclear war in October 1962 than previously known.[2]

---

1   Qtd. in Mozgovoi, "Cuban Samba".

2   The conference, titled 'The Cuban Missile Crisis: A Political Perspective after 40 Years', was held between October 11–13, 2002, in Havana, Cuba. It was organized jointly by the Cuban government and George Washington

Much closer.

Missile experts, journalists, historians and some of the key players during the missile crisis—including Cuban President Fidel Castro and former U.S. Secretary of Defense Robert McNamara—learned that a Russian submarine close to Cuba, had come to within an inch of launching its nuclear-tipped torpedo against the fleet of American ships that had located its position and was trying to force it to the surface.

The submarine in question, B-59, was the flagship of the 69th Torpedo Submarine Brigade, a small flotilla of four submarines that had departed from its base on the Kola Peninsula in northwest Russia on October 1, 1962 (USSR, "Report"). Each submarine was armed with 21 conventional torpedoes and one torpedo with a ten-kiloton nuclear warhead, with a range of 12 mi/19 km ("Report from General Zakharov"; House, 436). The flotilla's initial mission had been to strengthen the defense of Cuba against a possible U.S. invasion, but while en route it received new orders, to patrol positions in the Sargasso Sea, northeast of Cuba, supporting Soviet cargo ships delivering arms to the island ("Report from General Zakharov"; Savranskaya 2005).

That support was deemed necessary by the Soviet High Command after President Kennedy had ordered the Navy to enforce a blockade of Cuba, to prevent any more arms—specifically Russian nuclear warheads and missiles—from arriving on the island. It was the least drastic decision Kennedy could have made after photographs taken by a U-2 spy plane on October 14, 1962, proved Soviet missiles were being deployed on Cuba (McAuliffe, 155).

Relations between the U.S and Cuba had rapidly deteriorated since Fidel Castro had ousted Cuban President Fulgencio Batista almost four years earlier. Since then, the bearded

University's National Security Archive, in partnership with Brown University's Watson Institute for International Affairs.

revolutionary leader had wasted little time turning Cuba into a communist state and becoming a staunch ally of the Soviet Union. A Marxist-Leninist single-party state only 94 miles away from the shores of the United States at the height of the Cold War was simply unbearable for any U.S. administration, even for a relatively liberal one like that of newly elected President John F. Kennedy.

So, when, shortly after taking office, Kennedy was briefed on plans for a military invasion of Cuba, carried out by Cuban counter-revolutionaries trained and supported by the CIA, he authorized the Defense Department and CIA to *"review proposals for the active deployment of anti-Castro Cuban forces on Cuban territory"* (Bundy, "Memorandum").[3]

A few months later, on April 17, 1961, a small invasion force of some 1,500 Cuban paramilitaries landed at the southern coast of Cuba, in the *Bahía de Cochinos* (Bay of Pigs), to get rid of the *"communist menace that has been permitted to arise under our very noses, only 90 miles from our shores"*, as Kennedy had characterized Castro's revolution during his presidential campaign (Kennedy "Speech Cincinnati").[4]

But the counter-revolutionary paramilitaries were defeated just three days later by the Cuban army, commanded by Fidel Castro himself. It was a humiliating failure for the United States, attributed to underestimation of Castro and lack of support for the paramilitaries, in a rather quixotic attempt to retain plausible deniability.[5]

---

3   Kennedy was first briefed as President on January 28, 1961, but had also been briefed about the covert operation against Cuba during the campaign (Gleijeses, 13, 20).

4   The invasion was carried out by the 2506 Assault Brigade, numbering 1,511 anti-Castro Cuban exiles (Jones, 96).

5   When the situation of the anti-revolutionary forces on the beach became untenable, several urgent calls where made for U.S. air support, but no such support was authorized by the White House. *"We just can't become involved."* Kennedy insisted, to which a frustrated Admiral Arleigh Burke, Chief of Naval Operations, replied: *"Goddamnit, Mr. President, we are involved, and there is no way to hide it. We are involved!"* (qtd. in Jones, 117). But Kennedy would not

Even worse was that the half-hearted Bay of Pigs invasion made Kennedy look weak in the eyes of his Russian counterpart, Chairman Nikita Sergeyevich Khrushchev, an impression that would only strengthen two months later, when the two met for the first time in Vienna, Austria.

The son of poor peasants and a veteran of the infamous Battle of Stalingrad, Khrushchev was a very experienced politician who had not only survived Josef Stalin's Great Purge and impromptu paranoia, but had also bested several rivals in the power struggle that followed Stalin's death in 1953. Kennedy, by contrast, had been born into a wealthy family. His father was a banker and entrepreneur who in 1938 had been appointed U.S. Ambassador to the United Kingdom by President Franklin Roosevelt, his mother the eldest daughter of a prominent Bostonian politician. Having been a U.S. Senator since 1953 but President for only six months, JFK was still a relative light-weight in executive experience when the two political adversaries first met, mid-1961. On top of that, Kennedy was also 23 years younger than Khrushchev.[6]

Khrushchev planned to use the Vienna Summit of June 4 to show the young, silver-spooned, physically weak, freshly elected U.S. President who was boss, something he would have never dreamed of doing with Kennedy's predecessor, Dwight Eisenhower, a.k.a. Ike. Like Khrushchev, Eisenhower had been a military man, war hero and leader of men long before he became President (he was also three years older than Khrushchev). With Eisenhower, the Russian leader had

---

budge.

6   An illustration of the differences in career, hardship and experience between Kennedy and Khrushchev might come from mid-1941, when 47-year-old Khrushchev was personally appointed by Stalin as a member of the Military Council of the High Command of the Southwestern Area—to organize the defense against the advancing German Army during Operation Barbarossa—while 24-year-old JFK had just failed his physical for both the Army and the Navy on account of colon, stomach and back problems (Khrushchev, 332–33; Dallek, 82). With help from his father, JFK would nevertheless succeed in acquiring a post in the Navy.

had little success in pressuring the U.S. to leave the city of Berlin to East Germany (in which territory it was located), but with Kennedy, he felt he was presented with a new chance.

While Kennedy did not give in to the pressure applied by Khrushchev at the Vienna Summit, he did allow himself to be put on the defensive by the bullying Soviet leader, who did not give an inch and was adamant about the Soviet Union's intention to conclude a separate peace treaty with East Germany by the end of the year, after which—Khrushchev insisted—Berlin would fall under the sole jurisdiction of the German Democratic Republic and Western troops would have to leave (Sampson, Vol. XIV, doc. 32–33). Kennedy, meanwhile, repeatedly stressed his willingness to improve relations between their two countries and admitted that both were equally matched, which came off as weak to the Chairman. Not long after the summit, on August 13, the East German Army closed the border and began constructing the Berlin Wall, surrounding and closing off West Berlin from East Berlin, and East Germany.

According to Fyodor Burlatsky, one of Khrushchev's assistants, who was present at his debriefing after the Vienna Summit, Kennedy had seemed more like "*an adviser*" to Khrushchev, "*not a political decision maker or president.*" (qtd. in Absher, 10). Burlatsky thought Khrushchev looked down on Kennedy the way a self-made man looks down on a rich man to whom everything was handed on a silver platter. "*Khrushchev thought Kennedy too young, intellectual, not prepared well for decision making in crisis situations….too intelligent and too weak.*" (qtd. in Absher, 10).

In the aftermath of the Bay of Pigs invasion, Eisenhower asked Kennedy why he had not given more support to the counter-revolutionaries, to which Kennedy replied that he had been worried the Soviets would then perhaps retaliate in Berlin. Eisenhower responded "*that is exactly the opposite of what would really happen. The Soviets follow their own plans, and if they see us show any weakness, then is when they press the hardest…The failure of the Bay of Pigs will embolden the Soviets to do something that they would otherwise not do."* (qtd. in Absher, 10).

Eisenhower was right. In May 1962, Khrushchev proposed to Castro to station nuclear missiles in Cuba, so as to deter further invasion attempts by the United States.[7] Castro, fearing a second invasion might not be so easily defeated, agreed. A few months later, the launching pads, medium-range and intermediate-range ballistic missiles (MRBMs and IRBMs), nuclear warheads, bombers, fighter aircraft, anti-air defense units and mechanized infantry troops started to arrive in Cuba.

The military build-up was soon noticed by local Cuban spies and reported back to U.S. intelligence services. Definitive proof followed on the aforementioned October 14, when a U-2 spy plane succeeded in taking 928 pictures during a six-minute flight over suspected Cuban missile sites, several of which produced hard evidence that at least two MRBM sites were being developed near San Cristobal, in Pinar del Rio province (Absher, 46, 51–52; Merrill, 383).[8]

National Security Adviser McGeorge Bundy was notified about the new photographic evidence late night on October 15th, but decided to wait until early next morning to tell Kennedy, deciding that *"a quiet evening and a night of sleep*

---

7   Aside from Cuba, Khrushchev also wanted to protect Soviet prestige in Latin America, which would suffer a severe blow if Cuba was allowed to be invaded and occupied by the United States (Absher, 24). Still more important was that, by placing medium and intermediate-range ballistic missiles (MRBMs and IRBMs) in Cuba, the missile gap with the U.S. could be closed, since the U.S.S.R had only a handful of intercontinental ballistic missiles (ICBMs) at the time but plenty of MRBMs and IRBMs.

8   CIA memorandum "Probable Soviet MRBM Sites in Cuba" (October 16, 1962) mentions *"two areas in the Sierra del Rosario mountains about 50 n.m. west southwest of Havana which appear to contain Soviet MRBMs in the early stages of deployment."* (qtd. in McAuliffe, 139–44). A third area is identified as an apparent *"military encampment".*

were the best preparation", as he later wrote (qtd. in Zelikow, "Presidential Recordings", Vol. II, 396). Bundy informed the President around 9:00 a.m., who then told him to quietly round up several members from his cabinet and other key advisors for a meeting later that morning.[9] This group, soon called the Executive Committee of the National Security Council, or ExComm, would form Kennedy's core team throughout the crisis.

With the evidence clear, ExComm's first task was to come up with a proper response. Initially, all members favored bombing Cuba, they only differed on the scale of the attack. Some, including the President, favored a 'surgical strike', while others agreed with the Joint Chiefs of Staff that the best course of action would be to also take out air defense sites, fighters and bombers, in addition to bombing the missile sites, so as to limit losses to U.S. aircraft and prevent immediate air reprisal against U.S. bases in nearby Florida (Zelikow, "Presidential Recordings", Vol. II, 404ff.). Some of the Chiefs, like Air Force General Curtis LeMay, went even further and pressed for an immediate invasion of Cuba.[10]

On the third day of discussion, on October 18, Under Secretary of State George Ball voiced his opposition to an air strike without warning Khrushchev first. Comparing such an attack to Pearl Harbor, Ball said it was *"the kind of conduct that one might expect of the Soviet Union. It is not conduct one expects of the United States."* (qtd. in Zelikow, "Presidential Recordings", Vol. II, 539). Robert Kennedy—the Attorney

---

9   The following people attended the meeting: President Kennedy, George Ball, McGeorge Bundy, Marshall Carter, C. Douglas Dillon, Roswell Gilpatric, Sidney Graybeal, U. Alexis Johnson, Vice President Johnson, Robert Kennedy, Arthur Lundahl, Robert McNamara, Dean Rusk, and Maxwell Taylor (Zelikow, "Presidential Recordings", Vol. II, 397). Other people would sit in at several subsequent meetings.

10   Even after the crisis had been resolved peacefully LeMay still wanted to invade Cuba, calling the peaceful resolution of the crisis *"the greatest defeat in our history."* (qtd. in Hughes, 129).

General and the President's brother—and Secretary of State Dean Rusk agreed.

Doing nothing was not an option either though. As President Kennedy said the next day: "*If we do nothing, they have a missile base there with all the pressure that brings to bear on the United States and damage to our prestige.*" (qtd. in Zelikow, "Presidential Recordings", Vol. II, 581). It would also put Berlin in play, because doing nothing would significantly strengthen the hand of the old fox in the Kremlin, who would then likely try to gobble up Berlin in its entirety, which was all the Russians were really interested in, as Kennedy knew only too well: "*If you take the view, really, that what's basic to them is Berlin and there isn't any doubt* [about that]. *In every conversation we've had with the Russians, that's what . . . Even last night we* [Soviet foreign minister Andrei Gromyko and I] *talked about Cuba for a while, but Berlin— that's what Khrushchev's committed himself to personally.*" (qtd. in Zelikow, "Presidential Recordings", Vol. II, 581).

For the same reason, Kennedy held that the U.S. couldn't go into Cuba guns blazing either: "*If we attack Cuba, the missiles, or Cuba, in any way then it gives them a clear line to take Berlin, as they were able to do in Hungary under the Anglo war in Egypt. We will have been regarded as—they think we've got this fixation about Cuba anyway— we would be regarded as the trigger-happy Americans who lost Berlin. We would have no support among our allies. We would affect the West Germans' attitude towards us. And* [people would believe] *that we let Berlin go because we didn't have the guts to endure a situation in Cuba.*" (qtd. in Zelikow, "Presidential Recordings", Vol. II, 581).

And if the Russians moved in on Berlin, Kennedy figured he would have only one play left: "*Their just going in and taking Berlin by force at some point (...) leaves me only one alternative, which is to fire nuclear weapons - which is a hell of an alternative - and begin a nuclear exchange, with all this happening."* (qtd. in Zelikow, "Presidential Recordings", Vol. II, 581).

Thus stuck between a rock and a hard case, a new option began to emerge, one in which the U.S. would take the moral high ground by making it known to the world that the Soviet Union had placed missiles in Cuba, that these missiles must be removed and that a blockade would be enforced around Cuba to prevent the arrival of additional missiles.[11]

On October 22, both the Russians and U.S. allies were briefed on the decision to enforce a quarantine of Cuba, and in the evening Kennedy addressed the nation on television to inform the American people. Khrushchev publicly condemned the blockade, saying it put mankind on a path towards nuclear war. Privately, backchannels were opened to try and resolve the crisis without starting World War III. U.S. Armed Forces were put at DEFCON 3.[12]

But even if the quarantine was successful—i.e., merchant ships wouldn't try to run it and supporting Russian war-ships wouldn't (threaten to) open fire in the event a ship was boarded for inspection—even then it was only a temporary solution, giving Khrushchev some time to reconsider his gamble that Kennedy *"would make a fuss, make more of a fuss, and then agree"*, as he had told his son Sergei (qtd. in Smyser, 194).

It was a huge gamble on Khrushchev's part, one that might seem irresponsible in hindsight, but from the Soviet leader's point of view the potential payoff was well worth it. First of all, as Kennedy had already correctly assessed, it presented the Americans with an impossible dilemma: doing nothing would increase pressure on the U.S. and give Khrushchev

---

11   Kennedy later exchanged the term 'blockade' for 'quarantine', because a blockade is legally considered an act of war in International Law.

12   DEFCON, Defense readiness condition, is an alert state used by the U.S. Armed Forces. It has five graduated levels of readiness, with 5 being the lowest state of readiness and 1 being reserved for imminent nuclear war.

vital information about Kennedy's likely reaction to a Russian move on Berlin, while removing the missiles by force would give the Russians a great excuse to take Berlin in retaliation.

Secondly, the Soviet Union had far less ICBMs than the U.S. assumed and it was also behind in nuclear armed bombers and submarines. In short, the Mutually Assured Destruction was not that mutual after all, at least not at the time. But a couple of medium-range and intermediate-range nuclear missiles on Cuba—of which the U.S.S.R had more than enough—would solve that problem handsomely and give the Russians time to play catch-up.

Thirdly, some months earlier, in April 1962, the United States had stationed medium-range nuclear missiles in Turkey, right at the doorstep of the Soviet Union (Garthoff, 71, note 115).[13] Khrushchev therefore considered the missiles in Cuba an appropriate response to that provocative move.

Finally, and perhaps most importantly: he thought he could get away with it. Kennedy had been weak during the Bay of Pigs invasion, weak during the Vienna Summit and weak during the Berlin Crisis, so there was every reason to think he would be weak again. In the same vein, Khrushchev may have also believed that should it come to negotiations, he could probably get Kennedy to trade Berlin for the missiles in Cuba (Taubman, 530–31, 539).

Neither Kennedy nor Khrushchev wanted nuclear war though, and both of them knew it. They were basically playing a heads-up poker hand in which both players know neither one of them wants to go all-in. In other words, they could

---

13   Interestingly, the decision, late 1957, to station intermediate-range missiles in Europe in the first place, had been made because of a perceived missile gap with the Soviet Union, i.e., the exact same reason why Khrushchev wanted to station missiles in Cuba five years later (Garthoff, 71, note 115). Turkey had agreed to take fifteen Jupiter IRBM missiles in 1959, but negotiations, training and construction of the necessary facilities took several years, so that the missiles were basically obsolete by the time they arrived.

bet, raise, even re-raise, but both men knew their hand was only as strong as the other was willing to give it credit for. The future of mankind was at stake, yes, but both players thought they would be able to find a way to stop the game before one of them (or both) would have only one play left. In reality they were not the only players in the game though, and therefore not in control of its outcome, at least not entirely.

On October 24, the quarantine went into effect and Strategic Air Command (SAC) was put at DEFCON 2.[14]

Just after 10.00 a.m., McNamara reported that two ships, the Kimovsk and the Gagarin, were approaching the quarantine line and were being shadowed by a Soviet submarine, making the situation potentially explosive (Zelikow, "Presidential Recordings", Vol. III, 190–91). General Taylor, Chairman of the Joint Chiefs of Staff, explained to the other ExComm members that a signaling procedure for the surfacing of Russian submarines had been sent to the Soviets the night before, though it was unclear whether Moscow had relayed this procedure to its submarines (Zelikow, "Presidential Recordings", Vol. III, 192–93). McNamara said that in addition to the signaling procedure, U.S. destroyers would use practice depth charges, as a second warning and instruction to surface. Special Assistant to the President Kenneth O'Donnell asked what they would do in case the submarine still didn't surface, whether they would then attack it, but Kennedy was not prepared to go that far yet: *"I think we ought to wait on that today. We don't want to have the first thing we attack as a Soviet submarine. I'd much rather have a merchant ship."* (qtd. in Zelikow, "Presidential Recordings", Vol. III, 194).

---

14   Putting SAC at DEFCON 2 meant the crews of 1,436 strategic nuclear bombers and 134 ICBM missile silos were put on stand-by alert (Absher, 69). The missiles were ready for launch and one-eighth of the bombers were in the air at all times.

Meanwhile, Khrushchev, in an apparent effort to avoid confrontation as well, ordered several Russian ships to stop.[15] One ship close to the quarantine line, the Soviet oil tanker *Bucharest*, continued on course though and passed the quarantine line. McNamara reported the tanker had been hailed and had responded it was not carrying any prohibited items. The members of ExComm discussed at length whether or not the *Bucharest* should be stopped, boarded and searched (Zelikow, "Presidential Recordings", Vol. III, 244ff.). In the end the ship was allowed to continue, because it had already left port before the crisis began, had no deck cargo and its hatches were too small to accommodate missiles—and also to give the Russians a grace period to get their instructions clear.

On October 26, Kennedy received a letter from Khrushchev which had been delivered at the U.S. Embassy in Moscow more than six hours earlier (Zelikow, "Presidential Recordings", Vol. III, 349). In a staggering twelve—at times emotional and somewhat rambling—pages, Khrushchev proposed to remove the missiles from Cuba, in exchange for a public promise from the United States never to invade Cuba or aid others in doing so.[16]

On the morning of October 27—the day that would come to be known as *Black Saturday*—the American Embassy in Moscow received another, much shorter, letter, with another, much more concise proposal (Samson, Vol. VI, doc. 66). While the letter was still being translated at the embassy, Radio Moscow had already started broadcasting the proposal, the gist of which was that in addition to a pledge not to

---

15   Upon hearing the news that Khrushchev had apparently ordered the ships to hold and/or reverse course, Secretary of State Dean Rusk whispered to National Security Advisor McGeorge Bundy: "*We are eyeball to eyeball, and I think the other fellow just blinked.*" (qtd. in Zelikow, "Presidential Recordings", Vol. III, 197).

16   See Zelikow, "Presidential Recordings", Vol. III, 349–55, for the translated version of Khrushchev's letter used by ExComm.

invade Cuba, the Russians also wanted the U.S. to remove its missiles from Turkey.

The members of ExComm quickly agreed that the U.S. could not accept this proposal, as it would send the message that the United States was willing to sell out its allies. The problem was that Khrushchev's proposed trade of Russian missiles in Cuba for American missiles in Turkey sounded very reasonable, making a Cuban invasion "*an insupportable position*", according to Kennedy (qtd. in Zelikow, "Presidential Recordings", Vol. III, 363).

While they were debating the best response, news reached ExComm that a U-2 was shot down over Cuba, killing the pilot (Zelikow, "Presidential Recordings", Vol. III, 445–46). Several ExComm members—including Chairman of the Joint Chiefs of Staff Maxwell Taylor, Secretary of Defense Robert McNamara and Under Secretary of Defense Roswell Gilpatric—were clamoring for a retaliatory attack per the rules of engagement, and Kennedy came close to ordering one, but at the last moment decided not to, unless another plane was attacked.[17]

For decades, the U-2 incident was seen as probably the most decisive moment of the Cuban missile crisis, since U.S. retaliation—taking out Soviet-operated surface-to-air missile (SAM) sites on Cuban soil, to protect U.S. planes—would have likely resulted in Soviet casualties, followed by Soviet retaliatory attacks, as per the rules of engagement.

But that same day, around the same time, another incident occurred. One that would bring the world even closer

---

17   After much deliberation, Kennedy concluded: "*I think we ought to keep tomorrow clean, do the best we can with the surveillance. If they still fire and we haven't got a satisfactory answer back from the Russians, then I think we ought to put a statement out tomorrow that we are fired upon. We are therefore considering the island of Cuba as an open territory, and then take out all these SAM sites*" (qtd. in Zelikow, "Presidential Recordings", Vol. III, 492).

to nuclear war, without Kennedy or Khrushchev even being aware of it, let alone having any control over it.

While patrolling the Sargasso Sea, northeast of Cuba, a group of U.S. destroyers and the aircraft carrier USS Randolph discovered a Soviet submarine. Per their instructions, they subsequently moved in and began to tighten the circle around their now vulnerable prey (Mozgovoi, "Cuban Samba").

Submerged and in hiding, B-59 could not send or receive any radio traffic and was thus completely cut off from the world above. As it happened, the submarine had not received any communication from Moscow for days (Savranskaya, 246). It had picked up some broadcasts from U.S. radio stations though, which were filled with talk of an impending U.S. invasion of Cuba if Soviet nuclear missiles there were not removed, and of President Kennedy warning about the threat of thermonuclear conflict (Savranskaya, 242).[18]

Meanwhile, the destroyers, following the specific protocol prescribed by the Department of Defense to warn all submarines to surface in the quarantine area, started dropping practice depth charges (PDCs) to force B-59 to surface (Savranskaya, 245–46). About the size of a hand grenade, the PDCs were harmless, but B-59 had no way of knowing that. And although the Department of Defense had relayed its submarine protocol to Moscow four days earlier, B-59 had not received any information about it (Zelikow, "Presidential Recordings", Vol. III, 192–93).

Ominously, the ExComm discussion about the 'Submarine Surfacing and Identification Procedures', on the 24th, had been when the President had seemed the most worried. Robert Kennedy wrote down later that day that he thought

---

18   Savranskaya bases this part of her description of the situation aboard the Soviet submarines in the Sargasso Sea on Alexei Dubivko's, "In the Depths of the Sargasso Seas" in *On the Edge of the Nuclear Precipice* (1988). Dubivko had been the commander of submarine B-36, which, together with B-4, B-59 and B-130 formed the 69th submarine brigade.

"these few minutes were the time of greatest worry by the President. his hand went up to his face & covered his mouth and he closed his fist. His eyes were tense, almost gray, and we just stared at each other across the table." (qtd. in Zelikow, "Presidential Recordings", Vol. III, 193).

Kennedy had been right to be particularly worried about the submarines, because not only did the crew of B-59 not know that the destroyers were only using practice depth charges to try and force them to the surface, the destroyers, in turn, did not know B-59 was equipped with a nuclear-tipped torpedo with a 10-kiloton yield.

Moreover, the commander of B-59 had independent launching capability—there were no locks on the weapon—and had authority to launch in case he was 'hulled (Savranskaya, 240).[19-20] Should such a situation occur, the

---

19   As Captain Ryurik Ketov, commander of the B-4, one of the four submarines of the 69th submarine brigade, remembered Vice-Admiral A.I. Rassokha, Chief of Staff of the Northern Fleet, saying: *"Write down when you should use these. . . . In three cases. First, if you get a hole under the water. A hole in your hull. This is the first case. Second, a hole above the water. If you have to come to the surface, and they shoot at you, and you get a hole in your hull. And the third case – when Moscow orders you to use these weapons.(...) I suggest to you, commanders, that you use the nuclear weapons first, and then you will figure out what to do after that."* (qtd. in Savranskaya, 240).

20   There has been much debate about whether the submarine commanders really had the authority to launch the nuclear torpedo without specific orders from Moscow. According to Russian researcher Alexander Mozgovoi, author of *The Cuban Samba of the Quartet of Foxtrots: Soviet Submarines in the Caribbean Crisis of 1962* (2002), nuclear weapons could only be used on special orders from the Defense Minister, thus contradicting the testimony of B-4 commander Captain Ryurik Ketov, who stated Vice-Admiral Rassokha had given permission to fire in case they were hulled (see note above). Rear Admiral Georgi Kostev, veteran submarine commander and historian, has stated that Khrushchev was of the opinion that a Soviet submarine commander would be in his right to attack without further orders in the event he would be attacked himself. (Polmar, 204). Interestingly, an order from Soviet Defense Minister Marshal Rodion Y. Malinovsky, issued on October 27, 1962, at 16:30, to General Issa A. Pliyev, commander of the Soviet forces in Cuba, read: *"We categorically confirm that you are prohibited from using nuclear weapons from missiles, FKR* [cruise missiles], *"Luna" and aircraft without orders from Moscow. Confirm receipt."* (USSR, "Telegram TROSTNIK"). The order, issued on the

commander only needed confirmation from the submarine's political officer to launch the 'special weapon', as it was called (Savranskaya, 239). However, as fate would have it, B-59 also carried the chief of staff of the small flotilla of four submarines, Vasili Alexandrovich Arkhipov, meaning that on this particular submarine *three* people had to agree on any nuclear launch.

Three people on a hunted, cramped submarine with a malfunctioning cooling system, causing temperatures to rise to almost 50 °C/122 °F in the compartments and even 60 °C/140 °F in the engine room, adding to the already high stress levels on board (Mozgovoi, "Cuban Samba").

For Captain Valentin Savitsky, the exploding depth charges were the final straw. With no possibility of communicating with Moscow without surfacing the boat and attacked by (practice) depth charges which, according to Vadim Orlov—head of the special radio intercept team on B-59—*"felt like you were sitting in a metal barrel, which somebody is constantly blasting with a sledgehammer"*, an enraged Savitsky decided to launch the nuclear torpedo to destroy all the U.S. ships above them (qtd. in Mozgovoi, "Cuban Samba").

A heated argument subsequently erupted between Savitsky, Arkhipov and political officer Ivan Semenovich Maslennikov. According to Orlov, Arkhipov eventually succeeded in talking Captain Savitsky out of launching the nuclear torpedo and instead surface the boat (Savranskaya, 247). Nuclear war averted.

That evening, around 8:00 p.m. Washington time, Robert Kennedy met with Soviet Ambassador Anatoly Dobrynin at the Justice Department. Kennedy conveyed the U.S was

---

same day the incidents with the U-2 and B-59 occurred, implies that there was at least some unclarity among those in charge of the Soviet missiles on Cuba, about whether or not they had launching authority without special orders from Moscow. The same unclarity might very well have existed among Soviet submarine commanders.

willing to publicly promise not to invade Cuba if the Soviet Union would remove its missiles from Cuba. Saving the best for last, he then said that President Kennedy had been wanting to remove the missiles from Turkey for some time (seeing as they were obsolete anyway) and that the missiles would thus be removed *within a short time after this crisis was over*, but that this could not be part of the public deal (Kennedy, "Thirteen Days", 83).

Kennedy also stressed the White House would need an answer from Khrushchev the next day (Sunday), thus hinting at U.S. plans to attack Cuba on Monday (Kennedy, "Thirteen Days", 83). The Joint Chiefs had indeed prepared a strike plan for Monday the 29th, but several hours before Robert Kennedy's meeting with Dobrynin, ExComm had decided to wait until Tuesday with the attack (Zelikow, "Presidential Recordings", Vol. III, 437, 502–03).

The next day, Sunday October 28, at 9:00 a.m., Washington time, Khrushchev had a message broadcast over Radio Moscow that he had ordered work on the Cuban sites stopped and the missiles dismantled, crated and returned to the Soviet Union (Garthoff, 93). The crisis was over.

Arguably the most dangerous moment in human history, the Cuban Missile Crisis showed just how powerful the individual had become in the nuclear age. In the end, annihilation of our kind was averted by just a handful of people who decided not to push the button when they could have.

In the wake of the crisis, communication between the two superpowers improved, and in the late 1960s and early 1970s the first steps were taken to end the nuclear arms race, through the Strategic Arms Limitation Talks (SALT).

As of 2015, both the United States and Russia still possess thousands of nuclear weapons though, while the decision to use them still rests with just a handful of people.

Vasili Arkhipov died on August 19, 1998, aged 72. He was never awarded the title *Hero of the Soviet Union*.

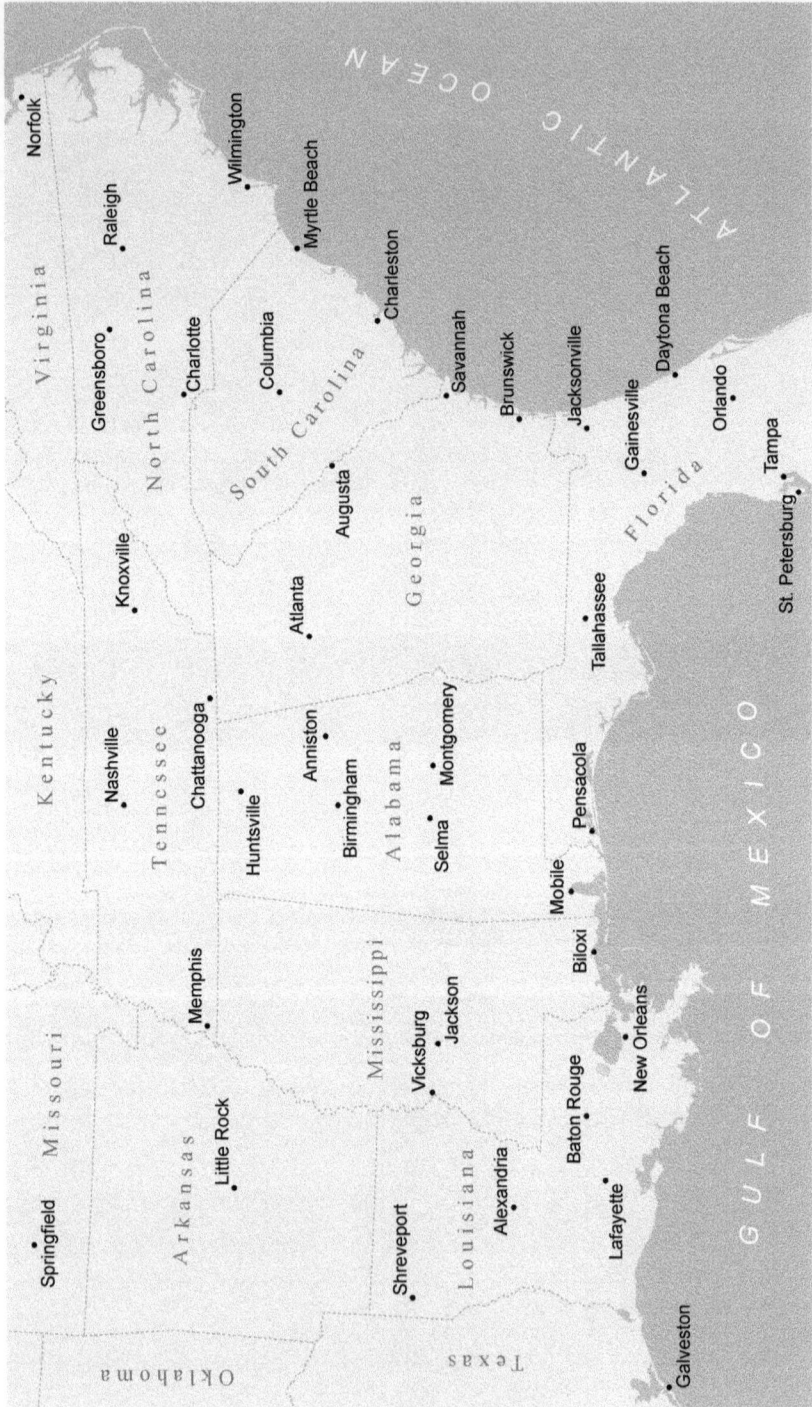

Map 13: The 'Deep South' of the United States

19

HE HAD A DREAM

"Tell them about the dream, Martin!"

Mahalia Jackson, August 28, 1963, Washington D.C.,
at the end of Martin Luther King's speech
during the March on Washington[1]

ON DECEMBER 11, 1967, IN THE MIDST of one of the most socially, culturally and politically volatile decades the world has ever seen, a movie premiered in New York City that cast both a disconcerting and hopeful light on an issue that was still dividing America to the bone, as it had been doing since its inception.

In the 1960s, the push for equality under the law was finally gathering momentum, but in the wake of several major victories for the African-American Civil Rights Movement, Stanley Kramer's 1967 movie *Guess Who's Coming to Dinner* showed that there was a difference between legal equality and *real* equality.

In the movie, a young woman introduces her fiancé, a celebrated doctor, to her parents. The woman's father owns a newspaper in San Francisco and her mother an art gallery. Intellectual, educated and liberal, they have brought their daughter up to be a kind, accepting, broad-minded, modern young woman. And they seem to have succeeded exceptionally well at this, because the man their daughter has chosen for her husband is an educated, well-spoken, empathic, charming black man.

---

1   Qtd in Hansen, "Mahalia Jackson".

After making inquiries, the father finds out that the fiancé is not just any doctor, he is an exceptional doctor. Graduated Maxima Cum Laude, worked at Johns Hopkins hospital, assistant professor at Yale Medical School, professor at the London School of Tropical Medicine, assistant director at the World Health Organization, author of textbooks and receiver of several medical society honors. In short, the dream of every parent. That is, if it weren't for the color of his skin.

As the story develops, it becomes clear that the father is against the marriage not because he disapproves of the fiancé, but because he fears the unforgiving world that awaits the young married couple, a feeling wholeheartedly shared by the doctor's father, who also comes to dinner. However handsome, accomplished, lovely and broad-minded their children are, all the fathers really see is a white woman and a black man who, as a married couple, would be vilified in the North and likely murdered in the South.

Their fear was not wholly unjustified, black people had been murdered for much less in the South. Just twelve years earlier, in non-fictional 1955, Emmet Till, a 14-year-old black boy, had been murdered in Mississippi just for flirting with a white woman, his two killers acquitted by an all-white jury.[2] And his case was hardly unique.

Ever since the first twenty African slaves had arrived on a Dutch trading vessel in Jamestown, Virginia, in 1619, blacks had been treated as inferior to whites in the New World. Inferior but useful, which is why about 600,000 African slaves would be imported to the United States between 1620 and 1865, most of them ending up on Southern plantations (Miller, 164, 182, 682).

---

2   Protected against double jeopardy, the murderers—the woman's husband Roy Bryant and his half-brother J.W. Milam—admitted to the killing in an interview published in Look magazine, a few months after the trial had ended (Huie 1956).

The Revolution of 1776 came and went, bringing independence, freedom from tyranny and a new nation, but only for white colonists. For blacks nothing changed until the Civil War, and even then the three historic steps forward were soon followed by two steps back.

Between 1865–70, three new amendments to the U.S. Constitution were adopted, collectively known as the Reconstruction Amendments. The Thirteenth Amendment, ending slavery, the Fourteenth Amendment, proclaiming all people who are born or naturalized in the United States citizens, with equal protection of the law, and the Fifteenth Amendment, forbidding to deny or abridge the right to vote based on *"race, color, or previous condition of servitude"* (US Const. amend. XV, sec. 1).[3]

But the effects of almost 250 years of slavery could not be wiped out so easily. In the defeated South, where most blacks lived, state legislatures bided their time, laying low as long as federal troops remained stationed in their states. But as soon as those troops had left, twelve years after the end of the Civil War, the advances that had been made during Reconstruction were quickly rolled back in the Southern States.[4] State legislatures across the South introduced a host of racial discrimination legislation known as Jim Crow laws, aimed at restoring the situation prior to the Civil War. Former Confederate States such as Mississippi, Alabama, Louisiana, North Carolina, South Carolina, Georgia and Florida knew

---

3   Important as the Fifteenth Amendment was, one other major discriminatory ground for withholding the right to vote was conspicuously absent from it. Women would have to wait another 50 years before the Nineteenth Amendment added the word 'sex' to the list of grounds on account of which the right to vote could not be denied or abridged.

4   The end of Reconstruction, in 1877, came after the intensely disputed presidential election of 1876 and the (alleged) 'Compromise of 1877', which gave the presidency to the Republican Rutherford B. Hayes, in exchange for the withdrawal of all federal troops from the Southern States, thus effectively handing control of the South to the Democratic 'Redeemers', who wanted to undo as much of Reconstruction as possible (Woodward, 3–21).

they could not reintroduce slavery—as that would likely start another war with the North—but they also realized people don't have to be *called* slaves to be *treated* as slaves.

Segregation laws institutionalized the inferior status of African Americans. Everything that could be segregated, was. Schools, work places, churches, hospitals, public transportation, restaurants, restrooms, even drinking fountains, everything was divided between 'white' and 'colored', with services and facilities for the latter always being second-rate, or worse.

To counter the Fifteenth Amendment, all kinds of barriers were put up to prevent black people from registering to vote, such as poll taxes, literacy tests and residency and record-keeping requirements.[5] African Americans were thus basically eliminated from political life, unable to vote, stand for election to public office or serve on a jury (which is how Emmet Till's murderers could be so 'lucky' to face an all-white jury in 1955, 85 years after the Fifteenth Amendment had been ratified).

As things stood, it was clear that anyone wanting to fight any of the Jim Crow laws in the South would come up against a brick wall in local and state courts, where white, Southern judges—the vast majority of whom agreed with segregation—presided. Of course the U.S. Supreme Court could be an altogether different matter, as its justices were not predominantly Southern. In fact, when a landmark case against segregation

---

5   The introduction of literacy tests and poll taxes caused black voter turnout in the Southern States to decline from between 45–80 percent in 1880 to 1–2 percent in 1912 (Valelly, 128, table 6.3). Of course these laws also potentially disenfranchised many poor white people, but restrictive voter laws often had loopholes that exempted those who had had the right to vote before 1866 (i.e., white people) or their lineal descendants, a.k.a. a 'grandfather clause'. In 1915, the Supreme Court ruled these kind of grandfather clauses in violation of the Fifteenth Amendment (Guinn v. United States, 238 U.S. 347), but Southern States quickly passed new voter registration restrictions that kept African Americans largely disenfranchised in the South until passage of the Voting Rights Act of 1965.

in public transportation was brought before the Supreme Court in 1896, only one of the nine justices hailed from a Southern State that had been part of the Confederacy.[6]

The case revolved around a man named Homer Plessy, who had bought a first-class ticket before boarding a 'whites only' car on a train in New Orleans, though he was classified as being one-eighth black, thus violating the Separate Car Act of 1890, a Louisiana State law segregating public transportation. It was a test case, provoked by a group of prominent black, creole and white people from New Orleans, who had united themselves in a Committee of Citizens (Medley, 14). Mr. Plessy was detained by a private detective hired by the Committee, to make sure there would be a clear case.

Sure enough, a New Orleans judge, John Howard Ferguson, convicted Mr. Plessy of violating the Separate Car Act and sentenced him to pay a fine of $25, a ruling subsequently confirmed by the Supreme Court of Louisiana. Next (and last) up was the U.S. Supreme Court.

One of Plessy's principal arguments was that the Separate Car Act violated his constitutional right to 'equal protection of the laws' as guaranteed by the Fourteenth Amendment, because it forced him to ride in the colored car (US Const. amend. XIV, sec. 1).

On this point, justice Henry Billings Brown, writing the majority opinion of the U.S. Supreme Court, contended that "*The object of the* [Fourteenth] *amendment was undoubtedly to enforce the absolute equality of the two races before the law, but, in the nature of things, it could not have been intended to abolish distinctions based upon color, or to enforce social, as distinguished from political, equality, or a commingling of the two races upon terms unsatisfactory to either.*" (Plessy v. Ferguson, 544). In other words, as long as social inequality and

---

6   Justice Edward Douglass White was from Louisiana. Justice John Marshall Harlan was from Kentucky, one of the four slave states that had not seceded from the Union.

separation did not lead to political inequality, the Fourteenth Amendment would not be violated.

Therefore, justice Brown continued, *"We consider the underlying fallacy of the plaintiff's argument to consist in the assumption that the enforced separation of the two races stamps the colored race with a badge of inferiority. If this be so, it is not by reason of anything found in the act, but solely because the colored race chooses to put that construction upon it."* (Plessy v. Ferguson, 551). The Court affirmed the ruling of the S.C. of Louisiana by 7 to 1.

With this *'separate but equal'* doctrine, the Supreme Court held that segregation was legal as long as the segregated services and facilities were of equal quality. Of course they almost never were, but Plessy v. Ferguson moved the burden of proof to the plaintiff, meaning that the mostly poor, uneducated and disenfranchised blacks now had to prove first that the quality of their hospitals, schools, restrooms and restaurants was inferior to those of whites. Plessy v. Ferguson thus shot a big hole through the Equal Protection Clause of the Fourteenth Amendment and legitimized racial segregation laws passed by state legislatures. It would be 48 years before the decision was overturned.

World War II changed things. Serving overseas, many young African Americans were for the first time in their lives introduced to a world that did not treat them as inferior, second-rate citizens, forced to use separate drinking fountains, restrooms, hotels, bars and restaurants. As James Jones, who served in the 761st Tank Battalion, put it: *"The French had a certain kind of openness and warmth that they exhibited towards minorities that was just unexplainable. You wouldn't know you were black when you were in their company."* (qtd. in Wormser, "Jim Crow Stories"). For many African Americans it was also the first time they could contribute in some other capacity than as a farmhand. They felt part of something greater than themselves, which in turn gave rise to a powerful feeling they had likely not experienced a lot riding the back of the bus at home: Pride.

Having returned to the United States after the war, many wanted more than just working on a farm like their fathers had done before them (and their fathers' fathers before them, and their fathers' fathers' fathers before them). They wanted to go to college, make something of their life and be treated as they had been in Europe and Australia. And when President Truman ended segregation within the United States Armed Forces in 1948, the time seemed ripe for a renewed push against the many segregation laws.[7]

The U.S. Supreme Court was to play a major role again, only this time it would strike a blow for the unabridged, equal protection of the laws as guaranteed by the Fourteenth Amendment, when, in 1954, in Brown v. Board of Education, it ruled unanimously that *"in the field of public education, the doctrine of "separate but equal" has no place. Separate educational facilities are inherently unequal."* (Brown v. Board of Education of Topeka, 495).[8]

The landmark decision did not lead public schools, colleges and universities in the South to swiftly end their segregational policies though, far from it. If anything, they dug their heels in even deeper, backed by state and local legislatures, mayors, governors, sheriffs and state troopers. But for the first time since Reconstruction, blacks could now invoke the full backing of the federal government if they wanted to enroll at a whites-only public school, college or university.

---

7   Executive Order 9981, issued on July 26, 1948, declared in article 1 that *"there shall be equality of treatment and opportunity for all persons in the armed services without regard to race, color, religion or national origin"*. The last all-black unit of the U.S. military was disbanded in 1954.

8   The class action lawsuit had been brought by the National Association for the Advancement of Colored People (NAACP) on behalf of the plaintiff, Oliver Brown, parent of one of the black children who had been denied access to one of the white schools of Topeka, Kansas. Thurgood Marshall, the NAACP's chief counsel, who argued the case before the Supreme Court, would become the first African-American justice of the Supreme Court in 1967.

If that makes the post-Brown v. Board of Education enroll-ment of blacks in white schools seem relatively open-and-shut, it is important to realize it was more like the opposite. The harsh reality was that a small group of African-American kids had to stomach the bravery of letting themselves be used as a crowbar to pry open a door that had remained shut for 335 years, facing hostile crowds of parents, students and teachers as they tried to enroll, without being protected by local or state police officers.

Like the 'Little Rock Nine', a group of African-American students who enrolled at Little Rock Central High School, in Little Rock, Arkansas, in 1957. Apart from said hostile crowds, Arkansas Governor Orval Faubus also deployed the Arkansas National Guard to prevent the nine teenagers from entering the high school, which in turn prompted President Eisenhower to order elements of the 101st Airborne Division—which had seen action of a different kind thirteen years earlier, in France, Holland and Belgium—to protect the nine black students on their way to school and between classes (Belknap, 46–47). Eisenhower also federalized the Arkansas National Guard, taking it away from the governor.

A few years later it was the State of Mississippi that became the unwilling frontline in the fight against segregation, after the Supreme Court on September 10, 1962, overturned a stay of a Fifth Circuit order for the admission of African-American student James Meredith to the all-white State University of Mississippi (Belknap, 46–47).[9]

Here too, local and state authorities refused to comply with the Supreme Court ruling, because three days later Mississippi Governor Ross Barnett declared on statewide television: "*We will not surrender to the evil and illegal forces of tyranny.*" (qtd. in Schlesinger, 318).[10]

---

9   Meredith had been trying to enroll at 'Ole Miss' since January 1961.

10   Just how vehemently Barnett was opposed to racial integration may be illustrated by a quote from his election campaign in 1959, when he said that

Barnett must have realized that the U.S. Justice Department, headed by President Kennedy's brother Robert F. Kennedy, could not let this refusal stand, but in a series of subsequent phone calls with the Attorney General he nevertheless tried to keep up his defiant stance.

The following conversation between Robert Kennedy and Barnett, held on September 25, 1962, may serve as an illustration of the untenable position Southern local and state officials found themselves in when defending segregation in public schools after Brown v. Board of Education:

Barnett: That's what it's going to boil down to—whether Mississippi can run its institutions or the federal government is going to run things...

Kennedy: I don't understand, Governor. Where do you think this is going to take your own state?

Barnett: A lot of states haven't had the guts to take a stand. We are going to fight this thing....This is like a dictatorship. Forcing him physically into Ole Miss. General, that might bring on a lot of trouble. You don't want to do that. You don't want to physically force him in.

Kennedy: You don't want to physically keep him out..... Governor, you are a part of the United States.

Barnett: We have been a part of the United States but I don't know whether we are or not.

Kennedy: Are you getting out of the Union?

Barnett: It looks like we're being kicked around—like we don't belong to it. General, this thing is serious.

"the Negro is different because God made him different to punish him. His forehead slants back. His nose is different. His lips are different, and his color is sure different." (qtd. in TIME, "Mississippi Mud").

Kennedy: It's serious here.

*Barnett: Must it be over one little boy—backed by commu-
nist front—backed by the NAACP which is a communist
front?.... I'm going to treat you with every courtesy but I
won't agree to let that boy to get to Ole Miss. I will never
agree to that. I would rather spend the rest of my life in a
penitentiary than do that.*

*Kennedy: I have a responsibility to enforce the laws of the
United States.... The orders of the court are going to be
upheld. As I told you, you are a citizen not only of the State
of Mississippi but also of the United States. Could I give you
a ring?*

Barnett: You do that.... Good to hear from you. (qtd. in
Schlesinger, 318–19).[11]

More than anything else, Barnett was concerned about his
own image. Having staked out a rebellious, uncompromising
position, frequently proclaimed in dramatic fashion on television and before large crowds of angry, revved up whites, he
now found it impossible to change tack without losing face.
So, when it became clear that the White House was not going
to back down, he asked Robert Kennedy for a large show of
force from the federal government and for U.S. marshals to
point their guns at him, so he could be seen as not having a
choice. When Kennedy asked if it would also suffice if just
one marshal drew his gun, while the others kept their hands
on their holsters, Barnett replied: "*They must all draw their
guns. Then they should point their guns at us and then we
could step aside. This could be very embarrassing down here
for us. It is necessary.*" (qtd. in Roberts, 288).

---

11   The conversation is a striking example of the shifting momentum in the
fight for racial equality and of how the same racist attitudes that had sparked
the Civil War a little over a hundred years before, would this time be defeated
through legal rather than military means; for the most part at least.

Barnett kept veering between feigned acquiescence and howling defiance, promising the Kennedys to help Meredith's registration go smoothly one moment, while firing up the segregationist mob and backpedaling from those same promises the next, not unlike talking to the fire department about helping with fire prevention while at the same time handing out matches and drums of gasoline to a group of pyromaniacs.

Early Saturday evening, September 29, Barnett suggested that Meredith be registered secretly, only to cancel it shortly after the Kennedys had reluctantly accepted it (Schlesinger, 321). That same evening, JFK federalized the Mississippi National Guard, like Eisenhower had done five years earlier with Arkansas' National Guard.[12]

The next day, Kennedy addressed the nation in a televised broadcast, signaling he would not accept the South's defiance of Federal law, no matter how strong and heartfelt: "*Americans are free, in short, to disagree with the law, but not to disobey it. For in a government of laws and not of men, no man, however prominent or powerful, and no mob, however unruly or boisterous, is entitled to defy a court of law.*" (Kennedy, "University of Mississippi").

Around the same time Kennedy gave this speech, riots broke out around the administration building on the campus of the University of Mississippi, where James Meredith and the 400 federal marshals protecting him were besieged by an angry mob of 2,500 segregationists (Sitton, "Shots"). A force of 200 state troopers that had previously been used by Governor Barnett to block one of Meredith's earlier

---

12   Rapping the table where he had just sat down to sign the executive order federalizing the Mississippi National Guard, Kennedy said to Norbert Schlei of the Office of Legal Counsel, who had brought over the document: "*You know, that's Grant's table.*" (qtd. in Schlesinger, 321). Schlei then went downstairs to inform waiting reporters about what had just happened. Moments later, Kennedy sprinted to the top balustrade and called down to Schlei: "*Don't tell them about General Grant's table.*".

registration attempts, stood by without interfering, before pulling back from the riot scene altogether, leaving the marshals to fend for themselves.[13]

Shortly after midnight, reinforcements began arriving in the form of units of the—now federalized—Mississippi National Guard and federal troops from Fort Bragg, Fort Dix, Fort Benning and Fort Campbell, until a total force of some 3,000 soldiers and guardsmen was able to quell the riot (Sitton, "Shots").

On October 1, James Meredith was finally able to register at the University of Mississippi, after which federal marshals escorted him to his first class, *Colonial American History* (Phillips, "Campus"). He graduated on August 18, 1963, with a degree in political science.

Brown v. Board of Education had a major impact on the fight against segregation, but it only applied to public education. To end segregation in other parts of life as well, such as public transportation, restaurants, restrooms etc., new legal challenges would have to be mounted.

Meanwhile, the NAACP, bolstered by its momentous victory in Brown v. Board of Education, had sought to keep the momentum by deploying a tried and tested weapon of the oppressed and powerless the world over: nonviolent resistance. Massive participation was required for it to work, but the NAACP knew that the African-American community was highly motivated to contribute. All that was needed was a spark.

On December 1, 1955, Rosa Parks, secretary of the NAACP in Montgomery, Alabama, refused to give up her seat on the bus to a white passenger. She was subsequently arrested and

---

13   On September 30, at 11.00 p.m., while the U.S. Marshals at Ole Miss were being attacked by the mob, Governor Barnett went on the air and instead of calling for restraint, said: "*I will never yield a single inch in my determination to win the fight we are engaged in. I call upon every Mississippian to keep his faith and his courage. We will never surrender.*" (qtd. in Roberts, 295).

taken to the city jail, where she was fingerprinted, booked and allowed a phone call, after which Ed Nixon, President of the Montgomery NAACP, arranged the bond for her release (Gray, 50–51).

Several key people of the African-American community of Montgomery quickly realized that if ever there was momentum to protest segregation on buses, it was now (Gray, 52). That same night, Jo Ann Robinson, President of the Women's Political Council, another Montgomery civil rights organization, created and mimeographed thirty thousand flyers aimed at igniting outrage over Mrs. Parks arrest. It read:

"This is for Monday, December 5, 1955

Another Negro woman has been arrested and thrown into jail because she refused to get up out of her seat on the bus for a white person to sit down.

It is the second time since the Claudette Colbert [Colvin] case that a Negro woman has been arrested for the same thing. This has to be stopped.

Negroes have rights, too, for if Negroes did not ride the buses, they could not operate. Three-fourths of the riders are Negroes, yet we are arrested, or have to stand over empty seats. If we do not do something to stop these arrests, they will continue. The next time it may be you, or your daughter, or mother.

This woman's case will come up on Monday. We are, therefore, asking every Negro to stay off the buses Monday in protest of the arrest and trial. Don't ride the buses to work, to town, to school, or anywhere on Monday.

You can afford to stay out of school for one day if you have no other way to go except by bus.

You can also afford to stay out of town for one day. If you work, take a cab, or walk. But please, children and grown-ups, don't ride the bus at all on Monday. Please stay off of all buses Monday." (qtd. in Gray, 54).

The boycott was initially meant for just the one day, but when city officials refused to give in despite its resounding success, it was decided to continue the protest until segregation on the Montgomery buses ended (Gray, 60–62). So, for the next 381 days, the black people of Montgomery walked, bicycled, carpooled and hitchhiked their way through town, led and inspired by the newly elected leader of the Montgomery Improvement Association, the young and charismatic Reverend Martin Luther King Jr.

In February 1956, while the bus boycott continued, the NAACP filed the federal civil action suit Browder v. Gayle in U.S. District Court, challenging the constitutionality of segregation laws for buses outright.[14] A few months later, on June 19, the court ruled in favor of Mrs. Browder, stating that enforced segregation on motor buses operating in the city of Montgomery indeed violated the Equal Protection Clause of the Fourteenth Amendment (Gray, 90–91).[15] On November 13, the U.S. Supreme Court upheld that ruling, ending segregation on Montgomery buses.[16]

---

14   Mrs. Browder had also been arrested for sitting in the white section of a public bus in Montgomery, some months before Rosa Parks. The other party in the case was the Mayor of Montgomery, W.A. Gayle. The NAACP lawyers filed the case because they could take it directly to federal court and focus on the question of constitutionality with regards to the segregation laws for the Montgomery buses (Gray, 70–73). The Rosa Parks case was left out intentionally, for fear of complicating the issue (Gray, 69).

15   Interestingly, the district court ruling of Browder v. Gayle thus overturned the Supreme Court ruling of Plessy v. Ferguson. One of the judges in Browder v Gayle, Frank M. Johnson, later noted that this was probably the first time in U.S. legal history a district court overruled a decision of the U.S. Supreme Court (Johnson, 16).

16   The bus protest did not end immediately with the Supreme Court ruling, because it took until December 20 until the district court entered an order

The Montgomery Bus Boycott had an enormous impact on the civil rights movement. It proved nonviolent activism could be a powerful force for change and propelled Martin Luther King Jr. into the national spotlight. The civil rights movement's choice for nonviolent but persistent resistance—and the graphic images that came with it, of black schoolkids and students being harassed by angry mobs, of silent black youngsters being dragged from their stools at whites-only lunch counters, hit and kicked into submission by crowds of whites—would also help garner sympathy from the large group of white Americans who neither fanatically opposed nor outright supported equal rights for blacks, as well as increase the pressure on the federal government to act.

In May 1961, following another U.S. Supreme Court decision, Boynton v. Virginia—which ruled all segregation in interstate bus transportation unconstitutional, including in restrooms, restaurants and bus terminal waiting rooms—a group of thirteen civil rights activists, called the Freedom Riders, boarded buses in Washington D.C. with the plan to ride to New Orleans, to challenge the continued segregation in interstate public transportation in the South.[17]

In each bus, a black Freedom Rider would sit in a seat reserved for whites and an interracial pair would sit in adjoining seats, while one Rider would abide by the segregationist customs such as they existed and act as an observer (Arsenault, 111–12). At each stop, a black passenger would use 'whites only' services such as restrooms and diners, while a white passenger would use the 'colored' services.

---

acknowledging receipt of the mandate from the Supreme Court, which officially ended the case of *Browder v Gayle*. On that day, Dr. King, Mrs. Parks and several others for the first time boarded and rode a bus in Montgomery on an integrated basis (Gray, 94).

17   One of the Supreme Court justices ruling in favor of Boynton was John Marshall Harlan II, grandson of John Marshal Harlan, the Supreme Court justice who had been the lone dissenter in Plessy v. Ferguson in 1896.

In several Southern cities the Freedom Riders were 'only' arrested for defying the local segregation laws—even though Boynton v. Virginia had already rendered these null and void—but in others, like Birmingham, Anniston and Montgomery (all in Alabama) they were awaited by angry mobs and beaten with fists, clubs, bricks, knives and lead pipes, sometimes to within an inch of their lives (Arsenault, 212–19). In Birmingham, the Commissioner of Public Safety, Eugene "Bull" Connor, allowed the local chapter of the Ku Klux Klan (KKK) to attack the Riders undisturbed by local police for fifteen minutes (Arsenault, 137). In Anniston, the KKK firebombed one of the buses; squeezing themselves through the windows, the passengers managed to escape with their lives, though several Freedom Riders had to be hospitalized (Arsenault, 144).

The attacks continued, but the Freedom Riders would not relent. Anticipating more brutality against the Riders in Jackson, Mississippi, Attorney General Robert Kennedy made a deal behind the scenes with James Eastland, the conservative long-serving U.S. Senator from Mississippi, not to oppose the Riders' arrest, in exchange for the latter's promise to protect them against further violence (Schlesinger, 299). Kennedy also urged the civil rights movement to call for a "*cooling off*" period, but the movement wanted to keep the pressure on and rejected any sort of armistice (qtd. in Schlesinger, 299). Meanwhile, the White House continued to put pressure on the Interstate Commerce Commission (ICC) to issue new rules that would end discrimination in interstate travel. It did so a few months later, with the new rules going into effect on November 1, 1961.

During the spring of 1963 the epicenter of the civil rights movement pivoted back to Birmingham, Alabama, once again, after reverend Fred Shuttlesworth—leader of the Birmingham civil rights movement and co-founder of the Southern Christian Leadership Conference (SCLC)—asked

Martin Luther King and the SCLC, of which King was president, to come to Birmingham and help in the fight against segregation (Eskew, 4).

Birmingham, the largest city of Alabama, was highly segregated. It also had a police commissioner—the aforementioned 'Bull' Connor—spoiled for a fight, a mayor who a few years earlier had preferred to close parks, playgrounds and swimming pools rather than comply with a federal court order to desegregate them, and a governor who had said, during his inaugural speech just a few months earlier: "*In the name of the greatest people that have ever trod this earth, I draw the line in the dust and toss the gauntlet before the feet of tyranny, and I say segregation now, segregation tomorrow, segregation forever.*" (qtd. in Carter, 11).

Dr. King and the SCLC, for their part, badly needed a victory in Birmingham, after a civil rights campaign in Albany, Georgia, had failed to produce any results the previous year. But Reverend Shuttlesworth assured King and the SCLC: "*Birmingham is where it's at, gentlemen. I assure you, if you come to Birmingham, we will not only gain prestige but really shake the country.*"(qtd. in Eskew, 209). In short, all the elements and players were there for a brutal confrontation.[18]

Through lunch counter sit-ins, church kneel-ins, boycotts and marches, the SCLC wanted to increase the pressure on the white business community and fill the jails with so many protesters that the city's political leaders would have no choice but to negotiate. The boycott indeed succeeded in pushing business leaders toward wanting to put an end to segregation in their stores, but it was Bull Connor who

---

18   In *But for Birmingham*, Eskew denies the SCLC was out for provocative confrontation, but Adam Fairclough convincingly argues in *To Redeem the Soul of America* that this seems unlikely, since the SCLC was familiar with "*the Ghandian stratagem of inviting the oppressor to inflict violence upon the non-violent protester*", and, moreover, knew that Birmingham "*was regarded as the most dangerous city in the South from the standpoint of the civil rights movement*", so that "*with or without Connor, SCLC was all but guaranteed a violent reception*" (Fairclough, 414).

would make the Birmingham Campaign the turning point of the civil rights movement, when he turned fire hoses and attack dogs on peaceful teenage protesters under the watchful eye of reporters and cameras (Haily, "Dogs and Hoses"; Washington Post, "Fire Hoses"). The vivid images that were subsequently broadcast on national television shocked the country and convinced many that this kind of repressive police action went much too far.

A few months after Birmingham, several civil rights organizations, including the NAACP, SCLC and the SNCC (Student Nonviolent Coordinating Committee), organized the massive 'March on Washington for Jobs and Freedom', to call for civil rights and an end to employment discrimination on a national level. On August 28, 1963, more than 200,000 demonstrators took part in the March and saw Martin Luther King speak from the steps of the Lincoln Memorial (Barber, 141). The event was widely televised.[19]

Dr. King started his speech by commemorating that 100 years after Lincoln's Emancipation Proclamation, "*the Negro still is not free.*" (King, "Dream", 1). He blamed America for having defaulted on its promise of "*unalienable rights of life, liberty and the pursuit of happiness*" "*insofar as her citizens of color are concerned*", and urged that "*this is no time to engage in the luxury of cooling off or to take the tranquilizing drug of gradualism*" (King, "Dream", 1–2). He passionately called for nonviolent action and for not being satisfied until full equality was achieved, even though he confided that he did not know how this was to be achieved, saying that "*somehow this situation can and will be changed*" (King, "Dream", 4).

Then he diverted from his prepared remarks and allowed himself a moment of dreaming.

---

19   In fact, with the networks using about 35 cameras, it was the biggest event since John F. Kennedy's inauguration (Adams 1963).

"I have a dream that one day this nation will rise up and live out the true meaning of its creed: "We hold these truths to be self-evident, that all men are created equal.""

"I have a dream that one day on the red hills of Georgia the sons of former slaves and the sons of former slave owners will be able to sit down together at the table of brotherhood."

"I have a dream that one day even the state of Mississippi, a state sweltering with the heat of injustice, sweltering with the heat of oppression, will be transformed into an oasis of freedom and justice."

"I have a dream that my four little children will one day live in a nation where they will not be judged by the color of their skin but by the content of their character."

"I have a dream today."[20]

Part of that dream would come true in Dr. King's lifetime. Together with the Birmingham Campaign, the March on Washington increased the pressure on the Kennedy administration to act, and the following year, on July 2, 1964, the Civil Rights Act was passed, outlawing all racial segregation.[21] The Voting Rights Act, prohibiting discrimination in voting, followed a year later.[22]

---

20   Excerpts from King's speech (4–5).

21   The act was signed into law by President Lyndon B. Johnson, after John F. Kennedy had been assassinated the previous year, on November 22, 1963.

22   The Selma to Montgomery marches of March 1965—touched off by the killing of civil rights activist Jimmie Lee Jackson and the continued obstruction against black voter registration in Alabama—were the immediate impetus for the Voting Rights Act of 1965. The violence against the peaceful marchers on 'Bloody Sunday' (March 7, 1965) convinced President Lyndon B. Johnson of the urgent need for a Voting Rights Act. In a speech to a joint session of Congress on March 15, 1965, Johnson told Congress he would send a law to Congress to *"eliminate illegal barriers to vote…"*, adding: *"But even if we pass this bill, the battle will not be over. What happened in Selma is part of a far larger movement which reaches into every section and State of America. It is the effort of American*

Though both laws were big steps towards racial equality, true societal change inevitably takes time, a reflection that might have crossed Martin Luther King's mind if he went to see *Guess Who's Coming to Dinner*, perhaps one night in December 1967.[23]

Societal change takes time. Sadly, Dr. King did not have any time left to see more of his dream come true. He was assassinated on April 4, 1968.

Would he have deemed it likely that a black president would be elected in 2008? Or that in 2013 New York City would elect a liberal white mayor with a black wife and two mixed-race children, one of them a son with a sizable Afro?

Perhaps he dreamed about that too.

Negroes to secure for themselves the full blessings of American life. Their cause must be our cause too. Because it is not just Negroes, but really it is all of us, who must overcome the crippling legacy of bigotry and injustice." (Johnson, "Voting Rights").

23   Stanley Kramer's *Guess Who's Coming to Dinner* premiered on December 11, 1967. Coincidentally, the Supreme Court had handed down an important decision on interracial marriage just a few months earlier (Loving v. Virginia), in which it ruled that all laws prohibiting interracial marriage were in violation of the Equal Protection Clause of the Fourteenth Amendment.

20

The Cultural Revolution

"There cannot be peaceful coexistence in the ideological realm. Peaceful coexistence corrupts."[1]

Jiang Qing, Chinese party official and
wife of Mao Zedong, April 1967

O N NOVEMBER 12, 2013, AT THE END of its Third Plenary
Session, the 18th Central Committee of the Communist
Party of China issued a communiqué stating its intention to
have markets play a "decisive" role in allocating resources,
thus basically acknowledging that markets are better at this
than government (Hui, "Market").

Historically, the Third Plenum—referring to the third
time the new leader of the Communist Party chairs a plenary
session of the Central Committee—has often marked the
starting point of major economic and political reforms. The
Third Plenum of the 11th Central Committee for instance,
decided in 1978 that China's economy would be opened up
and make the transition to a more market oriented economy,
while the Third Plenum of the 14th Central Committee in
1993 declared that the purpose of reforming China's economic system was to establish a 'socialist market economy',
leading to the dismantling of a large part of China's state-
owned economy (Jiwei, 142).

The 18th Central Committee's decision to further increase
the role of markets was not the only major reform announced.
President Xi Jinping made clear he also wanted to relax the

---

1   Qtd. in Andrews, 439.

334 — WORLD 2.0

one-child policy, abolish the *Laojiao* system of 'reeducation through labor'—with its detention centers involving forced labor for inmates, who are often sentenced without trial—and reform the system of land ownership, giving farmers more property rights over their land (Kroeber, "Ambitious Agenda").

Of course, if he could, Chairman Mao would turn in the crystal coffin in his mausoleum, contemptuously calling the current Chinese leaders 'capitalist roaders', 'revisionists', 'right-wingers', 'bourgeois elitists' and 'counter-revolutionaries', for straying from the true path of Marxism-Leninism and giving in to the false temptations of market capitalism. And then he would probably send the entire 18th Central Committee to one of the reeducation camps he established back in 1957 during the Anti-Rightist campaign, to purge the 'rightists' within the Communist Party.

The epithet 'rightist' has an interesting history of its own, going back all the way to the times of the French revolution, when those who supported the *Ancien Régime,* the monarchists, the clerics, the conservatives, the traditionalists—in short, the counter-revolutionaries—were seated to the right of the chair of the President of the Parliament.[2] Theirs was a politics of reaction to the ideas of those who sat to the left of the chair, the progressives, the revolutionaries. It was a label that stuck, making its way into the 20th century and beyond to denote the difference between the conservatives, capitalists and religious (the right wing) and the progressives, socialists, communists and environmentalists (the left wing).

For Mao Zedong, the fierce revolutionary who had had to fight two bloody civil wars against the conservative nationalists (1927–50) and another war against the Empire of Japan (1937–45) before finally realizing his lifelong dream of a communist China, being a rightist was about the worst

---

2   The term 'rightist' itself was first used in the 1930s.

thing one could be guilty of, short of murdering someone for pleasure. This was a man who in 1934–35 had marched 6,000 miles with 90,000 comrades in arms—more than 80,000 of whom would not survive the ordeal—just so he could continue the fight against Chiang Kai-shek.[3] To stain that hard-won victory by watering down the teachings of Marx and Lenin—let alone outright replace them with free markets and private property, the epitomes of capitalism—would be tantamount to treason in Mao's eyes.

To Mao, rightists and revisionists were a threat to the revolution because they wanted to change, to revise Marxism-Leninism, supposedly to make it more compatible with the real world. But why would you revise something that was already perfect? No, such dilution would only lead to imperfection and, ultimately, failure.

His vigilant worry about the simmering survival, even potential flourishing of revisionism—especially in the form of economic and democratic reform—further increased when, for a short period in 1956–57, the Communist Party of China (CPC) encouraged intellectuals to voice their lingering criticisms on government policies during what would become to be known as the Hundred Flowers campaign.[4]

At first, people were reluctant to speak out, but after Mao strongly supported open discussion of government policies, the flood gates opened and a tidal wave of critique started pouring in. Newspapers were filled with critical views, big character posters with political messages were put up on the walls of schools and public buildings, magazine articles about modernizing the economy and democratizing the government were published, debates were organized (Meisner,

---

3   For more on distance and survival estimates of the Long March, see chapter 12, Chinese Civil War Part I & II, note 9.

4   The name of the campaign comes from a quote from Mao Zedong, used in various speeches in the mid 1950s, in which he urged to "*let a hundred flowers bloom; let a hundred schools of thought contend.*"

174–75). For Mao, it was a classic example of 'be careful what you wish for'.[5]

Within a few months, the Hundred Flowers campaign was halted and Mao reversed course, moving to persecute the same intellectuals he had asked to criticize government policy—for criticizing government policy. Had it all been just a ruse to flush them out, or had Mao really been genuinely interested—at first at least—in getting input from people outside the inner circle of party hardliners? It is not entirely clear. Of course, inviting one's opponents to open up only to snap the trap on them later is an old trick, used by many a dictator. On the other hand, seeing as Mao was such a firm believer in the invincibility of Communism, it is also conceivable that he thought open discussion would only serve to show the superiority of Marxism-Leninism to a wider audience.[6] There is also some evidence that suggests Mao believed genuine opposition to the government to be small and that he could use the Hundred Flowers campaign to enlist the support of intellectuals for the policies he wanted to reform himself (Zhisui, 198–99).[7]

Whatever the reason, over 400,000 people would pay a heavy price for their well-meant openness, ranging from being forced to deliver self-criticisms and having their careers sidetracked, to being dismissed from their position

5   In *Mao's China and After*, Meisner argues that Mao's call for more open criticism from the non-Party intelligentsia was primarily meant to revive the revolutionary spirit of a Party leadership and apparatus that was becoming less and less receptive to his radical social and economic agenda (Meisner, 165). That would also explain why, apart from Mao, most of the CPC's highest leaders were opposed to the Hundred Flowers campaign, which they considered a threat to the Party's power base and their own positions (Meisner, 165–74).

6   That Mao saw little room for real political criticism may be illustrated by his warning, in an address to the Communist Youth League on May 25, 1957, that "*Any speech or action which deviates from socialism is entirely wrong.*" (qtd. in Meisner, 186).

7   For a discussion of possible reasons for breaking the promise not to retaliate against the intellectuals who spoke out during the Hundred Flowers campaign, see also Meisner, 183–84.

altogether, or sent to a reeducation camp where hard labor served as more than just a gentle nudge toward the 'right' direction.[8]

In January 1958, with the Anti-Rightist campaign in full swing, Mao launched the second five year plan, dubbed 'The Great Leap Forward'. Its primary goal was to rapidly industrialize China, while staying true to Marxism-Leninism, a transformation that required the peasantry to be mobilized en masse, since China was still a largely agricultural society. To increase its control over the peasants, the CPC therefore completely abolished private ownership of the agricultural means of production, land, labor and tools. The peasants were organized into large communes of up to 20,000 households, that were charged with both agricultural and industrial tasks, such as construction and steel production, the latter by using small blast furnaces known as 'backyard furnaces', so called because they were constructed in the backyards of the communes (Dikötter, xix).

Mao deemed steel of vital importance to China's industrialization and thus greatly encouraged its production by the communes. Unfortunately, the 'steel' produced by the communes was not actually steel but merely low value—and often low quality—pig iron. Producing high quality steel required additional steps, which could only be done at large-scale factories. When Mao found out about this he nevertheless decided to let the communes continue producing their backyard furnace pig iron, because he did not want to sap the zeal of the peasants (Zhisui, 290–91). The use of backyard furnaces was only phased out months later.

Of course, however zealous the peasants, there are only so many hours in a day. And with their involvement in the production of 'steel' as well as the construction of offices,

---

8   Exact figures are not available, but most estimates arrive at a figure of at least 400,000 people who were purged during the Anti-Rightist Campaign of 1957–58 (Teiwes, "Politics and Purges", 228, note h).

schools and so on, grain production suffered. Attempts at agricultural innovation, using untested—and later proven unsound—methods, made things even worse. But although harvest sizes thus decreased considerably, commune leaders, hoping to win praise from higher up political cadres, reported highly inflated production numbers. Consequently, almost the entire harvest was sent to the cities, leaving practically nothing for the peasants themselves (Zhisui, 283).

The result was massive famine, particularly in the country-side. Though Mao was aware of this, China remained a net exporter of grain between 1958–60 (Walker, 130, table 41). In fact, grain export even increased in 1959, because 'The Great Helmsman' did not want to have to admit his policies were a failure. While the death toll in the countryside was rising rapidly, Mao said: "*Tell the peasants to resume eating chaff and herbs for half the year*", and *after some hardship for one or two or three years things will turn around*". (qtd. in Jisheng, 337). By then, tens of millions of people had already died of starvation though.[9]

And so the Great Leap Forward actually became a Great Leap Backward. Due to this massive failure of Maoism—with its focus on the peasants and their revolutionary enthusiasm to bring about change—its chief advocate and namesake lost power and prestige within the Party for the first time, while moderates like Liu Shaoqi and Deng Xiaoping rose in prominence.

Liu Shaoqi succeeded Mao as President of China in 1959, but Mao retained his position as Chairman of the Central Committee, the Central Politburo and the Military Commission. Liu and Deng Xiaoping—who headed the

---

9   Estimates about the actual death toll vary widely, ranging from roughly 20 million to more than 45 million. Two of the more recent studies, one by Dutch historian and modern China expert Frank Dikötter (*Mao's Great Famine: The History of China's Most Devastating Catastrophe, 1958–1962*, 2010), the other by Chinese journalist Yang Jisheng (*Tombstone: The Great Chinese Famine, 1958–1962*, 2013), arrive at a death toll of 45 million and 36 million, respectively.

powerful CPC Secretariat—set out to restore the economy and increase agricultural production, reversing the collectivization and introducing reforms. By 1963, China's economy was growing again (Guo, 126, fig. 8.1).

Meanwhile, Mao was brooding over his diminished political status, which only worsened with the growing success of the policies of Liu Shaoqi, who by now was considered his heir apparent. Looking for a way to get back into the game, Mao once more focused on his strength and reputation as a communist ideologue, taking aim at the 'right wingers' and 'capitalist roaders' who were supposedly taking over the Party and destroying the revolution from the inside. In other words: his rivals.

Through covert tactics, such as nudging political allies towards criticizing his political opponents and their allies in newspaper articles and party meetings, and using the slightest whiff of bourgeois tendencies and revisionism to sack, demote or denounce non-allies in key positions within the Party and the military (with the goal of replacing them with staunch allies), Mao slowly moved his pieces in position for his great offensive against the moderates.[10]

On May 16, 1966, the Central Committee released a circular launching the 'Great Proletarian Cultural Revolution', to protect the socialist revolution from being watered down by the revisionists, who, according to the Committee, were attacking the proletarian left and shielding the bourgeois right, "*thereby preparing public opinion for the restoration of capitalism.*" ("Circular", 10). "*Those representatives of the bourgeoisie*", the circular continued, *who have sneaked into the party, the government, the army, and various cultural circles are a bunch of counter-revolutionary revisionists. Once conditions are ripe, they will seize political power and turn the*

---

10   For some examples of Mao's sometimes elaborate scheming, see Edward Rice's *Mao's Way* (185–86, 269, 286–87).

dictatorship of the proletariat into a dictatorship of the bour-
geoisie. Some of them we have already seen through, others we
have not.".

In other words, the socialist revolution was in danger. To
save it, "*the whole party must follow Comrade Mao Tse-tung's*
instructions, hold high the great banner of the proletarian
Cultural Revolution, thoroughly expose the reactionary bour-
geois stand of those so-called 'academic authorities' who oppose
the party and socialism, thoroughly criticize and repudiate the
reactionary bourgeois ideas in the sphere of academic work,
education, journalism, literature and art, and publishing, and
seize the leadership in these cultural spheres." ("Circular", 10).

The document effectively gave Mao a blank check to call
out whomever he wanted as a counter-revolutionary, revisionist, bourgeois, right-wing, capitalist roader. Academics,
journalists, artists, officers, nobody was save, not even senior
party officials—especially not senior party officials —because
the more power and prestige one had, the more likely that
envious enemies would set the bloodhounds on his trail by
calling him a revisionist or something else threatening the
revolution, an intellectual for example. Thus, as had been the
case with the French Revolution's Reign of Terror (1793–94)
and Joseph Stalin's Great Purge (1936–39), jockeying for political supremacy was once again disguised as an epic fight
against the 'enemies of the revolution'.

The bloodhounds of the Great Proletarian Cultural
Revolution came in the form of fanatical young university
and high school students, who had started to organize themselves as so-called Red Guards shortly after the May 16 circular and whose numbers quickly grew after they were openly
encouraged by Mao himself. Equipped with the Little Red
Book and donning themselves in green, army-like jackets
with red armbands on one of the sleeves, the Red Guards

rapidly evolved into paramilitaries loyal to nothing but pure Maoism and to no-one but Mao Zedong himself.[11]

On August 18, 1966, Mao cemented the messianic image the young fanatics had of him by holding a massive rally at Tiananmen Square. Standing atop Tiananmen Gate, wearing his old green army uniform—which he had not worn in years—he waved for hours to the hundreds of thousands of Red Guards gathered below.

The August 18 rally showed the Cultural Revolution was going to be more than just some shuffling of positions within the Communist Party and picking up a few thousand revisionists. These young radicals meant business. They had not yet been encapsulated by the system, had very little to lose and were at that time in life when one is most susceptible to being recruited for a cause.

The American journalist and activist Anna Louise Strong met some Red Guard representatives at Tiananmen Square in September 1966, just before things would get ugly for hundreds of thousands of local and senior officials, teachers, journalists, artists and others. One of the Red Guard leaders—who identified herself as Fighting Red—explained the Red Guards's straightforward logic and uncompromising philosophy: "*Chairman Mao has defined our future as an armed revolutionary youth organization, legal under the dictatorship of the proletariat...So if Chairman Mao is our Red-Commander-in-Chief and we are his red soldiers, who can stop us? First we will make China red from inside out and then we will help the working people of other countries make the whole world red...And then the whole universe.*" (qtd. in Strong, "Red Guards").

Mao directed the Red Guards to attack the 'Four Olds' of Chinese society: old customs, old habits, old culture and old

11   The Little Red Book, as it is known in the West, is a pocket book with famous Mao quotations. First published in 1964, its actual title is 'Quotations from Chairman Mao Tse-tung'.

thinking, because he considered them a hindrance to achieving a true communist state. Religion, tradition, rituals, all of these were just poison for people's minds, keeping them trapped in the social order of the bourgeois state.

The Red Guards took to their mission with zealous enthusiasm, changing the names of buildings, streets, even their own names, into something more revolutionary, destroying museums, churches, mosques, monasteries and temples, burning books and paintings, smashing religious statues (Yan, 71–74; Lee, 87). Party officials, local administrators, university professors, school officials, educated cadres, scientists, writers and other intellectuals were publicly humiliated and in many cases beaten, tortured, even murdered (Yan, 79–83). Everything needed to be changed, everything old was suspect.

During the summer of 1967, rebellion against everything institutionalized, especially Party cadres, reached a high point, with Red Guards locked into battle with other, more conservative mass organizations and local elements of the People's Liberation Army (PLA)—who generally supported the Party cadres and wanted to restore order—throughout the country (Meisner, 336–39).

The apex of these revolutionary tensions between the PLA and the Red Guards came in July 1967, when, in the city of Wuhan, things came to a head between a conservative organization of industrial workers called the Million Heroes— who were supported by the PLA—and Red Guard factions.[12]

On July 14, two members of the at that moment all-powerful Cultural Revolution Small Group, Xie Fuzhi and Wang Li,

---

12   The tensions had a significant impact on the economic productivity of Wuhan. According to one contemporary report, over 2,400 factories and mines in the Wuhan area had suspended production or saw their output decrease by half between April 19-June 3, while 50,000 workers were involved in armed conflict one way or another (Robinson, "Wuhan Incident", 418, note 19). Railway services across the vital First Yangtze River Bridge were also regularly interrupted (Robinson, "Wuhan Incident", 418–19).

arrived in Wuhan to resolve the situation (Rice, 398).[13] A few days later, they called a meeting with the highest ranking officers, notifying them of their—hardly surprising—decision to support the Red Guard factions in Wuhan and faulting the military for siding with the Million Heroes (Rice, 398–99). The next morning, the PLA occupied key points in the city, led an uprising of the Million Heroes and seized Xie Fuzhi and Wang Li (Rice, 399–400).[14] Beijing reacted immediately, sending the 8190 Airborne Division—which was stationed in the Wuhan area—the 15th Army from Xiaogan and units of the East China Fleet to deal with the insurgents (Robinson, "Wuhan Incident", 427). The mutiny was suppressed a few days later, but nevertheless served as a serious wake-up call for the powers that be in Beijing.

Initially, the Wuhan Incident gave the Cultural Revolution an even more powerful leftward impetus though, with calls for a large-scale purge of the PLA, the last stable bastion of the country. Jiang Qing—Mao's wife and member of the Cultural Revolution Small Group—advised the Red Guards to "*attack with words, but defend yourselves with weapons*" (qtd. in Meisner, 338). Red Guard factions throughout the country readily took this advice to heart and started seizing weapons left and right, including from military depots and military convoys bound for Vietnam (Meisner, 338–39). As a result, violence in the provinces actually increased in August, with heavily armed Red Guards fighting local PLA units, angry peasants attacking local administrative buildings and rebels overtaking the Foreign Ministry in Beijing and burning down

---

13   The Cultural Revolution Group was a quasi-official committee, established with the specific goal of guiding the Cultural Revolution. As such, it assumed many of the powers of the Central Committee and Politburo for a while (Meisner, 314–15). Some prominent members of the group were Chen Boda, Mao's wife Jiang Qing and Xie Fuzhi. For all fifteen members, see the *Historical Dictionary of the Chinese Cultural Revolution* (Jian, 85).

14   Wang Li was kicked and beaten during the kidnapping, leaving him with bruises and a broken left leg, while Xie Fuzhi apparently came away relatively unscathed (Robinson, "Wuhan Incident", 425).

the British Chancery, on August 22. Ever more unruly Red Guard factions were rolling over the country like a plague of locusts, purging intellectuals, party officials and military officers, while schools, universities and factories were closed.

It seemed the young People's Republic of China was rapidly sliding into anarchy, or, worse still, civil war. Realizing the seriousness of the situation, Mao opted for the restoration of order rather than another massive civil war in name of the revolution (Meisner, 339; Rice, 416–17).

On September 5, 1967, the Central Committee, the Central Military Commission, the State Council and the Cultural Revolution Group jointly ordered the PLA to use any means necessary to reestablish law and order in the country (Scobell, 431). The army subsequently carried out this order in the fashion armies usually carry out such orders: brutally.

By October 1968, all the provinces and autonomous regions were firmly under control of the People's Liberation Army again (Scobell, 431). The PLA's political influence also increased. In April 1969, when the Ninth Central Committee of the CPC first convened, 49 percent of its 279 full and alternate members were from the military (Wu, 203).

With the Red Guards gone, a new power struggle emerged in the upper echelons of the Communist Party, this time between Mao and Marshal Lin Biao, his second in command and designated successor.[15] To further increase Lin Biao's influence and political power base, his allies tried to secure the position of President of the People's Republic of China for him (or even for Mao, to strengthen Lin Biao's post-Mao era position), a post that had been vacant since the last holder of the office, Liu Shaoqi, had been purged in 1968.

But Mao, by now uncomfortable with Lin Biao's growing stature within the Party, resisted these efforts and instead

---

15   At the Ninth Party Congress, Lin Biao had been named as the only Vice-Chairman of the CPC and enshrined in the new Party constitution as Mao's "*closest comrade-in-arms and successor*" (qtd. in Gao, xxi).

started moving against his 'closest comrade-in-arms and successor', undermining his power base by discrediting and criticizing his allies (Yan, 313–14; Rice, 504–05). Early September 1971, after finding out Mao intended to seek a direct and decisive confrontation with Lin Biao, his allies (allegedly) responded by plotting to assassinate Mao (Meisner, 385).[16]

The plot failed however (again, if it indeed existed in the first place, no actual attempt on Mao's life was made) and Lin Biao and his family allegedly fled the country in a plane bound for the Soviet Union. The official version of the CPC is that the plane crashed in Mongolia on September 13, 1971, killing everyone inside.[17]

With Lin Biao out of the way, conflict now erupted between Mao's wife Jiang Qing and three other ultra-left wing radical ideologues—collectively known as the Gang of Four—and more moderate party officials such as the popular Premier Zhou Enlai, one of the last moderates left in the center of power, and Vice Premier Deng Xiaoping, who had been purged in 1969 but allowed to return a few years later.

With the party establishment working to undo much of the ideological disorganization that the Cultural Revolution Group and the Red Guards had plowed into the political system during the 1960s, and the Gang of Four in turn using the media to rail against that same party establishment and its 'revisionist' attitude, something of a stalemate emerged, paralyzing the government (Teiwes, "Politics and Purges", 485–86). Many officials feared taking any action whatsoever, not wanting to get caught on the wrong side of another

---

16   The existence of the plot, known as Project 5-7-1—so named because pronounced together the numbers rhyme with the characters for 'armed uprising' (Yan, 315)—appears likely, but evidence for it is too thin to be undisputed. For an elaborate description of the coup and how it came into being, see *Turbulent Decade: A History of the Cultural Revolution* (Yan, 310–26).

17   This official version remains disputed (Teiwes, "Lin Biao", 1).

revolution, while others did choose sides, thus contributing to further factionalization. Mao himself mostly supported the Gang of Four—no surprise there—but at the same time also made sure his wife's little clique did not become too powerful (Teiwes, "Politics and Purges", 484–86).

After Zhou Enlai died of cancer, in January 1976, the Gang of Four forbade all public signs of mourning. When, a couple of months later, a crowd nevertheless gathered around the Monument to the People's Heroes at Tiananmen Square to publicly mourn Zhou, the Central Committee violently suppressed the gathering (Jian, 287–88). Deng Xiaoping was also purged—again—for his alleged role in the 'Tiananmen Incident'.

But just a few months later the winds of change would blow through Beijing once more, when, on September 9, 1976, Mao Zedong died, aged 82, robbing the Gang of Four of their guardian angel. On October 6, less than a month after the Great Helmsman's death, the Gang of Four was arrested, ending whatever was left of the Cultural Revolution.[18] Jiang Qing, identified as the leader of the Gang, defended herself at her trial by maintaining that everything she had done had been for Mao, saying: "*I was Chairman Mao's dog. Whomever he told me to bite, I bit.*" (qtd. in Sterba, "Former Chinese Leaders").[19]

The Chinese people had finally had their fill of left-wing radicals, clearing the path for the moderate Deng Xiaoping to make yet another comeback and become the new, undisputed leader of the People's Republic of China in 1978. His subsequent reforms would put China on a path of spectacular economic growth for decades to come.

---

18   Some 400,000 people are estimated to have lost their lives due to the Cultural Revolution between 1966–76 (Meisner, 354).

19   Jiang Qing was sentenced to death in 1981, with a two-year suspension. Two years later the sentence was commuted to life imprisonment. She committed suicide in 1991.

Even today, the Great Leap Forward, the Great Famine and the Great Proletarian Cultural Revolution remain highly sensitive topics in China, with public discussion of them being severely limited.

A huge portrait of Mao Zedong still hangs at Tiananmen Gate.

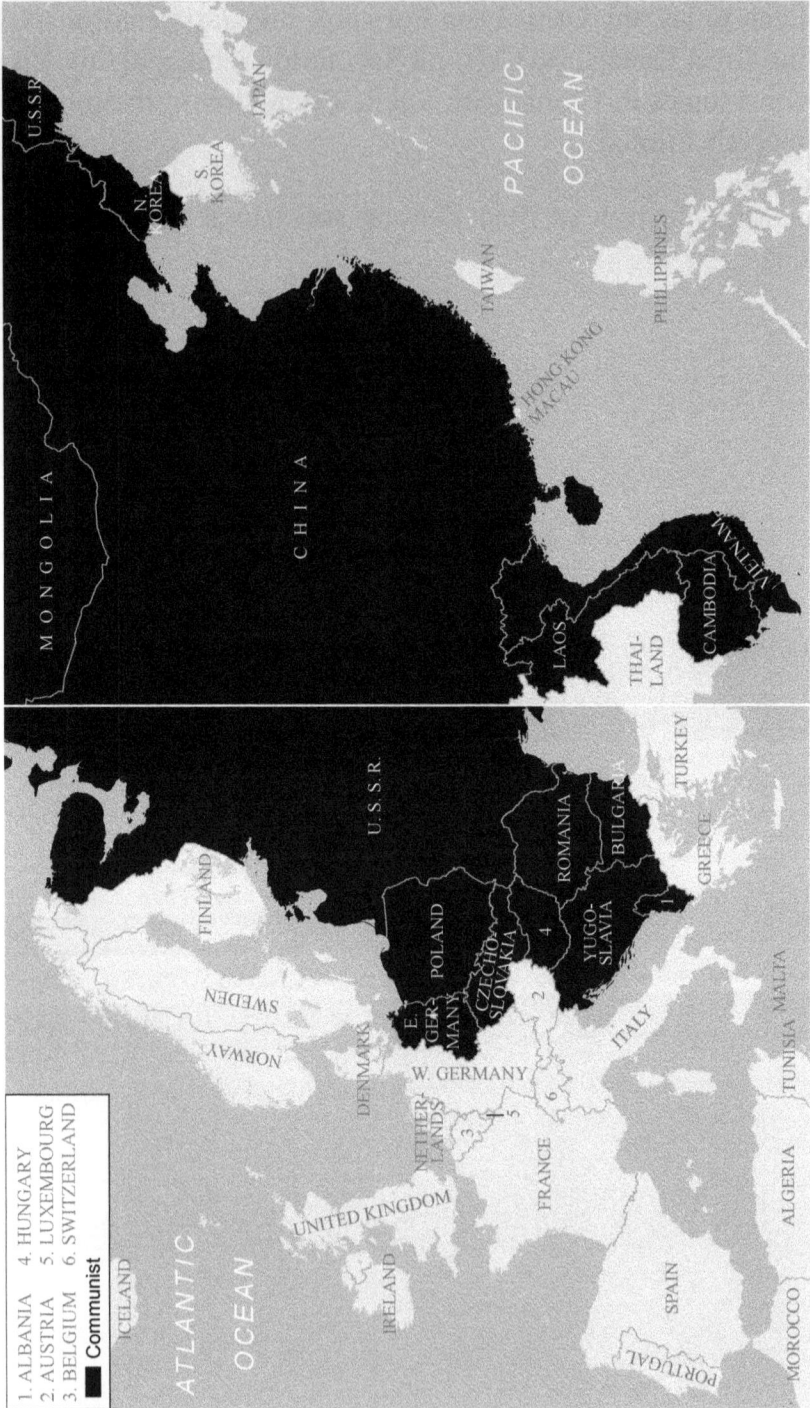

Map 14: Communist States in Europe and Asia, c. 1980s

21

THE END OF COMMUNISM

"The theory of the Communists may be summed up in the single sentence: Abolition of private property."[1]

The Communist Manifesto,
Karl Marx and Friedrich Engels, 1848

"Communism doesn't work because people like to own stuff."

Frank Zappa, musician, songwriter

IN APRIL 2009, NORTH KOREA REMOVED THE word 'communism' from its constitution, replacing it with the 'military first' doctrine, or *Songun*, which means exactly what it says. South Korean media quoted an official from the North as saying the change was made because the ideals of Communism were *"hard to fulfill"* (qtd. in Herskovitz, "North Korea").

And this coming from one of the last countries in the world that was still deserving of the moniker 'communist state', with its centrally planned economy, hardly any private property and state-provided housing, health care, education and food rations. But things change, even in the Democratic People's Republic of Korea (DPRK).

In May 2010, the North Korean government lifted all restrictions on private markets, allowing people to trade most products more freely (Harlan, "N. Korea lifts restrictions"). A significant step as well as a practical one, since most North Koreans were apparently deriving more than half of their

---

1   Marx, "Communist Manifesto", 30.

income from commercial activities at grass-roots market places located throughout the country anyway.[2] And in June 2012, a new agricultural policy was announced that would let farmers keep 30 percent of the target production, with the state taking 70 percent.[3] Moreover, under the new policy, farmers would be allowed to keep any surplus should the target production be exceeded.

Perhaps the DPRK's fanatic aversion against the root of all evil has dissipated somewhat under its new Supreme Leader, Kim Jong-un, who took over from his father, Supreme Leader Kim Jong-il (who had taken over from his father, Eternal President Kim Il-sung) after his demise in 2011. In any case, it seems that North Korea—like several other hard-core communist states from the roaring 20th century, China, Cuba, Vietnam, Laos—is trying to keep the marxist-leninist single-party state, only without the marxist-leninist part.

So what went wrong there? Well, for one thing, Communism didn't deliver. Or, more accurately, the prevailing theory of how to *get* to Communism, i.e., Marxism-Leninism, did not deliver; Communism itself—the stateless, classless, money-less Valhalla in which nobody owns anything because every-body owns everything—was never achieved. Anywhere.

Communist revolutions overthrew existing governments and created single-party socialist states that transferred ownership of the means of production to the state, banning capitalism, yes.[4] But instead of those socialist states 'wither-ing away' as they transformed into true communist societies, they actually grew stronger and more dominant than almost

---

2   In a 2008 survey of North Korean defectors, 69 percent of respondents reported over half their income in the hermit kingdom had come from market activities (Haggard, 10).

3   The new policy is part of the 'June 28 New Economic Management Measures', informally known as the '6.28 Policy' and reportedly implemented in October 2012 (Keck, "Agricultural Reforms").

4   Socialist states are sometimes called communist states. This is a misno-mer though, as there would no longer be a state in a true communist society.

any other form of government.[5] And instead of leading to a classless society, marxist-leninist states merely created a new upper class, the political class. Meanwhile, nothing changed for ordinary people (in the best case scenario, that is). As the much lauded economist John Kenneth Galbraith once said: "*Under capitalism, man exploits man. Under communism, it's just the opposite.*"

So, strong single-party states confiscating private property, suppressing freedom of speech and independent thinking, while nudging / herding / bullying / forcing their citizens to work collectively towards centrally planned goals. What's not to like?

A complicating factor for the socialist states was that they had to compete with the democratic, capitalist states of the West, their Cold War opponents. And not just for ideological, but also for technological and military superiority, as they could ill afford falling behind and risk 'imperialist' interference, or even outright war. This put pressure on socialist economies to be just as resilient, flexible and innovative allocating resources through forward planning by a central authority, as their capitalist counterparts were by chiefly relying on free and open markets. Famines, inferior products and mismatches between expected and actual supply and demand were the result.

And there was another problem: capitalist societies around the world did not collapse the way Marx had predicted.[6]

---

5   As Friedrich Engels wrote in *Anti-Dühring*: "*The first act in which the state really comes forward as the representative of society as a whole—the taking possession of the means of production in the name of society—is at the same time its last independent act as a state. The interference of the state power in social relations becomes superfluous in one sphere after another, and then ceases of itself. The government of persons is replaced by the administration of things and the direction of the process of production. The state is not "abolished", it withers away.*" (315).

6   In *Capital: A Critique of Political Economy* (*Das Kapital*, Vol. I. 1867), Marx wrote: "*Centralisation of the means of production and socialisation of labour at last reach a point where they become incompatible with their capitalist*

During the 19th century, Western countries, pressured by social reformers, slowly started paying heed to the appalling conditions of the large worker class Marx called 'the proletariat'. Over time, laws were enacted to prohibit child labor below a certain age, limit working hours, impose safety and health regulations, guarantee a minimum wage, etc.

Of course this did not happen overnight, or indeed without a fight. Persuading governments to redistribute some of the wealth and political power from the 'haves' to the 'have nots' took countless strikes, riots, marches and speeches, coupled with the rising importance of the economic theories of another highly influential economist, John Maynard Keynes, who argued that aggregate demand plays a vital role in economic growth and that if people don't have any money to spend, the economy will suffer.[7-8]

As a result of this redistribution of resources, life significantly improved for the working class in Western societies in the 20th century, creating a prosperous middle class and the blooming of opportunities for social advancement based on talent and ambition rather than one's station in life.

Between 1928–79 income inequality in the United States sharply declined, with the top one percent's share of total pre-tax income declining from a staggering 21.2 percent in

---

integument. This integument is burst asunder. The knell of capitalist private property sounds. The expropriators are expropriated." (837).

7　　This is an argument that has lately regained attention and support both in the United States and abroad, particularly in the wake of the so-called 'Occupy Wall Street' movement. The reasoning goes that the anemic economic recovery that followed the financial crisis of 2008 was at least partly caused by the growing gap between rich and poor. This may be illustrated by the fact that the U.S. minimum wage of 2015 was, at $7.25, significantly lower than the inflation-adjusted (CPI) $10.72 minimum wage of 1968.

8　　In The General Theory of Employment, Interest and Money (1936), Keynes argued that aggregate demand—rather than aggregate supply—is responsible for the level of employment, that markets cannot achieve full employment on their own if aggregate demand is deficient, such as during an economic downturn, and that government spending is needed in such a situation to increase aggregate demand and restore full employment.

1928 to 8.4 percent in 1976 (Piketty, "Income Inequality",
8–10, Table II). Between 1947–79, real family income in the
U.S. increased by 116 percent for the bottom twenty percent,
while it 'only' increased by 86 percent for the top five percent
(Reich, "Widening Inequality", 17). In other words, during
this period the poor grew richer at a faster rate than the
already rich did (relatively speaking of course), making less
people poor while still making rich people richer.

The irony is that while policies partly inspired by Marx's
theories markedly improved life of the working class in the
West, the full implementation of those theories made things
(much) worse for the working class in the socialist states of
the East, until moderate leaders there gained enough momentum to (re)introduce capitalism.

In China, for example, workers and peasants were still
reeling from the disastrous Great Leap Forward (1958–62)
and Cultural Revolution (1966–76), when Deng Xiaoping—
who had been purged twice by the Maoists—was finally able
to launch a program of much needed economic reforms in
1978, aimed at transforming the Chinese economy into a
more market oriented one.

Meanwhile, in Cambodia, the Khmer Rouge, apparently undeterred by the aforementioned Chinese failures,
had established a government based on Maoist principles,
ruling the country with an iron fist from 1975. Dreaming
of an agrarian-based communist society, the Khmer Rouge
forced millions of city dwellers to the countryside to take up
farming. Money and private property were abolished, religion, modern education and political dissent were forbidden,
schools, churches, mosques and temples were destroyed,
and the rich, intellectuals and soldiers who had fought the
Khmer Rouge in the civil war were executed (Kiernan, 8,
190, 223, 232, 284, 356). At least 1.5 million people thus
perished, before a Vietnamese invasion force defeated the
Khmer Rouge in 1979 (Kiernan, 456–60). After economic

reforms were carried out in the 1980s and early 1990s, the Cambodian economy started growing again.

In the same year the Khmer Rouge came to power in Cambodia, communist North Vietnam emerged victorious from its civil war with U.S. supported South Vietnam. But its subsequent efforts to collectivize agriculture and nationalize factories and services were a disaster, leading to economic chaos and rampant inflation (Alpert, 35–37). After a couple of years of trying to muddle through, the ideologue hardliners were replaced by more moderate leaders, who in 1986 initiated economic reforms to create a socialist-oriented market economy known as *Doi Moi* (Alpert, 37–38).

Vietnam's neighbor Laos was another marxist-leninist state that initially sought to get rid of capitalism altogether, until finding out the hard way that the road to Communism devastated the economy (Bourdet, 9). Like Vietnam, Laos started on a path of economic reform in 1986, decentralizing its economy and encouraging private enterprise.

1986 would also prove to be a watershed year for the country that had adopted Communism before all others, after its new leader, the relatively young Mikhail Sergeyevich Gorbachev, aged 54, announced the need for "*radical reform*" of the Soviet economy at the 27th Congress of the Communist Party of the Soviet Union, stating that mere "*changes in the economic mechanism*" would not suffice (qtd. in CIA, "27th CPSU Congress", 15).

Gorbachev came to power at a time the Soviet Union had been suffering from a stagnant economy for several years, caused in part by falling oil prices—thus reducing foreign currency revenue, which the U.S.S.R needed for importing grain and Western technology—a costly war in Afghanistan, and, perhaps most serious of all, the inability of the centrally planned economy to efficiently produce the wide variety of products and services characteristic for modern economies

(Strayer, 57–60).[9] Still, the new leader of the Soviet Union did not want to completely abandon the socialist economic model, merely to reform, to restructure, to reinvigorate it. He wanted to decentralize part of the economic decision-making process and stimulate individual creativity and innovation, without completely surrendering the economy to capitalism.

He wanted to allow state enterprises to determine for themselves how much to produce for example, based on customer demand. And to make them responsible for their own financing, instead of being propped up by Moscow regardless of their output or actual demand for their products. Gorbachev also moved to allow the establishment of private enterprises for the first time since the 1920s, acknowledging the importance of a private sector in increasing economic efficiency.[10]

Gorbachev's political reforms were characterized by the same kind of pragmatism. He did not seek to replace the single-party socialist state with a Western style democratic capitalist one, only to strengthen it, by allowing more openness from both the people and the central government, and by increasing people's participation in government through the introduction of some democratizing elements. *Perestroika* ('restructuring') and *Glasnost* ('openness'), those were the new magic words.

The same words would also come to define Gorbachev's foreign policy, in which he successfully strived for a détente with the West—reducing the nuclear weapons buildup

---

9 Between 1980–86, the oil price declined from a peak of $37 in 1980 to $14 in 1986. As one of the world's major oil exporters, the Soviet Union was hit hard by this price fall.

10 The 1988 Law on Cooperatives allowed for the creation of privately run, for-profit enterprises, operating much like Western companies. In *Russia's Capitalist Revolution*, Swedish economist Anders Åslund writes that one of the first new cooperatives in Moscow was a Russian restaurant on Kropotkinskaya Street (Åslund, 56–57). *"Unlike Soviet restaurants, it was cozy, had excellent service, and served the best of Russian food, but its prices were Western."* (Åslund, 57).

through the Intermediate-Range Nuclear Forces Treaty of 1987—an end to the war in Afghanistan and loosening Moscow's control over its satellite states, breaking with the so-called Brezhnev Doctrine.

This doctrine, established in 1968, had called for military intervention in Warsaw Pact countries whenever liberalization efforts threatened to undermine socialism. In a (perhaps coincidental) variation on the famous Article 5 of the North Atlantic Treaty—which states that an attack on one shall be considered to be an attack on all—Soviet leader Leonid Brezhnev had said in a speech at the 5th Congress of the Polish United Workers' Party, in November 1968, that "*When forces that are hostile to socialism try to turn the development of some socialist country towards capitalism, it becomes not only a problem of the country concerned, but a common problem and concern of all socialist countries*" (qtd. in Saul, 60). They weren't idle words either, as Brezhnev had already turned them into action a few months earlier, when the Soviet Union—together with Bulgaria, Hungary, Poland and the GDR—had invaded Czechoslovakia to end the Prague Spring, which had sprung up following Alexander Dubček's liberalization reforms.

When Gorbachev visited Prague in the spring of 1987, his own liberalization reforms already in full swing, a Western reporter asked him what the difference was between his reformist policies and those of Alexander Dubček. Gorbachev's spokesman famously replied: "*Nineteen years*" (qtd. in Gáti, 178).

Speaking in Strasbourg at the Council of Europe in July 1989, Gorbachev made clear what he thought of the Brezhnev Doctrine, saying that "*Social and political orders in one or another country changed in the past and may change in the future. But this change is the exclusive affair of the people of that country and is their choice. Any interference in domestic affairs and any attempts to restrict the sovereignty of states,* both friends and allies or any others, is inadmissible."(qtd. in Gáti, 169). With that, the Brezhnev Doctrine was laid to rest and replaced by a policy of non-interference sometimes jokingly called the Sinatra Doctrine, an allusion to Frank Sinatra's *I Did it My Way*, signifying that the satellite states within the Soviet Union would be allowed to go their own way (Keller 1989).

Gorbachev had not expected any of them to actually leave the Soviet Union though. But, as it turned out, he had greatly underestimated the long bottled-up frustration and longing for freedom and democracy in countries like Poland, Hungary, Eastern Germany, Bulgaria, Romania and Czechoslovakia. Empowered by Gorbachev's assurance that liberalization efforts would not be met by tanks and rifle fire this time, the peoples of these countries went 'once more unto the breach' in the closing months of the 1980s, demanding change. This time they succeeded.

On November 9, the Berlin Wall fell. The sight and sound of ordinary people hammering and chiseling away at that most notorious of Cold War icons symbolized the end not just for the forced separation of East and West Germany, but for the entire Eastern bloc. Less than two years later, on December 26, 1991, the Soviet Union was dissolved. The post-Soviet states each went their own way, some towards full democracy, others towards a little or no democracy, but all away from Communism.

It was not what Gorbachev had set out to achieve. He had just wanted to throw out the bath water, not the baby. Only what was the water and what the baby? To Gorbachev, the baby was the socialist state, but clearly he had not wanted to save it against any price, invading Eastern European countries with tanks, purging those who held different views and staying true to unreformed Communism no matter what, as his predecessors had done. So what *did* he want? For what else is a socialist state that champions private enterprise, freedom of expression and participation of the people in government, but a Western style capitalist democracy? Perhaps Gorbachev threw out just the bath water after all.

Of course this is exactly what single-party states like China, Cuba and North Korea are afraid of, that economic and political reforms will ignite social unrest and demands for ever more freedom, as it did in the Soviet Union. To these countries, the main lesson from Gorbachev's reforms is that they are very dangerous. Learning from this, China's ruling elite has been more successful than Gorbachev was in implementing far-reaching economic reforms without compromising its political power base (whether Cuba and North Korea can replicate China's success remains to be seen).

Interestingly enough, around the same time many socialist states started looking to the West for ways to reform their troubled economies, income inequality in the United States started growing again. Between 1980–2012, the gap between the wealthiest 1 percent and the other 99 percent rose to the highest since the 1920s (Saez, "Striking it Richer", fig. 2). Economist and Nobel laureate Robert Schiller has called the rising income inequality in the United States and elsewhere in the world "*the most important problem that we are facing now today.*" (qtd. in Christoffersen 2013).

So perhaps Communism is not quite dead yet. Just slumbering.

22

THE SECOND GREATEST INVENTION
OF THE MILLENNIUM

"By printing, one man alone can produce in a single day as much as he could have done in a thousand days of writing in the past." [1]

Sebastian Brant, Varia carmina, 1498

"We set up a telephone connection between us and the guys at SRI (…) We typed the L and we asked on the phone:
"Do you see the L?"
"Yes, we see the L," came the response.
"We typed the O, and we asked, "Do you see the O."
"Yes, we see the O."
"Then we typed the G, and the system crashed"...
Yet a revolution had begun"... [2]

Len Kleinrock about the first ARPANET
link on October 29, 1969

IN MARCH 1960, AT THE DAWN OF the Digital Revolution, computer scientist and psychologist J.C.R. Licklider published a paper about future *"cooperative interaction between men and electronic computers"* (Licklider, "Man-Computer

---

1   Qtd. in Halporn, 1.

2   Qtd. in Gromov 1995. In a 2009 video interview, Leonard Kleinrock also talks in detail about the very first building blocks of the ARPANET and sending that first message from UCLA to Stanford Research Institute (UCLA, "first internet connection").

Symbiosis", 4). A bold concept, considering there were only about 5,400 computers in the entire United States at the time, most of them much bigger than the average living room and costing hundreds of thousands of dollars (Flamm, 135, Tab. 5–1).[3]

The transistor had been invented only thirteen years earlier and was just beginning to replace the vacuum tubes then commonly used in computers. Another major game changer in the field of electronics, the integrated circuit, had been invented just two years earlier, and although it would make computers much faster, cheaper and smaller, the first ones equipped with them would not arrive until 1961.[4]

But the prohibitive cost of computers was precisely what had put Licklider on the trail of an idea that would help revolutionize knowledge-sharing on a scale not seen since Gutenberg had invented the printing press, roughly 500 years earlier. Because *"any present-day large-scale computer is too fast and too costly for real-time cooperative thinking with one man"*, Licklider suggested a network of *"thinking center[s]"*, functioning much like libraries and connected to each other as well as individual users (Licklider, "Man-Computer Symbiosis", 7).

As he envisioned: *"The picture readily enlarges itself into a network of such centers, connected to one another by wide-band communication lines and to individual users by leased-wire services. In such a system, the speed of the computers would be balanced, and the cost of the gigantic memories and the sophisticated programs would be divided by the number of users."* (Licklider, "Man-Computer Symbiosis", 7).

---

3   The IBM 1401 that came out in 1959 sold for about $370,000, almost $3 million in 2014 prices.

4   The first integrated circuit chips were built for the U.S. Air Force. They also started to be used in the nuclear-armed Minuteman missiles from the early 1960s. Another early customer was NASA. Its Apollo Guidance Computer—used in the Lunar Module and Command Module during the moon landing mission of 1969—was integrated circuit-based.

It was one of the earliest formulations of a computer network—if not the earliest.

Two years later, Licklider was hired by the Defense Advanced Research Projects Agency (DARPA), a research agency of the U.S. Department of Defense, to head up the newly established Information Processing Techniques Office, IPTO (Ceruzzi 2012, 75). While there, Licklider outlined his idea for an 'Intergalactic Computer Network' and convinced team members and later successors such as Ivan Sutherland, Bob Taylor and Lawrence G. Roberts—several of whom would come to play a key role in the creation of ARPANET, the progenitor of the internet—of its importance.[5]

Naturally, the Department of Defense was also very interested in the concept of networked computers. It therefore asked IPTO to come up with a way to link up the computers of the Pentagon, Strategic Air Command and the Department of Defense, to facilitate easier information sharing.

Around the same time, Paul Baran, an American engineer, performed a study on survivable communication networks for the U.S. Air Force, which was concerned about the elimination of such networks in the event of a nuclear attack. The key insight of Baran's study was that even a moderate degree of network redundancy would provide high immunity to such an attack (Baran 1960). To further increase the reliability of such a 'distributed network', Baran also came up with the idea of dividing messages into multiple *message blocks* that would be sent over the network separately and put back together again at the destination, still the basis for data communication around the world.[6]

---

5   Interesting reading in this respect is an eight-page memo Licklider sent to his colleagues on April 23, 1963, titled *Memorandum for: Members and Affiliates of the Intergalactic Computer Network*, in which he discussed several issues concerning the building of this 'Intergalactic Computer Network'.

6   Independently, Donald Watts Davies of the U.K. National Physical Laboratory came up with the same idea, calling it *packet switching*, which is the

Baran's ideas also made their way to Licklider's successors at IPTO, who used them in the creation of ARPANET. The first large-scale computer network, ARPANET initially consisted of just two host computers—one at the University of California's Network Measurement Center in Los Angeles, the other at the Stanford Research Institute—interconnected by two so-called Interface Message Processors, i.e., routers (UCLA, "first internet connection").[7] The first ARPANET link between these two host computers was established on October 29, 1969, a couple of months after Neil Armstrong had first walked on the moon.

About a year later ARPANET had grown to 10 nodes, 5 more were added in 1971—to connect a total of 23 host computers—and by 1972 there were 30 nodes (Ceruzzi 2003, 194). At that point ARPANET still consisted exclusively of American universities and government sites such as NASA, the Department of Defense, the National Science Foundation and the Federal Reserve Board, but in 1973 ARPANET went international, when it connected to the Norwegian Seismic Array (NORSAR) via satellite link.[8] The network kept expanding throughout the 1970s and by 1980 it counted 230 nodes (Korowajczuk, 16).

Meanwhile, other organizations had started building computer networks of their own, running on different network protocols.[9] This made interconnection difficult, a problem

---

name that stuck. Davies also played an important role in bringing the idea of packet switching to the attention of the ARPA engineers in the early stages of the creation of ARPANET (Harris 2009).

7   Another node was connected in November 1969, at the University of California's Culler-Fried Interactive Mathematics center in Santa Barbara (UCSB), and in December a fourth node was connected at the University of Utah's Computer Science Department (UCLA, "first internet connection").

8   A map of the ARPANET circa 1974 in *Computing: A Concise History* shows that its by then 60+ connections were concentrated in four regions: Boston, Washington D.C., Silicon Valley and southern California (Ceruzzi, 109, fig. 5.3).

9   Like IBM's Systems Network Architecture (SNA) and X.25, developed by

that could only be expected to increase over time. Something was needed to link different computer networks together more easily, while maintaining the open-architecture character of this rapidly growing 'network of networks'. Enter the 'Transmission Control Program' (TCP), a unifying network protocol that defined rules for processing data between networks, i.e., how to send, format, address and receive it.[10] First tested in 1975, TCP quickly became the *de facto* standard protocol for internet data processing, and still is today.[11]

In March 1982, the U.S. Department of Defense declared TCP/IP the standard for all military networking and on January 1, 1983, ARPANET changed its own protocol to TCP/IP as well (Korowajczuk, 16; Daigle 2013).[12] ARPANET's choice for TCP/IP was a game-changing step forward in the expansion of the network of computer networks, but it would take a couple of more years before the word 'internetworking', which had been in use since the mid-1970s to describe the interconnecting of different networks, would transform into a noun in its own right, to describe the global network that resulted from all that interconnecting: internet.[13]

ARPANET was a great success, but it was never meant to function as the backbone of a network of computer networks

---

the International Telecommunications Union (ITU).

10   TCP was designed by Vinton G. Cerf and Robert E. Kahn, who wrote a seminal paper on it in 1974, titled 'A Protocol for Packet Network Intercommunication'.

11   The original Transmission Control Program was later divided into different protocols, the two most important ones being the Transmission Control Protocol (TCP) and the Internet Protocol (IP), hence the informal designation 'TCP/IP' for what is officially known today as the Internet Protocol Suite.

12   There is no real D-Day for the creation of 'the' internet (or even a D-Year), but if there had to be one, January 1, 1983 would certainly be a good candidate.

13   The word 'internet'—as shorthand for 'internetwork'—was first used in the 1974 paper 'Specification of Internet Transmission Control Program', by the Network Working Group led by Vinton Cerf, one of the principal designers of the TCP protocol. In the late 1980s, the word 'internet' started to be used to designate the global TCP/IP network.

indefinitely. The mission of its creator, DARPA, was (and remains) to develop new technologies, not to become a glorified internet service provider. So, when it became clear that computer networks would continue to prosper and proliferate with or without the existence of ARPANET, the pioneering network began to look for a suitable successor to take over as backbone.

That successor was found in NSFNET, a nationwide computer network launched in 1986 by the National Science Foundation (Halabi, 7). Within a couple of years, NSFNET connected to a host of research and education networks both inside and outside the United States. NSFNET was also rapidly upgraded, with new backbone points added every year and transfer speeds increasing from 56-bit/s in 1986 to 1.5 Mbit/s in 1988 and 45 Mbit/s in 1991 (Halabi, 7). ARPANET was retired in 1990.

Commercial Internet Service Providers (ISPs) also began to emerge in the late 1980s, forcing the National Science Foundation to address the question of how to deal with commercial traffic on its network. It responded with an 'Acceptable Use Policy' that sought to ban all advertising—in many ways the backbone of today's internet—but allowed some other commercial traffic (Ceruzzi 2003, 320–21). It was hardly a clear line in the sand though, more of a murky smear in the mud.

In response, three Internet Service Providers (ISPs) created the Commercial Internet eXchange (CIX) in 1991, an internet exchange point for routing commercial internet traffic (Cronin, 253). CIX was operated based on a 'no-settlement policy', meaning traffic between parties was exchanged without compensation; instead, CIX members paid a fixed fee, a model that would later be adopted by most Internet Exchange Points regulating traffic between commercial ISPs.

Late 1991, NSFNET lifted its restrictions (Cronin, 253). Tension nevertheless largely remained between the commercial ISPs and the academic, non-profit NSFNET, until the latter was decommissioned in 1995. During this transitional period to a fully commercial internet, the NSF sponsored the creation of four public Network Access Points (NAPs) in the United States—two on the East Coast and two on the West Coast—to handle the growing traffic between Internet Service Providers (Frazer, 40–41). When there were enough commercially operated Internet Exchange Points to handle the ever increasing internet traffic load, the NAPs were decommissioned as well.[14]

Computer networking had made great strides in both quantity and quality between 1969–90 (the year ARPANET was retired), going from the very first message over the very first ARPANET link to countless messages over a global network of regional and national computer networks, connecting universities, government agencies and research facilities around the world. Still, for the internet to become the truly ubiquitous phenomenon it is today, one additional fundamental element was still missing: regular people.

But in 1990, getting on the internet could be challenging for novice users, not to mention using it. The available information on the internet was growing rapidly, yes, but knowing how to find it was a whole different matter. There were no search engines coughing up a list of relevant pages within 0.5 seconds of posing a question, or web browsers where you could simply enter a URL, or URLs for that matter, or webpages, or websites.

That is where British computer scientist Tim Berners-Lee comes in.

During a brief stint as a consultant at the European Particle Physics Laboratory (CERN) in 1980, Berners-Lee wrote a software program called *Enquire*, to bring some order in

---

14   As of May 2013, there are more than 350 Internet Exchange Points worldwide.

the informational chaos that resulted from 10,000 people working on different projects with different hardware and different software (Berners-Lee 1993/94). *Enquire* used hypertext—a database format that allows text to link directly to specific parts of information—to reveal relationships between people, programs and hardware.

When he returned to CERN in 1984 to work on a different project, Berners-Lee used *Enquire "to keep track of the modules, the users, the documents and everything I needed to note down about the project"* (Berners-Lee 1993/94). Still, even though he needed the program to keep track of everything that was going on, *Enquire* had its shortcomings, chief among them that it was not accessible to everyone and that the rules for updating it were too strict.

Berners-Lee realized there was a real need for a system that could link, retrieve and present information independently of the used hardware or software and that was accessible to everyone, much like the TCP/IP protocol had unified the transmission of information over the internet across different network platforms. *"This was the concept of the web"* (Berners-Lee 1993/94).

Between 1989–91, Berners-Lee was given the opportunity at CERN to work on his core idea of using hypertext to make data more accessible.[15] Calling the project World Wide Web, he wrote a protocol for transferring hypertext (HTTP), a web browser (called WorldWideWeb) to retrieve and present information and an application to set up the very first web server, capable of serving up web pages. He also created and launched the very first webpage, at http://info.cern.ch.[16]

---

15   In his proposal to persuade CERN management of the advantages of a global hypertext system, Berners-Lee called it 'Mesh'; he only decided on 'World Wide Web' when writing the code in 1990 (Berners-Lee 1989–90).

16   The first sentence on the first website read: *"The WorldWideWeb (W3) is a wide-area hypermedia information retrieval initiative aiming to give universal access to a large universe of documents."* (see: http://info.cern.ch/hypertext/ WWW/TheProject.html).

Fearing his 'documentation system' would fail to catch on at CERN because no one would put any information in it, Berners-Lee decided to set up a hypertext version of the CERN phone book, so that his system was useful from the get-go. "*So this was the way the web was first presented at CERN: as a rather simple user interface which allowed one to look up (mainly) telephone numbers. It was to be two years before it would shed that image.*"(Berners-Lee 1993/94).

Rather than claiming ownership, CERN decided the World Wide Web should benefit everybody, so on August 23, 1991—a date still celebrated as Internaut Day—the project was opened to new users.[17] In the years that followed, the number of internauts—those capable of using the internet—exploded, as did the number of *web*sites. There were only 10 websites in June 1992, but by June 1995 there were already more than 23,000 and two years after that more than 1,100,000 ("Total number of Websites"). As of June 2014, there are more than 968 million websites.

Part of the credit for the meteoric rise of the World Wide Web's popularity in the 1990s goes to Mosaic, the first web browser to display images inline with text instead of in a separate window (yes, it wasn't always so) and one of the earliest browsers available for the Windows operating system, at the time used by more than 80 percent of the world's computers (Reid, xxv).[18]

Since then, the internet's impact has become ever more indelible, reaching every corner of our lives, be it social, commercial, professional, recreational or educational. And

---

17   Two weeks earlier, Berners-Lee had already published a short summary of the WorldWideWeb project in a post on the alt.hypertext newsgroup, with links to the line-mode browser, a hypertext editor and documentation about the project, but it was not until August 23, 1991, that the web was opened to new users. On April 30, 1993, CERN announced it would publish its 'W3' software in the public domain, making it freely available to everybody.

18   Netscape Navigator, the dominant web browser of the 1990s, was based on Mosaic.

if the internet used to be something that you switched on and off and that was only available at work and at home, with the proliferation of broadband internet access and the smartphone most people have become connected wherever, whenever.

It seems the symbiosis between *"men and electronic computers"* that J.C.R. Licklider talked about is not too far off.

Or perhaps it's already here.

23

9/11

"The key to any strategy is accurate intelligence, and skilled professionals to get that information in time to use it. In seeking to guard this nation against the threat of catastrophic violence, our Administration gave intelligence officers the tools and lawful authority they needed to gain vital information. We didn't invent that authority. It is drawn from Article Two of the Constitution. And it was given specificity by the Congress after 9/11, in a Joint Resolution authorizing "all necessary and appropriate force" to protect the American people."[1]

Former Vice-President Dick Cheney, May 21, 2009

"But I don't want comfort. I want God, I want poetry, I want real danger, I want freedom, I want goodness. I want sin."
"In fact," said Mustapha Mond, "you're claiming the right to be unhappy."
"All right then," said the Savage defiantly, "I'm claiming the right to be unhappy."[2]

Brave New World, Aldous Huxley, 1931

O N SEPTEMBER 11, 2001, AT 8:49 A.M., CNN cuts short a commercial from sub-prime mortgage company Ditech, to show the first images of a plane-shaped hole in the upper part of the World Trade Center's North Tower. Black smoke is billowing out. Commentators cite "*unconfirmed reports*" that

---

1   Cheney, "Remarks".
2   Huxley, 211–12.

a plane has hit the tower (CNN, "9/11 News", 1:38). Moments later, Sean Murtagh—a CNN Vice President—confirms on the air that he saw a "*two-engined jet, maybe a 737*" crash into the tower (CNN, "9/11 News", 3:04).

During the next fourteen minutes, several other eyewitnesses confirm they saw a plane crash into the tower. One witness says she heard a "*sonic boom*", thinking at first that "*maybe the Concorde was back in service*" (CNN, "9/11 News", 8:05). Nobody uses words like 'terrorism', 'attack', or 'deliberate'. One of the CNN commentators simply calls it a "*horrible incident*" (CNN, "9/11 News", 7:48). Thus, although American Airlines Flight 11 had in fact been intentionally flown into the North Tower of the WTC at 8:46 a.m., most people remained on pre-9/11 time during those first seventeen minutes of the post-9/11 world.

That changed at 9:03 a.m.

The crash of the second plane is caught live on CNN, but the commentators—in the middle of a phone interview with an eyewitness—somehow miss the moment. The same happens at NBC, which shows the North Tower from another angle. There, viewers can see a second plane flying towards the WTC for six seconds, before it disappears behind the smoking North Tower. Another—surreal—four seconds go by, before the eyewitness on the phone screams "*Oh another one just hit! something else just hit, a very large plane just flew directly over my building and there has been another collision; can you see it?*"(NBC, "News Coverage", 9:47).

With the crashing of United Airlines Flight 175 into the South Tower, it becomes clear that the events unfolding are not accidental. At 9:30 a.m., President George Bush goes on air to deliver a hastily prepared statement, calling the crashing of the planes "*an apparent, terrorist attack on our country*" and promising "*to hunt down and to find those folks, who committed this act.*" (NBC, "News Coverage", 37:21, 37:44).

At 9:37 a.m., American Airlines Flight 77 crashes into the west side of the Pentagon. Minutes later, the networks show big clouds of smoke emanating from the building. People working on the other side of the Pentagon (the largest office building in the world) report hearing a loud explosion, thinking at first that perhaps a bomb has gone off.

At 9:59 a.m., CNN coverage of the Pentagon attack is interrupted when the South Tower of the WTC collapses. At 10:28 a.m., the North Tower follows its twin sibling. By then, United Airlines Flight 93 has already crashed in a field near Shanksville, Pennsylvania (at 10:03 a.m.). It would later become known the hijacker-pilot had decided to crash the plane into the ground as passengers were attempting to retake the plane. The intended target for United 93 had probably been either the White House or the Capitol.[3]

Meanwhile, the immediate response from local and federal government agencies and the military is focused on defense, containment and rescue. Within six minutes after the first plane hits the WTC, the New York City Transit subways and Port Authority Trans-Hudson (PATH) activate emergency procedures (Volpe, "Effects", 2). The subway station under the WTC is quickly closed. At 9:10 a.m., seven minutes after the second plane crash, the Port Authority of NY and NJ closes all its bridges and tunnels (Volpe, "Effects", 2). At 9:17 a.m., the Federal Aviation Administration (FAA) orders all NYC airports closed until further notice.

---

3   The hijackers had diverted the course of United 93 in the direction of Washington. The intended target remains uncertain, but it is generally believed that the target was either the White House or the Capitol. According to the 9/11 Commission Report, Osama Bin Laden had told Ramzi bin al-Shibh to advise Mohamed Atta—one of the leaders of the operation and hijacker-pilot of American Airlines Flight 11—that he preferred the White House over the Capitol (Nat. Com, *9/11 Commission Report*, 243). Atta deemed the White House too difficult a target though and had assigned Ziad Jarrah—the terrorist-pilot of United 93—the Capitol as target, according to bin al-Shibh (Nat. Com, *9/11 Commission Report*, 244).

At 9:42 a.m., the FAA directs all aircraft to land at the nearest airport, an unprecedented order (Nat. Com, *9/11 Commission Report*, 29). The entire U.S. airspace is now completely closed to all civil aviation, all departures from U.S. airports are halted, all of the approximately 4,500 aircraft in U.S. air space are guided to their nearest landing destinations and international aircraft are told not to enter U.S. territory but instead divert to Canadian air space.

At 10:20 a.m., NYC Transit suspends all subway service (Volpe, "Effects", 2). Ten minutes later, all rail service into Manhattan's Penn Station is halted as well. At 10:45 a.m., all activities of the PATH railroad service are suspended (Volpe, "Effects", 2). Meanwhile, Amtrak suspends train service nationwide and bus operator Greyhound cancels all its Northeast U.S operations.

The President, who is at the Emma E. Booker Elementary School in Sarasota, Florida, at the time of the attack, is rushed to Sarasota Airport, where Air Force One takes off at 9:54 a.m. without a clear destination, its only orders to reach high altitude as fast as possible (Nat. Com, *9/11 Commission Report*, 39). Around the same time, Vice President Dick Cheney is rushed to the Presidential Emergency Operations Center (PEOC), the bunker structure underneath the East Wing of the White House.[4]

Upon hearing that United 93 is 80 miles out of Washington D.C., Cheney orders the plane to be shot down. Ten years later, he would say about this decision: "*Frankly, I didn't pause to think about it very much. Once one of those aircraft was hijacked, it was a weapon…it was part of my responsibility*" (qtd. in "Cheney: Order"). Curiously, it remains unclear

---

4   Several accounts conflict with each other as to the exact time the vice president arrived at the PEOC. The 9/11 Commission Report concluded that the vice president arrived at the PEOC at 9:58 a.m., despite "*conflicting evidence*" (Nat. Com, *9/11 Commission Report*, 40).

whether or not Cheney actually had authorization already from President Bush at the time he issued the order.[5]

At Andrews Air Force Base, two F-16s are scrambled to shoot down United Airlines 93, but the fighters are not yet armed. While gearing up for takeoff, Col. Marc Sasseville says to Lt. Heather Penney: "*I'm going for the cockpit*". "*I'll take the tail*", Penney replies (qtd. in Hendrix 2011). When, not long after, those in the PEOC learn that an aircraft has crashed in a field in Pennsylvania, they wonder if it was indeed downed by fighters (Nat. Com, *9/11 Commission Report*, 41).

It was not. Nor would any other plane be. United 93 was the last of the hijacked planes.

With a death toll of 2,973 people (excluding the 19 dead hijackers) and more than 9,000 injured, the September 11 attacks remain the deadliest terrorist attack in U.S. history (Nat. Com, *9/11 Commission Report*, 311; Atkins, 435). Aside from the high cost in human lives and injuries, there was also extensive material damage. Of the World Trade Center complex, the North Tower (1 WTC), the South Tower (2 WTC), the Marriott hotel (3 WTC) and the 47 stories tall 7 WTC were destroyed. 4 WTC, 5 WTC, 6 WTC and the Deutsche Bank building on 130 Liberty street were severely damaged, as was the Pentagon, where the section hit by American Airlines Flight 77 collapsed. Several other buildings in the vicinity of the WTC were also damaged.

---

5   The 9/11 Commission Report states Cheney had a phone conversation with the President, "*sometime before 10:10 to 10:15*", during which National Security Advisor Condoleezza Rice heard the Vice President say: "*Sir, the CAPs* [Combat Air Patrol] *are up. Sir, they're going to want to know what to do*.", followed by him saying "*Yes sir.*" (qtd. in Nat. Com, *9/11 Commission Report*, 40). Between 10:10 and 10:15, the Vice President is asked for authorization to engage United 93 (unaware that the plane had already crashed several minutes earlier, at 10:03). Cheney readily gives it (Nat. Com, *9/11 Commission Report*, 41). On the suggestion of White House Deputy Chief of Staff Joshua Bolten, Cheney then places a logged call to the President, at 10:18, to obtain confirmation, which was given.

It did not take long to find out who was behind the attacks. In 1996, Osama Bin Laden, the leader of the militant islamist organization Al-Qaeda ('The Base'), had issued a fatwa—an Islamic religious decree, binding to those who follow the issuer—titled 'Declaration of War against the Americans Occupying the Land of the Two Holy Places'. In this more than 13,000 words long polemic, Bin Laden raged against the American *"occupation"* of the *"Land of the Two Holy Places "*—another name for Saudi Arabia, home to Islamic holy cities Mecca and Medina—and military activities of *"the USA and its allies"* against Muslims in other countries, such as the Philippines, Somalia, Eritrea, Chechnya and Bosnia-Herzegovina, calling upon all Muslims to concentrate on expelling the American enemy from the holy land (Bin Laden 1996).

Two years later, in February 1998, Bin Laden issued another fatwa, together with four others, among them Ayman al-Zawahiri, one of his top lieutenants.[6] This second fatwa, titled 'Declaration of the World Islamic Front for Jihad against the Jews and the Crusaders', again condemned U.S. *"occupation"* of *"the lands of Islam in the holiest of places"*, as well as the *"devastation"* the *"crusader-Zionist alliance"* had done in Iraq and the continued American support of Israel (Bin Laden 1998). The instructions of the second fatwa went much further than the first one, stating that *"The ruling to kill the Americans and their allies—civilians and military—is an individual duty for every Muslim who can do it in any country in which it is possible to do it"*. Six months later, on August 7, the eighth anniversary of the arrival of U.S. troops in Saudi Arabia—which had been sent there as part of Operation Desert Shield, following Iraq's invasion of Kuwait—suicide bombers connected to Al-Qaeda blew up trucks filled with explosives at the U.S. Embassies in Tanzania and Kenya,

---

6   Al-Zawahiri would succeed Bin Laden as leader of Al-Qaeda in May 2011, after the latter was killed by U.S. Navy SEALs.

killing 224 and wounding more than 4,000 others (Zenko, 59).

Though it was quickly clear that Osama Bin Laden and Al-Qaeda were also responsible for the September 11 attacks, bringing them to justice would be a whole different matter. U.S. intelligence (correctly) suggested Bin Laden and many of his fighters were hiding in Afghanistan, but how do you fight an enemy holed up in a mountainous, unruly, inhospitable country, ruled by Islamic fundamentalists?[7] Besides, even if Osama Bin Laden was in Afghanistan, Al-Qaeda also had people in several other countries and connections with a number of affiliated organizations, making it next to impossible to completely neutralize the threat it posed.

Still, whatever the difficulties, one thing was immediately clear: the response of the most powerful country in the world would be something more than simply bombing a couple of desert training camps where fanatical Islamic teenagers were learning to gird on a suicide vest and hit something other than sand or air with their AK-47.

On Sunday evening September 16, upon returning from a weekend war council at Camp David, President Bush declared: "*This crusade—this war on terrorism—is going to take a while. And the American people must be patient. I'm going to be patient. But I can assure the American people I am determined.*" (Bush, "Remarks"). The use of the word 'crusade' immediately triggered a backlash from the Muslim world, who interpreted it as though the United States were using the September 11 attacks to unleash a holy war against Islam. Two days later, the White House said the President regretted to have used the word 'crusade'. But crusade or not, war was coming. On September 20, in his address to a joint session of Congress, Bush said that "*Our war on terror begins with Al-Qaeda, but it does not end there. It will not end until every*

---

7   At the time, most of Afghanistan was controlled by the Taliban, another Islamic fundamentalist movement.

terrorist group of global reach has been found, stopped and defeated." (Bush, "Address").

And in that war, Bush made clear, the U.S. would make no distinction between terrorists and those who harbored them. "*We will pursue nations that provide aid or safe haven to terrorism. Every nation, in every region, now has a decision to make. Either you are with us, or you are with the terrorists. From this day forward, any nation that continues to harbor or support terrorism will be regarded by the United States as a hostile regime.*" (Bush, "Address").

It was not just idle talk. Neoconservatives such as Vice President Dick Cheney, Secretary of Defense Donald Rumsfeld and Deputy Secretary of Defense Paul Wolfowitz, had already started advancing an agenda aimed at protecting American national interest much more aggressively, and the September 11 attacks supplied them with an abundance of political capital for precisely that.

Cheney, for his part, wasted no time in demanding a multi-year military mandate for the war on terror, warning that "*This is not a war like the Gulf War, where we had a buildup for a few months, four days of combat, and it was over. This is going to be the kind of work that will probably take years because the focus has to be not just on any one individual; the problem here is terrorism*" (qtd. in Bazinet 2001). Cheney was also quick to point the finger to Afghanistan, saying that the United States believed that the government of Afghanistan had been harboring Osama Bin Laden and that "*They have to understand, and others like them around the world have to understand, that if you provide sanctuary to terrorists, you face the full wrath of the United States of America*" (qtd. in Bazinet 2001).

Rumsfeld went even further, preemptively claiming sheer unlimited operational legality when he said that "*They [the terrorists] may be operating in 50 or 60 countries, including the United States—and that means that we will have to use the full weight of the United States government—political, diplo-matic, financial, economic, military and unconventional, and I would underline that"* (qtd. in Bazinet 2001).

'Unconventional', a word that could mean anything, from spying on people indiscriminately to holding them without trial indefinitely and torturing them, from killing foreign nationals in countries the United States was not at war with to outright invading other countries. As it turned out, it would mean all those things.

On October 26, 2001, President Bush signed a comprehensive anti-terrorism bill into law, the USA PATRIOT Act. Among its most controversial parts were the power of indefinite detention the government gave itself and the expansion of its power to force organizations and other entities to give up information about third parties, through the issuance of a so-called National Security Letter (NSL).[8]

Special Agents in charge of a Bureau field office were authorized to issue such a Letter and demand organizations turn over various records and data pertaining to individuals (USA Patriot Act, Title V, sec. 505).[9] No probable cause or judicial oversight was required and the recipient of an NSL was forbidden from disclosing the letter was ever issued. Records show that 192,499 NSLs were issued by the FBI between 2003–06 (Yost 2010).

In 2004, the American Civil Liberties Union (ACLU) filed a lawsuit against the U.S. federal government on behalf of an

---

8   Per sec. 412, 236A.a.3 and 236A.a.6 of the Patriot Act, the Attorney General has, under certain circumstances, the power to detain immigrants for an indefinite number of six month periods, *"if the release of the alien will threaten the national security of the United States or the safety of the community or any person"* (USA Patriot Act, 236A.a.6).

9   Sec. 505 of Title V of the Patriot Act makes changes to U.S. Code: Title 18. sec. 2709 - Counterintelligence access to telephone toll and transactional records. Prior to the changes, an NSL could only be issued by the Director of the FBI or *"his designee not lower than Deputy Assistant Director"* (U.S. Code: Title 18. sec. 2709, b, c.1).

anonymous Internet Service Provider.[10] In Doe v. Ashcroft, the ACLU argued that the National Security Letters the Internet Service Provider had received—particularly in combination with the non-disclosure order—violated the First, Fourth, and Fifth Amendment to the United States Constitution.[11] The court ruled in favor of the ACLU, but the government appealed.

In May 2006, the 2nd Circuit Court of Appeals returned the case to the lower court, in light of changes made to the articles regulating the NSLs after the case was filed.[12] But in his concurring opinion, Judge Richard Cardamone did warn that "*a ban on speech and an unending shroud of secrecy in perpetuity are antithetical to democratic concepts and do not fit comfortably with the fundamental rights guaranteed American citizens.*" (Doe II v. Gonzales, 23).

In September 2007, the lower court again ruled in favor of the ACLU, deeming the revisions of the USA Patriot Improvement and Reauthorization Act of 2005 insufficient. The court took particular issue with the limited level of judicial oversight as allowed by the Act, through U.S.C. Title 18, section 3511. According to the court, section 3511(b) forced the judiciary into a substandard review of non-disclosure orders, thus preventing it from properly checking the constitutional validity of such an order, something that "*could serve as a precedential step toward the development of a much larger and more fearsome vehicle for legislative or executive intrusion into the business of the courts*", which would amount to "*the legislative equivalent of breaking and entering, with an*

---

10   In 2010 it was revealed the John Doe was Nicholas Merrill, of Calyx Internet Access (Zetter 2010).

11   The First Amendment protects free speech, the Fourth protects against unreasonable searches and seizures and requires a judicially sanctioned warrant supported by probable cause, the Fifth demands due process of law when the state deprives an individual of life, liberty or property.

12   By way of the USA Patriot Improvement and Reauthorization Act of 2005.

ominous free pass to the hijacking of constitutional values."
(Doe v. Gonzales, III.F.1.c).

Several remands, appeals and moves to reconsideration later, the U.S. District Court of New York ruled in March 2010 that the government had been partially incorrect in enforcing its non-disclosure requirement in the case of 'John Doe'.[13] Part of the attachment to the NSL remained under the non-disclosure order however, because the court found the government had sufficiently demonstrated that full disclosure would run the risk of informing "*current targets of law enforcement investigations, including the particular target of the Government's ongoing inquiry in this action, as well as, potentially future targets, as to certain types of records and other materials the Government seeks through national security investigations employing NSLs.*" (Doe v. Holder, 317).

In December 2014, 'John Doe' i.e., Nicholas Merrill filed a new complaint about his non-disclosure requirement.[14] On August 28, 2015—more than eleven years after he had first filed suit against his non-disclosure order—the U.S. District Court of New York ruled in favor of Merrill, finding the government had "*not satisfied its burden of demonstrating 'good reason' to expect that disclosure of the NSL Attachment in its entirety will risk an enumerated harm, pursuant to Sections 2709 and 3511.*" (Merrill v. Lynch).[15]

---

13   Specifically, the court ruled that the non-disclosure requirement had to be lifted where it concerned "*(1) material within the scope of information that the NSL statute identifies as permissible for the FBI to obtain through use of NSLs, and (2) material that the FBI has publicly acknowledged it has previously requested by means of NSLs.*" (Doe v. Holder).

14   Section 3511(b)(3) of 18 U.S.C., in effect between March 9, 2006-June 1, 2015, required NSL recipients to wait a year or more after unsuccessfully challenging a non-disclosure requirement before trying again. This restriction has since been lifted.

15   As of 2015, the non-disclosure order for recipients of an NSL remains, though the USA Freedom Act, signed into law by President Barack Obama on June 2, 2015, now permits recipients of an NSL to discuss it with: "*those persons to whom disclosure is necessary in order to comply with the request; an attorney in order to obtain legal advice or assistance regarding the request; other persons*

As for the government's power of indefinite detention of non U.S. citizens suspected of terrorism, this was legally dealt with in Title IV, section 412 of the USA Patriot Act.[16] Prisoners at Guantánamo Bay detention camp, Cuba, have been and continue to be held under this provision. As of January 2015, 35 Guantánamo detainees are designated to be held indefinitely (Human Rights First, "Guantánamo").

Several of Guantánamo's prisoners were previously held by the CIA, which operated a number of secret prisons outside the United States (a.k.a. black sites) between 2002–06 (Stout 2006). According to the International Committee of the Red Cross, which interviewed fourteen 'high value detainees' after their transfer to Guantánamo in 2006, these prisoners were subjected to torture (Int. Com., "ICRC Report", 5).

Early 2002, the CIA wanted to know if it could use 'enhanced interrogation techniques' (more commonly known as torture) to make interrogation of terrorism suspects more effective. The proposed techniques, including "*sensory deprivation, sleep disruption, stress positions, waterboarding, and slapping*", came from a program called SERE (Survival Evasion Resistance Escape), developed by the U.S. military in the early 1950s to help captured U.S. military personnel withstand abusive interrogation techniques (Com. On Arm., "Inquiry", xiv).

Use of these techniques on terrorism suspects was discussed by key people of the Bush administration, including Secretary of Defense Donald Rumsfeld, Director of Central Intelligence George Tenet, National Security Advisor

---

as permitted by the Director of the Federal Bureau of Investigation or the designee of the Director." (USA Freedom Act, Sec. 502. c.2). The issuance of an NSL still does not require a court order.

16   Through the National Defense Authorization Act for Fiscal Year 2012, the government's authority of indefinite detention was expanded to include U.S. citizens who committed or supported terrorist acts against the U.S. or its allies and who are captured outside the United States (Nat. Def., Title X, subtitle D, section 1021).

Condoleezza Rice and Attorney General John Ashcroft (Com. On Arm., "Inquiry"). They decided to allow enhanced interrogation techniques, reasoning that such techniques did not constitute torture under U.S. or international law. On December 2, 2002, Secretary Rumsfeld signed off on the recommendation of the Department of Defense's General Counsel's Office to approve the aggressive techniques (Com. On Arm., "Inquiry", xviii-xix).[17]-[18]

Internationally, the initial focus of the Bush administration was on Afghanistan. The emerging Bush Doctrine emphasized America's right to preemptively strike at its enemies—unilaterally if necessary—wherever they may be holed up (National Security Council, "Security to Terrorism", 15). According to this doctrine, the War on Terror was a global, ideological struggle between the West and its values of freedom and democracy, and extremist factions—particularly militant Islamists—bent on destroying those values. To win the war, the terrorists had to be weeded out wherever they were, while democratic change had to be promoted in countries ruled by autocratic regimes.

On September 12, 2001, NATO invoked article 5 of the North Atlantic Treaty for the first time in its history, declaring the September 11 attacks against the United States an attack on all NATO member countries.[19]

On October 7, the United States launched Operation Enduring Freedom, together with the United Kingdom. Other NATO allies later joined. Combat operations started

---

17   In a handwritten note that Rumsfeld added to his signed recommendation, he expressed his apparent disapproval to one of the limits proposed in the memo, writing: "*I stand for 8–10 hours a day. Why is standing limited to 4 hours?*" (qtd. in Com. On Arm., "Inquiry", xix).

18   On January 22, 2009, two days after assuming office, President Obama signed Executive Order 13491, which barred the use of enhanced interrogation techniques beyond those permitted by the U.S. military.

19   As of 2015, it remains the only time article 5 of the NATO treaty has been invoked.

with airstrikes in Afghanistan, targeting Al-Qaeda and the Taliban, the Islamic fundamentalists who ruled most of Afghanistan. On October 14, the Taliban offered to hand over Bin Laden to a third country if the U.S. would provide proof for his involvement and halt the bombing campaign. The U.S. rejected the offer. One day later, the Taliban offered to hand over Bin Laden for trial in a country other than the U.S., without demanding evidence, in return for a halt to the bombing campaign.[20] The U.S. rejected this offer as well.

In the ensuing weeks the Taliban were driven from power by the U.S. and its allies, with the Northern Alliance—a united front of Islamic factions that had been fighting the Taliban and Al-Qaeda since 1996—advancing under the cover of U.S. air support. In the night of November 12 the Taliban fled the capital of Kabul, where fighters of the Northern Alliance arrived the next day. Kunduz—the last Taliban stronghold in Northern Afghanistan —fell on November 26, Kandahar— the Taliban's birthplace and last remaining stronghold in the country—on December 7.

Meanwhile, Osama Bin Laden was believed to be hiding out in the mountains of Tora Bora, in Eastern Afghanistan. But although a five day bombardment of the area between December 12–17 left an estimated 200 Al-Qaeda and Taliban fighters dead, Bin Laden was not among them.[21] The Al-

---

20   This second offer was done by the more moderate Taliban foreign minister Wakil Ahmed Muttawakil, apparently without the approval of supreme Taliban leader Mullah Omar (Burns 2001). In July 2001, the same Wakil Muttawakil had also reportedly warned U.S. diplomats in Peshawar, Pakistan, of a large, imminent attack by Al-Qaeda in the United States. Muttawakil was apparently deeply unhappy with the presence of the Arab militants in his country and said he feared *"the guests were going to destroy the guesthouse"* (Clark 2002; Burke 2002).

21   A 2009 report by the Committee on Foreign Relations of the U.S. Senate stated it was never clear exactly how many Al-Qaeda fighters were at Tora Bora during the battle, but that the consensus figure was around 1,000 (Com. On For., "Tora Bora", 14). About 800 fighters were estimated to have escaped during an overnight pause in the bombing, which had been ordered to avoid killing Al-Qaeda fighters who were supposedly about to surrender, though this later

Qaeda leader was believed to have escaped to neighboring Pakistan, possibly on or around December 16 (Lynch 2008).[22]

The removal of the Taliban from power in Afghanistan would not be the end of the war there though. Having regrouped, the Taliban simply reverted back to the same kind of guerrilla warfare they had waged against the Russians in the 1980s. And, staying true to their beliefs, the Taliban continued to fight not only against the Afghan government and the International Security Assistance Force (ISAF), but also against the Afghan people, handing out harsh punishments for every violation of its strict Islamic code, including beheading people for activities such as celebrating with music and mixed-gender dancing (Salahuddin 2012). As of 2015, the Taliban insurgency is still ongoing.

Though the Taliban were a pain and Osama Bin Laden was possibly still hiding in Afghanistan, the neoconservatives considered Iraq a much greater threat than Afghanistan, believing Iraqi dictator Saddam Hussein was actively trying to acquire weapons of mass destruction (WMDs). In January 1998, for instance, the conservative American think tank Project for the New American Century had sent a public letter to President Bill Clinton, urging him to take action on the threat of Saddam Hussein possibly requiring the capability of delivering WMDs (Project, "Letter"). Among the signatories of the letter were soon-to-be Secretary of Defense Donald Rumsfeld, soon-to-be Deputy Secretary of Defense Paul Wolfowitz and soon-to-be Undersecretary of State for Arms Control And International Security Affairs John Bolton.

In the first hours after the planes had crashed into the Twin Towers, Secretary of Defense Donald Rumsfeld immediately ordered his aides to look for Iraqi involvement in the attacks.

---

turned out to be a hoax (Com. On For., "Tora Bora", 11). Only 20 fighters or so were taken prisoner after the battle (Com. On For., "Tora Bora", 14).

22   It would take almost ten years before U.S. special forces would finally kill 'OBL' in a private compound in Abbottabad, Pakistan, on May 2, 2011.

Notes taken by senior policy official Stephen Cambone, read: *"Best info fast. Judge whether good enough hit SH at same time - Not only UBL.",* and *"Need to move swiftly. Near term target needs - go massive - sweep it all up, things related and not."* (qtd. in Borger 2006).

The war in Iraq began on March 20, 2003, and would develop along a similar path as the one in Afghanistan, with only three weeks of major combat operations before the fall of Baghdad and the end of the 24-year rule of Iraqi dictator Saddam Hussein, on April 9, symbolized by the toppling of a large Saddam statue in Firdos Square, central Baghdad, that same day. No WMDs were found in Iraq though, nor any evidence of any connection between the regime of Saddam Hussein and Al-Qaeda.

Eight months later, on December 13, 2003, Saddam Hussein himself was captured by American forces. He was subsequently tried, found guilty of crimes against humanity, sentenced to death and hanged, on December 30, 2006. By then, an Islamic fundamentalist insurgency against the U.S coalition forces in Iraq had grown into a full-blown civil war. After the withdrawal of U.S. troops in December 2011, violence between Sunni and Shi'a Muslims continued.

In September 2014, a U.S.-led coalition launched a bombing campaign against the Sunni jihadist group known as the Islamic State of Iraq and Syria (ISIS, a.k.a ISIL, a.k.a IS), which had conquered large swaths of territory in civil war-torn Syria and Iraq in the preceding months. In November 2014, President Obama authorized doubling the number of military advisers in Iraq, from 1,500 to 3,000, as part of the expansion of the American military campaign against the self-proclaimed Islamic State (Cooper 2014).

When Obama assumed office in January 2009, he promised winds of change. But Guantánamo Bay detention camp still imprisons people without charge, the FBI can still issue National Security Letters without a court order and U.S.

drones are still killing foreign nationals in countries the U.S is not at war with. And although the U.S. did indeed withdraw its troops from Iraq (at least before it started sending them back in), the 'War on Terror'—declared by the Bush administration in the wake of 9/11—seems far from over. If anything, it is only just beginning.[23]

It's a brave new world.

---

23   As of November 2015, 107 detainees still remain at Guantánamo Bay ("US transfers").

EPILOGUE

Will we be alright?

Thinking about our future is almost impossible without thinking about our past. We have been shaped by it, continue to be influenced by it and try to draw lessons from it, to 'prevent history from repeating itself'.

Because, tellingly, we consider history repeating itself as something negative. Whenever someone says "*history repeats itself*", it is invariably to lament yet another war, another famine, another recession, another man-made disaster or some other thing we would prefer *not* to repeat itself.

History, it seems, is more often something to be ashamed of than to be proud of. Ashamed of all the massacres, persecutions and genocides, of all the oppression and exploitation, the intolerance, the hatred, the indifference. If we are able to step away for a moment from finger-pointing any one tribe for having committed this or that particular atrocity, we cannot but admit that as a species we have failed to live up to the expectations that come from being created in His own image (unless you believe in a very cruel god).

Thus, looking at our history easily elicits fear for our future.

Then again, the very fact that many now condemn what was once believed normal and natural, or at the very least inescapable—things like war, persecution, slavery, torture, dictatorial rule, the absence of the rule of law, racial segregation and gender inequality, to name but a few—can undeniably be called progress. Clearly, our ways are not set in stone and we are indeed learning from the past.

Still, how can we trust ourselves to steer our destiny in the right direction, knowing that less than a century ago we developed weapons to infect populations with the bubonic plague on a massive scale. Knowing that we carted off like cattle millions of Jews from all over Europe to concentration camps specifically constructed to exterminate people in an industrial-like fashion. Knowing that, in the end, all that stood between us and a nuclear holocaust was a Russian submarine commander who kept his cool when others did not.

Perhaps we cannot and perhaps we should not either. Perhaps, knowing what we know about our past—and our present, for that matter—it is best to remain unconvinced about our species' capability to completely overcome the primitive instincts lodged in the 'reptilian' part of our brain. Besides, whether we want to or not, we hold our collective destiny in our collective hands. We are like the small boys from William Golding's *Lord of the Flies*, stranded on a deserted island with no hope of being rescued.

It is up to us to write a different ending.

END

Homo Sapiens will return in

WORLD 1.0:
A HISTORY FROM CONQUEST TO REVOLUTION

WORKS CITED

Abbatiello, John. *Anti-Submarine Warfare in Wold War I: British Naval Aviation and the Defeat of the U.Boats.* London: Routledge. 2006. Print.

Absher, Kenneth Michael. *Mindsets and Missiles: A Firsthand Account of the Cuban Missile Crisis.* Lulu.com. 2012. Print.

Adams, Guy B, and Danny L. Balfour. *Unmasking Administrative Evil.* Third Edition. Armonk: M.E. Sharpe. 2009. Print.

Adams, Val. "TV: Coverage of March - Nielsen Reports 46% Higher Audience Than in Normal Daytime Hours." *The New York Times.* Aug. 29, 1963. Print.

Adamthwaite, Anthony P. *The Making of the Second World War.* New York: Routledge. 1992. Print.

Aldrich, Richard J. "OSS, CIA and European Unity: The American Committee on United Europe, 1948–60." *Diplomacy & Statecraft*, Vol. 8, No. 1 (March 1997): 184–227. London: Frank Cass. Published online Oct. 19, 2007 by Taylor & Francis Group. tandfonline.com. Web. Aug. 31, 2015.

Alexander, John K. *Samuel Adams: America's Revolutionary Politician.* Rowman & Littlefield. 2004. Print.

Allcorn, William. *The Maginot Line, 1928–45.* Oxford: Osprey Publishing. 2003. Print.

Allen, Larry. *The Encyclopedia of Money.* Santa Barbara: ABC-CLIO. 2009. Print.

Allen, Robert C. "The Great Divergence in European Wages and Prices from the Middle Ages to the First World War." *Explorations in Economic History.* Vol. 38. 2001: 411–447. Print.

Allison, Robert J. *The Boston Massacre.* Beverly: Commonwealth Editions. 2006. Print.

Alpert, William T, ed. *The Vietnamese Economy and its Transformation to an Open Market System.* Armonk: M.E. Sharpe. 2005. Print.

Anderson, Herbert L., Enrico Fermi, and Leo Szilard. "Neutron Production and Absorption in Uranium." *Physical Review.* Vol. 56. Aug. 1, 1939: 284–286. Print.

Andrews, Robert. *The Columbia Dictionary of Quotations.* New York: Columbia UP. 1993. Print.

Arad, Yitzhak. *Belzec, Sobibor, Treblinka: The Operation Reinhard Death Camps.* Bloomington: Indiana UP. 1987. Print.

Arad, Yitzhak, Israel Gutman, and Abraham Margaliot, ed. *Documents on the Holocaust: Selected Sources on the Destruction of the Jews of Germany and Austria, Poland, and the Soviet Union.* Eighth edition. Lea Ben Dor, trans. U of Nebraska P. 1999. Print.

Arsenault, Raymond. *Freedom Riders: 1961 and the Struggle for Racial Justice.* Oxford: Oxford UP. 2006. Print.

Articles of Confederation. March 1, 1781. Avalon Project, Yale Law. Web. June 2, 2015.

Ascher, Abraham. *The Revolution of 1905: Russia in Disarray.* Stanford UP. 1988. Print.

Ashraf, Quamrul, Oded Galor. "Dynamics and Stagnation in the Malthusian Epoch." *American Economic Review.* Vol. 101(5). 2011: 2003–41. Print.

Ashton, T.S. *Iron and steel in the industrial revolution.* Manchester: Manchester UP. 1924. Print.

Åslund, Anders. *Russia's Capitalist Revolution: Why Market Reform Succeeded and Democracy Failed.* Washington: Peterson Institute for International Economics. 2007. Print.

Atkins, Stephen E., ed. *The 9/11 Encyclopedia.* Second Edition. Santa Barbara: ABC-CLIO. 2011. Print.

Atomic Energy Commission. "Script from a radio broadcast sponsored by Gulf Oil Corporation. The script includes live interviews with employees who lived and worked at Oak Ridge during the development of the atom bomb." Records of the Atomic Energy Commission, 1923–1978. Feb. 9, 1947. research.archives.gov/id/281583?q=281583. ARC: 281583. NAIL Control Number: NRCA-326-OAK004-RADSCRIP. Web. Aug. 25, 2015.

Baran, Paul. "Reliable Digital Communications Systems Using Unreliable Network Repeater Nodes." RAND Corporation. P-1995. May 27, 1960. Print.

Barber, Lucy Grace. *Marching on Washington: The Forging of an American Political Tradition*. Berkely: U of California P. 2004. Print.

Barnes, Brooks. "In a Breathtaking First, NASA's Voyager 1 Exits the Solar System." *The New York Times*. nytimes.com. Sep. 12, 2013. Web. Sep. 6, 2015.

Barnes, Thomas G., and Gerald D. Feldman. *Nationalism, Industrialization, and Democracy, 1815–1914. A Documentary History of Modern Europe Volume III*. UP of America. 1980. Print.

Bartlett, John Russell. *A History of the Destruction of His Britannic Majesty's Schooner Gaspee, in Narragansett Bay, on the 10th June, 1772*. Providence. 1861. Print.

Bartley, Paula. *Emmeline Pankhurst*. New York: Routledge. 2002. Print.

Bartsch, Matthias, Dietmar Hipp, and Maximilian Popp. "Integration Case: Court to Rule on Swim Lessons for Muslim Girls." Paul Cohen, trans. spiegel.de. Sep. 9, 2013. Web. Mar. 5, 2015.

Bateman, Fred, and Thomas Weiss. *A Deplorable Scarcity: The Failure of Industrialization in the Slave Economy*. U of North Carolina P. 1981. Print.

Bazinet, Kenneth R. "A Fight VS. Evil, Bush and Cabinet Tell U.S." New York Daily News. Sep. 17, 2001. Web. Jan. 26, 2015.

BEA. "Texas". Bureau of Economic Analysis. U.S. Department of Commerce. bea.gov. Web. May 28, 2015.

Bears, Edwin C., and Bryce Suderow. *The Petersburg Campaign: The Western Front Battles, September 1864 - April 1865*. El Dorado Hills: Savas Beatie. 2014. Print.

Belknap, Michael R. *Federal Law and Southern Order: Racial Violence and Constitutional Conflict in the Post-Brown South*. U of Georgia P. 1995. First edition 1987. Print.

Bell, Christopher, and Bruce Elleman, ed. *Naval Mutinies of the Twentieth Century: An International Perspective*. Routledge. 2004. Print.

Bendersky, Joseph W. *A History of Nazi Germany: 1919–1945*. Rowman & Littlefield. 2000. Print.

Bennett, George D. *The United States Army: Issues, Background and Bibliography*. Huntington: Nova Science. 2002. Print.

Berg, Pierre, and Brian Brock. *Scheisshaus Luck: Surviving the Unspeakable in Auschwitz and Dora*. Amacom. 2008. Print.

Bernanke, Ben S. *Essays on the Great Depression*. Princeton: Princeton UP. 2000. Print.

Bernanke, Ben S. "Monetary Policy and the Global Economy." federalreserve.gov. Mar 25, 2013. Web. July 27, 2015.

Berners-Lee, Tim. "A Brief History of the Web." 1993/4. http://www.w3.org/DesignIssues/TimBook-old/History.html. Web. Oct. 10, 2015.

Berners-Lee, Tim. "Information Management: A Proposal." March 1989, May 1990. http://www.w3.org/History/1989/proposal.html. Web. Oct. 10, 2015.

Bernstein, Jeremy. *Hitler's Uranium Club: The Secret Recordings at Farm Hall*. New York: Copernicus. 2001. Print.

Berstein, Serge. *The Republic of de Gaulle 1958–1969*. Cambridge UP. 1993. Print.

Billington, James H., and Library of Congress. *Respectfully Quoted: A Dictionary of Quotations*. Dover Publications. 2010. Print.

Bin Laden, Osama, et al. "Declaration of the World Islamic Front for Jihad against the Jews and the Crusaders." Feb. 23, 1998. fas.org, trans. "Jihad Against Jews and Crusaders". Web. Jan. 26, 2015.

Bin Laden, Osama. "Declaration of War against the Americans Occupying the Land of the Two Holy Places." Aug. 1996. Newsdesk, trans. pbs.org. "Bin Laden's Fatwa." Web. Jan. 26, 2015.

Bismarck, Otto von. *Bismarck, the man and the statesman; being the reflections and reminiscences of Otto, Prince von Bismarck*. Vol. II. New York: Harper & Brothers. 1899. Print.

Black, Jeremy. *George III: America's Last King*. Yale UP. 2008. Print.

Blake, Robert, and Wm. Roger Louis, ed. *Churchill*. Oxford: Oxford UP. 1999. Print.

Blum, William. *Killing Hope: US Military and CIA Interventions Since World War II*. London: Zed. 2003. Print.

Blumenthal, Karen. *Six Days in October: The Stock Market Crash of 1929*. New York: Simon and Schuster. 2002. Print.

Bodart, Gaston. *Losses of Life in Modern Wars: Austria-Hungary; France*. Harald Westergaard, ed. Oxford: Clarendon Press. 1916. Print.

Boemeke, Manfred F., Gerald D. Feldman, and Elisabeth Glaser, ed. *The Treaty of Versailles: A reassessment after 75 Years*. Cambridge: Cambridge UP. 1998. Print.

Boldrin, Michele, and David K. Levine. *Against Intellectual Monopoly*. Cambridge: Cambridge UP. 2008. Print.

Bonekemper, III, Edward H. *A Victor, Not a Butcher: Ulysses S. Grant's Overlooked Military Genius*. Washington: Eagle. 2004. Print.

Booth, John. *The Battle of Waterloo: Containing the Accounts Published by Authority, British and Foreign, and Other Relative Documents, with Circumstantial Details, Previous and After the Battle, from a Variety of Authentic and Original Sources: to which is Added an Alphabetical List of the Officers Killed and Wounded, from 15th to 26th June, 1815, and the Total Loss of Each Regiment.* London: J. Booth. 1815. Print.

Borger, Julian. "Blogger bares Rumsfeld's post 9/11 orders." The Guardian. Feb. 24, 2006. Web. Jan. 28, 2015.

Bourdet, Yves. *The Economics of Transition in Laos: From Socalism to ASEAN integration.* Cheltenham: Edward Elgar. 2000. Print.

Branigan, Tania. "China's jasmine revolution: police but no protesters line streets of Beijing." theguardian.com. Feb. 27, 2011. Web. July 28, 2015.

Brown v. Board of Education of Topeka. 347 U.S. 483. Supreme Court of the United States. 1954. Supreme Court Collection. Legal Information Inst., Cornell U. Law School, n.d. Web. 15 Jan. 2016.

Brown, Weldon A. *Empire Or Independence: A Study in the Failure of Reconciliation, 1774–1783.* Port Washington: Kennikat Press. 1966. Print.

Browning, Christopher R. *The Origins of the Final Solution: The Evolution of Nazi Jewish Policy, September 1939-March 1942.* U of Nebraska P. 2007. Print.

Bundy, McGeorge. "Memorandum of Discussion on Cuba, Cabinet Room, January 28, 1961." Jan. 28, 1961. Washington. history.state.gov. Historical Documents, Foreign Relations of the United States, 1961–1963, Volume X, Cuba, January 1961-September 1962, Document 30. Web. Dec. 12, 2015.

Burgess, Colin, and Rex Hall. *The First Soviet Cosmonaut Team: Their Lives and Legacies.* Springer-Praxis Books. 2009. Print.

Burke, Edmund. *The Annual Register, or a View of the History, Politics, and Literature, for the Year 1804.* Vol. 46. J. Dodsley. 1806. Print.

Burke, Jason. "Warning of 9/11 'ignored." Sep. 8, 2002. theguardian.com. Web. Jan. 28, 2015.

Burns, John F. "Taliban Figure Asks Bombing Halt to Make Deal on bin Laden." Oct. 16, 2001. nytimes.com. Web. Jan. 28, 2015.

Burns, Richard Dean, and Joseph M. Siracusa. *A Global History of the Nuclear Arms Race: Weapons, Strategy, and Politics.* Santa Barbara: ABC-CLIO. 2013. Print.

Bush, George W. "Address to a Joint Session of Congress and the American People." georgewbush-whitehouse.archives. org. Sep. 20, 2001. Web. Jan. 26, 2015.

Bush, George W. "Remarks by the President Upon Arrival." georgewbush-whitehouse.archives.org. Sep.16, 2001. Web. Jan. 26, 2015.

Butcher, Tim. *The Trigger: Hunting the Assassin Who Brought the World to War.* New York: Grove Press. 2014. Print.

Cantelon, Philip L, Richard G. Hewlett, and Robert C. Williams, ed. *The American Atom: A Documentary History of Nuclear Policies from the Discovery of Fission to the Present."* Second Edition. U of Pennsylvania P. 1991. Print.

Caranci, Paul F. *North Providence: A History and the People Who Shaped It.* Charleston: The History Press. 2012. Print.

Carlyle, Thomas. *The French Revolution: A History.* London: Thomas Nelson & Sons. 1903. Print.

Carmichael, Joel. *A Short History of the Russian Revolution.* Basic Books. 1964. Print.

Carson, Jon. "Our States Remain United. Official White House Response to Peacefully grant the State of Texas to withdraw from the United States of America and create its own NEW government." petitions.whitehouse.gov. n.d. Web. May 26, 2015.

Carter, Dan T. *The Politics of Rage: George Wallace, the Origins of the New Conservatism, and the Transformation of American Politics*. LSU Press. 2000. Print.

Carter, Jimmy. "Voyager Spacecraft Statement by the President." July 29, 1977. presidency.ucsb.edu. Web. Sep. 13, 2015.

Caulaincourt, Armand de. *With Napoleon in Russia*. Mineola: Dover. 2005. Print.

Cerf, Vinton, Yogen Dalal, and Carl Sunshine. "Specification of Internet Transmission Control Program." *Network Working Group*. Dec. 1974. tools.ietf.org. Web. Oct. 9, 2015.

Ceruzzi, Paul E. *A History of Modern Computing*. Cambridge: MIT Press. 2003. Print.

Ceruzzi, Paul E. *Computing: A Concise History*. Cambridge: MIT Press. 2012. Print.

Chamberlain, Neville. "Peace for Our Time." Sep. 30, 1938. British Historical Documents. britannia.com. Web. Apr. 2, 2015.

Chamberlain, Neville. "Statement by the Prime Minister in the House of Commons on March 31, 1939." *The Avalon Project: The British War Bluebook*. avalon.law.yale.edu. n.d. Web. Apr. 2, 2015.

Chambers, John Whiteclay, ed. *The Oxford Companion to American Military History*. Oxford: Oxford UP. 1999. Print.

Chandler, David G. *The Campaigns of Napoleon*. New York: Simon and Schuster. 2009. Print.

Cheney, Richard B. "Remarks by Richard B. Cheney." *American Enterprise Institute*. May 21, 2009. Web. Jan. 23, 2015.

"Cheney: Order to Shoot Down Hijacked 9/11 Planes 'Necessary.'" foxnews.com. Sep. 4, 2011. Web. Jan. 25, 2015.

Chernow, Ron. *Alexander Hamilton*. New York: Penguin. 2004. Print.

Chesney, Charles Cornwallis. *Waterloo Lectures: A Study Of The Campaign Of 1815*. Third Edition. London: Longmans, Green. 1874. Print.

Chickering, Roger. *Imperial Germany and the Great War, 1914–1918*. Second Edition. Cambridge: Cambridge UP. 2004. Print.

"China police break up 'protests' after online appeal." bbc. com. Feb. 20, 2011. Web. July 28, 2015.

Chrisafis, Angelique. "Vive la révolution! French MP starts race to Napoleonland." theguardian.com. Feb. 14, 2012. Web. June 4, 2015.

Christoffersen, John. "Robert Schiller: Income Inequality Is 'Most Important Problem.'" huffingtonpost.com. Oct. 15, 2013. Web. Oct. 5, 2015.

Chuĭkov, Vasiliĭ Ivanovich. *The Beginning of the Road*. Macgibbon & Kee. 1963. Print.

Churchill, Winston S. "The Few." Aug. 20, 1940. The Churchill Centre. winstonchurchill.org. Web. Apr. 3, 2015.

Churchill, Winston S. *Their Finest Hour*. Volume II of the Second World War. New York: Houghton Mifflin Harcourt. 1986. Print.

Churchill, Winston S. *Triumph and Tragedy: The Second World War, Volume 6*. RosettaBooks. 2010. First edition 1953. Print.

Churchill, Winston S. "We Shall Fight on the Beaches". June 4, 1940. The Churchill Centre. winstonchurchill.org. Web. Apr. 3, 2015.

CIA. "The 27th CPSU Congress: Gorbachev's Unfinished Business." CIA. Directorate of Intelligence. SOV 86–10023. Apr. 1986. Print.

"Circular of the Central Committee Party of China on the Great Proletarian Cultural Revolution." Communist Party of China. May 16, 1966. marxists.org. Web. Sep. 26, 2015.

Clark, Christopher M. *Iron Kingdom: The Rise and Downfall of Prussia, 1600–1947*. Harvard UP. 2006. Print.

Clark, Gregory. *A Farewell to Alms: A Brief Economic History of the World*. Princeton UP. 2007. Print.

Clark, Kate. "Taleban 'warned US of huge attack.'" bbc.co.uk. Sept. 7, 2002. Web. Jan. 28, 2015.

Clausewitz, Carl von. *On War*. Michael Howard and Peter Paret, ed. and trans. Princeton UP. 1989. First German edition (Vom Kriege), 1832. Print.

CNN. "9/11 News CNN Sept. 11, 2001 8 48 am - 9 29 am September 11, 2001". youtube.com. Web. Jan. 23, 2015.

Coker, Rachel. "History professor: Civil War death toll has been underestimated." Binghamton University. binghamton.edu. Sept. 21, 2011. Web. June 18, 2015.

Committee On Armed Services United States Senate. "Inquiry Into The Treatment Of Detainees In U.S. Custody." Committee Print. Nov. 20, 2008. Print.

Committee On Foreign Relations United States Senate. "Tora Bora Revisited: How We Failed To Get Bin Laden And Why It Maters Today." Committee Print. Nov. 30, 2009. Print.

Constitution of the People's Republic of China. npc.gov.cn. Dec. 4, 1982. Web. July 28, 2015.

Constitution of the United States. The Constitution of the United States: A transcription. n.d. archives.gov. Web. June 4, 2015.

Cook, Frank W. "Lemuel Remembers Washington." n.d. burrcook.com. Web. June 16, 2015.

Cooper, Helene, and Michael D. Shear. "Obama to Send 1,500 More Troops to Assist Iraq." nytimes.com. Nov. 7, 2014. Web. Jan. 28, 2015.

Copeland, Jack, et al. *Colossus: The Secrets of Bletchley Park's Codebreaking Computers*. Oxford: Oxford UP. 2006. Print.

Craig, Gordon A. *The Battle of Königgrätz: Prussia's Victory Over Austria, 1866*. Philadelphia: U of Pennsylvania P. 2003. Print.

Craig, William. *Enemy at the Gates: The Battle for Stalingrad*. Old saybrook: Konecky & Konecky. 1973. Print.

Crawford, Samuel W. *The History Of The Fall Of Fort Sumter: Being An Inside History Of The Affairs In South Carolina And Washington, 1860–61*. New York: S.F. McLean. 1898. Print.

Creevey, Thomas and Herbert Maxwell, ed. *The Creevey Papers: A Selection from the Correspondence and Diaries of the Late Thomas Creevey*. Vol I. Cambridge: Cambridge UP. 2012. First edition published 1903. Print.

Crew, David F. *Nazism and German Society, 1933–1945*. London: Routledge. 1994. Print.

Cronin, Mary J, ed. *The Internet Strategy Handbook: Lessons from the New Frontier of Business*. Boston: Harvard Business School Press. 1996. Print.

Cushing, Harry Alonzo, ed. *The Writings of Samuel Adams*. Volume I. 1764–1769. New York: G.P. Putnam's Sons. 1904. Print.

Czech, Danuta. "The Auschwitz Prisoner Administration." In *Anatomy of the Auschwitz Death Camp*. Yisrael Gutman and Michael Berenbaum, ed. Bloomington: Indiana UP. 1994: 363–379. Print.

Daigle, Leslie. "30 years of TCP—and IP on everything!." *internetsociety.org*. Jan. 1, 2013. Web. Oct. 9, 2015.

Dale, Gareth. *Popular Protest in East Germany*. Abingdon: Routledge. 2005. Print.

Dallek, Robert. *An Unfinished Life: John F. Kennedy, 1917–1963*. Boston: Little, Brown and Company. 2003. Print.

Davidson, Greg, and Paul Davidson. *Economics for a Civilized Society*. Armonk: M. E. Sharpe. 1996. Print.

Dean, Peter J. "Napoleon as a Military Commander: the Limitations of Genius." napoleon-series.org. n.d. Web. June 8, 2015.

Declaration of Independence. archives.gov. Web. May 20, 2015.

Dewey, Davis Rich. *Early Financial History of the United States*. First Edition 1903. Washington: Beard Books. 2003. Print.

Dickson, Paul. *Sputnik: The Shock of the Century*. Bloomsbury Publishing USA. 2009. Print.

Dikötter, Frank. *Mao's Great Famine: The History of China's Most Devastating Catastrophe, 1958–1962*. New York: Walker. 2010. Print.

Dillon, Michael. *China: A Modern History*. London: I.B. Tauris. 2010. Print.

Doe v. Holder. 703 F. Supp.2d 313. U.S. District Court, S.D. New York. Mar. 28, 2010. clearinghouse.net. Web. Jan. 27, 2015.

Doe II v. Gonzales S III E. 449 F. 3d 415. U.S. Court of Appeals, Second Circuit. May 23, 2006. public.resource. org. Web. Jan. 26, 2015.

Doe v. Gonzales. 500 F. Supp. 2d 379. U.S. District Court, S.D. New York. Sep. 6, 2007. clearinghouse.net. Web. Jan. 27, 2015.

Dougherty, Kevin. *Military Leadership Lessons of the Charleston Campaign, 1861–1865*. Jefferson: McFarland. 2014. Print.

Dull, Paul S. *A Battle History of the Imperial Japanese Navy, 1941- 1945*. Annapolis: Naval Institute Press. 2013. Print.

Eastman, Lloyd E. *The Nationalist Era in China, 1927–1949*. Cambridge: Cambridge UP. 1991. Print.

Eicher, David J. *Robert E. Lee: A Life Portrait*. Lanham: Rowman & Littlefield. 2002. Print.

Eicher, David J. *The Longest Night: A Military History of the Civil War*. New York: Simon & Schuster. 2001. Print.

Einstein, Albert, and Leo Szilard. "Einstein's Letter to Roosevelt." osti.gov. Aug. 2, 1939. Web. Aug. 24, 2015.

Elliot, Jonathan, ed. *The Debates on the Adoption of the Federal Constitution in the Convention held at Philadelphia in 1787, with a Diary of the Debates of the Congress of the*

Confederation as reported by James Madison, revised and newly arranged by Jonathan Elliot. Complete in One Volume. Vol. V. Supplement to Elliot's Debates. Philadelphia. 1836. Print.

Ellis, John, and Michael Cox. *The World War I Databook: The Essential Facts and Figures for All the Combatants.* Aurum. 2001. Print.

"Emser Depesche." July 13, 1870. documentarchiv.de. Web. June 29, 2015.

"Encyclopedia Judaica: Haavara." jewishvirtuallibrary.org. n.d. Web. Aug. 17, 2015.

Engels, Friedrich. *Anti-Dühring; Herr Eugen Dühring's revolution in science.* New York: International Publishers. Translated from the third German edition by Emile Burns. C.P. Dutt, ed. First published in German as a book in 1878. Translation is from 1894 edition. Print.

Engelstein, Laura. *Moscow, 1905: Working-class Organization and Political Conflict.* Stanford: Stanford UP. 1982. Print.

Englund, Steven. *Napoleon: A Political Life.* New York: Simon & Schuster. 2004. Print.

Enys, John S. "Remarks on the Duty of the Steam Engines employed in the Mines of Cornwall at different periods." Published in: *Transactions of the Institution of Civil Engineers, Volume 3, Part 5.* Institution of Civil Engineers. London: J. Weale. 1842. Print.

Erdbrink, Thomas. "As Talks With U.S. Near, Iran Denies Nuclear Arms Effort." washingtonpost.com. Sep. 21, 2009. Web. Aug. 24, 2015.

Erdbrink, Thomas. "Iran's Leaders Signal Effort at New Thaw." *The New York Times.* Sept. 19, 2013. Print.

Ernesto. "Pirate Bay Takes Over Distribution Of Censored 3D Printable Gun." torrentfreak.com. May 10, 2013. Web. June 9, 2015.

Esherick, Joseph. *The Origins of the Boxer Uprising.* Berkely: U of California P. 1987. Print.

Eskew, Glenn T. *But for Birmingham: The Local and National Movements in the Civil Rights Struggle.* U of North Carolina P. 1997. Print.

"Estimated Impact of the American Recovery and Investment Act on Employment and Economic Output from October 2011 through December 2012." Feb. 2012. Washington: Congressional Budget Office. Web. July 25, 2015.

Espinasse, Francis. *Lancashire worthies.* London: Simpkin, Marshall, & Co. 1874. Print.

Exec. Order No. 6102, 3 C.F.R. (1933). Print.

Fairbank, John King, Albert Feuerwerker, and Denis Crispin Twitchett. *The Cambridge History of China, Vol. 13: Republican China, 1912–1949. Part 2.* Cambridge UP. 1986. Print.

Fairbank, John King, and Merle Goldman. *China: A New History, Second Enlarged Edition.* Harvard UP. 2006. Print.

Fairclough, Adam. *To Redeem the Soul of America: The Southern Christian Leadership Conference & Martin Luther King, Jr.* U of Georgia P. 2001. Print.

Ferro, Marc, and Brian Pearce. *Nicholas II: Last of the Tsars.* Oxford: Oxford UP. 1995. Print.

Fichte, Johann Gottlieb. *Addresses to the German Nation.* R.F. Jones and G.H. Turnbull, trans. Chicago: Open Court. 1922. Print.

Finkelman, Paul. *Slavery and the Founders: Race and Liberty in the Age of Jefferson.* Armonk: M.E. Sharpe. 2001. Print.

Fitton, R.S, and Alfred P. Wadsworth. *The Strutts and the Arkwrights, 1758–1830: A Study of the Early Factory System.* Manchester: Manchester UP. 1958. Print.

Fitzpatrick, John C. *The Writings of George Washington from the Original Manuscript Sources 1745–1799 Volume 29 September 1, 1786-June 19, 1788.* Best Books. 1939. Print.

Fitzpatrick, Sheila. *The Russian Revolution.* Oxford: Oxford UP. 2008. Print.

Flamm, Kenneth. *Creating the Computer: Government, Industry, and High Technology.* Washington: The Brookings Institution. 1998. Print.

Fleischman, Richard K., Warwick Funnell, and Stephen P. Walker, ed. *Critical Histories of Accounting: Sinister Inscriptions in the Modern Era.* New York: Routledge. 2013. Print.

Ford, Henry, and Samuel Crowther. *Edison as I know him.* New York: Cosmopolitan book corporation. 1930. Print.

Ford, Henry, and Samuel Crowther. *My Life and Work.* New York: Doubleday, Page & Company. 1923. Print.

Ford, Paul Leicester, ed. *The Works of Thomas Jefferson.* Vol. V. New York: G.P. Putnam's Sons. 1904. Print.

"Foreign Scientist Case Files 1945-1958 - 230/86/46/05 186 boxes." archives.gov/iwg/declassified-records/rg-330-defense-secretary/foreign-scientist-case-files.pdf. Nov. 30, 2010. Web. Sep. 8, 2015.

Förster, Stig, and Jörg Nagler. *On the Road to Total War: The American Civil War and the German Wars of Unification, 1861–1871.* Cambridge: Cambridge UP. 1997. Print.

Foster, Nigel G., and Satish Sule. *German Legal System and Laws.* Fourth Edition. Oxford: Oxford UP. 2010. Print.

Fox, Margalit. "Rochus Misch, Bodyguard of Hitler, Dies at 96." *The New York Times.* nytimes.com Sept. 6, 2013. Web. Apr. 1, 2015.

Frazer, Karen D. "NSFNET: A Partnership for High-Speed Networking: Final Report, 1987–1995." Merit Network. merit.edu. Web. Oct. 9, 2015.

Freedman, Russell. *The War to End All Wars: World War I.* New York: Houghton Mifflin Harcourt. 2013. Print.

Fremont-Barnes, Gregory. *Napoleon Bonaparte: Leadership, Strategy, Conflict.* Botley: Osprey. 2010. Print.

Friedman, Jonathan C. *The Routledge History of the Holocaust.* Abingdon: Routledge. 2011. Print.

Friedman, Milton, and Anna Jacobson Schwartz. *A Monetary History of the United States, 1867–1960*. Princeton UP 2008. First published 1963. Print.

Frisch, Otto, and Rudolf Peierls. "The Frish-Peierls Memorandum." web.stanford.edu. n.d. Web. Aug. 25, 2015.

Fritz, Stephen G. *Ostkrieg: Hitler's War of Extermination in the East*. UP of Kentucky. 2011. Print.

Fromkin, David. *A Peace to End All Peace: The Fall of the Ottoman Empire and the Creation of the Modern Middle East*. New York: Henry Holt. 2010. Print.

Fromkin, David. *Europe's Last Summer: Why the World Went to War in 1914*. London: Random House. 2005. Print.

Fugitive Slave Act 1850. Pub. L. 31–60. 9 Stat. 462–465. Sept. 18, 1850.

Gagliardo, John G. *Germany Under the Old Regime 1600–1790*. London: Routledge. 2013. Print.

Gallagher, Gary W., Robert Krick, and Stephen D. Krick. *Civil War: Fort Sumter to Appomattox*. Osprey. 2014. Print.

Gann, W. D. *New York Trend Detector*. Health Research Books. 1994. First Edition 1936. Print.

Gao, Yuan. *Born Red: A Chronicle of the Cultural Revolution*. Stanford: Stanford UP. 1987. Print.

Garthoff, Raymond L. *Reflections on the Cuban Missile Crisis: Revised to include New Revelations from Soviet & Cuban Sources*. Washington D.C.: The Brookings Institution. 1989. Print.

Garun, Natt. "In China, Noodle-Slicing Robots Are Taking Over Local Restaurants." Aug. 21, 2012. digitaltrends.com. Web. June 29, 2015.

Gáti, Charles. *The bloc that failed: Soviet-East European relations in transition*. Indiana UP. 1990. Print.

Geisst, Charles R. *Wall Street: A History*. Oxford: Oxford UP. 1997. Print.

"German Jewish Refugees, 1933–1939." *Holocaust Encyclopedia*. United States Holocaust Memorial Museum. n.d. ushmm.org. Web. Aug. 14, 2015.

Getty, J. Arch, Gabor T. Rittersporn, and Viktor N. Zemskov. "Victims of the Soviet Penal System in the Pre-War Years: A First Approach on the Basis of Archival Evidence." *The American Historical Review*. Vol. 98, No. 4 (Oct. 1993): 1017–1049. Print.

Giacomo, Carol. "In Saudi Arabia, Where Women's Suffrage Is a New Idea." *The New York Times*. nytimes.com. Nov. 2, 2015. Web. Nov. 21, 2015.

Gilbert, G.M. *Nuremberg Diary*. Da Capo Press. 1995. First Edition 1947. Print.

Glantz, David M. *Operation Barbarossa: Hitler's Invasion of Russia 1941*. The History Press. 2011. Print.

Gleijeses, Piero. "Ships in the Night: The CIA, the White house and the Bay of Pigs." *Journal of Latin American Studies*. Vol. 27, No. 1. 1995: 1–42. Cambridge UP. Print.

Godwin, Robert, ed. *Apollo 10: The NASA Mission Reports*. Apogee Books. 2000. Print.

Goldgar, Anne. *Tulipmania: Money, Honor, and Knowledge in the Dutch Golden Age*. U of Chicago P. 2007. Print.

Goldman, Merle, ed., and Elizabeth J. Perry, ed. *Changing Meanings of Citizenship in Modern China*. Harvard UP. 2002. Print.

Gray, Fred D. *Bus Ride to Justice: Changing the System by the System: the Life and Works of Fred Gray*. Montgomery: NewSouth Books. 2002. Print.

Gray, Jack. *Rebellions and Revolutions: China from the 1800s to 2000*. Oxford: Oxford UP. 2002. Print.

Gray, Randal. *Kaiserschlacht 1918: The Final German Offensive*. Botley: Osprey. 1991. Print.

Greene, A. Wilson. *The Final Battles of the Petersburg Campaign: Breaking the Backbone of the Rebellion*. U of Tennessee P. 2008. Print.

Greene, Jerome A. *The Guns of Independence: The Siege of Yorktown, 1781*. New York: Savas Beatie. 2005. Print.

Greer, Donald. *The incidence of the terror during the French Revolution; a statistical interpretation*. Harvard UP. 1935. Print.

Greif, Gideon. *We Wept Without Tears: Testimonies of the Jewish Sonderkommando from Auschwitz*. Yale UP. 2005. Print.

Grenville, John A. Soames. *The Major International Treaties of the Twentieth Century: A History and Guide with Texts, Volume I*. London: Routledge. 2001. Print.

Groen, Petra M. H. "Militant Response: The Dutch Use of Military Force and the Decolonization of the Dutch East Indies, 1945–50." *Emergencies and Disorder in the European Empires After 1945*. 30–44. R. F. Holland, ed. Routledge. 2012. Print.

Gromov, Gregory. "History of Internet and World Wide Web - The Roads and Crossroads of Internet History." netvalley. com. 1995. Web. Oct. 7, 2015.

Groves, L. R. "Memorandum For The Secretary of War, The Test." July 18, 1945. nsarchive.gwu.edu. Original source: U.S. National Archives. RG 77, MED Records, Top Secret Documents, File no. 4. Web. Aug. 26, 2015.

Guderian, Heinz. *Panzer Leader*. Da Capo Press. 2002. First published in New York in 1952. Print.

Guo, Rongxing. *Understanding the Chinese Economies*. Kidlington: Academic Press. 2013. Print.

Gutman, Yisrael, and Michael Berenbaum, ed. *Anatomy of the Auschwitz Death Camp*. Bloomington: Indiana UP. 1998. Print.

Guttmann, Robert. *Reforming Money and Finance: Toward a New Monetary Regime*. New York: M. E. Sharpe. 1997. Print.

Hagemann, Karen. *Revisiting Prussia's Wars against Napoleon: History, Culture, and Memory.* New York: Cambridge UP. 2015. Print.

Haggard, Stephen, and Marcus Noland. *Gender in Transition: The Case of North Korea.* Washington: Peterson Institute for International Economics. June 2012. iie.com. Web. Sep. 30, 2015.

Hailey, Foster. "Dogs and Hoses Repulse Negroes at Birmingham." *The New York Times.* May 4, 1963. Print.

Halabi, Bassam, Sam Halabi, and Danny McPherson. *Internet Routing Architectures.* Second Edition. Indianapolis: Cisco Press. 2001. Print.

Halporn, Barbara C, ed, trans. *The Correspondence of Johann Amerbach: Early Printing in Its Social Context.* U of Michigan P. 2000. Print.

Hall, Allan. "Muslim girl is ordered by German judge to wear a 'burkini' at her school swimming class after she refused to take part as it was against her religion." dailymail.co.uk. Sep 12, 2013. Web. Mar 5, 2015.

Hall, Christopher David. *British Strategy in the Napoleonic War, 1803–15.* Manchester UP. 1992. Print.

Hall, Rex, and David J. Shayler. *The Rocket Men: Vostok & Voskhod, The First Soviet Manned Spaceflights.* Springer-Praxis Books. 2001. Print.

Halpern, Paul G. *A Naval History of World War I.* Annapolis: U.S. Naval Institute. 1994. Print.

Hamilton, Alexander, John Jay, and James Madison. *The Federalist Papers.* n.p. n.d. Project Gutenberg. gutenberg.org. Web. June 2, 2015.

Hamilton, Thomas J. "Kennedy Asks Joint Moon Flight By U.S. And Soviet As Peace Step." *The New York Times.* Sep. 21, 1963. Print.

Hansen, Drew. "Mahalia Jackson, and King's Improvisation." *The New York Times.* nytimes.com Aug. 27, 2013. Web. Sep. 17, 2015.

Harcave, Sidney. *Count Sergei Witte and the Twilight of Imperial Russia: A Biography*. New York: M.E. Sharpe. 2004. Print.

Hardesty, Von, and Gene Eisman. *Epic Rivalry: The Inside Story of the Soviet and American Space Race*. National Geographic Books. 2008. Print.

Harlan, Chico, Blaine Harden, and Yoonjung Seo. "N. Korea lifts restrictions on private markets as last resort in food crisis." *The Washington Post*. washingtonpost.com. June 18, 2010. Web. Sep. 30, 2015.

Harrington, Peter. *Peking 1900: The Boxer Rebellion*. Botley: Osprey. 2001. Print.

Harris, Trevor. "Who is the Father of the Internet? The Case for Donald Davies." *Variety in Mass Communication Research*. 123–134. Yorgo Pasadeos, ed. Athens Institute for Education and Research. 2009. Print.

Harris, W.A. *The record of Fort Sumter, from its occupation by Major Anderson, to its reduction by South Carolina troops during the administration of Governor Pickens*. Columbia, S.C.: South Carolinian Steam Job Printing Office. 1862. Print.

Hartley, Janet M. *Russia, 1762–1825: Military Power, the State, and the People*. Westport: Praeger. 2008. Print.

Harvey, Brian. *Russia In Space: The Failed Frontier?* London: Springer. 2001. Print.

Headland, Ronald. *Messages of Murder: A Study of the Reports of the Einsatzgruppen of the Security Police and the Security Service, 1941–1943*. Cranbury: Associated UP. 1992. Print.

Heer, Hannes, and Klaus Naumann, ed. *War of Extermination: The German Military in World War II 1941–1944*. Berghahn. 2004. Print.

Helmreich, Paul C. *Wheaton College, 1834–1957: A Massachusetts Family Affair*. Cranbury: Cornwall Books. 2002. Print.

Henderson, W.O. *Zollverein Cb: The Zollverein.* Routledge. 2013. First published 1968. Print.

Hendrix, Steve. "F-16 pilot was ready to give her life on September 11." *The Washington Post.* washingtonpost. com. Sept. 8, 2011. Web. Jan. 26, 2015.

Henry, Patrick. *Jewish Resistance Against the Nazis.* Catholic U of America P. 2014. Print.

Herskovitz, Jon, and Christine Kim. "North Korea drops communism, boosts "Dear Leader"." *Reuters.* reuters.com. Sep. 28, 2009. Web. July 14, 2015.

Herold, J. Christopher. *Bonaparte in Egypt.* Tucson: Fireship. 2009. Print.

Hilberg, Raul. *The Destruction of the European Jews.* Volume III. Third Edition. Yale UP. 2003. Print.

Hill, Joseph Adna. *Women in Gainful Occupations, 1870 to 1920: A Study of the Trend of Recent Changes in the Numbers, Occupational Distribution, and Family Relationship of Women Reported in the Census as Following a Gainful Occupation.* Washington: G.P.O. 1929. Print.

Hillard, Elias Brewster. *The last men of the Revolution: a photograph of each from life, together with views of their homes printed in colors: accompanied by brief biographical sketches of the men.* Hartford: N.A. & R. A. Moore. 1864. Print.

Hills, Richard Leslie. *James Watt: Triumph through adversity, 1785–1819.* Landmark. 2006. Print.

Hills, Richard Leslie. *Power from Steam: A History of the Stationary Steam Engine.* Cambridge: Cambridge UP. 1989. Print.

History of the Seventy-ninth division, A.E.F. during the world war: 1917–1919. Compiled and Edited by History Committee 79th Division Association. Lancaster: Steinman & Steinman. 1922. Print.

Hitler, Adolf. *Mein Kampf.* John Chamberlain, ed. Reynal & Hitchcock. 1939. Print.

Hogan, Michael J. *The Marshall Plan: America, Britain and the Reconstruction of Western Europe, 1947–1952*. Cambridge: Cambridge UP. 1989. Print.

Holdstock, Douglas, and Frank Barnaby. *Hiroshima and Nagasaki: Retrospect and Prospect*. New York: Routledge. 2013. Print.

Holmes, Terence M. "Absolute Numbers: The Schlieffen Plan as a Critique of German Strategy in 1914." *War in History*. Vol. 21, 2. Apr. 2014: 193–213. Print.

Holton, Sandra Stanley. *Feminism and Democracy: Women's Suffrage and Reform Politics in Britain, 1900–1918*. Cambridge UP. 1986. Print.

Hosch, William L. *World War I: People, Politics, and Power*. Rosen Publishing Group. 2009. Print.

Hoss, Rudolf, Pery Broad, and Johann Kremer. *KL Auschwitz Seen by the SS*. Panstwowe Muzeum w Oswiecimiu. 1978. Print.

Hornick, John, and Dan Roland. "Many 3D Printing Patents Are Expiring Soon: Here's A Round Up & Overview of Them." 3dprintingindustry.com. Dec. 29, 2013. Web. June 9, 2015.

Hounshell, David. *From the American System to Mass Production, 1800–1932: The Development of Manufacturing Technology in the United States*. Johns Hopkins UP. 1985. Print.

House, Jonathan M. *A Military History of the Cold War, 1944–1962*. U of Oklahoma P. 2012. Print.

Hughes, R. Gerald. "'The best and the brightest': the Cuban missile crisis, the Kennedy administration and the lessons of history." *The Cuban Missile Crisis: A Critical Reappraisal*. 117–141. Len Scott, R. Gerald Hughes, ed. Abingdon: Routledge. 2015. Print.

Hui, Lu. "Market to play "decisive" role in allocating resources: communique." news.xinhuanet.com. Nov. 12, 2013. Web. Sep. 23, 2015.

Huie, William Bradford. "The Shocking Story of Approved Killing in Mississippi." *Look Magazine*. Jan. 1956. pbs.org. Web. Sep. 17, 2015.

Human Rights First. "Guantánamo by the Numbers." humanrightsfirst.org. 15 Jan. 2015. Web. Jan. 27, 2015.

Humphrey, John Peters. "Part One: The Contribution of the Universal Declaration." *Human Rights: Thirty Years After the Universal Declaration*. 21–40. B.G. Ramcharan, ed. The Hague: Martinus Nijhoff. 1979. Print.

Huxley, Aldous. *Brave New World*. New York: Random House. 2008. Print.

IMF. "Report for Selected Countries and Subjects." World Economic Outlook Database. imf.org. Apr. 2015. IMF. Web. May 28, 2015.

International Committee of the Red Cross. "ICRC Report On The Treatment Of Fourteen "High Value Detainees" In CIA Custody." nybooks.com. Feb. 2007. Web. Jan. 27, 2015.

"Iran and Nuclear Weapons." c-span.org. Aug. 14, 2002. Web. Aug. 24, 2015.

Isom, Dallas Woodbury. *Midway Inquest: Why the Japanese Lost the Battle of Midway*. Bloomington: Indiana UP. 2007. Print.

Jacobson, Timothy Curtis, and George David Smith. *Cotton's Renaissance: A Study in Market Innovation*. Cambridge: Cambridge UP. 2001. Print.

Jaffa, Harry V. *A New Birth of Freedom: Abraham Lincoln and the Coming of the Civil War*. Lanham: Rowman & Littlefield. 2004. Print.

Jankowski, Paul. *Verdun: The Longest Battle of the Great War*. Oxford: Oxford UP. 2013. Print.

Jefferson, Thomas. "Thomas Jefferson to John Holmes." Monticello. Apr. 22, 1820. loc.gov. Web. June 16, 2015.

Jian, Guo, Yongyi Song, and Yuan Zhou. *Historical Dictionary of the Chinese Cultural Revolution*. Lanham: Rowman & Littlefield. 2006. Print.

Jisheng, Yang. *Tombstone: The Great Chinese Famine, 1958–1962*. New York: Farrar, Straus and Giroux. 2012. Print.

Jiwei, Lou. *Chinese Economists on Economic Reform - Collected Works of Lou Jiwei*. China Development Research Foundation, ed. Routledge. 2013. Print.

Jocelyn, Ed, and Andrew McEwen. *The Long March: The True Story Behind the Legendary Journey that Made Mao's China*. Constable. 2006. Print.

Joffre, Joseph. "Plan of Action Proposed by France to the Coalition." Chantilly, France.Translation unknown. firstworldwar.com. Dec. 6, 1915. Web. July 21, 2015.

"John Adams to Abigail Adams, 3 July 1776." Founders Online, National Archives. founders.archives.gov. Web. May 26, 2015. Source: The Adams Papers, Adams Family Correspondence, vol. 2, June 1776–March 1778, ed. L. H. Butterfield. Cambridge: Harvard UP 1963: 27–29.

Johnson, Frank M. *Defending Constitutional Rights*. U of Georgia P. 2001. Print.

Johnson, Lyndon B. "Speech Before Congress on Voting Rights". millercenter.org. Mar. 15, 1965. Web. Sep. 23, 2015.

Jones, Eric M, ed. *Apollo 11 Lunar Surface Journal*. One Small Step. hq.nasa.gov. 1995. Web. Sep. 13, 2015.

Jones, Howard. *The Bay of Pigs*. Oxford UP. 2008. Print.

Jones, Vincent C. *Manhattan, the Army and the Atomic Bomb*. Washington: Center of Military History, U.S. Army. 1985. Print.

Journal of the Royal United Service Institution, Volume 5. Royal United Service Institution. London: W. Mitchell and Son. 1862. Print.

Journals of the Continental Congress: From 1774 to 1788. In Four Volumes. Volume I: From September 5, 1774, to December 31, 1776, inclusive. Washington: Way and Gideon. 1823. Print.

Jukes, Geoffrey. *Hitler's Stalingrad Decisions*. Berkeley: U of California P. 1985. Print.

Karlsbader Beschlüsse – Universitätsgesetz. Sept. 20, 1819. heinrich-heine-denkmal.de. Web. June 23, 2015.

Keck, Zachary. "North Korea Pushes Ahead on Agricultural Reforms." thediplomat.com. May 17, 2013. Web. Sep. 30, 2015.

Keegan, John. *The American Civil War*. London: Random House. 2010. Print.

Keller, Bill. "Gorbachev, in Finland, Disavows Any Right of Regional Intervention." *The New York Times*. Oct. 26, 1989. Print.

Kelly, Christopher. *History of the French Revolution and of the Wars Produced by that Memorable Event*. Vol. II. London: Thomas Kelly. 1820. Print.

Kennedy, John F. "Address at Rice University on the Nation's Space Effort." Sep. 12, 1962. jfklibrary.org. Web. Sep. 5, 2015.

Kennedy, John F. "Address on the Situation at the University of Mississippi". Sep. 30, 1962. millercenter.org. Web. Sep. 19, 2015.

Kennedy, John F. "Speech of Senator John F. Kennedy, Cincinnati, Ohio, Democratic Dinner." Oct. 6, 1960. presidency.ucsb.edu. Web. Sep. 14, 2015.

Kennedy, Robert F. *Thirteen Days: A Memoir of the Cuban Missile Crisis*. W.W. Norton & Company. 2011. First edition 1968. Print.

Keylor, William R. *The Legacy of the Great War: Peacemaking, 1919*. Houghton Mifflin. 1998. Print.

Khrushchev, Nikita, and Sergei Khrushchev, ed. *Memoirs of Nikita Khrushchev: Commissar, 1918–1945, Volume 1*. George Shriver, trans. Penn State Press. 2004. Print.

Kiernan, Ben. *The Pol Pot Regime: Race, Power, and Genocide in Cambodia under the Khmer Rouge, 1975–79*. Third Edition. New Haven: Yale UP. 2014. Print.

Kimes, Beverly Rae. *The Cars That Henry Ford Built.* Automobile Heritage Publishing & Communications. 2004. First published 1978. Print.

Kindleberger, Charles Poor. *Historical Economics: Art Or Science?* Berkeley: U of California P. 1990. Print.

King, Benjamin, and Timothy Kutta. *Impact: The History of Germany's V Weapons in World War II.* Da Capo. 2009. Print.

King, Martin Luther, Jr. "I Have A Dream." archives.gov. Aug. 28, 1963. Web. Sep. 23, 2015.

Kluckhohn, Frank L. "U.S. Declares War, Pacific Battle Widens." *The New York Times.* Dec. 8, 1941. Print.

Knight, Lionel. *Britain in India, 1858–1947.* London: Anthem. 2012. Print.

Knight, Will. "This Robot Could Transform Manufacturing." Sept. 18, 2012. technologyreview.com. Web. June 29, 2015.

Kolkey, Jonathan Martin. *Germany on the March: A Reinterpretation of War and Domestic Politics Over the Past Two Centuries.* Lanham: UP of America. 1995. Print.

Kolodziej, Edward A. *French International Policy under De Gaulle and Pompidou: The Politics of Grandeur.* Cornell UP. 1974. Print.

Korowajczuk, Leonhard. *LTE, WiMAX and WLAN Network Design, Optimization and Performance Analysis.* Chichester: Wiley. 2011. Print.

Krassenstein, Brian. "HP's Multi Jet Fusion Technology: New Details Unveiled On Future Plans, Capabilities & More." 3dprint.com. Apr. 20, 2015. Web. Oct. 22, 2015.

Kristensen, Hans M., and Robert S. Norris. "Worldwide deployments of nuclear weapons, 2014." *Bulletin of the Atomic Scientists.* Vol. 70(5) 96–108. thebulletin.sagepub.com. Web. Aug. 27, 2015.

Kroeber, Arthur. "Xi Jinping's Ambitious Agenda for Economic Reform in China." brookings.edu. Nov. 17, 2013. Web. Sep. 23, 2015.

Kuttner, Robert. "Simplify Banks and Bank Regulation." huffingtonpost.com. Oct. 16, 2011. Web, July 27, 2015.

Kwiet, Konrad, and Jurgen Matthaus, ed. *Contemporary Responses to the Holocaust*. Westport: Praeger. 2004. Print.

Laffan, Brigid, and Sonia Mazey. "European integration: the European Union - reaching an equilibrium?" *European Union: Power and Policy-Making*. 31–54. Jeremy Richardson, ed. Abingdon: Routledge. 2006. Print.

Lambert, Richard. "Crashes, Bangs & Wallops." The Financial Times. ft.com. Web. July 25, 2015.

Landau, Ronnie S. *The Nazi Holocaust*. New York: I.B. Tauris & Co. 2006. First edition 1992. Print.

Las Cases, Count de. *Memoirs Of The Life, Exile, And Conversations, Of The Emperor Napoleon*. Vol. II. London: Henry Colburn. 1836. Print.

Lawrence, Robert Z., Margareta Drzeniek Hanouz, and John Moavenzadeh. "The Global Enabling Trade Report 2009." World Economic Forum. 2009. Print.

Lee, Hong Yung. *The Politics of the Chinese Cultrual Revolution: A Case Study*. Berkely: U of California P. 1978. Print.

Leffler, Melvyn P., and Odd Arne Westad, ed. *The Cambridge History of the Cold War: Volume I, Origins*. Cambridge: Cambridge UP. 2010. Print.

"Lemuel Cook - The Last Revolutionary Patriot and Pensioner - Dead." Rochester Union Advertiser. May 22, 1866. burrcook.com. Web. June 16, 2015.

Lengel, Edward G. *General George Washington: A Military Life*. Random House. 2005. Print.

Lenin, V.I. "Letter to the Congress." Dec. 23, 1922-Jan. 4, 1923. marxists.org. Web. July 14, 2015.

Lerman, Katharine Anne. *Bismarck*. London: Routledge. 2013. Print.

Lew, Christopher R. *The Third Chinese Revolutionary Civil War, 1945–49: An Analysis of Communist Strategy and Leadership*. Abingdon: Routledge. 2009. Print.

Lew, Christopher R., and Edwin Pak-wah Leung. *Historical Dictionary of the Chinese Civil War*. Lanham: Rowman & Littlefield. 2013. Print.

Lichtblau, Eric. "The Holocaust Just Got More Shocking." *The New York Times*. Mar. 3, 2013. Print.

Licklider, J.C.R. "Man-Computer Symbiosis." IRE Transactions on Human Factors in Electronics. Vol. HFE-1, March 1960: 4–11. Print.

LIFE. "Defeat Ends In Surrender". Dec. 30, 1940. Web. Apr. 3, 2015.

Logsdon, John M. *John F. Kennedy and the Race to the Moon*. Palgrave Macmillan. 2011. Print.

Logsdon, John M., Roger D. Launius, and Robert William Smith, ed. *Reconsidering Sputnik: Forty Years Since the Soviet Satellite*. London: Routledge. 2000. Print.

Longerich, Peter. *Holocaust: The Nazi Persecution and Murder of the Jews*. Oxford: Oxford UP. 2010. Print.

Loss, Christopher P. *Between Citizens and the State: The Politics of American Higher Education in the 20th Century*. Princeton: Princeton UP. 2012. Print.

Luebke, Peter C. "Battle of Seven Pines–Fair Oaks." Encyclopedia Virginia. Virginia Foundation for the Humanities, Oct. 21, 2014. Web. Oct. 25, 2015.

Luzader, John. *Saratoga: A Military History of the Decisive Campaign of the American Revolution*. New York: Savas Beatie. 2010. Print.

Lynch, Stephen. "How Bin Laden Got Away." *New York Post*. nypost.com. Oct. 4, 2008. Web. Jan. 28, 2015.

MacDonald, William, ed. *Documentary Source Book of American History, 1606–1913*. New York: Macmillan. 1916. Print.

MacFarquhar, Neil. "Saudi Monarch Grants Women Right to Vote." *The New York Times*. nytimes.com. Sep 25, 2011. Web. Mar 6, 2015.

MacPherson, Robert. "Seventy years on, few Americans regret Enola Gay's mission." news.yahoo.com. Aug. 4, 2015. Web. Aug. 24, 2015.

Madsen, Daniel. *Resurrection: Salvaging the Battle Fleet at Pearl Harbor*. Annapolis: Naval Institute Press. 2003. Print.

Maier, Pauline. *Ratification: The People Debate the Constitution, 1787–1788*. New York: Simon & Schuster. 2010. Print.

"Majority of Russians still support Lenin's burial - poll." Apr. 23, 2014. rt.com. Web. July 14, 2015.

Malthus, Thomas Robert. *An Essay on the Principle of Population*. 1798. Library of Economics and Liberty. econlib.org. Web. June 11, 2015.

Mann, James A. *The cotton trade of Great Britain: its rise, progress and present extent*. London: Simpkin, Marshall & Co. 1860. Print.

Mansch, Larry D. *Abraham Lincoln, President-elect: The Four Critical Months from Election to Inauguration*. McFarland. 2005. Print.

Marrus, Michael Robert, ed. *The Nazi Holocaust. Part 6: The Victims of the Holocaust, Volume 2*. Walter de Gruyter. 1989. Print.

Marshall, Samuel L. A. *World War I*. New York: American Heritage. 1964. Print.

Martel, Gordon. *The Month That Changed The World*. Oxford: Oxford UP. 2014. Print.

Marx, Karl. *Capital: A Critique of Political Economy. Vol. I, The Process of Capitalist Production*. Translated from the third German edition by Samuel Moore and Edward Aveling. Frederick Engels, ed. Original title: *Das Kapital, Kritik der politischen Ökonomie*. Chicago: Charles H. Kerr & Company. 1915. Print.

Marx, Karl, and Friedrich Engels. *The Communist Manifesto*. The Floating Press. 2009. First published 1848. This version from an 1888 edition. Print.

Massie, Robert K. *Nicholas and Alexandra*. New York: Random House. 2011. First published 1967. Print.

Mastny, Vojtech, Sven G. Holtsmark, and Andreas Wenger, ed. *War Plans and Alliances in the Cold War: Threat Perceptions in the East and West*. Abingdon: Routledge. 2006. Print.

M.A.U.D. Committee. "Report by M.A.U.D. Comittee on the Use of Uranium for a Bomb." London: Ministry of Aircraft Production. July 1941. fissilematerials.org. Web. Aug. 25, 2015.

Maurer, John H. *The Outbreak of the First World War: Strategic Planning, Crisis Decision Making, and Deterrence Failure*. Greenwood PG. 1995. Print.

May, Ernest R. *Strange Victory: Hitler's Conquest of France*. London: I.B. Tauris & Co. 2000. Print.

McAuliffe, Mary S, ed, and CIA History Staff. *CIA Documents on the Cuban Missile Crisis*. DIANE Publishing. 1992. Print.

McKinsey Global Institute. "Disruptive technologies: Advances that will transform life, business, and the global economy." May 2013. McKinsey & Company. Print.

McLynn, Frank. *Napoleon*. London: Random. 1998. Print.

McPherson, James M. "Antebellum Southern Exceptionalism: A New Look at an Old Question." Civil War History. Vol. 50, no. 4. 2004: 418–433. Print.

McPherson, James M. *The Illustrated Battle Cry of Freedom: The Civil War Era*. Oxford: Oxford UP. 2003. Print.

McRaney, W, and J. McGahan. *Radiation Dose Reconstruction U.S. Occupation Forces in Hiroshima And Nagasaki, Japan, 1945–1946*. Washington: Defense Nuclear Agency. Aug. 6, 1980. Print.

Medley, Keith Weldon. *We as Freemen: Plessy v. Ferguson.* Gretna: Pelican. 2003. Print.

Meisner, Maurice. *Mao's China and After: A History of the People's Republic.* Third Edition. New York: Simon & Schuster. 1999. Print.

Merrill, Dennis, and Thomas Paterson. *Major Problems in American Foreign Relations, Volume II: Since 1914.* Seventh Edition. Cengage Learning. 2009. Print.

Merrill v. Lynch, 14-CV-9763. Aug. 28, 2015. United States District Court. isp.yale.edu. Web. Dec. 22, 2015.

Michman, Dan. *The Emergence of Jewish Ghettos during the Holocaust.* Cambridge: Cambridge UP. 2011. Print.

Miller, Donald L. *D-Days in the Pacific.* New York: Simon & Schuster. 2008. Print.

Miller, Harry W. *Railway Artillery: A Report on the Characteristics, Scope of Utility, Etc., of Railway Artillery.* Volume I. United States Army. Ordnance Dept. Washington: Government Printing Office. 1921.

Miller, John C. *Alexander Hamilton and the Growth of the New Nation.* First edition 1959. Brunswick: Transaction. 2004. Print.

Miller, John C. *Origins of the American Revolution.* Stanford: Stanford UP. 1959. Print.

Miller, Randall M., and John David Smith, ed. *Dictionary of Afro-American Slavery.* Westport: Praeger. 1997. Print.

Milyukov, Pavel. *Political memoirs, 1905–1917.* U of Michigan P. 1967. Print.

Misa, Thomas, J. *A Nation of Steel: The Making of Modern America, 1865–1925.* Johns Hopkins UP. 1998. Print.

Misch, Rochus. *Hitler's Last Witness: The Memoirs of Hitler's Bodyguard.* Pen & Sword Books, trans. Frontline Books. 2014. Print.

Mitchell, Allan. *The Great Train Race: Railways and the Franco-German Rivalry, 1815–1914.* Berghahn Books. 2006. Print.

Molotov-Ribbentrop Pact. *Modern History Sourcebook: The Molotov-Ribbentrop Pact, 1939.* Web. Apr. 2, 2015.

Mombauer, Annika. *Helmuth Von Moltke and the Origins of the First World War.* Cambridge: Cambridge UP. 2001. Print.

Montholon, Charles Tristan. *Récits de la captivité de l'empereur Napoléon à Sainte-Hélène.* Volume 1. Paris: Paulin. 1847. Print.

Montrie, Chad. *Making a Living: Work and Environment in the United States.* U of North Carolina P. 2008. Print.

Moon, David. *Abolition of Serfdom in Russia: 1762–1907.* New York: Routledge. 2014. Print.

Morgan, Edmund S., and Helen M. Morgan. *The Stamp Act Crisis: Prologue to Revolution.* U of North Carolina P. 1953. Print.

Morrow, John H. Jr. *The Great War: An Imperial History.* London: Routledge. 2004. Print.

Morse, Jedidiah. *Annals Of The American Revolution Or A Record Of The Causes And Events Which Produced And Terminated In The Establishment And Independence Of The American Republic.* Hartford: s.n. 1824. Print.

Mozgovoi, Alexander. "The Cuban Samba of the Quartet of Foxtrots: Soviet Submarines in the Caribbean Crisis of 1962." Military Parade, Moscow. 2002. Svetlana Savranskaya, trans. National Security Archive. nsarchive. gwu.edu. Web. Sep. 13, 2015.

NASA. "Voyager Mission Operations Status Report # 2014–07–25 Week Ending July 25, 2014." voyager.jpl. nasa.gov. Web. Sep. 6, 2015.

National Commission on Terrorist Attacks. *The 9/11 Commission Report: Final Report of the National Commission on Terrorist Attacks Upon the United States (Authorized Edition).* New York: W.W. Norton & Company. 2011. Print.

National Defense Authorization Act For Fiscal Year 2012. Pub. L. 112–81. Dec. 31, 2011. Print.

National Security Council, United States. *From U.S. Security to Terrorism: A Three-Part Series.* Cosimo, Inc. 2005. Print.

NBC. "NBC News Coverage of the September 11, 2001, Terrorist Attacks (Part 1 of 2)." youtube.com. Web. Jan. 25, 2015.

Nester, William R. *The Great Frontier War: Britain, France, and the Imperial Struggle for North America, 1607–1755.* Westport: Greenwood. 2000. Print.

Neufeld, Michael J. *The Rocket and the Reich: Peenemünde and the Coming of the Ballistic Missile Era.* New York: Simon & Schuster. 1995. Print.

Neumeyer, Joy. "A Visit to Moscow's Brain Institute." vice.com. Apr. 10, 2014. Web. July 2, 2015.

New York Times. "1,028 Economists Ask Hoover To Veto Pending Tariff Bill." *The New York Times.* May 5, 1930. Print.

New York Times. "Hitler is Pleased to Get Rid of Foes." *The New York Times.* Mar. 27, 1938. Print.

New York Times. "Last Union Army Veteran Dies; Drummer at 17, he Lived to 109." *The New York Times.* Aug. 3, 1956. Print.

Nicosia, Francis R. *Jewish Life in Nazi Germany: Dilemmas and Responses.* Berghahn Books. 2010. Print.

Northrup, Cynthia Clark, ed. *The American Economy: A Historical Encyclopedia, Volume I.* Santa Barbara: ABC-CLIO. 2011. Print.

Odekon, Mehmet. *Booms and Busts: An Ecyclopedia of Economic History from the First Stock Market Crash of 1792 to the Current Global Economic Crisis.* Third Edition. Routledge. 2015. Print.

Official papers, relative to the preliminaries of London and the Treaty of Amiens. London: J. Debrett. 1803. Print.

Osborn, Andrew. "Russians want Lenin removed from Red Square." Jan 23, 2011. Telegraph.co.uk. Web. July 14, 2015.

Osborne, Roger. *Iron, Steam & Money: The Making of the Industrial Revolution*. London: Random House. 2013. Print.

Osiander, Robert. "From Vengeance 2 to Sputnik I: The Beginnings." *Handbook of Space Engineering, Archaeology, and Heritage*. 209–228. Ann Garrison Darrin and Beth Laura O'Leary, ed. Taylor and Francis Group. 2009. Print.

Overy, Richard. *Russia's War: A History of the Soviet War Effort: 1941–1945*. New York: Penguin Group. 1998. Print.

Pankhurst, Emmeline. "Freedom or Death." Nov. 13, 1913. *Political Dissent: A Global Reader: Modern Sources*. 121–147. Derek Malone-France, ed. Lanham: Rowman & Littlefield. 2012. Print.

"Peacefully grant the State of Texas to withdraw from the United States of America and create its own NEW government." n.d. petitions.whitehouse.gov. Web. May 26, 2015.

Pershing, John J. *My Experiences in the World War*. Vol. II. New York: Frederick A. Stokes Company. 1931. Print.

Persico, Joseph E. *Eleventh Month, Eleventh Day, Eleventh Hour: Armistice Day, 1918 World War I and Its Violent Climax*. New York: Random House. 2004. Print.

Pflanze, Otto. *Bismarck and the Development of Germany: The Period of Unification 1815–1871*. Vol. 1. Princeton UP. 1968. Print.

Phillips, McCandlish. "Campus A Bivouac As Negro Enters, 2,000 Troops Stand Guard—Meredith Eats Alone." *The New York Times*. Oct. 2, 1962. Print.

Philpott, William. *Three Armies on the Somme: The First Battle of the Twentieth Century*. New York: Random House. 2011. Print.

Piketty, Thomas, and Emmanuel Saez. "Income Inequality in the United States, 1913–1998." *The Quarterly Journal of Economics*. Vol. 118 (1). 1–41. 2003. Print.

Pinkus, Oscar. *The War Aims and Strategies of Adolf Hitler*. Jefferson: McFarland & Company. 2005. Print.

Piper, Franciszek. "Gas Chambers and Crematoria." *Anatomy of the Auschwitz Death Camp*. Yisrael Gutman and Michael Berenbaum, ed. Bloomington: Indiana UP. 1994. 157–182. Print.

Pipes, Richard. *Communism: A History*. Modern Library Edition. New York: Random House. 2001. Print.

Piston, William Garrett, and Richard W. Hatcher III. *Wilson's Creek: The Second Battle of the Civil War and the Men Who Fought It*. U of North Carolina P. 2000. Print.

Piszkiewicz, Dennis. *The Nazi Rocketeers: Dreams of Space and Crimes of War*. Mechanicsburg: Stackpole Books. 2006. Print.

Plessy v. Ferguson. 163 U.S. 537. Supreme Court of the United States. 1896. Supreme Court Collection. Legal Information Inst., Cornell U. Law School, n.d. Web. 15 Jan. 2016.

Ploeckl, Florian. "The Zollverein and the Formation of a Customs Union." *University of Oxford Discussion Papers in Economic and Social History*. No. 84. Aug. 2010. Department of Economics and Nuffield College, University of Oxford. Print.

Polmar, Norman, and Kenneth J. Moore. *Cold War Submarines: The Design and Construction of U.S. and Soviet Submarines*. Washington, D.C.: Potomac Books. 2004. Print.

Population of the United States in 1860; Compiled from the Original Returns of the Eighth Census. Washington: Government Printing Office. 1864. Print.

Preston, Richard. "First World War centenary: the assassination of Franz Ferdinand, as it happened." June 27, 2014. telegraph.co.uk. Web. July 14, 2015.

Proclamation of Rebellion. Aug. 23, 1775. archives.gov. Web. Jan. 1, 2016.

"Proceedings of Commissioners to Remedy Defects of the Federal Government: 1786." Avalon Project, Yale Law. n.p. n.d. avalon.law.yale.edu. Web. June 2, 2015.

"Program of the National Socialist German Workers' Party." Avalon Project, Yale Law. n.p. n.d. avalon.law.yale.edu. Web. Aug. 13, 2015.

Project for the New American Century. "Letter from the Project for the New American Century to the Honorable William J. Clinton, President of the United States." informationclearinghouse.info. Jan. 26, 1998. Web. Aug. 4, 2015.

Quartering Act; May 15, 1765. Great Britain: Parliament. Avalon Project, Yale Law. avalon.law.yale.edu. Web. May 28, 2015.

Radziwill, Princess Catherine. *The Taint of the Romanovs.* Cassell. 1931. Print.

Reich, Robert B. "Community Perspective: Widening Inequality Hurts us All." *Community Investments.* Vol. 23 (2). 2011. 17–21. Federal Reserve Bank of San Francisco. frbsf.org. Web. Oct. 1, 2015.

Reid, Robert H. *Architects of the Web: 1,000 Days that Built the Future of Business.* New York: John Wiley & Sons. 1997. Print.

"Report from General Zakharov and Admiral Fokin to the Presidium, Central Committee, Communist Party of the Soviet Union, on the Progress of Operation Anadyr." Sep. 25, 1962. Volkogonov Collection, Library of Congress, Manuscript Division, Reel 17, Container 26. Translated by Gary Goldberg for the Cold War International History Project of the National Security Archive. nsarchive.gwu. edu. Web. Sep. 13, 2015.

"Rethink Robotics Revolutionizes Manufacturing with Humanoid Robot." Sept. 18, 2012. Press release from Rethink Robotics. rethinkrobotics.com. Web. June 29, 2015.

Rhodes, Richard. *The Making of the Atomic Bomb: 25th Anniversy Edition*. New York: Simon & Schuster. 2012. Print.

Rice, Edward E. *Mao's Way*. Berkely: U of California P. 1974. Print.

Richards, Denis. *The Royal Air Force 1939–1945 Vol. I: The Fight At Odds*. London: H.M. Stationery Office. 1953. Print.

Richards, Leonard L. *Shay's Rebellion: The American Revolution's Final Battle*. U of Pennsylvania P. 2002. Print.

Risjord, Norman K. *Jefferson's America, 1760–1815*. Lanham: Rowman & Littlefield. 2010. Print.

Risser, Nicole Dombrowski. *France Under Fire: German Invasion, Civilian Flight, and Family Survival during World War II*. Cambridge: Cambridge UP. 2012. Print.

Roberts, Andrew. *Napoleon and Wellington: The Battle of Waterloo - and the Great Commanders who Fought it*. New York: Simon & Schuster. 2001. Print.

Roberts, Andrew. *Napoleon & Wellington: The Long Duel*. London: Orion. 2002. Print.

Roberts, Gene, and Hank Klibanoff. *The Race Beat: The Press, the Civil Rights Struggle, and the Awakening of a Nation*. New York: Random House. 2007. Print.

Roberts, Geoffrey. *Stalin's Wars: From World War to Cold War, 1939–1953*. Yale UP. 2006. Print.

Roberts, Geoffrey. *Victory at Stalingrad: The Battle that Changed History*. Harlow: Pearson Education Limited. 2002. Print.

Robinson, Janet, and Joe Robinson. *Handbook of Imperial Germany*. Bloomington: AuthorHouse. 2009. Print.

Robinson, Thomas W. "The Wuhan Incident: Local Strife and Provincial Rebellion during the Cultural Revolution." *The China Quarterly*. No. 47. Jul.-Sep., 1971: 413–438. Cambridge UP. Print.

Rogers, Simon. "Nasa budgets: US spending on space travel since 1958." theguardian.com. Feb. 1, 2010. Web. Sep. 13, 2015.

"Roll of Honour of "The Few"." *The Battle of Britain Historical Society*. battleofbritain1940.net. Web. Apr. 3, 2015.

Roosevelt, Franklin D. "Address Accepting the Presidential Nomination at the Democratic National Convention in Chicago." July 2, 1932. *The American Presidency Project*. presidency.ucsb.edu. Web. July 27, 2015.

Roosevelt, Franklin D. "Day of Infamy Speech". Records of the United States Senate. SEN 77A-H1, Record Group 46, National Archives. archives.gov. Dec. 8, 1941. Web. Apr. 4, 2015.

Rothbard, Murray N. *History of Money and Banking in the United States: The Colonial Era to World II*. Ludwig von Mises Institute. 2002. Print.

Rose, John Holland. *The Life Of Napoleon I*. London: G. Bell and Sons. 1910. Print.

Roser, Max. "Child Mortality." ourworldindata.org. 2015. Web. July 1, 2015.

Roser, Max. "Life Expectancy." ourworldindata.org. 2015. Web. July 1, 2015.

Rozett, Robert, and Shmuel Spector. *Encyclopedia of the Holocaust*. Jerusalem Publishing House. 2000. Print.

Rudoren, Jodi. "Proudly Bearing Elders' Scars, Their Skin Says 'Never Forget'." *The New York Times*. nytimes.com. Sept. 30, 2012. Web. Aug. 13, 2015.

Russian Fundamental Laws of 1906. Royal Russia and Gilbert's Royal Books. angelfire.com. n.d. Web. July 7, 2015.

Sablinsky, Walter. *The Road to Bloody Sunday: The Role of Father Gapon and the Petersburg Massacre of 1905*. Princeton UP. 1976. Print.

Saez, Emmanuel. "Striking it Richer: The Evolution of Top Incomes in the United States." UC Berkeley. eml.berkeley. edu. Jan. 25, 2015. Web. Oct. 5, 2015.

Saich, Tony, and Benjamin Yang. *The Rise to Power of the Chinese Communist Party: Documents and Analysis*. M.E. Sharpe. 1995. Print.

Salahuddin, Sayed. "Taliban beheads 17 Afghan partygoers; 2 NATO troops killed." *The Washington Post*. washington-post.com. Aug. 27, 2012. Web. Jan. 28, 2015.

Sampson, Charles S., and Glenn W. LaFantasie, ed. *Foreign Relations of the United States, 1961–1963, Volume XIV, Berlin Crisis, 1961–1962*. Washington: United States Printing Office. 1993. Print.

Sampson, Charles S., and Glenn W. LaFantasie. *Foreign Relations of the United States, 1961–1963, Volume VI, Kennedy-Khrushchev Exchanges*. Washington: United States Printing Office. 1996. Print.

Sarkar, Tapan K., Robert J. Mailloux, et al. *History of Wireless*. Hoboken: John Wiley & Sons. 2006. Print.

Saul, Norman E. *Historical Dictionary of Russian and Soviet Foreign Policy*. Lanham: Rowman & Littlefield. 2015. Print.

Savranskaya, Svetlana V. "New Sources on the Role of Soviet Submarines in the Cuban Missile Crisis." *Journal of Strategic Studies*, 28:2, 2005: 233–259. Print.

Schlesinger, Arthur M., Jr. *Robert Kennedy and His Times*. New York: Houghton Mifflin. 2002. First edition 1978. Print.

Schmemann, Serge. "Soviet Disarray; Preserving Lenin, the High-Tech Icon." *The New York Times*. nytimes.com. Dec. 17, 1991. Web. July 2, 2015.

Schmuhl, Hans-Walter. *The Kaiser Wilhelm Institute for Anthropoloy, Human Heredity and Eugenics, 1927–1945: Crossing Boundaries*. Springer. 2008. Print.

Schnoor, Stefan, and Boris Klinge. "The last survivor of Hitler's downfall - The Fuhrer's bodyguard gives last interview." express.co.uk. May 15, 2011. Web. Apr. 1, 2015.

Schofield, Hugh. "Napoleon…the theme park." BBC News. bbc.com. Mar. 27, 2012. Web. June 5, 2015.

Schouler, James. *History of the United States of America. Vol. VI. 1861–1865.* New York: Dodd, Mead & Company. 1899. Print.

Schüddekopf, Otto Ernst. *Der Erste Weltkrieg.* Bertelsmann Lexikon-Verlag. 1977. Print.

Schwartz, Stephen I, ed. *Atomic Audit: The Costs and Consequenses of U.S. Nuclear Weapons Since 1940.* Washington: Brookings Institution. 1998. Print.

Sciolino, Elaine. "North of Paris, a Forest of History and Fantasy." *The New York Times.* nytimes.com. Nov. 2, 2008. Web. 3 Apr. 2015.

Scobell, Andrew. "Seventy-five Years of Civil-Military Relations; Lessons Learned." *The Lessons of History: The Chinese People's Liberation Army at 75.* 427–450. Laurie Burkitt, Andrew Scobell, Larry M. Wortzel, ed. Strategic Studies Institute. U.S. Army War College. 2003. Print.

Scott-Smith, Giles, and Hans Krabbendam. *The Cultural Cold War in Western Europe, 1945–1960.* London: Frank Cass. 2003. Print.

Scott v. Sanford, 60 U.S. (19 How.) 393 (1857).

Sears, Stephen W. *Gettysburg.* New York: Houghton Mifflin. 2004. Print.

Sears, Stephen W. *Landscape Turned Red: The Battle of Antietam.* New York: Houghton Mifflin. 2003. Print.

"Second Crash New York 'Change - Frenzied Trading - Panic Spreads Quickly." Oct. 28, 1929. *The Sydney Morning Herald.* trove.nla.gov.au. Web. July 25, 2015.

"Security Council Committee established pursuant to resolution 1737 (2006)." un.org. n.d. Web. Aug. 24, 2015.

Service, Robert. *A History of Modern Russia from Nicholas II to Vladimir Putin.* Harvard UP. 2005. Print.

Shapiro, Fred R. *The Yale Book of Quotations.* Yale UP. 2006. Print.

Shedlock, Mike. "Incredible Burger-Flipping Robot Wants To Steal Our Jobs." Febr. 4, 2013. businessinsider.com. Web. June 29, 2015.

Sherman, A. J. *Island Refuge: Britain and Refugees from the Third Reich 1933–1939*. Routledge. 2013. Print.

Siddiqi, Asif A. *The Red Rockets' Glare: Spaceflight and the Russian Imagination, 1857–1957*. Cambridge: Cambridge UP. 2010. Print.

Simpson, Colin. "Lusitania: A Great Liner With Too Many Secrets." Life Magazine. Vol. 73. No. 15. Oct. 13, 1972. Print.

Sitton, Claude. "Shots Quell Mob—Enrolling of Meredith Ends Segregation in State Schools." *The New York Times*. Oct. 2, 1962. Print.

Smith, Harold L. *The British Women's Suffrage Campaign, 1866–1928*. Second Edition. Harlow: Pearson Education. 2007. Print.

Smith, Jean Edward. *Grant*. New York: Simon & Schuster. 2001. Print.

Smyser, W. R. *Kennedy and the Berlin Wall*. Lanham: Rowman & Littlefield. 2009. Print.

Snow, Edgar. *Red Star Over China*. New York: Grove Press. 1968. First edition 1938. Print.

Sondhaus, Lawrence. *World War One: The Global Revolution*. Cambridge: Cambridge UP. 2011. Print.

Sparks, Jared, ed. *The Writings of George Washington. Vol. VI*. Boston: Ferdinand Andrews. 1840. Print.

Sperber, Jonathan. *Rhineland Radicals: The Democratic Movement and the Revolution of 1848–1849*. Princeton: Princeton UP. 1991. Print.

Stalin, Joseph. "Order No. 227 by the People's Commissar of Defence of the USSR". July 28, 1942. wikisource.org. Web. Apr. 4, 2015.

"Statistical Abstract of the United States 1937." Washington: U.S. G.P.O. 1937. Print.

"Statistical Abstract of the United States 1942." Washington: U.S. G.P.O. 1942. Print.

Stedman, C. *The History Of The Origin, Progress, and Termination Of The American War. In Two Volumes*. Vol. I. London: n.p. 1794. Print.

Steinberg, Mark D. *Voices of Revolution, 1917*. Yale UP. 2003. Print.

Steinweis, Alan E. *Studying the Jew: Scholarly Antisemitism in Nazi Germany*. Harvard UP. 2006. Print.

Steinweis, Alan E., and Robert D. Rachlin. *The Law in Nazi Germany: Ideology, Opportunism, and the Perversion of Justice*. Berghahn Books. 2013. Print.

Stephens, A. Ray. *Texas: A Historical Atlas*. U of Oklahoma P. 2010. Print.

Sterba, James P. "Former Chinese Leaders Given Long Prison Terms." *The New York Times*. Jan. 26, 1981. Print.

Stewart, John Hall. *A Documentary Survey of the French Revolution*. New York: Macmillan. 1951. Print.

Stiglitz, Joseph E. "Capitalist Fools." Vanity Fair. vanityfair. com. Jan. 2009. Web. July 27, 2015.

Stillion Southard, Belinda A. *Militant Citizenship: Rhetorical Strategies of the National Woman's Party, 1913–1920*. Texas A&M UP. 2011. Print.

Stone, Dan. *The Liberation of the Camps: The End of the Holocaust and Its Aftermath*. Yale UP. 2015. Print.

Stout, David. "C.I.A. Detainees Sent to Guantánamo." *The New York Times*. nytimes.com. Sep. 6, 2006. Web. Jan. 27, 2015.

Strachan, Hew. *The First World War*. New York: Penguin Group. 2004. Print.

Strayer, Robert W. *Why Did the Soviet Union Collapse?: Understanding Historical Change*. Armonk: M.E. Sharpe. 1998. Print.

Strickland, Mary, and Jane Margaret Strickland. *A memoir of the life, writings, and mechanical inventions of Edmund Cartwright*. London: Saunders and Otley. 1843. Print.

Strong, Anna Louise. "I Join the Red Guards." *Letters from China*. No. 41. Sep. 20, 1966. Quoted in *China's Great Proletarian Cultural Revolution: Master Narratives and Post-Mao Counternarratives*, 105. Woei Lien Chong. Rowman & Littlefield. 2002. Print.

Swarup, Bob. *Money Mania: Booms, Panics, and Busts from Ancient Rome to the Great Meltdown*. New York: Bloomsbury. 2014. Print.

Szatmary, David P. *Shays' Rebellion: The Making of an Agrarian Insurrection*. U of Massachusetts P. 1980. Print.

Szilard, Leo. "Petition to the President of the United States." July 17, 1945. trumanlibrary.org. Original source: U.S. National Archives, Record Group 77, Records of the Chief of Engineers, Manhatten Engineer District, Harrison-Bundy File, folder #76. Web. Aug. 26, 2015.

Taubman, William. *Khrushchev: The Man and His Era*. New York: W.W. Norton & Company. 2004. Print.

Taylor, Jay. *The Generalissimo: Chiang Kai-shek and the Struggle for Modern China*. Harvard UP. 2009. Print.

Taylor, Robert J, Greg L. Lint, and Celeste Walker, ed. *Papers of John Adams, Volume 3, May 1775-January 1776*. Cambridge: Harvard UP. 1979. Print.

Teiwes, Frederick C. *Politics and Purges in China: Rectification and the Decline of Party Norms, 1950–1965*. Armonk: M.E. Sharpe. 1993. Print.

Teiwes, Frederick C. *The Tragedy of Lin Biao: Riding the Tiger During the Cultural Revolution*. Honolulu: U of Hawaii P. 1996. Print.

Texas v. White, 74 U.S. 7 Wall. 700 (1868).

"The Electric Light." *New York Herald*. Jan. 4, 1880. P. 6, Col. 2. Print.

Thompson, Robert. "Two Days in April." civilwar.org. n.d. Web. Oct. 27, 2015.

TIME. "Elections: Mississippi Mud." *Time.* Sep. 7, 1959. Vol. 74, no. 10. Print.

TIME. "Vanguard's Aftermath: Jeers and Tears." *Time.* Dec. 16, 1957. Vol. 70, no. 25. Print.

"Total number of Websites." Internet Live Stats. internetlivestats.com. n.d. Web. Oct. 10, 2015.

"Treaty of Brest-Litovsk." 1918. Avalon Project, Yale Law. Avalon. law.yale.edu. Web. July 14, 2015.

Trenear-Harvey, Glenmore S. *Historical Dictionary of Atomic Espionage.* Lanham: Rowman & Littlefield. 2011. Print.

Trial of the Major War Criminals before the International Military Tribunal. Nuremberg, 14 November 1945–1 October 1946. Nuremberg. 1947. loc.gov/rr/frd/Military_Law/NT_major-war-criminals.html (gives access to all 42 volumes). Web. 2 Apr. 2015.

Trotsky, Leon. *1905.* Anya Bostock, trans. marxists.org. n.d. First publishesd 1907. Web. July 7, 2015.

"Troubled Asset Relief Program (TARP) Monthly Report to Congress - December 2012." United States Department of the Treasury. treasury.gov. Jan 10, 2013. Web. July 25, 2015.

Truman, Harry S. "Address in San Francisco at the Closing Session of the United Nations Conference." June 26, 1945. trumanlibrary.org. Web. Aug. 27, 2015.

Truman, Harry S. "Statement by the President on the Situation in Korea," June 27, 1950. The American Presidency Project. presidency.ucsb.edu. Web. Aug. 11, 2015.

Tucker, Spencer. *Blue & Gray Navies: The Civil War Afloat.* Annapolis: Naval Institute P. 2006. Print.

Tyng, Sewell. *The Campaign of the Marne, 1914.* New York: Longmans, Green. 1935. Print.

UCLA. "The first internet connection, with UCLA's Leonard Kleinrock." UCLA. Jan. 13, 2009. youtube.com. Web. Oct. 7, 2015.

Uhalley, Stephen. *A History of the Chinese Communist Party*. Hoover Press. 1988. Print.

Union of Utrecht Treaty. Signed Jan. 23, 1579. Published on constitution.org from *The Low Countries in Early Modern Times: A Documentary History*. Herbert H. Rowen. New York: Harper & Row. 1972: 69–74. Print.

United Nations. "Universal Declaration of Human Rights." un.org. Dec. 10, 1948. Web. Sep. 2, 2015.

United States. "Dropshot - American Plan for War with the Soviet Union, 1957." n.p. 1949. allworldwards.com. Web. Aug. 28, 2015.

United States Bill of Rights. National Archives and Records Administration. United States. Web. 19 Mar. 2015.

United States Government. *Peace and War: United States Foreign Policy, 1931–1941*. Dept. of State. Washington: United States Government Printing Office. 1943. Print.

United States Government. *U.S. Strategic Bombing Survey: The Effects of the Atomic Bombings of Hiroshima and Nagasaki, June 19, 1946*. War Department. Print.

United States. *Pentagon Papers. Part II. U.S. Involvement in the Franco-Viet Minh War, 1950–1954*. NAI: 5890486. Vietnam Task Force. Office of the Secretary of Defense. 1967–69. Published on archives.gov. Web. Sep. 2, 2015.

United States. *Pentagon Papers. Part IV. A. 2. Evolution of the War. Aid for France in Indochina, 1950–54*. NAI: 5890489. Vietnam Task Force. Office of the Secretary of Defense. 1967–69. Published on archives.gov. Web. Sep. 2, 2015.

United States. *Pentagon Papers. Part IV. A. 4. Evolution of the War. U.S. Training of Vietnamese National Army, 1954–59*. NAI: 58990491.Vietnam Task Force. Office of the Secretary of Defense. 1967–69. Published on archives.gov. Web. Sep. 2, 2015.

United States. *Pentagon Papers. Part IV. C. 4. Evolution of the War. Marine Combat Units Go to DaNang, March 1965*. NAI: 5890503. Vietnam Task Force. Office of the Secretary of Defense. 1967–69. Published on archives.gov. Web. Sep. 2, 2015.

United States. *Pentagon Papers. Part IV. C. 5. Evolution of the War. Phase I in the Build-up of U.S. Forces: March - July 1965.* NAI: 5890504. Vietnam Task Force. Office of the Secretary of Defense. 1967–69. Published on archives.gov. Web. Sep. 2, 2015.

U.S. Code: Title 18. Sec. 2709. United States. 2006. law.cornell.edu. Web. Mar. 9, 2015.

"US transfers five Guantánamo Bay detainees to United Arab Emirates". theguardian.com. Nov. 15, 2015. Web. Dec. 23, 2015.

USA Freedom Act. Pub. L. 114–23. United States. June 2, 2015. Print.

USA Patriot Act. Pub. L. 107–56. 115 Stat. 272. United States. Oct. 26, 2001. Print.

USA Patriot Improvement and Reauthorization Act of 2005. Pub. L. 109–177. 120 Stat. 192. United States. Mar. 9, 2006. Print.

USSR. "Telegram TROSTNIK to PAVLOV." Oct. 27, 1962. Archive of the Russian Federation, Special Declassification, Apr. 2002. Svetlana Savranskaya, trans. nsarchive.gwu.edu. Web. Sep. 17, 2015.

USSR Northern Fleed Headquarters. "Report about participation of submarines "B-4," "B-36," "B-59," "B-130" of the 69th submarine brigade of the Northern Fleet in the Operation "Anadyr" during the period of October-December, 1962." Svetlana Savranskaya, trans. National Security Archive. nsarchive.gwu.edu. n.d. Web. Sep. 13, 2015.

Valelly, Richard M. *The Two Reconstructions: The Struggle for Black Enfranchisement.* Chicago: U of Chicago P. 2004. Print.

Vernon, J. R. "Unemployment Rates in Post-Bellum America: 1869–1899." *Journal of Macroeconomics* 16: 701–714. 1994. Print.

"Versailles Treaty June 28, 1919." Avalon Project, Yale Law. Avalon. law.yale.edu. Web. July 23, 2015.

Viner, Jacob. *The Customs Union Issue.* Oxford: Oxford UP. 2014. Print.

Voline. *The Unknown Revolution, 1917–1921.* Montreal: Black Rose Books. 1975. Print.

Volpe Center (John A. Volpe National Transportation Systems Center). "Effects of Catastrophic Events on Transportation System Management and Operations: Cross Cutting Study." Cambridge, Mass, 2003. Web. Jan. 25, 2015.

Vries, Jan de. *European Urbanization, 1500–1800.* Routledge. 2007. Print.

Waddell, Steve R. *United States Army Logistics: From the American Revolution to 9/11.* Santa Barbara: ABC-CLIO. 2010. Print.

Wakeman, Rosemary. "The Fourth Republic." *The French Republic: History, Values, Debates.* Edward Berenson, Vincent Duclert, Christophe Prochas, ed. Cornell UP. 2011. Print.

Walker, Kenneth R. *Food Grain Procurement and Consumption in China.* Cambridge: Cambridge UP. 2010. First published 1984. Print.

Ward, Bob. *Dr. Space: The Life of Wernher von Braun.* Annapolis: Naval Institute Press. 2009. Print.

Washington Post. "Fire Hoses and Police Dogs Quell Birmingham Segregation Protest." *The Washington Post.* May 4, 1963. Print.

Wawro, Geoffrey. *The Austro-Prussian War: Austria's War with Prussia and Italy in 1866.* Cambridge: Cambridge UP. 1996. Print.

Wawro, Geoffrey. *The Franco-Prussian War: The German Conquest of France in 1870–1871*. Cambridge: Cambridge UP. 2005. Print.

Wettig, Gerhard. *Stalin and the Cold War in Europe: The Emergence and Development of East-West Conflict, 1939–1953*. Lanham: Rowman & Littlefield. 2008. Print.

Wheeler-Bennett, John W. *Brest-Litovsk: The Forgotten Peace, March 1918*. London: Macmillan. 1938. Print.

White, Matthew. *Atrocities: The 100 Deadliest Episodes in Human History*. New York: W.W. Norton & Company. 2012. Print.

Wicker, Elmus. *Banking Panics of the Gilded Age*. Cambridge: Cambridge UP. 2000. Print.

Wigmore, Barrie A. *The Crash and Its Aftermath: A History of Securities Markets in the United States, 1929–1933*. Westport: Greenwood. 1985. Print.

Wilford, John Noble. "Russians Finally Admit They Lost Race to Moon." *The New York Times*. Dec. 18, 1989. Print.

Wilson, Woodrow, and Arthur Roy Leonard, ed. *War Addresses of Woodrow Wilson*. Boston: Ginn and Company. 1918. Print.

Winkler, Heinrich August. *Der lange Weg nach Westen: Deutsche Geschichte vom Ende des Alten Reiches bis zum Untergang der Weimarer Republik*. Vol. I. Munich: C.H. Beck. 2000. Print.

Witkop, Philipp, and Jay Winter. *German Students' War Letters*. First edition 1929. This edition published by U of Pennsylvania P. 2002. Print.

Wolf, Eric R. *Peasant Wars of the Twentieth Century*. U of Oklahoma P. 1969. Print.

Wolff, Richard D. *Democracy at Work: A Cure for Capitalism*. Chicago: Haymarket. 2012. Print.

Woodward, C. Vann. "Editor's Introduction." *Battle Cry of Freedom: The Civil War Era*. James McPherson. Oxford: Oxford UP. 1988. Print.

439

Woodward, C. Vann. *Reunion and Reaction: The Compromise of 1877 and the End of Reconstruction*. Oxford: Oxford UP. 1991. First published 1951. Print.

"World Urbanization Prospects: The 2009 Revision. Highlights." New York: United Nations. ESA/P/WP/215. 2010. Print.

Wormser, Richard. "The Rise and Fall of Jim Crow. Jim Crow Stories. U.S. in World War II." pbs.org. n.d. Web. Sep. 18, 2015.

Wu, Yiching. *The Cultural Revolution at the Margins*. Harvard: Harvard UP. 2014. Print.

Xiang, Lanxin. *The Origins of the Boxer War: A Multinational Study*. London: Routledge. 2003. Print.

Yahil, Leni. *The Holocaust: The Fate of European Jewry, 1932–1945*. Ina Friedman and Haya Galai, trans. Oxford: Oxford UP. 1990. Print.

Yan, Jiaqi, and Gao Gao. *Turbulent Decade: A History of the Cultural Revolution*. D.W.Y. Kwok, ed. and trans. U of Haiwaii P. 1996. Print.

Yost, Pete. "FBI Access To Email And Web Records Raises Privacy Fears." huffingtonpost.com. July 30, 2010. Web. Jan. 26, 2015.

Young, Robert W., and George D. Kerr. *Reassessment of the Atomic Bomb Radiation Dosimetry for Hiroshima and Nagasaki—Dosimetry System 2002*. Vol. 1. Hiroshima: Radation Effects Research Foundation. 2005. Print.

Young, Roy A. "The Present Credit Situation." Sept. 20, 1928. Federal Reserve Bank of Philadelphia. federalreservehistory.org. Web. July 24, 2015.

Yurchak, Alexei. "Bodies of Lenin: The Hidden Science of Communist Sovereignty." *Representations*. Vol. 129, No. 1, 2015: 116–157. U of California P. Print.

Zarrow, Peter. *China in War and Revolution, 1895–1949*. Abingdon: Routledge. 2005. Print.

Zedong, Mao. *Selected Works of Mao Tse-Tung, Volume 2.* Oxford: Pergamon. 1965. Print.

Zedong, Mao. "Smash Chiang Kai-Shek's Offensive By A War Of Self-Defense." n.p. July 20, 1946. marxists.org. Web. Aug. 11, 2015.

Zelikow, Philip, Ernest R. May, and Timothy Naftali, ed. *The Presidential Recordings: John F. Kennedy: The Great Crises, Volume Two, September-October 21, 1962.* New York: W.W. Norton & Company. 2001. Print.

Zelikow, Philip, and Ernest May, ed. *The Presidential Recordings: John F. Kennedy: The Great Crises, Volume Three, October 22–28, 1962.* New York: W.W. Norton & Company. 2001. Print.

Zenko, Micah. *Between Threats and War: U.S. Discrete Military Operations in the Post-Cold War World.* Stanford: Stanford UP. 2010. Print.

Zetter, Kim. "'John Doe' Who Fought FBI Spying Freed From Gag Order After 6 Years." wired.com. Aug. 10, 2010. Web. Jan. 26, 2015.

Zhao, Suisheng. *A Nation-state by Construction: Dynamics of Modern Chinese Nationalism.* Stanford: Stanford UP. 2004. Print.

Zhisui, Li. *The Private Life of Chairman Mao.* Tai Hung-Chao, trans. New York: Random House. 2011. Print.

Zuber, Terence. *Inventing the Schlieffen Plan: German War Planning 1871–1914.* Oxford: Oxford UP. 2002. Print.

Zuber, Terence. *The Real German War Plan: 1904–14.* The History Press. 2011. Print.

Zuckerman, Larry. *The Rape of Belgium: The Untold Story of World War I.* New York: New York UP. 2004. Print.

INDEX

454

www.ingramcontent.com/pod-product-compliance
Lightning Source LLC
Chambersburg PA
CBHW021037090426
42738CB00006B/128